PARLIAMENT AND FOREIGN POLICY IN THE EIGHTEENTH CENTURY

Drawing on a wide range of British and foreign archival sources, this book tackles the role of Parliament in the conduct of eighteenth-century foreign policy, the impact of this policy on parliamentary politics, and the quality of parliamentary debates. The study is important for our assessment of eighteenth-century Britain, and also, more generally, for an understanding of the role of contingency in the assessment of political systems.

'I shall never bear the smell of the House of Commons.' James Duff made this remark in 1784 having already served as an MP in the small and stuffy chamber for thirty years. It serves as a reminder that Parliament had many facets, some of which are difficult to recover. Reflecting over a quarter-century of work on parliamentary sources, this book highlights the influence of Parliament, positive and negative, direct and indirect, on foreign policy and politics. It also has great contemporary relevance as we consider the effectiveness of democratic states when confronting authoritarian rivals, and the rights of representative bodies to be consulted before wars are launched.

JEREMY BLACK MBE is Professor of History, University of Exeter. A prolific author, his many books include *Maps and History* (1997) and *War and the World 1450–2000* (1998).

PARLIAMENT AND FOREIGN POLICY IN THE EIGHTEENTH CENTURY

JEREMY BLACK

CAMBRIDGE
UNIVERSITY PRESS

CAMBRIDGE UNIVERSITY PRESS
Cambridge, New York, Melbourne, Madrid, Cape Town, Singapore, São Paulo

Cambridge University Press
The Edinburgh Building, Cambridge CB2 8RU, UK

Published in the United States of America by Cambridge University Press, New York

www.cambridge.org
Information on this title: www.cambridge.org/9780521833318

First published 2004
This digitally printed version 2007

A catalogue record for this publication is available from the British Library

Library of Congress Cataloguing in Publication data

Black, Jeremy.
Parliament and foreign policy in the eighteenth century / by Jeremy Black.
p.   cm.
Includes bibliographical references and index.
ISBN 0 521 83331 0
1. Great Britain – Foreign relations – 18th century.   2. Great Britain.
Parliament – History – 18th century.   I. Title.
DA480.B559   2004
327.41´009´033 – dc22   2003060808

ISBN 978-0-521-83331-8 hardback
ISBN 978-0-521-54076-6 paperback

For
Isabel and Oliver Letwin

Contents

Preface

Having now worked on this period for close to a quarter-century, there is a sense of coming back to old friends when writing on this subject. Yet, at the same time, in providing both a narrative and thematic account of British foreign policy in the eighteenth century, focusing on the role of Parliament in the making of that policy, I am trying to tackle at book-length a subject that has not hitherto received adequate attention. There are first-rate articles on various aspects of the relationship between Parliament and foreign policy, especially those of Graham Gibbs, but no comprehensive treatment, and none that takes my theme and follows it through the century. This reflects the difficulty of the task and the extent to which the subject matter demands the expertise of both the diplomatic historian and the domestic political historian. In this book, I consider the role of Parliament in the conduct of foreign policy, the impact of this policy on parliamentary politics, and the quality of parliamentary debates. These are important questions for our understanding of eighteenth-century Britain: our contemporary fashion for social and cultural topics does not obviate the centrality of Parliament, foreign policy and war in the politics of the period. The issues I discuss are also relevant today, not least because they relate to the important question of the effectiveness of democratic states when confronting authoritarian rivals. Moreover, in 2002–3, the right of Parliament to be consulted before Britain engaged in hostilities with Iraq, and the nature and role of that consultation, became important political issues.

The range of research on which this work is based ensures that I must thank a number of bodies. The British Academy, the Leverhulme Foundation, the Wolfson Foundation and the Universities of Durham and Exeter have provided valuable assistance, as has Merton College Oxford, the Huntington Library and the Beinecke Library, each of which elected me to visiting fellowships. I am most grateful to Her Majesty the Queen, the late Duke of Northumberland, the Marquess of Bute, the late Earl Harrowby, the late Earl Waldegrave, the Earl of Malmesbury, Lady Lucas,

Sir Hector Monro, John Weston-Underwood, Richard Head and the Trustees of the Bedford Estate for permission to work on papers belonging to them. I would also like to record my gratitude to numerous archivists at home and abroad, not least for the opportunity to work in three major archives when they were shut to the public. I benefited from the opportunity to advance earlier ideas at the 38th Conference of the International Commission for the History of Representative and Parliamentary Institutions, held in Durham in 1988, and at the 1997 colloquium on the Treaty of Rijswijk, held at the Institut für Europäische Geschichte in Mainz. I am most grateful to Bob Harris and Bob McJimsey for commenting on draft chapters, to two anonymous readers for helpful reflections and criticisms, to William Davies, a prince among publishers, and to David Watson, a most skilful copy editor. It is a great pleasure to dedicate this book to two good friends and university contemporaries, one of whom is a distinguished parliamentarian.

Notes on dates, spelling and titles

The New Year is always taken as starting on 1 January. Until the reform of the calendar in 1752 Britain conformed to the Julian Calendar. Dates recorded in this calendar are referred to as old style and designated (os). All other dates are new style, the Gregorian Calendar, which was ten days ahead before 1700 and eleven days ahead from then. Where possible, well-established anglicised forms have been used for both place and personal names. The length of proper noble titles and of titles of office has dictated their shortening. Individuals who held aristocratic titles could be MPs. For example, they could be the eldest son of a peer, as with Frederick, Lord North, or could hold an Irish peerage, as with John, 2nd Earl of Egmont. Place of publication is London unless otherwise indicated.

Abbreviations

152M/C	Addington (Sidmouth papers), Exeter, Devon CRO.
Add.	Additional Manuscripts
AE.	Paris, Archives du Ministère des Affaires Etrangères
AN.	Paris, Archives Nationales
Ang.	Angleterre
AST.	Turin, Archivio di Stato
Aylesbury	Aylesbury, Buckinghamshire Record Office
Berlin	Berlin-Dahlem, Geheimes Staatsarchiv Preussischer Kulturbesitz
BL.	London, British Library
Bod.	Oxford, Bodleian Library
Bowood	Papers of the 1st Marquess of Lansdowne, from Bowood House, now in British Library.
Cawdor	Carmarthen, Dyfed Record Office, Cawdor papers
Chewton	Chewton Hall, Chewton Mendip, papers of James, 1st Earl Waldegrave
Cobbett	W. Cobbett (ed.), *Parliamentary History of England* (36 vols., London, 1806–20)
CP.	Correspondance Politique
CRO.	County Record Office
CUL.	Cambridge, University Library
Dresden	Dresden, Hauptstaatsarchiv, Geheimes Kabinett, Gesandschaften
Eg.	Egerton Manuscripts
Farmington	Farmington, Connecticut, Lewis Walpole Library
HHStA.	Vienna, Haus-, Hof-, und Staatsarchiv
HL.	San Marino, Huntington Library
HMC.	Historical Manuscripts Commission
HP.	London, History of Parliament Transcripts

Hayton	D. W. Hayton (ed.), *The House of Commons 1690–1715* (5 vols., Cambridge, 2002)
Ing.	Inghilterra
KAO.	Maidstone, Kent Archive Office
LM.	Lettere Ministri
Marburg	Marburg, Staatsarchiv, Bestand 4: Politische Akten nach Philipp d. Gr.
Munich	Munich, Bayerisches Hauptstaatsarchiv
Namier	L. B. Namier and J. Brooke (eds.), *The House of Commons 1754–1790* (3 vols., 1964)
NAS.	Edinburgh, National Archives of Scotland
NLS.	Edinburgh, National Library of Scotland
os	old style
Osnabrück	Osnabrück, Staatsarchiv, Repertorium 100, Abschnitt 1
PRO.	London, Public Record Office
RA.	Windsor Castle, Royal Archives, Stuart Papers
Sedgwick	R. R. Sedgwick (ed.), *The House of Commons 1715–1754* (2 vols., 1970)
SP.	State Papers
Thorne	R. G. Thorne (ed.), *The House of Commons 1790–1820* (5 vols., 1986)
UL.	University Library
Williamwood	Williamwood, Sir Hector Munro, Ewast papers
WW.	Sheffield, Archives, Wentworth Woodhouse papers

Introduction

'I shall never bear the smell of the House of Commons'.[1] James Duff made this remark in 1784 having already served as an MP in the small and stuffy chamber for thirty years. It serves as a reminder that Parliament had many facets, some of which are difficult to recover. It was a social centre as well as a place of business, and parliamentarians made an impact in many ways other than through their speeches. This needs to be borne in mind when we concentrate on Parliament's political role and, more specifically, on the debates. Indeed, the political importance of MPs was not simply measured by their participation, let alone skill, in debate, and, as also today, this was particularly so of parliamentarians in government. Similarly, votes in divisions were not solely the product of party alignments and of responses to the issues debated. In 1735, James, Earl of Morton complained that his son Robert, MP for Orkney and Shetland, where the Earls were the hereditary stewards, had been 'taking such flirts in Parliament by voting against our friends by the influence of a parcel of women'. Two years later, he threatened Robert that if the latter voted contrary to his wishes 'he would never see my face, nor possess a furrow of ground that belongs to me'.[2] The threat succeeded in bringing Robert into line.

Parliament, in its debates, political influence and constitutional powers, has justifiably played a major role in studies on British history. The role of Parliament was seen as central to the constitution, and indeed as a touchstone of British identity. In recent decades, however, Parliament has been displaced from centre stage as attention has been devoted to the world of popular politics and consciousness, particularly in its more dramatic manifestations of demonstrations and riots. Yet, fine work continues to

---

[1] Fife to William Rose, 11 May 1784, A. and H. Tayler (eds.), *Lord Fife and his Factor* (1925), p. 166.
[2] Morton to his heir James, Lord Aberdour, 25 Mar. (os) 1735, 15 Mar. (os) 1737, NAS. GD. 150/3476/52x, 85.

be produced on parliamentary politics, much of which can be approached through the journal *Parliamentary History* (1982–).

This book looks at Parliament and foreign policy because it was important to contemporaries, has received insufficient scholarly attention in recent decades, and is a topical issue today, as the question of the respective powers of executive and legislature over foreign policy is rightly seen as important, particularly, but not only, in the United Kingdom and the United States. Furthermore, many of the issues that were discussed in the eighteenth century, such as the extent to which parliamentary debate compromised national interests and also challenged the equation of reputation and security, are again subjects for consideration. Foreign policy itself may seem distant from the concerns of most eighteenth-century voters, let alone of the remainder of the population, but it helped lead to war or peace, the crucial factor in public finances and the most important aspect of state activity for the bulk of the population.

Approaching the issue from a different perspective, much of the problem in defining and assessing the formulation and conduct of foreign policy in eighteenth-century Britain hinges on the question of the influence of Parliament, both positive and negative. That influence was both direct and indirect. The monarch had the right of making war and peace, signing treaties, appointing, dismissing and paying diplomats, giving them instructions, and receiving their reports, and all without consulting Parliament. These rights were firmly asserted by the great jurist Sir William Blackstone in his influential *Commentaries on the Laws of England* (1765–9).[3]

Parliament, in contrast, had responsibility in the field of finance, and thus for supporting the military expenditure and subsidies to foreign powers that were judged necessary for the pursuance of policies. Treaties that entailed either a financial charge or a change in British law had to be brought before both Houses (House of Commons and House of Lords). With the majesty of legal authority, Philip, 1st Earl of Hardwicke, a longstanding Lord Chancellor and a key member of the 'Old Corps' Whigs, who had dominated British politics for four decades, told the House of Lords in 1755:

The King is not obliged by our constitution to ask either the consent or the approbation of Parliament to any treaty he makes, nor even to communicate it to Parliament, unless it requires a grant or an Act of Parliament, and even then he is

[3] Blackstone, *Commentaries on the Laws of England* (5th edn, Oxford, 1773) I, 252–3, 257–8.

obliged to communicate the treaty only when he applies for the grant or the Act thereby required.[4]

Thus Parliament was to play a role in giving effect to policy, but at a time set by the Crown. Sir Robert Walpole, First Lord of the Treasury and longstanding head of the 'Old Corps' Whig ministry, warned, in 1738, on prudential grounds against an extension of parliamentary power: 'a future House of Commons may assume to themselves a power of calling for papers during the dependence of a negotiation; and if this should ever come to be our case, I am sure no foreign prince or state will ever enter into any secret negotiation or treaty with our government'.[5]

Treaties were communicated to Parliament after they had been ratified, which limited the value of parliamentary discussion, and certainly of any advice that might be given. On a number of occasions, individual parliamentarians and others called for an extension of Parliament's formal role. In 1738, Sir William Wyndham, the Tory leader in the Commons, argued that the prerogative arose from the circumstances of feudalism, stated that 'sovereigns now make war at the expense of the nation', and pressed for communication of treaties prior to their ratification.[6] In 1743, Philip, 4th Earl of Chesterfield, a Whig and former diplomat, then in opposition, repeated the call. Both employed parliamentary debates as occasions for their remarks. Chesterfield told the Lords that 'to execute measures first, and then to require the approbation of Parliament, instead of advice, is surely such a degree of contempt as has not often been shown in the most arbitrary reigns'.[7] In 1752, John, Earl Granville (formerly Lord Carteret), the Lord President of the Council, warned, however, that the communication of treaties for parliamentary approval prior to their ratification 'would be a total subversion of our constitution'.[8] In 1760, an anonymous pamphlet appeared setting out *Reasons Why the Approaching Treaty of Peace should be debated in Parliament; As a Method most Expedient and Constitutional.*[9] The charge of this pamphlet was ignored.

Such calls were rare, and pressure for a constitutional change in Parliament's position was slight. Instead, the emphasis was on the value to government of parliamentary support, and therefore on an extension of parliamentary competence by permission; rather than any alteration of the

---

[4] Cobbett, XV, 652.   [5] Cobbett, X, 590, cf. 612.   [6] Cobbett, X, 858.
[7] Cobbett, XII, 1135, 1145.   [8] Cobbett, XIV, 1185, cf. Hardwicke in 1743, XII, 1170.
[9] G. C. Gibbs, 'Laying Treaties Before Parliament in the Eighteenth Century', in R. M. Hatton and M. S. Anderson (eds.), *Studies in Diplomatic History: Essays in Memory of David Bayne Horn* (1970), pp. 116–37.

royal prerogative in this field. In 1739, Richard, 2nd Earl of Scarborough, a Whig close to George II, told the Lords:

Your lordships know that the power of peace and war is in the Crown . . . and that our constitution always understands that the Crown has a right to make either without the participation of Parliament. No wise King will indeed venture upon this; but, my Lords, no dutiful Parliament will refuse to thank such a king for his condescension in thus making the Parliament as it were partners in his prerogative,[10]

the latter a formulation that captured political reality and constitutional mutability.

A memorandum on peace treaties in the papers of Sir Gilbert Elliot MP, a supporter of John, 3rd Earl of Bute, the leading minister in 1762–3, claimed:

The King's prerogative undoubtedly empowers him to conclude peace without laying the terms before Parliament. He may however ask their advice. The question therefore merely upon usage. Anciently, articles [in peace treaties] few and simple, not unusual to ask advice. In modern times, more complicated and branched into more particulars, scarce possible certainly not expedient to ask advice. Accordingly for 150 years hardly an instance Treaty of Utrecht [1713] excepted.[11]

This was a distinctly conservative approach to politics, and it is necessary to appreciate its widespread appeal in order to avoid a misleading perspective that emphasises support for change. In 1749, Henry Pelham, the First Lord of the Treasury, and a minister who was sensitive to the mood of the House of Commons, made a robust defence of the government's refusal, the previous year, to communicate the preliminaries of the Treaty of Aix-la-Chapelle. In his eyes, any encroachment on prerogative would be a dangerous constitutional innovation.[12]

As a separate issue, although the approval of treaties was at stake, the question of whether the Crown had the right to part with territories without parliamentary authority was raised, particularly over the loss of the Thirteen American Colonies.[13] Another aspect of the implementation of treaties related to obligations to provide military assistance. A pamphlet referred to the promise to do so under the Anglo-Prussian treaty of 1788, noting 'as they may be demanded when Parliament is not sitting, a King of England

[10] Cobbett, X, 900.   [11] NLS. Mss. 11036 fol. 26.   [12] Cobbett, XIV, 598.
[13] *Edinburgh Advertiser*, 27 Sept., *Morning Chronicle*, 2 Nov. 1782.

may be put under the necessity either of breaking faith with his ally, by not sending troops . . . or of breaking faith with his people, by raising troops without consent of Parliament'.[14]

To see the subject in terms of a struggle to extend parliamentary competence would be to adopt a modern approach to politics and a teleological account of the past, neither of which were appropriate in this case. Radical prospects were, indeed, to be outlined in the revolutionary crisis of the 1790s, and the American Revolution (1775–83) showed the constitutional and political structures and practices that could develop in the English-speaking political world, but the extent to which the radical possibilities of the Glorious Revolution of 1688–9 for the role of Parliament were not teased out is the most striking aspect of the situation. Indeed, the unsuccessful Peerage Bill of 1719 was the last major attempt to give constitutional form to the potential for ongoing change opened up by the manner of James II and VII's removal from his thrones in 1689.

Treaties were not the sole issue for Parliament in the field of diplomacy. Foreign policy was debated in both Houses, being the single most important topic in many of the major parliamentary debates, such as a large number of those on the Addresses of Thanks.[15] Thus, foreign policy posed, in an acute form, the serious problem of parliamentary management.

Parliament's indirect influence is harder to gauge, and was an issue over which contemporaries were understandably divided. The extent to which British policy, and the foreign response to British views that played such a large role in shaping British policy, were affected by the existence of Parliament, and the consequent need for government to consider how best to win parliamentary support or reply to parliamentary criticisms, was unclear to contemporaries, who were having themselves to respond to the dynamic character of British political developments. Thus, at the close of 1726, the British ministry hastened to assure its French ally that a Spanish attack on the British possession of Gibraltar would receive a firm response even though Parliament was not sitting:

neither need the Cardinal [Fleury, France's leading minister] apprehend that we shall be in any distress on account of the Parliament's not being assembled, the King having received from both Houses, in the last session, such strong assurances of support, and having so much reason to depend upon their being of the same

---

[14] Anon., *Considerations on the Prussian Treaty* (1789), pp. 3–4.
[15] The best introduction is Gibbs, 'Parliament and Foreign Policy in the Age of Stanhope and Walpole', *English Historical Review*, 77 (1962), pp. 18–37.

mind at their next meeting, considering the prudent measures that have been taken in consequence of those assurances.[16]

Parliament was often cited in discussion of foreign policy, whether by ministers stressing the need to settle matters before the sessions, British diplomats concerned about the detrimental consequences for their government's image of parliamentary contentions, or foreign diplomats seeking to assess the stability and intentions of the British ministry. The major setpiece occasions of the debate over foreign policy occurred in Parliament. It was in the House of Commons that the government was most seriously assailed, whether over relations with France in 1730 and with Spain in 1739, Hanoverian subsidies in 1742 and 1744, peace with France in 1762, or the prospect of war with Russia in 1791, although the Lords took centre stage for the struggle in 1711–12 over ending the War of the Spanish Succession.

And yet the significance of parliamentary discussion can be qualified. This study positions itself between scholars, such as the late Ragnhild Hatton, who have emphasised the Crown's freedom of manoeuvre in diplomacy and, more generally, in foreign policy, and others who have stressed the significance of popular and public engagement with foreign affairs, which might, inelegantly, be termed the 'public sphere' approach. Against the former, it is necessary to draw attention to the constitutional necessity (given the power of the purse) and political reasons for foreign policy to be a collaboration of Crown and Parliament, and to be seen to be such. Against the latter, it is important to emphasise that Parliament functioned less as an organ for popular expression than as an arena for the disagreements and contestations within the government. Indeed, this leads to a questioning of the usefulness of the very idea of a parliamentary foreign policy.

Equally important, it can be suggested that any assessment of Parliament's role requires a more specific approach, one that is more sensitive to particular issues and years. This emphasis on contingency requires a stress on the archival research that aids an understanding of the dynamics of specific moments. In addition, a reliance on manuscript material has an analytical importance in its own right, as it redresses the bias towards newspapers, pamphlets and other printed material which have played too large a role in the populist account of foreign policy.

The qualification of Parliament's importance has various sources. At one level, it is but part of the more general realisation that the tendency to stress

---

[16] Thomas, Duke of Newcastle, Secretary of State for the Southern Department, to Thomas Robinson, 20 Dec. (os) 1726, BL. Add. 32748 fol. 475.

public spheres of discussion can be misleading. They were less frequently spheres of decision-making, or sources of the decisions that were taken, than is generally appreciated. Nevertheless, there is a marked reluctance among scholars to accept this situation, or to consider its consequences. Instead, there is a powerful sense that the public sphere, Parliament, the culture of print and the world of campaigns, agitation, propaganda and public opinion, must somehow have been not solely important, but, instead, central to the processes of decision-making; and that if Parliament had a role it was in large part because it was receptive to this public sphere, and thus represented it.

It would be foolish to deny the importance of the public sphere, both in Britain and, more generally, in Europe;[17] but, equally, the stress on it sometimes seen can be described rather as an act of faith than as an assessment based on an understanding of the steps by which decisions were usually taken. Furthermore, there is a related tendency to focus on crises in Britain in which public manifestations of opposition to the government were notable, which presents a misleading view of the difficulties that ministries encountered. This view concentrates on the relationship between policy and public, especially popular, opposition, and on the pressures that the latter could produce. As the crises are automatically defined by the strength of the latter, an impression is created that the central political problem was that of defending policy in such contexts, and that the political chronology of the period can be readily traced from crisis to crisis. A 'structure of politics' has indeed been advanced for this public opposition, one based on urban institutions, sociability and manifestations: clubs, petitions, newspapers, instructions and addresses. In addition, a corresponding ideology has been discerned, most prominently for the 1730s–1750s, one of 'closely intertwined . . . Patriotism, nationalism, and commercial expansion'.[18]

These factors were indeed of importance. To consider foreign policy without paying attention to the range, intensity and impact of public debate would be misguided, but this impact has been exaggerated, not least in terms of its role in defining a chronology of crisis and an agenda for study. Thus, the period 1738–63 apparently becomes a matter of the Jenkins'

[17] T. C. W. Blanning, *The Culture of Power and the Power of Culture. Old Regime Europe 1660–1789* (Oxford, 2002), pp. 103–82; H. Barker and S. Burrows (eds.), *Press, Politics and the Public Sphere in Europe and North America 1760–1820* (Cambridge, 2002), pp. 1, 17, 93–7.
[18] N. Rogers, *Whigs and Cities. Popular Politics in the Age of Walpole and Pitt* (Oxford, 1989), p. 397. See also J. Brewer, *Party Ideology and Popular Politics at the Accession of George III* (Cambridge, 1976), and K. Wilson, *The Sense of the People. Politics, Culture and Imperialism in England, 1715–1785* (Cambridge, 1995).

Ear agitation for war with Spain of 1738–9, the upsurge of opposition to Hanover in 1742–4, the Pittite onslaught on the Duke of Newcastle, the head of the ministry in 1754–6, and his policies, and the response, first, to Pitt's fall in 1761, and, then, to peace with France in 1762–3. Each of these was indeed important, but it is misleading only to study crises, or to suggest that such crises defined Parliament's relationship with foreign policy.

Parliament's role is mistaken if it is presented largely in terms of a forum for the advancement or rejection of public aspirations, a sphere in short for the conduct of public politics. This was clearly of consequence, but its role has been exaggerated, for, by focusing on the debate between government and opposition, and then largely in terms of this as an aspect of a wider struggle between antithetical values and 'consciousnesses', the importance of Parliament to discussion and contention within government has been underrated. Instead, it is clear that parliamentary attitudes, and the real and alleged problems of parliamentary management, played a major role in discussions over policy within the government. Ministerial cohesion and successful parliamentary management were linked, John, 2nd Earl of Stair reporting in January 1724:

The session of Parliament we are told is to be a very short one and in appearance a very quiet one. His Majesty [George I] confides entirely in Mr. [Robert] Walpole for the management of his affairs. There is not the least struggle in that manner.[19]

Parliament and the executive were not separate. Aside from their close relationship, as working parts of the state, as well as the linkage arising from the presence of government figures, including diplomats, in both Houses of Parliament, both Parliament and the executive were affected by the arguments advanced in public debate. Indeed, part of the importance of Parliament rested in its role as the sounding-board for ideas, and as a setting in which they took on consistency and coherence, and became political ammunition. Newspapers and pamphlets in part fulfilled these functions, but they lacked the authority and validation provided by public exposition in Parliament by senior politicians. Politics involved far more than issues of policy but, in so far as these played a role, Parliament was the public forum in which these issues were given weight and clear partisan alignment.

Parliament was also therefore the forum in which tensions within partic-ular traditions of approaching foreign policy were noted and shifts marked.

[19] Stair to 3rd Earl of Loudoun, 18 Jan. (os) 1724, HL. Loudoun papers 7664.

In 1723, Horatio Walpole, a prominent diplomat, Whig MP and brother to the leading minister, Robert Walpole, provided Philip, Duke of Orléans, the leading French minister, with an uncomplicated account of party alignments in Britain:

> I had an opportunity of touching upon the principles of the Whigs and Tories, that indeed the first had been during the last war [1702–13] against France as absolutely necessary for preserving the present establishment of their government, but that the peace at Utrecht [1713] and the treaties since made in consequence of it had made and must make upon that foot the Whigs for keeping well with France and particularly friends to his Royal Highness [Orléans] and the Tories must of consequence as far as they were Jacobites be against his interest.[20]

In practice, as numerous debates in Parliament were to show, the Whig response to the Anglo-French alignment of 1716–31 proved divided and contentious.

There is no doubt of the influence of Parliament as a whole in the conduct of foreign policy. Despite repeated claims that ministries were certain of parliamentary support, because of the widespread distribution of places and pensions, Parliament's independence should not be underestimated. More generally, parliamentary views on policy could be of considerable consequence. Nevertheless, a tendency in work from the 1970s to refocus the traditional view of the sovereignty of the King in Parliament, by stressing the independence of royal action in the field of diplomacy, means that it would be mistaken to claim that Britain followed a parliamentary foreign policy in the sense of one based simply on a consideration of what Parliament would accept.

The constitutional and political roles of Parliament in the conduct of foreign policy were still significant. Paradoxically, the principal constitutional necessity, that of voting the funds necessary for the military forces, British and foreign, that were expected to give substance to foreign policy, would have been emasculated had the 'Country' strategy, advocated with varying degrees of plausibility by Tories and opposition Whigs, of dispensing with a standing army and limiting treaty commitments, been carried out. The following of a contrary policy from 1714, albeit with significant variations, by successive Court Whig ministries, instead, ensured that Parliament had to be approached frequently with requests for financial assistance.

In response to these, and other, requests, parliamentarians were not simply manoeuvring to their own personal or factional advantage: they had

---

[20] Horatio Walpole to Duke of Newcastle, 20 Nov. 1723, BL. Add. 32686 fol. 408.

opinions on policy. These were not simply on party lines: for example, the recently published papers of William Hay reveal him as a committed ministerial Whig MP, who disapproved of the opposition Whig 'Patriots', but could also be critical of the government. He exercised independent judgement as an MP, and, to gain his support, the ministry had to rely on principle and policy, not bribery or intimidation.[21] The same was true of many other parliamentarians.

The role of initiating fiscal legislation was restricted to the Commons. In that constitutional or legal sense, the Commons possessed a formal authority in the field of foreign policy significantly greater than that of the Lords, although, in 1735, it was correctly pointed out in the Lords that the House had an important role that ensured that treaties entailing expense also had to be communicated to it:

if it was necessary for his Majesty to lay this treaty before the other House, because it was to be attended with some expense, the very same reason made it necessary for his Majesty to order it to be laid before this House; for, although grants of money are first made by the other House, no such grant can be effectual, without the consent of this.[22]

Much of the parliamentary discussion of foreign policy took place during Commons' debates on fiscal measures designed to ensure an adequate military strength for the furtherance of this policy. Furthermore, the sensitivity of these measures led to attempts to manage news in order to help the government. John Boteler MP reported on the Commons' discussion in June 1721 of such a governmental request for money:

Mr. [Robert] Walpole to sweeten this draught told us there was no ways and means wanting and . . . he also took this opportunity to tell the House that the peace with Spain was actually signed, that he had it this morning in his hands, and that he did not question but the preliminaries between the Swede and the Czar [Peter the Great] were also by this time agreed upon.[23]

Fortunately for the government, which was faced by the consequences of the bursting of the South Sea Bubble, international problems indeed eased greatly that year.

The role of Parliament was not restricted to its constitutional prerogatives. As with much in the British political system, the 'constitution', itself no immutable or clear entity, was related to a set of political practices and

---

[21] S. Taylor and C. Jones (eds.), *Tory and Whig: the Parliamentary Papers of Edward Harley, Third Earl of Oxford, and William Hay, MP for Seaford, 1716–1753* (Woodbridge, 1998).
[22] Cobbett, IX, 667–8.
[23] Boteler to Cowper, 17 June (os) 1721, Hertford, CRO. D/EP F53 fol. 46.

conventions that affected the parliamentary discussion of foreign policy; although the flexibility this offered was constrained by an emphasis on precedence:

proceedings are regulated and governed by laws not written, as well as by . . . standing orders . . . The law and the practice of all courts are derived from the nature and objects of their institution – They exist in the received and acknowledged usage – In the opinion of grave and learned men . . . in the memory and experience of persons who have sat long in Parliament, and in the history of the debates of those who have gone before them.

This reassuring advice, offered in 1796 by the Commons' clerks when the Speaker, Henry Addington, sought advice on whether an MP could force a division,[24] did not do justice to the extent to which government interpretations could be challenged, and to which the challenges could affect policy.

For example, the view that parliamentary supervision entailed scrutiny led to repeated opposition calls for laying papers about negotiations before Parliament, which, although defeated, helped to encourage ministries to offer selected papers for consideration, although, in turn, that led to repeated debate over the range of papers that was provided.[25] The possibility of such scrutiny encouraged ministers and envoys to correspond privately, although this practice would have been important irrespective of the role of Parliament, for it provided a valuable means to expound opinion and to supplement official correspondence. Partly as a consequence of this private correspondence, much evidence that is relevant to the formulation of foreign policy and to the influence of Parliament cannot be found in the state papers.

Conversely, the role of Parliament was extended by other factors. The habit of speaking at length upon unrelated subjects ensured that, even when parliamentarians were asked to discuss only very limited subjects, they tended to consider the whole range of foreign policy, and ministerial speakers had to be prepared to respond to discussion and criticism accordingly. Alongside criticism, Parliament represented the best forum for the public presentation of government policy, a position that owed much to its national scope, which contrasted with the provincial origin and character of many comparable bodies on the Continent. The national scope of the Westminster Parliament was enhanced after the Act of Union with Scotland came into effect in 1707. Parliament thus represented the power

---

[24] John Ley to Addington, 1 Mar., John Hatsell to Addington, 1 Mar. 1796, 152M/C 1796/OZ 16, 10.
[25] P. D. G. Thomas, *The House of Commons in the Eighteenth Century* (Oxford, 1971), pp. 24–5, 38–9.

of a new state.[26] This was an age when European states, whether 'absolutist' or in possession of important agencies of representative government, were increasingly concerned to achieve a good public defence of policy, not least in the field of foreign policy.

Both Houses of Parliament participated in the wider political role of presenting government views on foreign policy. As it was a role that lacked a formal constitutional place or a specific institutional expression, there is, and was, a considerable subjective element involved in the judgement of Parliament's general (and indeed frequently specific) impact. Nevertheless, Parliament was crucial to the process by which support was elicited and demonstrated, and foreign policy was a key area in which this support was both sought and contested.

---

[26] J. Brewer, *The Sinews of Power: War, Money and the English State, 1688–1783* (1989), e.g., pp. 246–7; D. Hayton, 'Contested Kingdoms, 1688–1756', in P. Langford (ed.), *The Eighteenth Century 1688–1815* (Oxford, 2002), p. 67.

2

The Revolution Settlement, Parliament and foreign policy, 1689–1714

Parliament's role in foreign policy became more prominent as a result of the Glorious Revolution in 1688–9, the political and constitutional changes that accompanied the invasion of England in 1688 and the replacement of James II (r. 1685–8; James VII of Scotland) by his nephew and son-in-law William of Orange, William III (r. 1689–1702). However, a parliamentary monarchy could not simply be legislated into existence. It required the development of conventions and patterns of political behaviour that would permit a constructive resolution of contrary opinions within a system where there was no single source of dominant power. The slowness of the development of these patterns was particularly serious, as Britain was at war from 1689 until 1697 and again from 1702 until 1713, and as Jacobitism, the cause of the exiled male line of the Stuarts, was a significant force. The Revolution Settlement (the term for the set of constitutional and political arrangements that followed the Glorious Revolution) created the constitutional basis for an effective parliamentary monarchy, with parliamentary control over the finances of the state: the aim of many of the critics of Charles II (r. 1660–85). However, the instability of the ministries of the 1690s, 1700s and 1710s suggests that the political environment within which such a monarchy could be effective had not been created. Looked at differently, the process of ministerial change was peaceful, and the instability of ministries reflected not simply 'structural' constitutional problems, but also the serious nature of the issues in dispute.

There was no immediate extension of Parliament's formal competence in the specific field of foreign policy, but, in 1692, William III thought it sensible to provide Parliament with a copy of the Treaty of the Grand Alliance he had negotiated with Austria and the Dutch in 1689 in order to create the coalition then fighting against France in the Nine Years' War.[1] This was despite the fact that the treaty did not contain financial provisions,

---

[1] H. Horwitz (ed.), *The Parliamentary Diary of Narcissus Luttrell, 1691–1693* (Oxford, 1972), p. 250.

the sphere that was within Parliament's competence. Nevertheless, it seemed appropriate to try to cement and underline parliamentary backing for government policy.

Parliament's part in the debate over foreign policy greatly increased in the last years of William's reign. This reflected political circumstances, specifically the royal need to win support for a contentious foreign policy.[2] However, the necessary precondition had occurred earlier in William's reign, with the establishment of Parliament on a permanent basis after the Glorious Revolution. Prior to that, Parliament could play a major role in foreign policy, not least by the negative criteria of measures taken to prevent it meeting; but this role was episodic and generally limited to one of seeking to thwart royal policy. In February 1681, the Austrian minister Count Königsegg told the English envoy, Charles, 2nd Earl of Middleton, that the prorogation of Parliament by Charles II would probably oblige the King to 'close with France', as Charles would find no other way to support himself. A peevish Middleton replied that Charles's revenues were better than those of Leopold and that Charles was able both to subsist honourably and to make his friendship very advantageous to his allies.[3]

This was bluster. Charles had to turn to Louis XIV to take French subsidies and to accept French gains on the Continent in order to avoid the compromises and contention that a resort to Parliament would have entailed. Without parliamentary financial support, it was impossible for Charles to follow an active foreign policy in a period of tense international relations, and, specifically, to fulfil his commitment to Spain under a 1680 treaty of mutual assistance.

More generally, in the late seventeenth century, the role of Parliament in both constitution and political system was unclear, and it still appeared possible that it would follow the path of many representative bodies on the Continent and become, at best, an occasional presence. The Diet of Baden, for example, was not convened during the eighteenth century, and had not met since 1626. The Portuguese Cortes did not meet between 1698 and 1820, despite the fact that the Cortes of 1697–8 agreed to an increase in taxation. Cosimo III of Tuscany (r. 1670–1723) convened the Senate only once. The Estates of Savoy, Piedmont and Nice had all ceased to meet before

---

[2] The best introduction is provided by R. J. McJimsey, 'A Country Divided? English Politics and the Nine Years War, 1689–1697', *Albion*, 23/4 (1991), pp. 61–74, 'Crisis Management: Parliament and Political Stability, 1692–1719', *Albion*, 31 (1999), pp. 559–88, and 'Shaping the Revolution in Foreign Policy: Parliament and the Press, 1680–1730', unpublished paper. I am most grateful to Bob McJimsey for providing me with a copy of the last.

[3] PRO. SP. 80/16 fol. 269.

the century began. In England, indeed, from 1679 to 1688 the Commons conducted business on only 171 days.[4]

The financial settlement after his accession left William III with an ordinary revenue that was too small for his peacetime needs, obliging him to turn to Parliament for support. So also did the prohibition of a standing (permanent) army unless permitted by Parliament. The Declaration of Rights of 1689 had declared that 'the raising or keeping a standing army within the kingdom in time of peace, unless it be with consent to Parliament, is against law', a determined assertion of the role of Parliament as the arbiter of military strength.

The Nine Years' War with France (1689–97) further encouraged a development in Parliament's role. The war led to a massive increase in British military activity and the resulting cost. Parliament was willing to pay for a substantial army and for what became the largest navy in the world. Whereas Charles II's army had cost £283,000 in 1684 and James II's £620,322 per annum, all figures for peacetime, between 1691 and 1697 the army and the navy each cost an annual average of £2.5 million.[5] Thanks to an Act of 1691 sponsoring naval shipbuilding, from 1695 England had a clear lead in new launchings over both the Dutch and the French, although that also owed something to a switch in French priorities.[6]

The war also led to a reorganisation of public finances that introduced principles of openness and parliamentary responsibility. Although it was not to be a permanent feature, the creation of a Commission of Public Accounts in the 1690–1 session represented an important extension of parliamentary scrutiny of the executive. More significantly, the funded national debt, based on the Bank of England, which was founded in 1694, was guaranteed by Parliament. In the short term, the fiscal needs of William's foreign policy had been met by institutionalising the role of Parliament as financial provider. Money was obtained on the basis of future revenue, but that security could only be offered by Parliament. As a result, it would be necessary for the latter to meet regularly in order to vote taxes unless the principal of the loan was to be repaid, but it was rapidly apparent that this was not possible. Furthermore, the Crown had to concede the presentation of estimates to the Commons and the examination of them by the latter. This provided the

---

[4] A. R. Myers, *Parliaments and Estates in Europe to 1789* (1973); M. A. R. Graves, *The Parliaments of Early Modern Europe* (Harlow, 2001); J. Hoppit, *A Land of Liberty? England 1689–1727* (Oxford, 2000), p. 7.

[5] J. Childs, *The British Army of William III* (Manchester, 1987).

[6] J. Glete, *Navies and Nations. Warships, Navies and State Building in Europe and America, 1500–1860* (2 vols., Stockholm, 1993), I, pp. 223, 225; G. J. Symcox, *The Crisis of French Seapower, 1688–97: From Guerre D'escadre to Guerre de Course* (The Hague, 1974).

opportunity for scrutiny, although the detailed examination of accounts by a Commons' public accounts commission proved shortlived.

In the long term, the creation of a parliamentary-guaranteed national debt helped lead to stronger public finances and thus to an ability to borrow at a low rate of interest.[7] In 1723, a French envoy referred to 'une parfaite correspondance' between Treasury and Bank.[8] This relationship was crucial to the financial stability of the state, and therefore to its international potency. It was a relationship founded on confidence, the key to a successful relationship with financial markets; and the ministerial ability to manage Parliament was essential for sustaining this confidence. The politics of confidence put a premium on stability.

Parliament's governmental and political roles were transformed from the Glorious Revolution. From 1689 to 1698, the Commons did business on nearly 1,300 days. The number of statutes similarly greatly increased, and this helped ensure the centrality of Parliament's political position, and the greater importance of parliamentary service.[9] Procedures were debated and regularised, and Parliament's infrastructure improved.

The foundation of the Bank, and the parliamentary union with Scotland in 1707, were aspects of a modernisation of governmental and political systems and practices that, in large part, arose from conflict with France, and thus prefigured what were arise from the later modernisation of the 1790s and 1800s: income tax, national mapping, parliamentary union with Ireland, and the beginning of the national census. In both cases, parliamentary developments were greatly affected by the competitive international context.

The Triennial Act of 1694 was also a crucial political change, as it limited the life-span of Parliament to a maximum of three years. Passed against the wishes of William III, the Triennial Act looked towards a post-war situation when the financial pressures to turn to Parliament would be less severe, but when, thanks to the Act, frequent elections would be necessary. The Act testified to Parliament's determination to fix its constitutional role and assert its political importance. It led to more regular and developed electoral politics, which, in turn, affected expectations about the parliamentary conduct of MPs, and thus the nature of parliamentary politics. There were ten elections in England and Wales between 1695 and 1715, a frequency that

---

[7] P. G. M. Dickson, *The Financial Revolution in England: A Study in the Development of Public Credit, 1688–1756* (1967).

[8] Chammorel to Charles, Count of Morville, French foreign minister, 15 Nov. 1723, AE. CP. Ang. 346 fol. 253.

[9] Hoppit, *Land of Liberty?*, p. 7.

encouraged popular participation in national politics, as well as a sense of political volatility. The increased frequency of new Parliaments made parliamentary management more significant and its skills more important to a ministry. The Act also limited the royal power to dissolve Parliament.

Prior to the Act, there had been no constitutional provision for frequent elections; the changes of 1689 had not ensured this in England or Scotland. In Ireland, indeed, no Parliament was called by William and his wife (and co-ruler until her death in 1694) Mary until 1692 and the calling of Parliament remained completely at the discretion of the monarch; although a compromise in which the Crown retained its prerogative to initiate legislation while the Commons alone were able to introduce money bills and also establish a committee of accounts developed from 1695.[10]

In England, war with France forced a measure of co-operation on Crown and Parliament, and so did the royal succession. The failure both of William to have children and of Anne (r. 1702–14), his sister-in-law and designated successor, to have children who survived infancy, ensured that the Act of Settlement was passed in 1701 in order to establish the succession in the house of Hanover, a Protestant dynasty descended through the female line from James I and VI that did not have the best dynastic claim to succeed to the throne.

However, despite this co-operation, the political history of William's reign was markedly unstable in terms both of Parliament and of his British ministers. This instability diminished the chances of mutual trust developing. They were further hindered by William's knowledge and suspicions concerning the Jacobite links of many leading political figures, although, as the possibility existed of a return to the male line of the Stuarts on the death of William or Anne, these were commonly, although not solely, developed for insurance purposes. The conspiratorial activities of numerous British politicians, both in 1688, when his uncle, James II and VII, had been toppled, and subsequently, fostered William's distrust, and made him conscious of the danger of trusting British politicians, whether in or out of government.

William tried initially to rule through a 'mixed ministry' composed of Whigs and Tories and organised on the basis of royal selection not party

[10] D. Hayton, 'Contested kingdoms, 1688–1756', in P. Langford, *The Eighteenth Century* (Oxford, 2002), p. 39; C. I. McGrath, *The Making of the Eighteenth-Century Irish Constitution. Government, Parliament and the Revenue, 1692–1714* (Dublin, 2000) and 'Parliamentary Additional Supply: The Development and Use of Regular Short-Term Taxation in the Irish Parliament, 1692–1716', in D. Hayton (ed.), *The Irish Parliament in the Eighteenth Century: The Long Apprenticeship* (Edinburgh, 2001), pp. 27–53.

alignment. This, in part, appears to have reflected his view that he could overcome the partisan divisions over religion and party animosity. William, indeed, favoured a 'politique' position on toleration which was the counterpart to his support for a 'mixed ministry'. The political groupings of the period, however, had developed in mutual hostility during the Exclusion Crisis of 1678–81; although they remained in a state of flux in which circumstances played a major role. The opponents of Charles II in that crisis were known as Whigs, an abusive term referring to Scottish Presbyterian rebels, originally used by their opponents, the Tories, initially another abusive term referring to Irish Catholic brigands. In fact, Tory perceptions of the nature of authority drew on Anglican tradition, particularly with reference to support for legally constituted authority. Toryism found it difficult to cope with the consequences of the overthrow of the King in the Glorious Revolution. Some Tories were prepared to accept that the legally constituted authority was now that of William III, but others sought his overthrow. This tension in Toryism remained strong until Jacobitism received a fatal blow at the battle of Culloden in 1746, but it did not prevent the development of a Tory parliamentary politics opposed to the Whigs. In William's reign, a Tory–Whig polarity was complicated, if not confused, by an additional opposition between the Court (or governmental) interest and the anti-authoritarian Country tendency with its suspicion of government. In the late 1690s, the Country Whigs were largely absorbed by the Tories, so that a Tory–Whig division was central to Anne's reign. These political trends were not simply a matter of tensions and alignments in politics at the centre. In addition, across the country, the political world was increasingly split along party lines, affecting both the formal processes of politics, particularly elections, as well as sociability.[11]

The 1690s saw increased party organisation, in part because of more frequent parliamentary sessions. William's attempt to govern without relying on an individual party fell foul of partisanship, but he also became disillusioned with what he saw as a lack of parliamentary support for his goals. In 1689, Parliament's refusal to endorse a declaration of war that specified the misdeeds of Louis XIV was an issue; their focus, instead, was on preventing the return of James II. In 1690, William felt that his expedition to conquer Ireland received insufficient support. William's subsequent troubles over naval matters confirmed his frustration with partisan politics. However, the difficulties he faced in the session of November 1692 to March 1693 in

11 S. E. Whyman, *Sociability and Power in Late-Stuart England. The Cultural Worlds of the Verneys 1660–1720* (Oxford, 1999).

trying to govern through a mixed ministry, and concern in late 1693 about the ability of his Tory ministers to help him obtain money from Parliament, led William to turn to party government. By the summer of 1694, a largely Whig government was in power, and the clear party character of the government became more marked with ministerial changes in 1696–7. This was divisive, and also accentuated William's tendency to rely on a small group of trusted advisers.

Due to the latter, parliamentary government, in the sense of government by those able to manage Parliament, was restricted in its scope. Nevertheless, Parliament's criticism of war aims was wide-ranging, and involved matters of strategy and conduct. Issues such as the number of French warships that survived their defeat at Barfleur in 1692, the failure of the proposed English 'descent' (amphibious operation) of 1692, and the Smryna convoy disaster of 1693 allowed for criticism of commanders and allies, and Parliament could consider these episodes. It sought to manage operational deployment and warship design. Appeals to the Crown for redress after failure were met by William dismissing first Admiral Edward Russell and then the Tory admirals. Nevertheless, Parliament's investigations of the war's conduct, although irritating, were a conventional aspect of consultation and review in which both Crown and Parliament had a recognised stake and over which there were established and understood ways of proceeding. Setting grievances right depended upon such co-operation. Furthermore, William and Parliament were held together by Jacobite plots, especially the Fenwick Plot of 1696.

By the late 1690s, the so-called Junto, the group of Whig leaders, was holding frequent meetings in order to maintain party consistency. These meetings suggested that party might provide the structure and ethos necessary to offer clear leadership and agreed policy in government, and thus to compromise the monarch's continued role as the arbitrator of Court factionalism and the ministerial struggle for influence.[12] Nevertheless, the prominence of the continued role of the monarch as arbitrator was to be demonstrated by Anne's importance in 1714 in the bitter struggle between Bolingbroke and Harley for primacy within the Tory ministry.

After the Nine Years' War had ended in 1697, there was a serious parliamentary attack on Williamite foreign policy, more specifically its secretive

---

[12] J. P. Kenyon, *Revolution Principles: The Politics of Party 1689–1720* (Cambridge, 1977); H. Horwitz, *Parliament, Policy and Politics in the Reign of William III* (Manchester, 1977); T. Harris, *Politics under the Later Stuarts: Party Conflict in a Divided Society 1660–1715* (Harlow, 1993); Hayton, 'The "Country" Interest and the Party System, 1689–c. 1720', in C. Jones (ed.), *Party and Management in Parliament 1660–1784* (Leicester, 1984), pp. 37–85.

character. This character appeared to link William to his Stuart predecessors, and to vindicate concerns about his intentions. William, however, was a true Stuart and an intensely private man, whose experience with representative institutions in his native United Provinces was far from happy. William, instead, preferred his own counsel and the advice of trusted intimates. He saw parliamentary limitations as impertinences and readily vetoed legislation he disliked.

William was criticised in Parliament and his requests contested. In the Commons on 19 November (os) 1691, Paul Foley, MP for Hereford and a prominent Whig who was to be Speaker in 1695–8, queried the request for 65,000 troops for the 1692 campaign,[13] while, that month, Sir Thomas Clarges, MP for Oxford University and a leading Country Tory, explicitly compared what the Parliament was being asked to do (consider the estimates as a whole) with the treatment of the *Parlement* of Paris by Louis XIV, the touchstone of contemporary British ideas about unacceptable government. Clarges was a critic of England's allies and argued that England paid a disproportionate share of the burdens of the alliance.[14]

This was a pointed comparison. Between 1673 and 1713, Louis did not visit the Grand-Chambre of the Parlement, and his solemn receptions for its delegates came to be defined as acts of extreme generosity on his part. As a consequence of *parlementaire* resistance to Louis' fiscal demands at the outset of the Dutch War of 1672–8, Louis had imposed new rules about registration procedures that pushed the *parlements* away from any position of real influence, while the coercive ethos and practice in the royal government was seen in forced loans and other attacks on the economic interests of the judges who comprised the membership of these non-elective bodies.[15]

William was no Louis XIV, but for him to have turned to Parliament to discuss the treaties for the future of the Spanish Habsburg territories he negotiated with Louis in 1698 and 1700 – the Partition treaties[16] – would have been to abandon the discretion and authority he sought to retain in order to be able to direct policy. Furthermore, the Spanish succession was a contentious issue that would invite attempts by foreign envoys to influence parliamentarians, and where there were no agreed national interests, nor any process by which such agreement could be readily elicited.

---

[13] Hayton, III, 1060.   [14] Hayton, III, 567–8.

[15] J. J. Hurt, *Louis XIV and the Parlements. The Assertion of Royal Authority* (Manchester, 2002).

[16] For detailed documentation, H. Reynald, *Succession d'Espagne, Louis XIV et Guillaume III* (2 vols., Paris, 1883), and A. Legrelle, *La Diplomatie française et la succession d'Espagne* (2nd edn, 6 vols., Braine-le-Comte, 1895–9).

The absence of clear national interests is an important point that was long obscured by scholarly commitment to a particular Whig interpretation of history. This commitment can be seen in valuable work published in the third quarter of the twentieth century, especially a brief essay by Mark Thomson, 'Parliament and Foreign Policy 1689–1714', which appeared in 1953. Nine years later, his approach was taken forward chronologically in a more substantial article by Graham Gibbs, the seminal work on the subject, entitled 'Parliament and Foreign Policy in the Age of Stanhope and Walpole', and, in 1968, Gibbs added an essay on 'Parliament and the Treaty of Quadruple Alliance'.[17] Adopting a teleological approach, Thomson felt able to refer to the Commons in 1701 as being slow-witted but 'not unpatriotic'. Gibbs, in turn, wrote of 'aims consistent with British interests', and, again, of 'specifically British interests', as though these were apparent to contemporaries and should be so to modern scholars.[18] By assuming the existence of these interests, Gibbs suggested that an objective standard existed against which the views and policies of William, Anne and the Hanoverians could, and can, be judged. Thus, the measure of Parliament's influence became its success in ensuring that these views and policies conformed, or could be made to conform, to the national interest. A similar approach characterised much work on the period, for example assessments of Philip V of Spain (r. 1700–46) and the relevance of his Italian policies for Spanish interests.[19]

Subsequent scholarship has made this approach appear in need of some modification. Our understanding of the politics of the period has greatly deepened as a result of work on political structures and ideology. A number of scholars, pre-eminently Edward Gregg and Ragnhild Hatton, directed attention to the continued political significance of the Crown and, therefore, of the royal Court,[20] although it remains the case that Anne's veto of the Scottish militia bill in 1708 was the last by the Crown. Similarly,

[17] M. A. Thomson, 'Parliament and Foreign Policy, 1689–1714', *History*, new series, 38 (1953), pp. 234–43, reprinted in R. M. Hatton and J. S. Bromley (eds.), *William III and Louis XIV. Essays 1680–1720 by and for Mark A. Thomson* (Liverpool, 1968), pp. 130–9; G. C. Gibbs, 'Parliament and Foreign Policy in the Age of Stanhope and Walpole', *English Historical Review*, 77 (1962), pp. 18–37, and 'Parliament and the Treaty of Quadruple Alliance', in R. M. Hatton and J. S. Bromley, *William III and Louis XIV. Essays 1680–1720 by and for Mark A. Thomson* (Liverpool, 1968), pp. 287–305. See also, E. R. Turner, 'Parliament and Foreign Affairs, 1630–1760', *English Historical Review*, 34 (1919); Gibbs, 'Newspapers, Parliament and Foreign Policy in the Age of Stanhope and Walpole', in *Mélanges offerts à G. Jacquemyns* (Brussels, 1968), pp. 293–315; D. H. Wollman, *Parliament and Foreign Affairs, 1697–1714* (Ph.D. thesis, University of Wisconsin, 1970).
[18] Thomson, 'Parliament and Foreign Policy', p. 134; Gibbs, 'Stanhope and Walpole', pp. 20, 22.
[19] For a recent study, H. Kamen, *Philip V of Spain* (New Haven, 2001).
[20] E. Gregg, *Queen Anne* (1980); Hatton, *George I* (1978).

attention was directed to the House of Lords;[21] and the relative importance of the Commons, both as a sphere of political activity and debate
and as a source of policy, was diminished, although it remained, and remains, the most studied of the two Houses. More pertinently, from the
point of assessing national interests, the ideological hegemony of Whiggish
notions was challenged, as indeed was their uniformity. While a more
sophisticated assessment of Whig thought was offered, the vitality of Toryism was also stressed, and Jacobitism became a major topic for scholarly
study.[22]

One does not need to sympathise with the exiled Stuarts and their British
supporters, both in and out of Parliament, to appreciate that an approach
that took Whig perspectives for granted was unsatisfactory. Thomson and
Gibbs were naturally aware that Parliament was divided on issues of foreign
policy, but they failed to stress the extent to which these divisions expressed
not dissent over the means to achieve agreed aims, but, instead, fundamental disagreement as to national interests. In part, this reflected a tendency
not to treat the Tories seriously, either as politicians or as representatives of
a specific attitude to foreign policy. Thus, Gibbs wrote of the most influential Tory contribution to the printed debate over foreign policy in 1727,
'Bolingbroke's arguments, which, in so far as they amounted to anything
worthy of being called an argument, represented a plea for permanent isolation from Europe', and dismissed them as violent and destructive, but
not very effective.[23] Gibbs's assessment was in no way unusual, for Tory
views on foreign policy were generally neglected or derided, particularly for
the period after the Hanoverian accession in 1714. There appeared to be a
widespread supposition that these ideas were ignorant and prejudiced, and
the nineteenth-century historian Thomas Macaulay's view of the foolish
provincial Tory squire was never more influential than in the assessment of
Tory views on foreign policy.

This approach was exacerbated by the sources employed. The archival
basis for recreating the perceptions and views of opposition politicians
is often limited, certainly in comparison with those of their ministerial
counterparts. The resulting emphasis, in work on the eighteenth century, on
governmental sources for foreign policy encouraged a failure to understand

[21] C. Jones, 'The House of Lords and the Growth of Parliamentary Stability, 1701–42', in Jones (ed.),
Britain in the First Age of Party 1680–1750 (1987), pp. 85–110.
[22] L. Colley, *In Defiance of Oligarchy: The Tory Party, 1714–60* (Cambridge, 1982); E. Cruickshanks,
Political Untouchables. The Tories and the '45 (1979); P. Monod, *Jacobitism and the English People*
(Cambridge, 1989).
[23] Gibbs, 'Stanhope and Walpole', pp. 35–6.

debates on national interest. In essence, opposition views were presented from outside, and treated as ridiculous and/or inconsequential.

However, once the views of those who disagreed with government policy, particularly, though not only, the Tories, are given due weight, then it becomes increasingly difficult to present Britain as possessing clear-cut interests, interests that should have been defended and financed by Parliament without question. It therefore becomes questionable to present a set of policies as the obvious agenda for furthering national interests. Parliament's role, instead, becomes that of definer of often shifting partisan views as national interests. The increased discussion of foreign policy in Parliament, particularly from 1701, reflected a new set of political circumstances and perceptions that encouraged and necessitated such processes of definition. Instead, therefore, of the political focus being simply one of the relationship between Crown and Parliament, the former finding it necessary to convince the latter, there was a more complex process. Part of this arose from the need to use Parliament to influence the extra-parliamentary debate over national issues.

From 1689 until 1722, British parliamentary politics were in an extraordinary state of flux. In particular, the identity, nature and aspirations of political groupings were far from constant. Distinguished modern historians have devoted much effort to discussing the validity of a description in terms of defined political parties, but this has not been without controversy. It is important to consider the terms employed by contemporaries, especially Whigs and Tories, but these were far from uniform in meaning. However, the very existence of a government tended to produce one rough distinction: between those who supported the government of the day and those who opposed it, however divided these two groups might be. John Ellis, an Under-Secretary of State, who was later an MP, adopted a Court perspective when he wrote from Whitehall in December 1701 to George Stepney, envoy in Vienna, concerning 'this contentious place that peaceable men can hardly live in, without being mauled by one side, or other'.[24]

Parliament served then as an institution in which political groups could define their identity and present their views, and also one in which ministerial schemes could be expounded as national interests to both domestic and international audiences in order to rally support. Ministers and diplomats generally believed that parliamentary debates were of influence abroad, although they knew that this was not invariably the case. Ellis wrote in 1701, 'I hope we shall take such resolutions, when we meet in Parliament, as the

[24] Ellis to Stepney, 19 Dec. (os) 1701, BL. Add. 7074 fol. 73.

present great conjuncture requires, and as may inspire our confederates with the courage that is necessary for the preservation of us all.' Two years later, Sir Rowland Gwynne, a former Whig MP, hoped that 'the resolutions of the Parliament may give some new life to the allies':[25] the Emperor and the Dutch. In 1708, Charles, 1st Duke of Manchester, Ambassador in Venice, wrote to a Secretary of State, Charles, 3rd Earl of Sunderland: 'I am glad both Houses of Parliament have taken notice of sending Prince Eugene. If anything will prevail with the Court of Vienna, I should think that should; but I am far from thinking it will.'[26]

The public dimension of politics was accentuated by the expansion in printed discussion. This helped shape, define and debate the goals of British policy. Pamphlet controversy provided a high-tempo discussion of policy,[27] while the politicians within Parliament could only raise issues occasionally. The press also served as a medium between Crown and Parliament, and ensured that both acted, to at least a partial degree, in a public sphere. The printing of the rejected proposal for war with France in 1689 raised the ire of parliamentarians who had turned down the specific terms. When Parliament gathered in 1696, everyone knew from the newspapers that peace negotiations were underway, and that William had to appeal for subsidies to help make the talks serve the goal of a satisfactory settlement.

The use of Parliament as a sounding board for policy ensured that the Glorious Revolution gave England, and then Britain, a parliamentary foreign policy, a policy that was expounded and debated in Parliament for political reasons that were not related solely to Parliament's fiscal powers. This, however, was a process associated with Anne's reign, rather than William's, and the different views of the two monarchs were important.[28] William's attitude has been criticised by scholars. Thomson wrote of William and the two Houses of Parliament: 'he made no attempt to secure their support for . . . the Partition Treaties. Convinced of the desirability of this policy and relying on the undoubted treaty-making power of the crown, he ignored signs of a change in opinion'. Gibbs saw the parliamentary crisis over the treaties and related issues as arising from a failure to convince Parliament

---

[25] Ellis to Stepney, 2 Dec. (os) 1701, BL. Add. 7074 fol. 63; Gwynne to Lord Halifax, 20 Dec. (os) 1703, BL. Eg. 929 fol. 51.

[26] Manchester to Sunderland, 27 Jan. 1708, Huntingdon CRO. DD M36/8.

[27] D. Coombs, *The Conduct of the Dutch. British Opinion and the Dutch Alliance during the War of the Spanish Succession* (The Hague, 1958). For a recent account, J. Metzdorf, *Politik-Propaganda-Patronage. Francis Hare und die englische Publizistik im spanischen Erbfolgekrieg* (Mainz, 2000).

[28] Thomson, 'Parliament and Foreign Policy', p. 135. On William see, more generally, G. Davies, 'The Control of British Foreign Policy by William III', in *Essays on the Later Stuarts* (1958), pp. 91–122.

that British interests were being considered 'during the period 1698–1701 when William III was made to see very clearly the serious disadvantages attached to policies inspired and conducted without regard to Parliament, and complained, seemingly unaware of his own responsibility in the matter, that indifference and parochialism' were general in Britain.[29]

More than the Partition Treaties was at issue. William's failure to seek parliamentary approval for the terms of the 1697 Rijswijk peace settlement also helped inflame anger, and, in addition, the consequences of continued international readiness, in the shape of a large army, were contentious. The king's lack of interest in Parliament's view on the size of the army led to bitter divisions that weakened his international position. Domestic critics were concerned not so much about foreign policy, as about the possible consequences of a large army for domestic politics, an issue with a long resonance in English politics.[30] On 2 December (os) 1697, at the opening of the session, William told Parliament that the maintenance of a standing force was essential.[31] He believed it was necessary in order to provide security against France and the Jacobites. Nine days later, however, the Commons decided to disband all land forces that had been raised since 1680. There was a strong desire for a peace dividend, as well as longstanding opposition to a large army. As a result, the English establishment was cut to 10,000 men.

A year later, after the general election of 1698 had seen a revival in Tory numbers and a strengthening of 'Country' attitudes, best described as hostility to central government, the Commons again attacked on the issue, which was dear to William as well as crucial to tax levels. The 'New Country Party' of Paul Foley and Robert Harley and their Tory allies won some Whig support for their attacks, although this 'Country' alliance was in practice largely a Tory movement.[32] The Commons decided to reduce the English establishment to 7,000, and its Irish counterpart to 12,000, and to restrict the army to native troops, thus ensuring that Dutch regiments would have to return home, a humiliating blow that William unsuccessfully sought to reverse. William complained to Parliament that 'the nation is left too much exposed'.[33]

[29] Thomson, 'Parliament and Foreign Policy', pp. 131–2; Gibbs, 'Stanhope and Walpole', p. 20.
[30] L. G. Schwoerer, *No Standing Armies: the Antiarmy Ideology in Seventeenth-Century England* (Baltimore, 1974).
[31] Cobbett, V, 1166.
[32] D. Hayton, 'The Country Party in the House of Commons 1698–1699: a Forecast of the Opposition to a Standing Army?', *Parliamentary History*, 6 (1987), pp. 141–4.
[33] Cobbett, V, 1193.

In contrast, the Dutch army was kept at 45,500. There was little doubt where William's views were more influential, and his disillusionment with British politics was readily apparent. This, however, led him to give far too little attention to parliamentary management, a failure exacerbated by the length of time he spent in the United Provinces.[34] As a result, with the ministry bereft of royal support, and now without the enforced cohesion stemming from the threats from France and the Jacobites, the political initiative was left with parliamentary critics.

As a reminder of the different directions in which parliaments could develop in the British Isles, the Dublin Parliament did not meet between 1698 and 1703 because of ministerial concern about Irish demands for autonomy. These dates themselves testify to the importance of foreign policy for constitutional developments, because the financial pressures following British entry into the War of the Spanish Succession in 1702 made it necessary to call this Parliament again in 1703.

The contrast between parliamentary opposition in Westminster and government views can be glimpsed in letters from Edward Villiers, 1st Earl of Jersey, a plenipotentiary for the Rijswijk negotiations, to Richard Hill, envoy in Brussels. In November 1697, he wrote:

You know the necessity of having an army; everybody here is not of that mind . . . here are horrible cabals on all sides. It is hoped that the Parliament will give the number of troops that is wanted, and His Majesty his revenue – though neither without a good deal of opposition.

The following January, Jersey added that he was 'peevish . . . at the mistaken notions of our wise senators, who think English militia better than any French regular troops . . . the parties are as they were – one jealous of their power [the Whigs], and the other not trusted' by William (the Tories). Parliamentary moves on government revenues also aroused Jersey's anger.[35]

More was at issue than William's attitudes. Any discussion of relations between Crown and Parliament carries with it the danger that the position of the latter is made to appear consistent, that, in short, a sound basis existed for defining a relationship with the monarchy, and for settling the ambiguities produced by the contrary pressures of constitutional convention and political exigency. This was not so. Moreover, for William to turn to Parliament over the Partition Treaties and other issues of foreign policy

---

[34] An important source for this period is D. Hayton (ed.), *The Parliamentary Diary of Sir Richard Cocks, 1698–1702* (Oxford, 1996).

[35] Jersey to Hill, 26 Nov. (os) 1697, 18 Jan. (os), 8 Feb. (os) 1698, London, Greater London Record Office Acc. 510/71–2, 74.

was to risk surrendering his political initiative, at home and abroad. Immediate post-war periods were classically difficult in diplomatic and domestic political terms in an age when total victory was rare and when peace thus entailed contentious compromises. The situation was made worse from 1697 by the crisis over the Spanish succession – the contested inheritance to the Spanish empire – which revealed the bankruptcy of the notion of obvious, let alone agreed, British national interests.[36] The prospect of a Bourbon succession to all or part of the succession focused the contentious issues of Louis XIV's intentions and France's relative strength, and raised the issue of the desirability and prudence of different possible responses.

William had to manoeuvre in a difficult diplomatic situation made more volatile by the domestic and international recriminations following the peace of 1697, the prospects for international realignment that it offered, and the opportunities presented by the Spanish succession. To have taken Parliament into his trust would have involved manoeuvring in public, and might have entailed limitations to his room in manoeuvre.

William had to convince foreign rulers that he was securely in control when it was by no means clear that a majority of parliamentary opinion would follow the tergiversations of his partition diplomacy. Being forced to accept the Disbandment Act of 1699 and the resumption of his grants of Irish forfeited estates in 1700, were public humiliations that risked compromising William's international position. Foreign envoys were certainly sensitive to the parliamentary situation. Arriving in London in March 1698, the French envoy Camille d'Hostun, Count of Tallard reported, that month, that William was less powerful than was believed in France. He claimed, correctly, that the parliamentary opposition wished to prevent William becoming 'le maître', and he stressed William's unpopularity. Tallard presented a volatile situation: a two-party system, the Whigs opposed to royal authority and the Tories unhappy about the Glorious Revolution, a monarch who found it difficult to find ministers whom he could rely upon, and 'un mouvement perpetuel' in the political sphere.[37]

Given the sensitivity of the Spanish Succession negotiations, and the need to keep them secret from the childless Charles II of Spain, for fear that he would take unwanted steps over the succession to his territories,[38] there were important 'external' reasons, aside from the 'internal' factor of William's

---

[36] W. Roosen, 'The Origins of the War of the Spanish Succession', in J. Black (ed.), *The Origins of War in Early-Modern Europe* (Edinburgh, 1987), pp. 151–75.

[37] Tallard to Louis XIV, 31 Mar., 8 Apr., 9 May 1698, 3 May 1699, AE. CP. Ang. 174 fols. 106, 128, 175, 181 fol. 14.

[38] Tallard to Louis, 8 May, 17 Sept. 1698, AE. CP. Ang. 175 fol. 30, 177 fols. 76–7.

difficulties with British politicians, that help to explain why William chose to confide in only a few, principally Dutch, ministers.[39] Tallard stressed likely parliamentary opposition to William's plans. In addition, claiming, correctly, that English politics altered during the parliamentary session,[40] Tallard argued that, as a result, any agreement over the succession would have to be made before the session.[41]

Any agreement would, indeed, have led to parliamentary criticism. In the event, in 1700, Louis XIV accepted the will of Charles II of Spain after he died. The will ignored the Second Partition Treaty of that year and left the entire inheritance to the Bourbon claimant, Philip, Duke of Anjou, Louis' younger grandson (who became king as Philip V). This ensured that William had the worst of both worlds. He was condemned for the manner of his diplomacy, and was himself unhappy with its failure and with the consequences. William was criticised within Britain for failing to take adequate advice before concluding the treaty. In April 1701, the leading Whig ministers, the Earls of Halifax and Orford and John, Lord Somers, all members of the Junto, as well as William's favourite Dutch minister, William, 1st Earl of Portland, were impeached for their alleged responsibility in the signing of the Partition Treaties, and, in addition, the Lords criticised the agreement to allow France territorial gains. Ellis commented in March 1701,

It may be supposed that when the Addresses of the House are made intelligible to the princes abroad, they will scarce think it safe to conclude treaties without the concurrence of the Parliament, and sure nothing can be a secret there, who will enter into negotiation with us?[42]

Tallard came to a similar conclusion, telling the Portuguese envoy that the unreliability of any alliance negotiated with England should make Portugal turn to France.[43] It did so until 1703 (when it switched to the Allied camp), but this was not due to parliamentary attacks on the government.

After the Tories gained control of the Commons in the general election held in January and February 1701, they made their attitude to William clear. In May 1701, the Kentish petitioners who called for support for William's foreign policy were put into custody by the Commons. The Act of Settlement, passed in June, included a further criticism of William's

[39] Tallard to Louis, 8 Apr., 9 May 1698, AE. CP. Ang. 174 fol. 130, 175 fols. 38–9.
[40] Tallard to Louis, 15 May 1699, AE. CP. Ang. 181 fol. 62.
[41] Tallard to Louis, 4, 10 Sept. 1700, AE. CP. Ang. 188 fols. 301, 357.
[42] Ellis to Stepney, 28 Mar. (os) 1701, BL. Add. 7074 fol. 7.
[43] Tallard to Louis, 17 Mar. 1701, AE. CP. Ang. 191 fol. 71.

approach to foreign policy: monarchs were only to be able to leave their realm with parliamentary consent. In practice, this did not affect the ability of monarchs to conduct negotiations in person abroad, as Anne never sought to travel there, while the clause was repealed for the Hanoverians, but the measure reflected the willingness of Parliament to define royal prerogatives and defy royal wishes. So also did the provision under which judges only became removable after Parliament had played a role.

Concern about international implications encouraged the search for a domestic political consensus, but so also did a greater accommodation on the part of the Crown as relations with France deteriorated. On 18 March (os) 1701, William sent Parliament a report on diplomatic discussions at The Hague, giving, as his reason, his 'gracious intention to acquaint you, from time to time, with the state and progress of those negotiations'. William knew he needed parliamentary support, not least for the expansion of the army, which was crucial if Britain was to play a military role on the Continent as he intended. Without such a commitment, the Dutch would be very vulnerable to French attack, and therefore less likely to defy Louis.

William's approach, combined with growing popular hostility in England to inopportune French moves, that greatly increased fears about Louis' intentions and the consequences of the Bourbon succession to the Spanish empire, produced results. There was concern and anger about a number of developments including the replacement of the Dutch garrisons in the Barrier fortresses in the Spanish Netherlands (modern Belgium) by French forces in February 1701, and the permission granted the following month for French warships to sell goods in Spanish American ports. In the 1701 session, the Commons resolved to support the Dutch with the assistance specified in the Anglo-Dutch treaty of 1678, voted more money than had ever hitherto been voted in time of peace, and gave William a free hand in the negotiation of alliances, prefiguring the shift towards military commitment on the Continent that was to be seen, during the Seven Years' War, in 1758.

On 12 June (os) 1701, William thanked Parliament for 'repeated assurances' of support for alliances to preserve 'the liberty of Europe'. The Commons responded by promising backing for such alliances as he should negotiate 'in conjunction with the Emperor and the States-General, for the preservation of the liberties of Europe, the prosperity and peace of England, and for reducing the exorbitant power of France'. This was an important mark of support. On 17 June (os), Somers was acquitted, bringing to an end the impeachment of those criticised for the Partition Treaties.

After Whig success in the second general election of 1701, that held in November and December, there was more pronounced parliamentary support for war in the session that began on 30 December (os) 1701, as well as the raising of new taxes, and the passage of an Act requiring the abjuration of the new Jacobite Pretender, 'James III and VIII', whom Louis had recognised when James II and VII died in September 1701. This second general election had been influenced by the circulation of a 'black list' of Tory MPs allegedly unwilling to prepare for war with Louis XIV. In May 1702, the declaration of war on France was made by the authority of Queen Anne (who had succeeded two months earlier), but in response to the Addresses and resolutions of both Houses of Parliament; a pattern in some respects matching that of the political consequences of the constitutional position over foreign policy.

It was from the session of 1701 that Thomson dated a new, more open relationship between Crown and Parliament in foreign policy. However, it is necessary not to exaggerate the change that took place. Parliament was only given general details about policy. Furthermore, policies and actions were concealed from it. In 1706, for example, in an important indication of both policy and attitudes, Victor Amadeus II of Savoy-Piedmont was given, besides his agreed subsidy, 'fifty thousand pounds sterling, for which no provision was made by Parliament'.[44]

The parliamentary politics of William's last years were cited in debate subsequently, not least in the Lords' debate on the Address on 15 November (os) 1739. Thomas, Duke of Newcastle, Secretary of State for the Southern Department, cited William in support of his call for unity in the newly declared war with Spain, only for John, 4th Duke of Bedford to argue that there was no comparison, not least as the particular crisis that had led to the impeachment of ministers had not been repeated.[45]

The significance of 1701 for the development of Parliament's role in foreign policy has been over-emphasised in part as a result of the war between England and France that began the following year, a war that Sir Michael Warton, an MP with Country sympathies, described in 1703 as a 'legacy the late King left us'.[46] This conflict increased the need for parliamentary support, both in order to raise funds and to impress foreign

---

[44] Harley to Stepney, 24 May (os) 1706, BL. Add. 7059 fol. 101; G. Symcox, 'Britain and Victor Amadeus II: or, the Use and Abuse of Allies', in S. Baxter (ed.), *England's Rise to Greatness, 1660–1763* (Berkeley, 1983); Gibbs, 'Laying Treaties', pp. 121–2.

[45] *A Collection of the Parliamentary Debates in England from 1668 to the present Time*, XVII (1741), pp. 338–9, 349–50.

[46] Warton to Thomas Pitt, 14 Apr. (os) 1703, BL. Add. 22852 fol. 63.

powers. In addition, turning to Parliament provided the Crown with a relatively popular basis for eliciting cooperation. Tallard had warned Louis in 1698 that, whatever his current domestic and parliamentary difficulties, William would be able to raise all the money he asked on the day that war began with France.[47] Five years later, Edward Harrison, a captain in the India trade and later an MP, noted 'things have gone smooth in the main this session I mean as to raising money and men and that is the sinews of war'.[48]

The shift in 1702 from the unpopular William to his sister-in-law Anne was important. She was able to emphasise her Englishness and her Anglicanism. Indeed, Anne told her first Parliament, 'I know my own heart to be entirely English', a declaration made more appropriate by its setting. Anne, who frequently attended Lords' debates, was also readier than William to accept that the implications of parliamentary management entailed, firstly, finding ministers who could enjoy the confidence of Parliament, and, secondly, responding to national party politics as represented, through an imperfect electoral process, in the composition of the Commons. This limited the choice of ministers and thus of policies.

More specific factors also helped improve relations from 1701. Louis XIV's recognition of 'James III' helped cement British support for opposition to Louis, and made it more difficult to criticise the declaration of war on France the following May or, at least initially, the war goals. This support was carried forward by dramatic successes, especially the victories of John Churchill, 1st Duke of Marlborough, particularly Blenheim (1704), Ramillies (1706), and Oudenaarde (1708), which contrasted with William III's failures in the Low Countries in terms of both prestige and results, and helped the Whigs make important gains in the general election of 1705, and win a clear majority in that of 1708.

If royal disclosure of policy to Parliament increased from 1701 it was, nevertheless, the case, as both Thomson and Gibbs pointed out, that Parliament was not told the whole truth. Indeed, statements could be made that were inaccurate, and known to be such, as with Anne's speech opening the session on 7 December (os) 1711 in which she claimed that her allies supported the current effort to negotiate peace.[49] The Crown retained the initiative in foreign policy, and, in practical terms, the reasons for monarch

---

[47] Tallard to Louis, 22 May 1698, AE. CP. Ang. 175 fol. 83.
[48] Harrison to Pitt, 14 Feb. (os) 1703, BL. Add. 22852 fol. 75.
[49] Thomson, 'Parliament and Foreign Policy', p. 135; Gibbs, 'The Revolution in Foreign Policy', in G. Holmes (ed.), *Britain after the Glorious Revolution 1689–1714* (1969), p. 73.

and ministers to remain hesitant about discussing policy remained. There was no automatic parliamentary support for government policy and, in addition, the particular grievances of specific constituencies could cause difficulties. In 1704, Harley wrote to Stepney concerning a petition from Exeter and several other West Country boroughs complaining about Austrian tariffs on their woollen cloths:

there is the greater reason to consider the petitions, and endeavour to obtain redress herein, because, besides the general interest of the nation, the members from the West have a great influence in the resolutions of the House of Commons, and especially in the granting of money.[50]

Money was indeed crucial to Parliament's role. The War of the Spanish Succession, in which Britain was engaged from 1702 until 1713, was considerably more expensive than the Nine Years' War, as Britain took a greater role, in conflict on the Continent, in subsidies to foreign allies, and in operations outside Europe. This ensured that it was more necessary than in the previous war to turn to Parliament in order to raise loans, and thus underwrite the servicing of a rising debt, as well as to increase taxes. Excise duties were extended during the wars with France. Among new duties, salt was taxed from 1694, seaborne coal from 1695, and leather from 1697.[51]

Policy was linked to interest and party, but debate over foreign policy during the war essentially shrank to the progress of the war and, more specifically, to the conduct of the allies. Thus, in 1703, Anne was pressed to insist that the Dutch stop trading with France and Spain.[52] Supporters of Continental interventionism advocated a multilateralism that contrasted with the unilateralism of those who preferred a maritime option, the 'blue-water' policy of amphibious operations and attacks on Bourbon colonies and trade.[53]

It was understandable that the war came to dominate the attention of parliamentarians, but, as a result, singularly little attention was devoted to other important changes in Europe, especially the rise in Russian power after Peter the Great's crushing victory over Charles XII of Sweden at Poltava in 1709. The consequences of this were greatly to affect foreign policy during the reign of George I (1714–27) and to be the source of parliamentary controversy. It was already clear in Anne's reign that the rise of Russia

[50] Harley to Stepney, 10 Nov. (os) 1704, BL. Add. 7059 fol. 45.
[51] D. W. Jones, *War and Economy in the Age of William III and Marlborough* (Oxford, 1988).
[52] D. Coombs, *The Conduct of the Dutch. British Opinion and the Dutch Alliance during the War of the Spanish Succession* (The Hague, 1958).
[53] J. B. Hattendorf, *England in the War of the Spanish Succession: A Study of the English View and Conduct of Grand Strategy, 1701–1712* (New York, 1987).

would be of future consequence for Britain, as the Hanoverian succession had been established under the Act of Settlement and Hanover was greatly concerned in the fate of the Swedish empire. However, this was not a pressing issue during Anne's reign, while the volatility of Eastern European developments discouraged any firm building of consequences upon them: Charles XII had beaten the Russians at Narva in 1700, while, in 1711, Peter was to be defeated by Charles's Ottoman (Turkish) allies at the River Pruth.

The combination of policy and party in debating diplomatic (and other) issues could create serious problems for parliamentary management. In 1710, there was a political change, with Whigs dismissed from office in favour of Tories, and a general election that October that saw support dramatically switch to the latter. Prefiguring John, 3rd Earl of Bute's peace policy in the early 1760s, and his sense that war was no longer producing desirable gains, the Tories, in 1710–11, were determined on peace, and willing to negotiate without the consent of their allies; but the process was far from easy. On 7 December (os) 1711, the government was defeated in the Lords on a division of 62 to 54 over Daniel, 2nd Earl of Nottingham's motion that 'No peace could be safe or honourable to Great Britain or Europe, if Spain and the West Indies were allotted to any branch of the House of Bourbon.'[54] That, indeed, was what was intended by the government.

This crisis led to an expedient that could only be practised in the Lords, the creation of new parliamentarians, in this case twelve peers at the close of the year (thirteen peerages were in fact offered). Parliament therefore provided the occasion for an important public display of royal favour for the government, and this helped ensure that the political crisis over the peace could be overcome. The following May, an opposition motion that the war be prosecuted 'with the utmost vigour' was defeated in the Lords by 68 to 40 votes.[55]

In June 1712, when Anne revealed the outline of the peace, there was an attack in the Lords, specifically on the provisions designed to prevent Philip V of Spain from holding both the French and the Spanish thrones. They were regarded as inadequate, while the peace terms were seen as a violation of the Treaty of the Grand Alliance under which the war had been waged. Twenty-four Whig Lords signed a protest, but the government's majority ensured that the protest was expunged on a division of 90 to

---

[54] G. Holmes, 'The Commons' Division on "No Peace without Spain", 7 December 1711', *Bulletin of the Institute of Historical Research*, 33 (1960), pp. 223–34.
[55] Cobbett, VI, 1135–8; Gregg, *Queen Anne*, p. 357.

54.[56] Opposition in the Lords in part reflected Whig strength there, but it would be misleading to understand politics simply in terms of Whig–Tory animosity. There was also an important role, particularly in the Lords, for those who saw themselves as above party, an attitude that accorded with powerful cultural pressures in favour of harmony and against faction, as well as classical notions of public service.

In practice, however, the pressures of partisan politics led many to party alignments. The same pressures affected those who saw themselves primarily as the servants of Crown and government.[57] Yet, the inability of parties, especially the Tories, to ensure cohesion was important: Nottingham was a disaffected Tory.

The peace terms faced fewer problems in the Commons. The 'No Peace without Spain' motion was defeated. Jonathan Swift claimed credit for this with the publication of his pamphlet *The Conduct of the Allies* in November 1711, which was timed to influence the session. The pamphlet, which sold more than 11,000 copies in two months, was indeed used as the source of Tory arguments, and Swift claimed that the votes 'would never have passed, if that book had not been written'.[58] However, in practice, war-weariness was strong, and took precedence over concern about specific terms.

Opposition to the continuation of the war helped define what was subsequently seen as the Tory position on foreign policy: caution towards foreign commitments, particularly alliance politics and warfare on the Continent. In practice, as was always the case, there was, in the formulation and expression of attitudes, a complex and not completely comfortable interaction of short-term exigencies and opportunities with longer-term developments. The war policy that was rejected had been associated with Marlborough and Sidney, 1st Earl of Godolphin, the Lord Treasurer, both of whom were Tories, albeit Tories willing to align with Whigs in order to remain in power and secure their policies. By focusing on a rapid and unilateral peace, Harley and his allies secured an issue around which most Tories could rally, while the Tory divide from Whigs could be satisfactorily clarified in order to

---

[56] Cobbett, VI, 1141–51, 1165; Gregg, *Anne*, pp. 357–8.
[57] J. H. Plumb, *The Growth of Political Stability in England 1675–1725* (1967); C. Roberts, *Schemes and Undertakings: A Study of English Politics in the Seventeenth Century* (1985); G. Holmes, *British Politics in the Age of Anne* (2nd edn, 1987); D. Hayton (ed.), *The History of Parliament. The House of Commons 1690–1715* (5 vols., 2002).
[58] H. Davis *et al.*, *The Prose Works of Jonathan Swift* (16 vols., Oxford, 1939–68), XVI, 480–2; J. A. Downie, '*The Conduct of the Allies*: The Question of Influence', in C. T. Probyn (ed.), *The Art of Jonathan Swift* (1978), pp. 108–28.

win popular support. The Tories were able to demonstrate their care for national interests, and also address the long-term problem of finding a set of coherent Tory policies.

The difficulties that the Commons could still create for government were amply demonstrated in 1713 when the Anglo-French commercial treaty was rejected on 18 June (os) by 194 to 185 votes.[59] This defeat was a significant blow against the diplomatic realignment that the ministry sought after the dissolution of the Grand Alliance, and it exposed the unpopularity of the Tory government's attempt to improve relations with France. The correspondence of officials provides a valuable indication of their perception of an absence of control in the face of parliamentary opposition. On 12 June 1713, Richard Warre, one of the Under-Secretaries, wrote to Robert, 2nd Lord Lexington, the Ambassador in Spain:

The Commons in a Grand Committee have for 2 or 3 days sat late in hearing what some merchants had to say upon the Treaty of Commerce, wherein some have shown they little understand trade as to the nation's interest, how able so ever they may be in their private concerns, which may have misguided them, and made them lay a greater stress on some parts of trade then the things will bear. We shall quickly see, what effect their speeches will have had with the members; the majority hitherto has appeared considerably for making good articles; and as little has been said that was not known before, few perhaps will be moved to change their opinion.

Four days later, Warre's colleague, Erasmus Lewis, soon to be a Tory MP, added,

There having been no open trade between Britain and France these five and twenty years I find the treaty now made is not comprehended by the generality of people. It is natural where people are ignorant they should be diffident and that is the state of our case. The adverse party is against it, because the present ministry made it, but the misfortune is our friends are much divided in their sentiments. Your Excellency knows the cry of Popery or woollen manufacturing will raise this nation into a ferment at any time.

[59] D. A. E. Harkness, 'The Opposition to the 8th and 9th Articles of the Commercial Treaty of Utrecht', *Scottish Historical Review*, 21 (1923–4), pp. 219–26; E. C. Bogle, *A Stand for Tradition: The Rejection of the Anglo-French Commercial Treaty of Utrecht* (Ph.D. thesis, University of Maryland, 1972); D. C. Coleman, 'Politics and Economics in the Age of Anne: The Case of the Anglo-French Trade Treaty of 1713', in Coleman and A. H. John (eds.), *Trade, Government and Economy in Pre-Industrial England: Essays Presented to F. J. Fisher* (1976), pp. 187–211; G. Holmes and C. Jones, 'Trade, the Scots and the Parliamentary Crisis of 1713', *Parliamentary History*, 1 (1982), pp. 47–77; T. J. Schaeper, 'French and English Trade after the Treaty of Utrecht: The Missions of Amisson and Fénellon in London, 1713–1714', *British Journal for Eighteenth-Century Studies*, 9 (1986), pp. 1–18. For the developing role of foreign trade in political debate, P. Gauci, *The Politics of Trade: The Overseas Merchant in State and Society, 1660–1720* (Oxford, 2001).

In the event, the Bill was defeated:

Several voted and some spoke against the Bill of whom it was little expected, which turned the scales. Many boroughs are strangely possessed with an opinion, of great prejudice threatened by this Treaty to our woollen manufactures abroad, which others think they can prove will be advanced by it. However some may think that by voting against it, they have the better secured their interest in the next election,[60]

the latter a reminder of the role attributed to electoral calculations when parliamentary votes were assessed. The defeat was due to the willingness of close to eighty moderate Tories to break ranks. They were referred to as 'whimsical'; the attitudes of these 'Hanoverian' Tories reflected the role of issues. The unity and popularity seen in the pressure for peace, that helped the Tories to a sweeping victory in the general elections of 1710 and, even more clearly, September 1713, did not extend to questions of post-war policy. Had the Tories remained in power from 1714, instead of being swept from office after George I succeeded Anne, who died on 1 August (os) at the age of forty-nine, then their serious divisions over policy, tactics and personality would probably have extended further to details of foreign policy. The negotiation of peace had served them as war had earlier served their Whig rivals, bringing a measure of unity; but, as circumstances changed, so divisive issues came to the fore.

Whereas the crucial division on the trade treaty occurred in the Commons, more generally in 1711–14, the major parliamentary debates on foreign policy took place in the Lords where the ministry had a small or non-existent majority.[61] This was true of the 'No Peace without Spain' motion, the so-called desertion of the allies and the motion to expel the Pretender from Lorraine. The Whigs forced the debates on the Tory ministry because of their strength in the Lords.

The events of 1711–14 might appear to prove that the Revolution had given Britain a parliamentary foreign policy, which William III had managed to delay, but not prevent. In 1712, Anne presented the general plan of peace to Parliament, declaring 'the making peace and war is the undoubted prerogative of the Crown. Yet, such is the just confidence I place in you . . .' On 9 May (os) 1713, the Treaties of Utrecht with France and Spain were laid before both Houses. This was very different to the Treaty of Rijswijk of 1697, which had not been communicated to Parliament. The Harley ministry was motivated by a desire to associate itself clearly with the

---

[60] Warre to Lexington, 12 June (os), Lewis to Lexington, 16 June (os), Warre to Burch, Lexington's secretary, 19 June (os) 1713, BL. Add. 46546 fols. 71, 22, 74.

[61] For the background, C. Jones and G. Holmes (eds.), *The London Diaries of William Nicolson Bishop of Carlisle 1702–1718* (Oxford, 1985), pp. 62–105.

popularity of peace, in order both to strengthen its own position and to demonstrate to foreign powers that the peace was popular. Furthermore, parliamentary backing would make subsequent impeachment of the ministers who had negotiated the treaty by a Whig-dominated Parliament less easy. The decision to communicate the treaties can also be related to Harley's policy towards the press. Rather than re-imposing the pre-publication censorship that had lapsed in 1695, Harley preferred to introduce taxation with the Stamp Act of 1712. This choice has been attributed to his understanding of the value of the press as a means of propaganda.[62]

A contrast with the situation in France was readily apparent. In June 1712, the month in which Harley's peace policy was decisively endorsed by both Houses of Parliament, Louis XIV's foreign minister, Jean Baptiste Colbert, Marquis of Torcy, wrote to Henry St John, one of the Secretaries of State, who was soon to be created Viscount Bolingbroke, to inform him that Louis was opposed to the idea that his grandson Philip V of Spain's renunciation of his rights in the French succession should be ratified by an Estates General:

Les Estats en France ne se meslent point de ce qui regarde la succession à la Couronne, ils n'ont le pouvoir ny de faire, ny d'abroger les loix; quand les Roys les convoquent, on marque dans les lettres que c'est *pour ouyr les plaintes des bons et fideles sujets, et chercher des remedes aux maux presens*. Les exemples des siècles precendens ont fait voir que ces sortes d'assemblées ont presque toujours produit des troubles dans le Royaume, et les derniers etats tenûs en 1614 finirent par la guerre civile . . . l'assemblée des Estats, qui n'ayant point êté convoquez depuis pres de cent ans, sont en quelque maniere abolis dans le Royaume.[63]

Indeed, the Estates General was not to meet again until 1789 and then only due to a crisis of authority and power in the French state. When Louis excluded Philip from the French succession, and again, in 1714, when he legally promoted his bastards to the status of princes of the blood, adding them to the order of succession, and again challenging dynastic and legal principles, neither act was carried out in a *lit de justice*, and the association of Crown and Parlement symbolised by this royal act in the Grand-Chambre of the Palais de Justice was ended. In contrast to the revisionism seen in late-twentieth-century scholarship that sought to limit the impression, created by earlier studies, of authoritarianism in Louis' treatment of the *parlements*, it has recently been argued that he subjugated them.[64]

---

[62] J. A. Downie, *Robert Harley and the Press* (Cambridge, 1979).
[63] Torcy to St John, 22 June 1712, PRO. SP. 78/154 fols. 318–19.
[64] S. Hanley, *The Lits de Justice of the Kings of France* (Princeton, 1983), p. 328; J. J. Hurt, *Louis XIV and the Parlements. The Assertion of Royal Authority* (Manchester, 2002), p. 196.

The contrast is clear, but caution is necessary before pressing the case for a parliamentary foreign policy in Britain too far. The implications of the passage, by the Edinburgh Parliament in 1703, of the Act Anent Peace and War, which laid down that, after Anne's death, the consent of that Parliament would be necessary for negotiating alliances and treaties and making war, were ended by the Act of Union of 1707 which contained no such stipulations. This ended the possibility of an independent foreign policy for Scotland. The legislation of the Edinburgh Parliament in the early 1700s had tended in this direction. The Wine Act had maintained links with France, while the Act of Security of 1704 reserved the right to alter the Hanoverian Succession.

In England, significant defeats for governmental policy did not begin with the Revolution Settlement. Indeed, although the subject does not readily lend itself to quantification, in so far as governmental initiatives in the field of foreign policy were affected by Parliament, they were checked, when Parliament was in session, more frequently prior to 1689 than after it, and, in particular, after the consolidation of a new political order with the Hanoverian succession in 1714, the formation of the first of a series of 'Old Corps' Whig ministries, and the Septennial Act of 1716, which ensured that elections could be held as infrequently as every seven years.

After 1689, a measure of self-congratulatory complacency was produced by the fact that governmental composition and policy reflected that of the parliamentary majority, or, as Ellis put it in 1701, 'the Governing part of our ruling Senate'.[65] That was indeed the supposition made by Whig apologists for the Revolutionary settlement and the 'Old Corps' Whig ascendancy during the reigns of Georges I and II. Several criticisms of this appealing thesis must be advanced. The Revolution Settlement did not prevent monarchs from following a secret personal policy *secret du roi*, with or without the knowledge of some of their ministers. It was impossible to disprove suspicions that Parliament was being kept in the dark, and reports to that effect circulated. In addition, what successive ministries told Parliament in the field of foreign policy remained limited.

Nevertheless, however unpopular he was, William III was no James II. Unlike his predecessor, he had no option of trying to rule without Parliament, but, also unlike James, he understood the need to seek acceptable managers; and this search helped to increase the volatility of ministerial politics. William was driven to anger, but not violence, by Parliament. Once peace had been won in 1697, there was no attempt to stage either a military

---

[65] Ellis to Stepney, 30 May (os) 1701, BL. Add. 7074 fol. 25.

or a political coup. Conversely, English fears of his intentions lessened as William's willingness to heed the implications of parliamentary power became clearer. He sought to evade parliamentary scrutiny, but not to overthrow Parliament; and his reign closed with Parliament and Crown closer together over policy than they had been earlier in the reign.

As war with Louis XIV approached again, William III told the Parliament that met on 30 December (os) 1701, 'the eyes of all Europe are upon this Parliament; all matters are at a stand, till your resolutions are known'.[66] Parliament responded then, but also took steps on other occasions that helped to define political options, as in March 1708 when the Whig-dominated Commons passed an Address stating what they saw as necessary peace conditions. These were dynastic – Louis XIV's recognition of Anne's title and the Hanoverian succession, and the expulsion of the Pretender, 'James III'; territorial – Philip V's abandonment of his quest for Spain; and commercial/strategic – the slighting of Dunkirk, France's leading privateering base and a potential invasion port.

The process by which, in the Nine Years' War and the War of the Spanish Succession, Parliament acquired a position of greater importance in the discussion of foreign policy reflected not so much a gaining of the initiative in the face of royal and ministerial opposition as a development that served different interests at the same time that it caused episodic political difficulties. The eliciting of parliamentary support for public definitions of policy was associated with the organisation of a system of public finance that increased the capabilities of British foreign policy. This was in political terms more significant than the weakening of the royal prerogative discerned by Thomson, and adds an important dimension to Gibbs's suggestion that 'the advent of a parliamentary foreign policy added an element of instability, as well as inflexibility, to a system which appeared in European eyes to be chronically unstable'.[67]

The wider political role of Parliament in the discussion of foreign affairs persisted from 1713. Foreign policy continued to be a contentious issue in domestic political debate with the Whig attack on the Peace of Utrecht and the political tensions created after 1714 by the Hanoverian commitments of George I.

---

[66] Cobbett, V, 1330.
[67] Thomson, 'Parliament and Foreign Policy', pp. 135–6; Gibbs, 'Revolution in Foreign Policy', p. 75.

3

The Walpolean system, Parliament and foreign policy, 1714–42

The management of Parliament was seen as a central task of government. However party alignments were defined, ministerial majorities were uncertain. Victory in elections, and the subsequent opening of the bazaar of patronage to parliamentarians, did not necessarily entail either quiescent sessions or, more seriously, stable majorities. In some moments of crisis, governmental majorities fell, in part due to defections by MPs to the opposition, but, more generally, due to a rise in the number of abstentions. The latter were crucial in Sir Robert Walpole's two major parliamentary defeats: the enforced withdrawal of the excise legislation in the Commons in 1733, and his own loss of control in the Commons in the winter of 1741–2. Once the parliamentary majority of a ministry began to fall and rumours circulated of government changes, it proved very difficult to retain the loyalty of Whig MPs keen to make bargains with those they believed were about to take power, who were bound to be prominent Whigs. Indeed, various statements were attributed to Walpole to the effect that if the majority fell below forty or fifty his power was lost.[1]

It was widely argued by the opposition in Britain, as well as in Jacobite circles and in Europe, that the ministry was able to dominate Parliament thanks to corruption and to the tempting prizes it could offer. This was an argument rejected by the government. The ministry claimed that it enjoyed its majorities thanks to an ability to persuade Parliament of the wisdom of its policies. Charles, 2nd Viscount Townshend, Secretary of State for the Northern Department from 1721 to 1730, informed Stephen Poyntz, envoy in France, in February 1729, that Cardinal Fleury, the leading French minister, was

mistaken if he thinks that the Parliament is influenced by money to be thus unanimous in the supporting His Majesty in all he has done. This zeal proceeds

[1] HMC. *The Diary of the First Earl of Egmont* (3 vols., 1920–3), II, 150; Duke to Duchess of Newcastle, 10 Dec. (os) 1741, BL. Add. 33073 fol. 186; *St. James's Chronicle*, 18 Apr. 1769.

from the chief men in both houses being convinced, that the measures His Majesty has hitherto taken are right; but these persons, though they have heartily concurred in what has been done hitherto, are under the greatest anxiety, at the uncertain state of our affairs; and will not be kept much longer in suspense.

Townshend was writing in order to persuade Fleury to act 'a friendly part towards the king', but that does not make his claim without value. Later in the year, Townshend replied with similar arguments to the French suggestion of a secret declaration promising peacetime subsidies to the Archbishop-Elector of Cologne, and he made the same point in 1730 over Swedish subsidies.[2] Foreign diplomats often argued that the ministry exaggerated its difficulties in order to persuade allies not to press issues, such as the restitution to Spain of Gibraltar, which had been conquered in 1704 and ceded to Britain in the Utrecht settlement. While not without value, this argument underrated the independence of parliamentarians.

Concern over parliamentary management led to two different and sometimes clashing themes in the field of foreign policy: the need for a stress on a clear-cut defence of what were seen as national interests and a wish to restrain expenditure. These could coincide, as in the reluctance to support subsidies to foreign powers, but also clashed, as in 1739, when concern about the parliamentary response to the continuing crisis with Spain took precedence over anxiety about financial considerations.

The course of foreign policy made parliamentary management more of a problem and increased the chances of parliamentary difficulties and the risks of ministerial division. This was very much seen in the early years of the reign of George I (r. 1714–27), as the negotiation of an alliance with France in 1716, and a subsequent controversy over the extent to which the government's foreign policy reflected Hanoverian interests, both caused difficulties. The Act of Settlement of 1701, under which the House of Hanover succeeded after the death of Queen Anne in 1714, had placed Parliament at the centre of the constitutional safeguard of British interests, and thus enhanced its position in foreign policy. Entitled programmatically, 'An act for the further limitation of the crown, and better securing the rights and liberties of the subject', it had stipulated 'that in case the crown and imperial dignity of this realm shall hereafter come to any person, not being a native of this kingdom of England, this nation be not obliged to engage in any war for the defence of any dominions or territories which do not belong to the crown

---

[2] Townshend to Poyntz, 12, 21 Feb. (os) 1729, W. Coxe, *Memoirs of the Life and Administration of Sir Robert Walpole, Earl of Orford* (3 vols., 1798), II, 639, BL. Add. 48982; Townshend to Duke of Broglie, French envoy, 3 Nov. (os) 1729, and to Edward Finch, envoy in Sweden, 3 Feb. (os) 1730, PRO. SP. 100/9, 95/54.

of England, without the consent of Parliament'. Thereafter, any supposed distortion of British interests for Hanoverian goals was not only brought up in Parliament as a political matter by opposition politicians, but could also serve to illustrate their charge that the ministry was failing to defend the constitution. Negotiations and commitments could be criticised as likely to provoke a situation in which Britain would support Hanover.

Domestic difficulties, in turn, affected the apparent stability of British policy. An important element in foreign policy was the need to conceal weaknesses and to emphasise strength in order to win the compliance, or at least respect, of other states. This was particularly difficult for countries where representative institutions had a significant role to play, as many statesmen who held office in states where such institutions had been destroyed or lessened regarded these institutions with intense suspicion, viewing them as inherently factious, and, unless they could be controlled, as a dangerous threat to the stability of the state. Substance was lent to such attitudes by the role of Parliament, as well as of the Dutch Estates and the Swedish and, more particularly, Polish Diets in making their countries apparently difficult to govern.

The Septennial Act of 1716, which established that general elections had to be held at least every seven years instead of every three, as under the Triennial Act of 1694, reflected concern about the problems of electoral management and, thus, of parliamentary volatility, as well as the determination of the Whig government to hold on to power. Ministers, indeed, could be driven to exasperation by Parliament. In March 1718, James, Viscount Stanhope, First Lord of the Treasury, was led to exclaim 'combien notre constitution est défectueuse'.[3] The previous month, he had directly linked foreign policy with parliamentary politics in a letter to the envoy in Paris:

It very much behoves us in England to be very cautious how we engage in any war, when I shall tell you that the united strength of the Tories and discontented Whigs, headed and animated by one you may guess [Robert Walpole], are to give us battle tomorrow in the House of Lords upon the bill for punishing mutiny and desertion. Upon this occasion they intend by disagreeing with the preamble of the bill sent up by the Commons to lessen very considerably the number of forces for which the Commons have provided pay. We think ourselves sure of carrying the question, but I am sorry to tell you that 'twill be a slender majority. The happiest thing therefore is to hide from foreign nations if possible our nakedness.[4]

[3] Bonet, Prussian envoy, to Frederick William I, 15 Mar. 1718, Berlin, Rep. XI, vol. 41.
[4] Stanhope to Stair, 17 Feb. (os) 1718, Maidstone, Kent Archives Office, U1590/O145/24.

Regarding British institutions as shaky, foreign diplomats were dubious about the stability of its ministries and the continuity of its policies, particularly down to the consolidation of the Walpole ministry in 1722–4. At times, this led them to express scepticism about the value of Britain as an ally. Simon van Slingelandt, the leading Dutch politician, commented on the danger that Parliament would force the British Court to change its policies, while his colleague Sicco van Goslinga argued that recent history had established that no faith could be placed on the stability of a British ministry. These men were not politicians and diplomats concerned to discredit the value of Britain as an ally, as were for example Jacobites and Spanish diplomats. Instead, they supported a British alliance and favoured a Whig ministry. Similar views were held by the French, who, in 1717–18, questioned the value of Britain as an ally.[5] Through its system of postal interception and decyphering, the government was aware of the views of foreign diplomats. Similarly, diplomats paid attention to the popular context of parliamentary activity and its capacity to affect both Crown and Parliament. In 1726, the Wolfenbüttel envoy argued from the popular cries when George I went to open Parliament that the populace sought war.[6]

The Whig ministry was faced from 1714 with a foreign ruler whose knowledge of British conditions was limited, but whose expectations, particularly in the field of foreign policy, presented difficulties in terms of domestic politics, while, at the same time, they had to cope with a fast-changing international situation and were also engaged in establishing Whig hegemony. Under Queen Anne, political debates on foreign policy had focused on the needs of the war with France and on the subsequent controversy over peace. A new situation had emerged with the dual developments of an alliance with France and the accession of a Hanoverian ruler with German and Baltic interests of his own. This forced British politicians to define their attitudes towards states they knew little about.

The government split in the winter of 1716–17 over ministerial competition and differences concerning foreign policy. The latter were treated as tests of loyalty. In April 1717, the ministry was determined to use the 'Gyllenborg Plot' – the conspiracy it had exposed in which Charles XII of Sweden agreed to help the Jacobites in return for money from them – in order to secure a definite commitment from Parliament to support George's anti-Swedish policy. A large money supply was to be voted and British

[5] W. A. van Rappard (ed.), *Briefwisseling tussen Simon van Slingelandt en Sicco van Goslinga 1697–1731* (The Hague, 1978), pp. 151–3; Lord Mahon, *History of England from the Peace of Utrecht 1713–83* (7 vols., 1858), II, lvi–lvii.
[6] Report by Thom, 5 Feb. 1726, Wolfenbüttel, Staatsarchiv 1 Alt 6 nr. 87 fol. 50.

trade with Sweden was to be prohibited. When, on 8 and 9 April (os) 1717, money was sought to enable George to concert measures with his allies against hostile Swedish designs, the opposition, however, accused George's Hanoverian ministers of using British money to serve Hanoverian territorial interests in the duchies of Bremen and Verden, conquered Swedish possessions, accusations that had considerable weight. Due to opposition not only by the Tories but also by some Whigs, as well as the abstentions of most of the Prince of Wales's household, the majority dropped to four on the 9th. According to the report sent to George's brother, Ernst August, Prince-Bishop of Osnabrück, opposition to the measure by Spencer Compton, the Speaker, and a protégé of the Prince of Wales, was largely responsible for the narrowness of the latter vote.[7] Indeed, a sense that control over the Commons was being lost led the ministry to think of removing Compton to the Lords.[8]

The government was keen to remedy the damaging impression that had been created. Already, in 1716, Stanhope had told the Commons that when parliamentary zeal for the Crown slackened, 'foreign powers would assist the Pretender'.[9] When, on 4 June (os) 1717, the government held off an opposition attack in the Commons by ten votes, Joseph Addison, the newly appointed Secretary of State for the Southern Department, as well as an MP and an essayist of note, informed John, 2nd Earl of Stair, the envoy in Paris, that the opposition had thought they would have a majority of fifty or sixty, adding, in a message that was clearly designed to be passed on: 'As this was the utmost effort of all parties united against the present interest, I believe it is not hard to guess which of the two sides is likely to grow the strongest for it'.[10]

As the new session drew near in November 1717, ministers hoped that firm support by the King would help them overcome the crisis. Opposition attacks in the session concentrated on foreign policy and the army, issues on which it was possible to unite opposition Whig and Tory views and to present foreign policy as being distorted for Hanoverian ends. There was a revival of the traditional 'Country' platform, with both Tories and opposition Whigs objecting to the large size of the army. Foreign commentators were aware of the importance of the relationship between these groups.[11]

[7] Report to Ernst August, 20 Apr. 1717, Osnabrück, Staatsarchiv, vol. 204 fols. 57–8.
[8] Schulenburg to Görtz, 17 Aug. 1717, Darmstadt, Staatsarchiv, Gräflich Görtzisches Archiv F23 153/6 fol. 83.
[9] 4 Feb. (os) 1716, BL. Add. 47028 fol. 135.
[10] Addison to Stair, 6 June (os) 1717, NAS. GD 135/141/9.
[11] Marquis de Chateauneuf to Chammorel, 28 Dec. 1717, BL. Add. 61574 fol. 157.

The government was also aware of the need to create an impression of control. Ministerial success in Parliament was highlighted by William, Lord Cadogan in a letter written in French so that the envoy could show it to Dutch ministers. In this, Cadogan referred to the need to understand the British constitution: 'il est aisé à nos amis de Hollande et surtout à ceux qui connoissent un peu notre constitution, de juger par ce trait si la cour n'emportera pas tout ce qu'elle entreprendra'.[12]

Conscious of foreign attention, the ministry made use of the recess to attempt to gain MPs with offers of places and pensions. Foreign interest in Parliament could not be doubted. When, on 14 February (os) 1718, the capital penalty clause of the Mutiny Bell was taken by the Commons in a Committee of the Whole House, Guillaume Dubois, the French foreign minister, attended the debate in person. He carefully described the outcome:

La Chambre des Communes estoit composées le jour là de quatre cent quatre vingt six membres . . . L'affirmative proposée par le parti de la cour, l'emporta de . . . dix huit . . . Tous les domestiques du Prince de Galles et les gens qui lui sont attachés donnerent leurs soix au parti opposé à la cour.[13]

Yet, as a reminder of the difficulty of influencing foreign views, Bonet, the Prussian envoy, reported that the opposition was satisfied with the result that day as they had got such a large vote.[14] Furthermore, the belief that the majority had been obtained by distributing money[15] helped make it seem precarious.

On 17 March (os) 1718, when the Commons received a message from George I requesting additional supplies to equip a fleet, with no indication to where the fleet was to be sent, only two MPs spoke against the Address to provide the additional expense: Walpole and the Tory Joseph Herne. They complained that no previous notice had been given, and argued that war must be avoided, as it would lead to increased taxation and contracting new debts. They went on to suggest that the ministry try and pay off the national debt first, and that Parliament should examine treaties concluded with the Emperor, Charles VI, to ascertain whether support for Austria was in the national interest. The implication was that it was intended to use the fleet to win Austrian backing for Hanover. Walpole and Herne, however, were

---

[12] Cadogan to Whitworth, envoy in The Hague, 10 Dec. (os) 1717, BL. Add. 37366 fols. 216–18.
[13] Dubois to Orléans, 17 Feb. 1718, AE. CP. Ang. 312 fols. 69–71.
[14] Bonet to Frederick William, 18 Feb. 1718, Berlin, Rep. XI, vol. 41, cf. 4, 8 Mar., 5 Apr., 17 May 1718.
[15] Chammorel to d'Huxelles, 11 Mar. 1718, AE. CP. Ang. 312 fol. 110.

not supported, and the Address was carried without a division.[16] Parliament was not to receive the opportunity to rule on the alliance.

The parliamentary crisis seriously endangered not only the government's schemes at Westminster, but also foreign policy, as doubts grew about governmental stability. The Austrian diplomat Johann, Baron Pentenriedter, who came to London to negotiate an Austro-Spanish peace plan with the British government, had been optimistic at first, reporting on 4 December 1717 that the opening of the session augured 'un bon succès pour les mesures que les conjonctures demanderont, de sorte qu'il y a lieu de croire que ceux qui voudroient entreprendre de rebrouiller de nouveau l'Europe n'y trouveront pas leur compte'. Ten days later, however, he was deploring the instability of British politics, thinking that it would be harmful to European affairs. Even after the voting of supplies, Pentenriedter was still complaining about British stability:

si le Roy d'Angleterre ne prend pas le parti de se reconcilier avec le Prince son fils, de choisir un ministère agréable à la nation et la ramener à luy les grands seigneurs, il est impossible qu'il n'arrive quelque troubles don't les suites peuvent être très fâcheuses.[17]

It is significant that he did not specifically refer to Parliament, but choosing a ministry agreeable to the nation entailed this, as parliamentary developments were the way in which foreign diplomats assessed Britain's political stability. They paid most attention to the Commons, as that was where the ministry was placed under greatest pressure during the reign of George I. Bonet, however, pointed out that in the Lords more Protests had been entered than at any time since the beginning of the reign.[18]

The parliamentary attack on government policy in the winter of 1717–18 encouraged Montéléon, the Spanish envoy, to believe that British policy could be affected by the impact of Spanish moves on domestic opinion. He reported that a threat to confiscate British investments in Spain and to close ports to British ships would cause confusion and complaints in London. In his view, this lent credence to the argument that trade with Spain was too important to allow any anti-Spanish moves. Montéléon's assessment was influenced by Compton's assurance that any measures resulting in disruption of trade with Spain would meet with bitter opposition throughout

[16] Bonet to Frederick William, 29 Mar. 1718, Berlin, Rep. XI, vol. 41; *House of Commons Journals*, XVIII, 767; BL. Add. 37367 fol. 251, 47028 fol. 228; Craggs to Stair, 17, 31 Mar. (os) 1718, NAS. GD. 135/141/13B.
[17] Pentenriedter to Königsegg, 4, 14, 30 Dec. 1717, HHStA. Frankreich, Varia 10 fols. 22, 31, 44–5; Pentenriedter to Charles VI and Rialp, 26 Dec. 1717, HHStA. Ek. 53.
[18] Bonet to Frederick William, 5 Apr. 1718, Berlin, Rep XI, vol. 41.

the country. Montéléon followed Compton's advice by warning Stanhope that the arrival of a British fleet in the Mediterranean would be regarded as a declaration of war and would lead to a confiscation of British goods.[19] Montéléon's strategy, however, failed. Walpole was unable to enlist much support for opposition to the naval supply, and a fleet was sent.

Contemporaries directly linked parliamentary politics to international developments. Stair was informed by his Spanish counterpart that his government had been sure that Parliament would not support the ministry in an anti-Spanish policy. After the British had destroyed a Spanish fleet off Cape Passaro in Sicily in August 1718, the Spanish envoy at The Hague was still confident that Spain could build a new fleet, instigate trouble within France, and 'qu'il travailleroit pendant l'hyver à faire des caballes en Angleterre pour embarasser les affaires du Roy au Parlement'.[20] All the British ministers believed that there was a strong relationship between the internal British political situation and Britain's ability to conduct a foreign policy successfully.[21] Stair was delighted by the King's message to the Commons of 17 March (os) 1718 on the dispatch of a fleet, and the Commons' answer: 'la réponse de la chambre basse va donner un crédit et un éclat infini aux affaires du Roi dans les pais étrangers'. He thought there was no surer way to avoid a war as seeming not to be frightened of it: credit and confidence were all.[22] Equally, this seemed the best way to retain the support of France.

The 1718 crisis underlined the centrality of foreign policy issues to the political and parliamentary events of particular years. The need for increased taxation to finance a controversial foreign policy created parliamentary difficulties for the ministry, which was indeed fortunate that the war with Spain (1718–20) proved so successful. It is difficult to conceive how the ministry could have maintained itself in Parliament had the war been unsuccessful. However, success in war helped still criticism, while, in 1719, foreign policy was overshadowed by the contentious domestic legislative programme of the ministry.[23]

Significant parliamentary debates over foreign affairs in this period were held generally in the Commons. There are few signs that managing the Lords in this field presented as much of a problem as dealing with the

[19] Montéléon to Grimaldi, 7 Feb. 1718, Archivio General de Simancas, Estado, Legajo 6841.
[20] PRO. SP. 78/161 fol. 197; BL. Add. 37369 fols. 298–9.
[21] J. M. Graham (ed.), *Annals and Correspondence of the Viscount and the First and Second Earls of Stair* (2 vols., 1875), I, 283; George Bubb to Stair, 22 July 1715, NAS. GD. 135/1413A.
[22] Stair to Stanhope, 6 Mar. 1718, KAO, U1590/0145/24; PRO. SP. 78/161 fols. 190–1, 197; BL. Stowe Mss. 246 fol. 99, Add. 37367 fols. 254, 279, 295.
[23] Duke of Montrose to Mungo Graham, 14 Mar. 1719, NAS. SRO. GD. Z20/5/828.

Commons, and foreign diplomats reported that unwelcome legislation could be blocked by the government in the Lords. A comparison between the two Houses over the discussion, in 1729, of Spanish depredations on British trade in the West Indies and, in 1730, of the repair of the harbour of Dunkirk by France, in defiance of the Treaty of Utrecht, is instructive in this respect. In the former case, the greater sensitivity of the Commons to commercial issues, the representation of London in the House, and the opportunities that this permitted for the use of petitions and Addresses as devices to link parliamentary and extra-parliamentary views, all help explain the emphasis on the Commons. In 1730, however, there was no doubt that the centre of the political storm over Dunkirk was located in the Commons when there was no obvious reason why it should not have been in the Lords. Walpole, who was reconciled to the Crown in 1720, becoming the leading minister from then and, more clearly, from 1722, until his fall in 1742, and holding office as First Lord of the Treasury from 1721 to 1742, remained in the Commons, and this helped to ensure that it remained the focus of political attention. Nevertheless, there was criticism of government policy throughout the period in the Lords, and it was particularly important in the early 1720s, as William, 1st Earl Cowper played a prominent role in continuing opposition Whig condemnation of policy. Cowper attacked what he saw as a subservience to French interests. For example, in January 1722, he claimed that the construction of ships for the French in British yards was dangerous.[24]

Foreign policy in the period 1714–42 was often contentious, and it frequently lacked widespread popularity. The Walpole ministry's close identification with the French alliance until it collapsed in 1731 produced considerable criticism. The Commons' debates on the Treaty of Hanover in February 1726 saw opposition claims that France was an unreliable ally whose aggrandisement was dangerous.[25] A case could be made for supporting the government in war with Spain in 1718 and confrontation with Russia in 1720 and Austria in 1725, but they were not, particularly the last two, very popular. In addition, the failure to come to the assistance of Austria when attacked by France and Spain in the War of the Polish Succession (1733–5) was controversial, and led to serious complaints that the Walpole government was heedless of the European balance of power. Far more serious charges of neglecting national interests were pressed in 1738–9, as the

---

[24] Hertford CRO. D/EP F. 182 fols. 96–104. That volume contains other material on Cowper's opposition and on relevant Lords' debates.
[25] A. N. Newman (ed.), *The Parliamentary Diary of Sir Edward Knatchbull 1722–1730* (1963), pp. 52, 59; Le Coq, Saxon envoy, to Augustus II, 5 Feb. 1726, Dresden 2674.

government, ultimately unsuccessfully, strove to avoid war with Spain over colonial and maritime disputes.

Foreign policy, a controversial branch of activity, made more so, and more volatile, by the kaleidoscopic nature of international relations in this period, was a significant topic of parliamentary debate. This was even more so due to the limited amount of contentious legislation proposed by ministries after the unsuccessful highpoint of the Sunderland/Stanhope ministry's efforts in 1719. At the same time, foreign policy was not always the cause of political storms. Some sessions, such as that of 1724, were relatively placid.[26]

Ministers felt a need for public parliamentary support, both because of the frequent vigour of the domestic debate over foreign policy, and because the commitments stemming from a Hanoverian dynasty and a French alliance entailed novel international confrontations that did not match traditional suppositions of British conduct. No attempt was made to place new restrictions on Parliament's position in the discussion of foreign policy.

Ministers were not all equally concerned about parliamentary support. There was a tension between those, such as Stanhope and, later, John, Lord Carteret, Secretary of State for the Northern Department in 1742–4, for whom diplomatic exigencies came first, and colleagues, particularly those responsible for management of the Commons, such as Walpole and Henry Pelham, who were more inclined to emphasise the need to temper such exigencies to the problems of management. However, the extent of this clash should not be exaggerated, other than for particular conjunctures. It is necessary to recall that the process of policy formulation and execution is never free from tension. In addition, differences expressed over policy might owe their seriousness, and indeed provenance, to other issues, such as the competition for predominance.

Tension has been detected between Walpole and his brother-in-law until 1726, Townshend, not least in 1725 when Walpole was displeased by the financial consequences of Townshend's expensive attempt to recruit allies by means of subsidies.[27] In fact, Townshend, an experienced debater in the Lords, was fully aware of the political difficulties of persuading Parliament to grant peacetime subsidies to foreign powers. He showed this in 1726 over discussions about offering Bavaria such subsidies, and the envoy from Hesse-Cassel, General Ernst Diemar, found him very firm in negotiations over subsidies and concerned about parliamentary attitudes. Chammorel,

---

[26] *London Journal*, 2 May (os) 1724.   [27] Coxe, *Memoirs*, I, 549–50.

the French Chargé d'Affaires, pressing Townshend in March 1726 against a projected tax upon French cloth imports, reported that the minister was very concerned about the possibility of the opposition exploiting the issue.[28] Such foreign pressure against projected legislation generally related to the Westminster Parliament, as in 1722 with taxation on Catholics;[29] although there was also sensitivity by foreign powers about the measures of its Dublin counterpart, especially the treatment of Catholics and economic legislation.[30]

Politicians were aware of the great importance attached on the Continent to parliamentary developments, and the consequent need to control them. In addition, envoys were instructed to publicise ministerial accounts of parliamentary events. In 1727, James Dormer, envoy in Lisbon, was told to stress Parliament's support of British foreign policy. He translated the relevant parliamentary resolutions into Portuguese.[31] Foreign envoys were convinced that government policy was dominated by concern about parliamentary consequences. In 1723, Anne-Théodore Chevignard de Chavigny, the French envoy, reported that, because of popular concern about Austrian commercial plans, Townshend feared pressure in Parliament and therefore only wanted to make an agreement over their Ostend Company that could be readily justified. The Jacobites also thought that government policy in the matter was heavily influenced by concern about Parliament.[32]

Similarly both Houses were expected to support government policies with public gestures. In November 1725, Townshend, the Secretary of State with George I in Hanover, pressed his London counterpart, the Duke of Newcastle, on the need for parliamentary support for the recently negotiated Treaty of Hanover. Townshend claimed that it would

when approved by both Houses, discourage our enemies, and let our friends see that we are in earnest, and that they may depend upon their engagements with us, provided the resolutions of the Parliament are followed with the fitting out a strong fleet, without which I can assure you (according to the notion at present

[28] Townshend to St. Saphorin, 14 Jan. (os) 1726, and to Chesterfield, 29 Apr. (os) 1729, PRO. SP. 80/57, 84/304; Townshend to Horatio Walpole, 22 Aug. (os) 1728, BL. Add. 32757; Chammorel to Morville, 11 Mar. 1726, AE. CP. Ang. 354.

[29] Perceval to Charles Dering, 1 Dec. (os) 1722, BL. Add. 47029 fol. 141.

[30] Waldegrave to Delafaye, 11 Feb. 1732, PRO. SP. 78/200 fol. 35.

[31] Townshend to William Finch, 21 Jan. (os) 1726, to Du Bourgay, 22 Feb. (os) 1726, to Cyril Wich, William Finch and Diescau, all 20 Feb. (os) 1728, Dormer to Delafaye, 10 Apr. 1727, Harrington to Thomas Robinson, 28 Jan. (os) 1731, PRO. SP. 84/289, 90/22, 82/45, 84/299, 95/50, 89/32, 80/71.

[32] Chavigny to Morville, 21 Oct. 1723, AE. CP. Ang. 346 fol. 185; Hay to John Walkingshaw, 15 Feb. 1724, RA. 72/114.

universally entertained of us abroad) all the Parliament can say will make very little impression in our favour.[33]

The relationship of parliamentary and international developments was underlined by Townshend two months later when he pressed William Finch, envoy in The Hague and an MP, on the trouble that would be faced in Parliament if the Dutch did not accede to the Treaty of Hanover before the session. Such an accession was believed necessary in the diplomatic community before Parliament could meet. In the event, Parliament readily backed government policy, leading Finch to respond:

Some people here, it may be, thought the example of the Dutch was necessary to make the Parliament of England approve of the defensive alliance, but I believe the sense of the two Houses expressed in their address, which I took care to communicate immediately, has [instead] given the conclusive stroke to this day's resolution [to accede].[34]

The extent to which Parliament was followed abroad also led British envoys to seek explanations of obscure developments there.[35]

The reiteration by British envoys of the convention that ministerial success in Parliament would have an effect abroad,[36] in part reflected their awareness of what it was sensible to say; but, even if that cynical view is taken, nevertheless this reiteration contributed to an important convention. Furthermore, this was enhanced by knowledge of the extent to which hostile foreign powers sought to use Parliament to their own ends.[37] Conversely, the failure of hostile hopes, whether domestic or foreign in provenance, helped affirm the strength of the government,[38] and was presented in this light by the ministry.[39] The *London Journal* of 5 March (os) 1726 claimed,

The mails this week have brought very little from abroad, the papers being filled up with the proceedings of the British Parliament, which have not a little surprised

---

[33] Townshend to Newcastle, 27 Nov. 1725, PRO. SP. 43/8 fols. 80–1, 122.

[34] Townshend to Finch, 14 Jan. (os), Finch to Townshend, 8 Feb. 1726, PRO. SP. 84/289 fols. 29, 73; Newsletter amidst reports of Gansinot, Wittelsbach envoy in The Hague, to Ferdinand, Count Plettenburg, leading minister of Elector of Cologne, 25 Jan. 1726, Münster, Staatsarchiv, Dep. Nordkirchen, NB. 259 fol. 163; Hay to Daniel O'Brien, 23 Jan. 1726, RA. 90/12.

[35] Dayrolles, reporting views of Chesterfield, to Tilson, 28 Mar. 1731, PRO. SP. 84/310 fol. 71.

[36] Delafaye to Poyntz, 30 Jan. (os) 1729, BL. Add. 75451; Wich to Tilson, 4 Mar. 1729, PRO. SP. 82/46 fol. 37.

[37] Hay to James Hamilton, 26 Jan. 1726, RA. 90/27.

[38] Count Albert, Bavarian envoy in Paris, to Baron Malknecht, 9 Feb. 1726, Munich, Kasten Schwarz 17087; Gansinot to Plettenberg, 12 Feb. 1726, Münster, Dep. Nordkirchen, NB. 259 fol. 191; William Wood (Paris) to Mylord, 15 Mar. 1726, CUL. Cholmondeley (Houghton) papers, correspondence, no. 1286.

[39] Townshend to Du Bourgay, 31 Jan. (os) 1729, PRO. SP. 90/24.

some foreign powers who had flattered themselves that no such vigorous resolutions would have been taken there. Meanwhile, they look upon them to be the surest means of securing a peace in Europe, it not being thought that any power will care for attacking his Britannick Majesty, or any of his allies.

In contrast, concern about the failure of Britain and France to obtain promised concessions from Spain led to the proroguing of the 1728 session until the international situation became clearer. It was widely believed then that Walpole's parliamentary success would depend upon satisfaction being obtained. Duncan Forbes MP wrote from London 'whether we shall in the ensuing Parliament have any heats will probably depend upon the state of foreign affairs'.[40] In the event, and as a potent warning to opposition hopes for advantage from international developments, the news of Spain agreeing to most of the British demands provided the government with an opportunity to seize the initiative. George II was able to tell Parliament that he had received from Britain's allies, France and the United Provinces, 'the greatest proofs of their sincerity, and a renewal of the strongest assurances imaginable, that they would effectually make good all their engagements', and, also, that 'a general pacification' was at hand.

In response, the Commons' Address in 1728 was a lengthy defence of ministerial foreign policy, arguing for 'the absolute necessity of supporting your allies' and stating that 'the late disagreeable situation of affairs' could not have been prevented by 'human prudence'. This was an answer to opposition arguments that the government had been responsible for the diplomatic imbroglio Britain had been trapped in. Walpole's view that negotiation was preferable to war led to the passage in the Address which referred to the 'noble self-denial of all the success and glory that might attend your Majesty's arms in the prosecution of a just and necessary war, when put in balance with the ease, quiet, and prosperity of your subjects. It is a disposition of mind truly great in your Majesty . . . to choose rather to procure peace for your subjects, than to lead them to victories.'[41]

The debates on the Addresses were a triumph for the government.[42] Ministerial success was attributed to the new diplomatic situation. Newcastle informed James, Lord Waldegrave, then in Paris en route to his embassy

---

[40] Duncan to John Forbes, 6 Jan. (os) 1728, D. Warrana (ed.), *More Culloden Papers*, III (Inverness, 1927), pp. 27–8.

[41] *House of Lords Journals*, XVIII, 167–8; *House of Commons Journals*, XXI, 30.

[42] Delafaye to Waldegrave, 29 Jan. (os) 1728, Chewton; Townshend to William Finch, 30 Jan. (os) 1728, PRO. 84/299; Visconti to Sinzendorf, 10 Feb. 1728, HHStA. Englische Korrespondenz 65.

in Austria, that 'the good news you have sent us, has made the opening of our Parliament very successful'.[43]

Ministerial foreign policy was fully debated in Parliament. Horatio Walpole, back for the session from his posting in Paris, spoke at length in defence of the French alliance. According to the newsletter sent to George II's uncle, Ernst-August, Horatio persuaded most MPs that it was a sound policy. The opposition 'let themselves into the whole state of public affairs from north to south', but their attacks were without success. The debates convinced foreign diplomats that the government was in control. Marquis Scaramuccia Visconti, the Austrian representative, claimed that the degree of harmony between ministry and Parliament was unprecedented.[44]

The royal speech proroguing Parliament in May 1728 predicted a successful peace congress solving international differences, but the failure of the Congress of Soissons to do so created a dangerous political situation as the next session approached, with a serious debate in the press in the autumn of 1728 about foreign policy. As a result, it was widely held in diplomatic circles that the government would encounter major difficulties with Parliament in 1729. Philip, 4th Earl of Chesterfield, envoy at The Hague, was told there by an Austrian supporter, 'that if nothing were concluded before the meeting of the Parliament, the nation, that was already uneasy at the expense, would be extremely exasperated at the continuance of it'. Count Philip Kinsky, the Austrian envoy in London, informed Prince Eugene, one of the leading Austrian ministers, that the government was worried about what it would be able to tell Parliament and feared that the continued uncertainty of affairs would lead to unpopularity. Chesterfield wrote to Townshend that it was believed at The Hague that there would be trouble in Parliament, and that Slingelandt had asked him whether the government majorities were secure in both Houses. Poyntz reported, 'The court of Madrid have received letters from England which give them great hopes from divisions in the insuing session with an account of a strong Imperial party in England, and the approaching ruin of Los Walpole'. St Saphorin, earlier envoy in Vienna, had noted that 'la Cour Impériale se flattoit, à chaque ouverture du Parlement, que les choses y prendroient un tour désagréable à feu Sa Majesté'. Cyril Wich, envoy in Hamburg, wrote to Townshend,

[43] Newcastle to Waldegrave, 29 Jan. (os) 1728, Chewton.
[44] Newsletter, 2 Mar. 1728, Osnabrück, 295; William Finch to Tilson, 2 Mar., and to Townshend, 29 Mar., PRO. SP. 84/299; Broglie to Chauvelin, 26 Feb., 15 Mar., Chauvelin to Chammorel, 4 Mar. 1728, AE. CP. Ang. 362, supplément 8; D'Aix to Victor Amadeus II, 15 Mar. 1727, AST. LM. Ing. 35; Visconti to Sinzendorf, 5 Mar. 1728, HHStA. EK. 65.

I do not doubt, but that it has been generally observed by all those who have had the honour to serve His Majesty abroad, that our enemies have more depended upon a prospect of seeing difficulties arise at home and creating discontents and divisions among us, than upon their own force.

The Jacobites spread reports that there would be trouble in Parliament.[45]

Indeed, in the coming session, Sir Robert Walpole was to attack those who sought 'to encourage His Majesty's enemies with the hopes that the Parliament would not approve of the late measures taken by him and to put it out of the King's power to give the support and assistance to his allies, which his own honour and the most solemn engagements oblige him to perform'.[46]

Given these expectations, it was obvious that the ministry had to ensure a successful session in order to maintain their credibility in Europe. Chesterfield wrote 'to suggest the necessity of the strongest addresses imaginable from both houses at the meeting of the Parliament, in order to undeceive people abroad'.[47]

The opening of the 1729 session indeed saw a sustained attack upon the government's foreign policy. The opposition Whigs launched a furious assault. Edward Vernon attacked the French as a threat to British commerce and a false ally; John Norris proposed that George II should be addressed to break the alliance with France; and Sir Wilfred Lawson argued that it was dangerous to trust to French mediation, adding that, if war broke out, France would never support Britain against Spain, a view also held by many diplomats. William Pulteney 'questioned the steadiness of France'. William Stanhope and Horatio Walpole, who were MPs as well as leading diplomats, rebutted these views and 'they both gave assurances of the readiness of His Most Christian Majesty [Louis XV] to concur . . . in any measures that should be judged requisite for obtaining a general peace'. Sir Robert Walpole confessed there was uneasiness about the international situation, but added that 'when the negotiations at [the Congress of] Soissons came to be laid before the House, they would be better understood than at present'. There was no division in the Lords and a substantial government majority in the

---

[45] Chesterfield to Townshend, 1 Oct., 28 Dec. 1728, Poyntz to Delafaye, 25 Dec. 1728, 29 Jan. 1729, St Saphorin to Townshend, – Aug. 1727, Wich to Townshend, 15 Feb. 1729, PRO. 84/302, 78/188, 190, 80/61; Kinsky to Eugene, 25 Sept., Fonseca to Eugene, 14 Nov. 1728, HHStA. GK 94(b), 85(a); Anon., French mémoire, 8 Nov. 1728, AE. CP. Ang. 364.

[46] *Knatchbull*, p. 82.

[47] Chesterfield to Townshend, 28 Dec. 1728, PRO. 84/302; Delafaye to Poyntz, 30 Jan. (os) 1729, BL. Add. 75451.

Commons,[48] but attacks upon the government persisted. The entire tenor of foreign policy was challenged: 'Mr. Pulteney and his friends entered into a debate upon the whole state and management of the foreign affairs since the present disturbances began.'[49] Sir Thomas Saunderson, who had been refused a peerage, went over to the opposition and launched a strong attack on the French alliance, there was pressure over Spanish depredations on British trade in the West Indies,[50] and, in the Commons, Lord Morpeth pressed (unsuccessfully) for an Address to enquire about the help France had given Britain for the preservation of Gibraltar, a measure designed to focus attention on the unreliability of France as an ally.

The Walpoles defended the alliance against strong attacks by claiming that France was a good ally as a result of structural factors in the international system, an argument that directed attention away from the issue of trust. Horatio Walpole 'affirmed France to be the most faithful to us through the whole course of these late differences, and for a good reason, she being the irreconcilable enemy to Austria'. Sir Robert Walpole declared 'that where some had compared Gallica fides with Punica fides [French faithfulness with that of notoriously unfaithful Carthage], we were to consider that states govern themselves by their interest and that the close alliance of Austria, the ancient enemy, with Spain made them as entirely sure to our alliance as heretofore they were enemies when they aimed at universal monarchy'.[51]

This argument was challenged by growing public distrust of France, which handed the opposition a potent political weapon. Edward Harrison, a placeman and former MP close to Townshend, observed 'we go on swimmingly in Parliament for the present, but the uneasiness daily increases, and spreads far and near'.[52] The extent to which Parliament forced the ministry to appear in control without a break was captured in the 1729 session as foreign diplomats and ministers came to sense that the government was losing control of the situation.[53] Philip, Count Sinzendorf, the Austrian Chancellor, felt that parliamentarians had positive views of their own about what policy should be as well as negative ones directed against the policies followed by the British ministry. He told the Dutch envoy that his government 'thought the Parliament of England might advise His Majesty to

[48] *Wye's Letter*, 23, 25 Jan. (os) 1729; *Egmont*, III, 330–2; *Knatchbull*, pp. 80–1; Kinsky to Eugene, 2, 8 Feb. 1729, HHStA. GK 94(b), fols. 21, 24.
[49] Townshend to Du Bourgay, 31 Jan. (os) 1729, PRO. SP. 90/24.
[50] R. R. Sedgwick (ed.), *The House of Commons 1715–1754* (2 vols., 1970), II, 230.
[51] *Egmont*, III, 338, 347.   [52] Harrison to Poyntz, 3 May (os) 1729, BL. Add. 75449.
[53] Broglie to Chauvelin, 7 Mar. 1729, AE. CP. Ang. 305.

rupture with Spain, but was in no apprehension that the Parliament would meddle with the Emperor'.[54]

This belief played a role in Austrian opposition the following spring to accepting the terms of the Treaty of Seville of November 1729 by which Britain, France and Spain had settled their difficulties and proposed a new settlement for Italy. The Austrians were convinced that it was unnecessary to accept terms as the ministry would be defeated in the 1730 session, while the British government was intensely suspicious of links between the opposition and the envoys of Austria and Prussia. Indeed, in 1727, the Jacobite envoy in Vienna had asked the Austrian government to give the Tories copies of its critical reply to George I's speech opening Parliament.[55]

It was unnecessary to believe that the opposition was manipulated by foreign envoys in order to realise that the relationship between foreign policy and parliamentary developments was close. Horatio Walpole referred to 'the relation which the affairs here in Parliament must have with those abroad'.[56] Initially, in the winter of 1729–30, this led to a measure of government optimism. Horatio claimed that the opposition had planned to attack the ministry 'for their indolence and neglect in suffering so patiently the insults of the Spaniards' upon British trade, but that the Treaty of Seville had forced them to change their tactics. There is no evidence for this assertion, but it seems reasonable. Girolamo Vignola, the Venetian envoy, noted that the treaty plunged the opposition into confusion.[57]

The 1730 session began on 13 January (os) with a royal speech setting out the benefits of the Treaty of Seville. In the Commons' debate on the Address, Thomas Wyndham for the opposition failed to persuade the House 'to confine whatever assurances the Parliament should give His Majesty of making good his engagements, and of standing by him to attempts upon his Britannic dominions'; in other words not Hanover. The ministry claimed to be well satisfied with the debates, British envoys were instructed to convey an optimistic view, and Britain's allies were certainly impressed by the governmental success.[58] However, although there had been no division in the Lords, the opposition amendment in the Commons attracted a

---

[54] Waldegrave to Townshend, 15 Jan. 1729, Chewton.
[55] Graeme to Hay, 8 Mar. 1727, RA. 104/113.
[56] Horatio Walpole to Waldegrave, 13 Mar. (os) 1730, Chewton.
[57] Horatio Walpole to Waldegrave, 13 Mar. (os) 1730, Chewton; Vignola to Senate of Venice, 9 Dec. 1729, Venice, Archivio di Stato, LM. Ing. 98; Lord Kinnoull to Delafaye, 14 Dec. (os) 1729, PRO. SP. 97/25.
[58] Trevor to Poyntz, 15 Jan. (os) 1730, BL. Add. 75449; *Knatchbull*, pp. 97–8; *Egmont*, I, 3–6; H. McMains, *The Parliamentary Opposition to Sir Robert Walpole 1727–31* (Ph.D. thesis, Indiana State University, 1970), pp. 163–5; Townshend to Du Bourgay, 13 Jan. (os), and to Edward Finch, 13 Jan. (os) 1730, PRO. SP. 90/26, 95/54.

considerable vote, reflecting the success of the opposition Whigs' plan to create a workable alliance with the Tories. Edward Weston, one of the Under-Secretaries, referred to this alliance as designed 'to counterbalance the Treaty of Seville'.[59]

In subsequent debates in both Houses, the government saw off attacks on foreign policy, leading to an optimism that, however, was to be badly dented by the unexpected storm that was to arise over the French restoration of Dunkirk. Since 1725, the harbour facilities had been restored, despite specific prohibitions in the Treaties of Utrecht (1713) and The Hague (1717). The government had been well aware of this restoration, and had complained to the French in 1727, 1728 and 1729. The issue had been exploited by the opposition press over the previous three years, and it was widely known that the harbour was capable of receiving fairly large ships.[60] The ministry were aware that Dunkirk might be used as an issue by the opposition in the session of 1730, although they appear to have taken few precautions to ensure that they could deflect criticism. When the issue was drawn to Horatio Walpole's attention as envoy in Paris, he attributed the improvement of the port to tidal action and unauthorised work, and, with little prescience, complained that the ministry was 'transported and frightened with the least good or bad thing, and without considering the real state of the matter we call for help from abroad upon trifles'.[61]

On 10 February (os) 1730, the Commons formed itself into a Committee of the Whole House to consider a motion from Sir William Wyndham, Tory leader in the Commons, for an examination of the state of the nation, the first Committee on the State of the Nation since the Hanoverian succession in 1714. After a lengthy attack upon the policies and practices of the ministry, Wyndham turned to the restoration of Dunkirk's harbour as a proof of the government's failure to protect national interests. The unsuspecting ministerial speakers lost control of the House and were unable to prevent the hearing of evidence about the restoration. On the following day, it was resolved to address George II for the laying of all correspondence about Dunkirk before the House. In order to give time for this to be prepared, the debate on the state of the nation was adjourned for a fortnight.[62]

The seriousness of the situation, and its capacity to derail both the ministry and British foreign policy, was clear. The opposition had found a topic that captured the concern of many MPs over the French alliance.

---

[59] Weston to Poyntz, 29 Dec. (os) 1729, 30 Jan. (os) 1730, BL. Add. 75450.
[60] Newcastle to Horatio Walpole, 14 May (os), – July (os) 1728, PRO. SP. 78/189.
[61] Horatio Walpole to Delafaye, 14 Dec. (os) 1729, PRO. SP. 78/192.
[62] Notes of Wyndham's speech, BL. Add. 35875 fol. 22; *Knatchbull*, pp. 104–6; *Egmont*, I, 34–8.

Long-established anxiety over the use of Dunkirk as a privateering base made the issue a concrete and readily grasped instance of the more general opposition; criticisms of the government. François-Marie, Duke of Broglie, the French envoy, reported 'La chambre en général a paru approuver les raisons du parti opposé', John, Viscount Perceval, MP for Harwich, an independent-minded Whig, referred to 'so popular and national a point', and Charles Howard, another supporter of the ministry, noted that most of his fellow MPs believed France to be restoring the harbour. Support for the government fell. On 12 February (os), Anthony Duncomb, a ministerial MP, complained that 'he saw the members fall every day from the Court, and . . . at last there would be a majority against it'. An air of anticipation hung over Westminster. Opposition leaders scented the prospect of office, and foreign envoys speculated about the fall of the ministry.[63]

On 16 February (os) 1730, indeed, the opposition won the division on a bill they had introduced against office-holders sitting in the Commons by 144 to 134, thanks to ministerial MPs abstaining or defecting. Kinsky was sufficiently impressed to send a courier to Vienna with the news of the defeat, and in Austria expectations were raised of the collapse of the Walpole ministry. Austrian supporters made similar claims elsewhere, for example at The Hague. Giovanni Zamboni, agent for a number of rulers in London, suggested that the government would be unable to win a majority in the Commons when the debate on the state of the nation was resumed.[64]

The ministry was therefore threatened not only with a loss of control in the Commons, but also with a collapse of European confidence in its ability to control Parliament. As a result, the French were pressed hard. Colonel John Armstrong, the military representative at Paris, who was a Dunkirk expert, was informed by Newcastle that nothing would 'more contribute to damage the efforts of those who oppose His Majesty's measures and have chiefly in view to discredit our alliance with France' than securing the demolition of the works.[65]

British diplomatic pressure succeeded. Fleury gave an official assurance that the works had been performed without the authorisation of Louis XV, who now ordered their demolition. Copies of this order were sent to

---

[63] Broglie to Chauvelin, 22 Feb. 1730, P. J. Mantoux, *Notes sur les Comptes Rendus des Séances du Parlement Anglais au XVIIIe siècle, conservés aux archives du ministère des affaires étrangères* (Paris, 1906), p. 52; *Egmont*, I, 38–40; HMC. Manuscripts of the Earl of *Carlisle* (1807), p. 67; Chammorel to Chauvelin, 27 Feb., 2 Mar. 1730, AE. CP. Ang. 369.

[64] Waldegrave to Tilson, 15, 18 Mar., Holzendorf to Tilson, 7 Mar. 1730, PRO. 80/67, 84/307; Zamboni to Saxon minister, Count Manteuffel, 3 Mar. 1730, Bod. Ms. Rawlinson letters, 120.

[65] Newcastle to Armstrong, 12 Feb. (os) 1730, BL. Add. 32765.

Britain.[66] When the Commons resumed their deliberations on Dunkirk, Wyndham produced fresh evidence of the French works, but a ministerial proposal for an Address to thank George II for his care of the national interest over the issue and to 'declare satisfaction in the firm union and mutual fidelity which so happily subsist, and are so strictly preserved, between the two crowns' was carried by 270 to 149.[67]

This victory was seen by the ministry as a testimony to the willingness of MPs to respond to developments; and therefore a response to those who claimed that support rested on financial inducements. Newcastle informed Harrington that 'many of our friends that had before left us came back upon this occasion', while Charles Delafaye, an Under-Secretary, predicted that the French order would 'perfectly reconcile to our alliance some weak though well meaning men, who by false insinuations had been prejudiced against it'.[68] British envoys were instructed to cite the debate as a demonstration of parliamentary support for the Anglo-French alliance.

The government's victory set the tone for the rest of the session. When the examination of the state of the nation was resumed on 10 March (os) 1730, a desultory debate on the Anglo-French dispute over the West Indian island of St Lucia ended with a government majority of 112. St. Lucia lacked the importance of Dunkirk, its position in international agreements was obscure and contested, and there was no way in which the theme of national betrayal so powerfully advanced over Dunkirk could be repeated.[69]

Opposition failure over St Lucia led to the end of the Committee on the State of the Nation, and, as a testimony to the political importance of foreign policy at this point, to the departure of many opposition MPs from London. The session became more quiescent, although it still saw 'skirmishes'[70] that involved foreign affairs. On 17 March (os) 1730, the Loan Bill, a measure designed to prevent loans to foreign powers without royal licence and, in particular, to block Austrian moves to borrow money in London, was passed by the Commons, after only a short debate, with the government defeating an opposition amendment in a division of 176–76.[71] The following month, the division was 197–78 when an opposition motion for an Address to George II to lay before the House the secret and

---

[66] 'Order from the King of France', 27 Feb. 1730, BL. Add. 32765.
[67] *Knatchbull*, pp. 109–10; *Egmont*, I, 71–5; *Carlisle*, pp. 68–9.
[68] Newcastle to Harrington, 2 Mar. (os), Delafaye to Poyntz, 21 Feb. (os), 2 Mar. (os) 1730, BL. Add. 32766, 75451.
[69] *Knatchbull*, pp. 112–13; *Egmont*, I, 78.
[70] Horatio Walpole to Waldegrave, envoy in Paris from 1730, 21 Apr. (os), 1 May (os) 1730, Chewton.
[71] *Knatchbull*, pp. 113–14; *Egmont*, I, 81–2; Diemar to William of Hesse-Cassel, 4 Apr. 1730, Marburg, England 199.

separate articles of the Treaty of Seville, and thus discover if it was possible to embarrass the ministry on the issue, was defeated. Horatio Walpole concluded 'it plainly appeared by the debate and by the complexion of the House that they will support His Majesty in fulfilling his engagements for the execution of the Treaty of Seville'.[72]

The French alliance had been attacked in previous sessions of the Parliament, but never with the ferocity seen in 1730. The opposition chose well, striking a popular chord, and also reflecting tensions within the ministry where there was considerable disquiet about the impact on Britain's interests of war with Austria. Although the government had survived the parliamentary onslaught, the opposition claim that the nation would not accept an endlessly uncertain diplomatic situation and a dangerous and expensive alliance system had come close to fruition.

This led to pressure from ministerialists to avoid any repetition of the crisis. John Selwyn MP was capturing a common theme when he wrote 'it behoves us to look a little forward and to prevent such an attack in another sessions, which will not turn out so favourable to us'. Delafaye noted 'We cannot help insisting upon Dunkirk; our letters may be called for next winter', a clear indication of concern about the possibility of parliamentary scrutiny of diplomatic correspondence. Horatio Walpole warned of the danger if the Dunkirk issue was not settled: of 'the greatest confusion in England but also in all Europe next winter by the dissolution of the present system of affairs, for it is impossible to imagine that the nation will grow cooler on this head'.[73]

It was normal, particularly in the early winter, as the session neared, to exercise such fears, but, in 1730, the level of anxiety was higher than in preceding years. Ministers anxiously surveyed issues, such as Dunkirk or recruitment in Ireland for the French army, that might lead to trouble in the forthcoming session.

In light of these political problems, it is interesting to turn to the bland remarks about the mutual benefits brought by parliamentary consultation expressed in two pamphlets of 1730,

As to the right of making peace and war, the same is allowed and granted to be part of the King's high prerogative, though we find that the wisest of our monarchs have very rarely entered into any war without the approbation and consent of their parliaments: for who can give better and more wholesome advice and counsel in such arduous affairs?[74]

[72] *Egmont*, I, pp. 5–6; *Carlisle*, p. 71; Horatio Walpole to Waldegrave, 21 Apr. (os) 1730, Chewton.
[73] Selwyn to Poyntz, 5 Mar. (os), Delafaye to Poyntz, 2, 14, 30 Apr. (os), Horatio Walpole to Poyntz, 21 May (os) 1730, BL. Add. 75451.
[74] M. Gordon, *The True Crisis* (1730), p. 7.

Though the making of peace is acknowledged to be without the prerogative of the Crown, yet it will most certainly be brought before you for your approbation; which ministers always esteem to be some kind of security to them.[75]

These were reasonable statements, although they excluded mention of the financial benefits in the shape of support of taxation that could arise from seeking 'wholesome advice and counsel'. A fuller statement was made by a leading London ministerial paper, the *Daily Courant*, in its issue of 1 October (os) 1734:

In the military part of the domestic indeed, and in both the branches of our foreign policy or government, which regulates our leagues and treaties, our wars or peace with other states, the King has a greater latitude; for, as they are almost all of them individual points or cases, which admit of very few, or no invariable general rules, and do also require the utmost dispatch, and the greatest secrecy, he is therein invested with the entire power of determining both what shall be done, and who shall execute those determinations; subject nevertheless to the regulation of the legislature as to the expense which the public shall furnish towards those transactions; and by which subjection it usually becomes necessary to the Crown to consult their inclinations, in a general manner at least, in most of the momentous undertakings of that sort.

The constitutional and general political situation of Parliament was naturally mediated through specific political circumstances. This can be seen by comparing the sessions of 1730 and 1731. Having surmounted the attack on the French alliance in the former session, ministers faced the challenge of having to defend it anew. Parliament was seen as a challenge, but also as an opportunity to give force to government policy. Aware of the 'clamour that may arise against our joining with France to pull down the house of Austria', which was refusing to yield to Anglo-French pressure to accept the entry of Spanish garrisons into Tuscany and Parma, Horatio Walpole, nevertheless, urged that, in order to intimidate Austria, Parliament should be summoned to meet early, in November 1730, and asked to vote supplies sufficient to permit the raising of another 10,000 British troops.[76] Instead, the potentially fatal domestic repercussions of the continuance of the French alliance helped lead the ministry to explore the possibilities of reconciliation with Austria.

Their success in doing so in March 1731 helped draw the opposition sting in the 1731 session. The sensitivity of the issue had been indicated at the outset when the opposition unsuccessfully moved amendments to

[75] Anon., *The Remembrancer: Caleb's Sensible Exhortation* (1730), p. 4.
[76] Horatio to Robert Walpole, 16 Aug., 16 Sept. 1730, BL. Add. 63849, and to Newcastle, 10 Sept. 1730, BL. Add. 32769.

the Address to urge that there be no attack on the Austrians north of the Alps, and made reference to past national efforts to keep France out of the Austrian Netherlands.[77] This was a skilful use of historical resonance in order to present the government as neglecting national interests and, indeed, betraying the Whig tradition.

Alliance with Austria also led to a relatively easy session in 1732. Exploiting the new diplomatic alignment, Horatio Walpole accused the opposition of being unable to praise the government for following the course they had earlier pressed for. The politics of foreign policy ensured that the opposition was unable to mount a strong case, at the same time that genuine problems with governmental policy, especially the failure to incorporate France into the Anglo-Austrian alignment, were not adequately probed. There was no division on the Address in either House. The army estimates passed the Commons without a division, in part because the government sought support for fewer troops than had been anticipated.[78]

Newcastle's account of the royal speech opening the 1732 session was designed to demonstrate harmony between Crown and Parliament, but also to use it to defend policy in discussions with the French government:

the King has been pleased to give his Parliament a very particular account of the late negotiations and of the engagements entered into by the Treaty of Vienna, which, his Majesty has very justly observed, neither tend to aggrandize or reduce the power or weight of any potentate, but are calculated purely for preserving a due balance of power in Europe . . . no speech from the throne was ever perceived with more universal applause.[79]

Augustus II of Saxony-Poland commented on the air of satisfaction in the royal speech, in a deciphered instruction to the Saxon envoy in London that underlined to the British government the close attention paid to the content of the speech.[80] Foreign envoys noted that domestic issues dominated the 1732 session,[81] and their reporting was correspondingly reduced. Nevertheless, the ministry took pains to put the best gloss on small Commons' majorities over the revival of the Salt Duty, in order to avoid any

[77] *Carlisle*, p. 80.
[78] *Egmont*, I, 215; Delafaye to Waldegrave, 13, 27 Jan. (os), 14, 17, 21, 24 Feb. (os), 9, 13 Mar. (os), Thomas Pelham to Waldegrave, 24 Jan. (os) 1732, Chewton; *Carlisle*, p. 88; Wich to Tilson, 1 Feb. 1732, PRO. SP. 82/49 fol. 34; Zamboni to Lagnasc, Saxon minister, 1 Feb. 1732, Dresden, 637 fol. 170.
[79] Newcastle to Waldegrave, 13 Jan. (os) 1732, BL. Add. 32776 fol. 59; cf. 27 Jan. (os), 9 Mar. (os) fols. 100, 168.
[80] Augustus II to Watzdorf, 10 Feb. 1732, PRO.SP. 107/5. For a more critical view, Grumbkow to Degenfeld, 9 Feb. 1732, PRO.SP. 107/5.
[81] Kinsky to Sinzendorf, 19 Feb. 1732 (wrongly endorsed 1733 on back), Kinsky to Charles VI, 11 Mar. 1732, PRO. SP. 100/11, 5.

impression of governmental weakness. Delafaye misleadingly claimed that the legislation was 'not a ministerial point'.[82] Displaying an appreciation of Britain's social politics, some envoys explained how the Salt Duty would strengthen the government politically by enabling it to cut land tax.[83] The hostile Chavigny attributed the ministerial dominance of the Commons to corruption, and, at the same time, eagerly noted signs of weakness.[84] Chavigny warned that the next session would be very troublesome.[85]

As foreign policy also focused the issue of Hanoverian commitments, it provided a way to challenge, or assert, the underlying legitimacy of the regime. The relationship between royal rights as King and obligations as Elector of Hanover constituted a new area for debate over the prerogative, one that was defined only after much disagreement. The terms of the Act of Settlement proved very ambiguous and unhelpful in practice. The government's view was clearly set out in the 1726 Commons' Address, which was, like other Addresses, printed. The Address carefully focused on the threat to Britain posed by the recent treaties between Austria and Spain and presented that as the basis for an alliance with Prussia and for a guarantee to Hanover, which was not actually mentioned:

The engagements which Your Majesty has entered into by the said defensive alliance with the Most Christian King, and the King of Prussia [Treaty of Hanover], in order to obviate and disappoint the dangerous views and consequences of the Treaty of Peace between the Emperor and the King of Spain, and to preserve the many valuable rights and privileges of this nation, against the fatal tendency of the said Treaty of Commerce, calculated for the entire destruction of the chief branches of the British trade, and in breach of the several solemn treaties now in force, call upon us to express our most unfeigned and grateful sense of Your Majesty's concern for the preservation of the balance and peace of Europe, the Protestant religion, and the particular interests of your British subjects.

And when we reflect upon Your Majesty's prudence and resolution, in not letting any attempts or insinuations whatsoever divert you from consulting and steadily pursuing the good and welfare of these your kingdoms, we think ourselves obliged, by the strongest tyes of duty and affection to assure Your Majesty that we will, in justice and vindication of the honour and dignity of the British crown, stand by and support Your Majesty against all insults and attacks that any prince or power (in resentment of the just measures which Your Majesty has so wisely taken) shall make upon any of Your Majesty's territories or dominions, tho' not belonging to the Crown of Great Britain.

[82] Delafaye to Waldegrave, 10 Feb. (os) 1732, Chewton.
[83] Rantzau, Danish envoy, to Rosenkrantz, Danish Foreign Minister, 22 Feb. 1732, PRO. SP. 107/5; Watzdorf to Augustus II, 26 Feb. 1732, Dresden 2676 III fol. 72.
[84] Chavigny to Chauvelin, 11, 18 Feb., 26 May 1732, AE. CP. Ang. 376 fols. 214–16, 233, 377 fol. 191.
[85] Chavigny to Chauvelin, 2 June 1732, AE. CP. Ang. 377 fol. 237.

It is clear from reports of debates that parliamentarians took note of the precise terms of such speeches.[86]

Claims of Hanoverian influence on British policy resonated through a number of controversies. In the 1710s, relations with Sweden were discussed in these terms, and in the late 1720s and early 1730s subsidies to Hesse-Cassel were a crucial issue. Hesse-Cassel had the second-best army in northern Germany, after that of Prussia, and this was seen as a vital source of security for Hanover against Prussian attack when relations with Prussia became hostile from 1726. The subsidy treaty, signed on 1 March (os) 1726, provided for the Hessians holding 12,000 troops ready for use. The need to secure parliamentary consent for the voting of funds with which to pay the annual subsidy ensured that the issue was frequently discussed. The ministry came under heavy attack. In 1727, the Commons' division was 191–98, in 1728, 280–86, in 1729, 298–91, and, in 1730, 248–169, the lowest government majority in a major debate for ten years. It was claimed that if the majority was not large, or the opposition vote exceeded 150, then the government would fall.[87]

Anxiety over the issue did not reflect any particular animosity to Hesse-Cassel. In the discussion about the use of Hessians during the War of American Independence (1775–83), opposition was to be voiced to the then Landgrave, Frederick II, as a ruler who could hire out his subjects for money. Earlier in the century, opposition, instead, focused on what appeared to be an instance of Hanoverian influence. The annual retainer of £125,000 paid to ensure the first call on the Hessians' services was attacked as an expense that led to an outflow of bullion, and one that could be ill-afforded during a period of economic difficulties. The opposition alleged that the cost of the Hessians was equivalent to 6d ($2\frac{1}{2}$ new pence) in the pound on the land tax, a figure that represented one-eighth of that tax's load in the late 1720s. Sir Edward Knatchbull MP recorded that, in the debate on 7 February (os) 1729, the opposition argued that the Hessian subsidy 'was giving foreign princes access to our treasury here, and exporting too much money and impoverishing the nation'.[88] A year later, the opposition returned to the theme, and Walter Titley, a diplomat, responded to the news that the Hessian subsidy had been carried by noting 'That is such a camel for a country squire to swallow, that I am extremely glad to find it went down

---

[86] Alan Brodrick to his father Alan, 22 Jan. (os) 1726, Guildford, Surrey CRO., Brodrick Mss. 1248/6.

[87] Zamboni to Manteuffel, 29 Mar. 1729, Bod. Ms. Rawlinson letters, 120 fol. 59.

[88] *Knatchbull*, p. 84.

so easily.'[89] These criticisms were justified given the heavy cost: £241,000 for 1731.[90]

Although these sums were significant, particularly given the minimal nature of Anglo-Hessian commerce, which ensured that little of the money returned through trade, it was the political consequences that aroused most disquiet. Ministerial MPs argued that the Hessians were not simply hired to protect Hanover, but that they were part of a wider strategic plan: 'Secretary [at War, Henry] Pelham . . . showed that the true design of the Hessian troops was never to defend Hanover, but to guard one part of Europe from the ambitious views of another.'[91] In particular, it was claimed that the Hessians were designed to protect Britain's Dutch ally from Prussian or Austrian attack. This argument was used in the lobbying of ministerial supporters,[92] valuable evidence for which survives in the diary of Viscount Perceval, MP for Harwich. He tended to support the ministry, but also preserved considerable independence. In February 1730, Horatio Walpole paid a visit to the wavering Perceval to urge him to stand fast. Far from relying on the blandishments of ministerial favours, Walpole emphasised the geopolitical situation. He told Perceval that the Hessians

are not kept as the malcontents pretend to defend the Hanover dominions, but really to fulfil our engagements with the Dutch, who having nobody to fear but the Emperor, would not in reason accede to the Treaty of Seville, till they were sure they should be defended from the Emperor's attacks by land; that unless a formidable army covered them on the side of Germany, they would in case of an attack be obliged to accommodate themselves with the Emperor, and so be obliged against their wills to quit our alliance, a thing to be prevented by all means.[93]

This argument throws light on the quality of parliamentary argument, and thus on what was expected from debate. The reference to the opposition as 'malcontents' reflected the ambiguous character of opposition in the face of the persistence of traditional assumptions about the illegitimate nature of faction.

Horatio Walpole's argument was specious. In the correspondence of the Hessian envoy, Diemar, there are no signs that the British ministers, with whom, especially Sir Robert Walpole, he enjoyed close personal relations, intended that the Hessians should be used to aid the Dutch. Rather, it is clear that they were intended for the defence of Hanover. This point was reiterated with vigour by the opposition in all the major

[89] Titley to Tilson, 28 Feb. 1730, PRO. SP. 75/54 fol. 119; *Knatchbull*, pp. 103, 151.
[90] Cobbett, VIII, 842.   [91] *Egmont*, I, 25–6.
[92] For lobbying in 1727, Diemar to Landgrave Karl, 21 Jan. 1727, Marburg, England 175.
[93] *Egmont*, I, 21.

debates of the period. As the Jacobite MP William Shippen baldly put it in 1730, 'To me plain that these are only for the defence of the foreign dominions'.

The opposition argued that the distortion of British policy for Hanoverian ends represented by the Hessian subsidies was illegal and unconstitutional. In the debate on 4 February (os) 1730, George Heathcote, a wealthy West India merchant, and hitherto a ministerial MP, went into opposition, with what another MP described as 'a flaming speech against the Court, which he had collected from a common-place book on tyranny and arbitrary power and extracts of treatises on a free government'. Heathcote claimed that George II's right to the throne was based upon his observance of a contract with the population, a contract stipulated in the Act of Succession. He stated 'that the not defending Hanover at the expense of England' was included in the contract, and that therefore, by subsidising the Hessians, George was in breach of his right to the crown.[94] Robert Vyner, MP for Lincolnshire and an opposition Whig, claimed that voting for the Hessian subsidies was committing treason 'against the people'.[95]

Thus the debates over the Hessians provided an opportunity for discussing, or rather declaiming upon, the constitutional position of the monarch. By encapsulating the issue of relations between Britain and Hanover, the Hessian subsidies provoked consideration of the relationship between George II, in his ambivalent position as King and Elector, and the elected representatives of the people of Britain. George's strong personal interest in, and determination to control, foreign policy increased the importance of the issue. The debates did not reveal much knowledge of the intricacies of German politics, but prudential points about subsidies were raised. In the 1736 Commons' debate on the Navy Estimates, the opposition Whig Walter Plumer advanced a line held in private by some ministers:

I have always observed, that no foreign prince would lend us any of his troops, without our engaging not only to pay them, but to grant him a subsidy, perhaps greater than the pay of those troops, upon their own footing, would have amounted to; and that even in cases where the prince stood obliged, perhaps by former treaties, to assist us with troops at his own expense, and often in cases where his own preservation was more immediately concerned in the event of the war than ours.[96]

[94] Earl of Ilchester (ed.), *Lord Hervey and his Friends 1726–38* (1950), p. 47; *Egmont*, I, 27–8.
[95] *Knatchbull*, p. 151.
[96] Cobbett, IX, 1003. For sensible opposition criticisms in 1732 about money owed to Denmark, *Egmont*, I, 250.

Parliamentary opposition to the Hessian subsidies was used by the Prussians in an attempt to dissuade Hesse-Cassel from supporting George II. In 1729, the Prussian Resident in Cassel informed the Hessians 'that the Parliament will never support His Majesty in any war he may undertake in defense of his German dominions', and argued very strongly that the Hessian troops being voted for by Parliament were not to act in any cause 'that did not regard Great Britain in particular'.[97] Irrespective of its accuracy, the impression created abroad about parliamentary decisions and debates was clearly important.

The role of Parliament in the granting of subsidies and other payments was frequently referred to by British ministers and diplomats in this period. In 1726, when St Saphorin, envoy in Vienna, was sent to Munich to attempt to arrange an alliance with Bavaria, Townshend told him that he could not offer peacetime subsidies as Parliament would never consent, and that, without Parliament, they could not be afforded. Four years later, Edward Finch, envoy in Stockholm and MP for Cambridge University, informed the Swedish government that peacetime subsidies were impossible as Parliament would never accept them.

Parliament also frequently provided a convenient excuse. In 1723, Townshend was discouraging about the payment of arrears owed to allies for expenditure during the campaigning of the 1690s. He referred to the impact of his predecessors' criticisms of the Dutch on that head in Parliament, claiming that the criticism had been made in response to diplomatic disagreements:

les feu My Lords Sunderland et Stanhope et Monsr. Craggs, en revanche de ce que les Hollandois ne vouloient pas acceder à la Quadruple Alliance [1718] ont tant fait au parlement pour decrediter leurs comptes et pretensions, que non seulement les Torys, qui se prevalent toujours des occasions de les chagriner, mais aussi un grand nombre des Whigs ont eté fortement prevenus contre eux.[98]

The Hessian issue was also symptomatic of a deeper rift in British attitudes towards international relations. In 1716–30, the response to the growing power of Russia and Austria was frequently the central issue in British diplomacy. However, this response did not strike much favourable resonance in terms of parliamentary and press debate, in part because of concern arising from the alleged consequences of the Hanoverian connection, and also because of the continued potency of suspicion of France

---

[97] Caillaud to Tilson, 5 Sept. 1729, PRO. SP. 81/123.
[98] Townshend to St. Saphorin, 14 Jan. (os) 1726, Townshend to d'Eltz, 18 Oct. 1723, PRO. SP. 80/57, 43/5 fol. 138.

as an organising theme and inspiration for parliamentary and press discussion, and that despite the Anglo-French alliance of 1716–31. In fact, within a very volatile international situation, the dynastic amalgam of Britain-Hanover was hard pressed by Russian, Austrian and Prussian assertiveness. Georges I and II were fearful of attack, but also anxious not to be simply passive or reactive, both because they feared that they would miss out from possible gains and because they were concerned that inaction would simply increase their vulnerability and weakness. Retaining the Hessians served their policy. However, from the collapse of the Anglo-French alliance in 1731, British ministers moved closer to public debate than to the royal position, as the question of how best to respond diplomatically and militarily to French power became the dominant issue for policymakers.

Although the arithmetic of parliamentary power was crucial, a sense of Parliament as responding to public discussion emerges clearly in some surviving accounts of particular debates. In this respect, foreign policy was clearly not a separate sphere, James Hamilton, a jaundiced Jacobite, was not totally wrong when he reported of one opposition attack in early 1726, 'though the courtiers had little to say against the reasonableness of this motion, they called for the question and carried it by two to one'.[99] However, parliamentary debate at the time of the Excise Bill in 1733 resonated strongly to wider currents, and the same was also true of the controversy over Spanish depredations on British trade in 1738–9, a controversy that fatally affected the government's room for manoeuvre,[100] not least because the crisis coincided with the 1739 session.

The latter has been extensively covered, so it is useful to turn to the session of 1729 in order to probe the character of the parliamentary treatment of foreign policy. Two letters by Thomas Winnington MP indicate the extent to which the familiar sources can be supplemented. They are found among the Ilchester papers deposited in the Dorset County Record Office at Dorchester,[101] and were written on 24 March (os) 1729[102] and 9 April (os) 1729 to Lord Hervey and Stephen Fox respectively. The two MPs were travelling together in Italy. Neither letter was published by the Earl of Ilchester when he produced a collection of correspondence by Hervey and his friends.[103]

---

[99] Hamilton to Philip, Duke of Wharton, 15 Feb. (os) 1726, RA. 90/118.
[100] P. L. Woodfine, *Britannia's Glories. The Walpole Ministry and the 1739 War with Spain* (Woodbridge, 1998).
[101] D124/box 240. I would like to thank Lady Theresa Agnew for permission to cite them.
[102] Not 1728 as dated.   [103] Ilchester, *Lord Hervey and his Friends 1726–38* (1950).

The first letter contains an account of the Commons' debates on the Address and the Army Estimates that is fuller than the Knatchbull account, and, although shorter, contains material not in the Egmont diary. The second, containing a long account of the Commons' consideration of the issue of Spanish depredations, is valuable as it is longer and more detailed than the Knatchbull account, and as the Egmont diary does not survive for this period. The letters stress the divisions within opposition ranks that contrast with the ideology of a united opposition propagated by Bolingbroke and the *Craftsman* newspaper:

The first day the Address (which I suppose you have seen in the foreign prints)[104] was moved by Sir George Oxenden who . . . took particular notice of some expressions made use of in the public papers representing the majority of the House of Commons as hirelings and betraying their country for a sum of money . . . Sir Wilfred Lawson[105] took notice of the ill situation of our affairs abroad and the manifest decay of trade.[106] That a bully was the worst character in private life and that the English nation had now acted that part. That the distinguishing mark of the English was formerly that we were slow to provoke . . . that we now had been precipitate in provoking our enemies and slow and patient in revenging the injuries and insults thrown upon us by the Spaniards. He thought the present words moved were not strong enough and therefore hoped there would be some words added in the Address in relation to our trade and the losses our merchants had sustained. Oglethorpe said[107] there were a great many particulars in the Address which ought to be considered and moved to adjourn the debate till tomorrow . . . Pulteney[108] said he was afraid adjourning the debate would look like want of respect to his Majesty and be of ill consequence to his affairs abroad and therefore hoped gentlemen would retract their motion. And if it was not to be understood that gentlemen should be precluded in future debates from offering their opinions about the state of public affairs he should be glad to agree to pay this compliment to the King . . . Shippen . . . had heard a great deal said today against some weekly papers as if they had retarded the progress of our negotiations but surely such a doctrine could never be advanced by any friends of the administration that a few pamphleteers should have a greater influence upon foreign powers than the consummate wisdom of our wise and experienced ministers . . . Barnard[109] took notice of the great disadvantages trade lay under that the losses of the merchants were great and in the present question unprovided for and moved that these words <u>And thereby to restore the commerce of this kingdom and obtain just and ample satisfaction for the many and great losses sustained by his trading subjects</u> might be

[104] On the Spanish envoys in Paris reading the *Craftsman*, Poyntz to Delafaye, 29 Jan. 1729, PRO. SP. 78/190 fol. 92.

[105] Opposition Whig.   [106] A frequent theme in the opposition press, *Craftsman* 28 Dec. (os) 1728.

[107] James Oglethorpe, opposition Whig.   [108] William Pulteney, leader of the opposition Whigs.

[109] John Barnard, MP for London, opposition Whig.

added ... Strickland[110] said he was against adding these words because no notice was taken of this affair in the King's Speech. Jekyll[111] said he was for it for the reasons Strickland gave against it that we might have something of our own in the Address and not all of it dictated by the Ministry.

Walpole pressed for 'secure' rather than 'restore', defeating the opposition on a division.

On 31 January (os) 1729, the Commons debated the Army Estimates. Winnington responded to the opposition. Unsurprisingly his account of his speech, which was not mentioned by Knatchbull, is the best:

thought the uncertain and dangerous situation of our affairs required us as Englishmen to give all possible assistance to the administration to extricate us out of our present difficulties ... that the immediate diminution of our troops might encourage Spain in their obstinacy who had never given any instances of their inclinations for peace but when our fleet was at their ports or our armies ordered to march into Flanders. That as we had with some reason been represented loaden with debts and decayed in trade the only consequence our enemies could draw from the diminution of our troops at this conjecture would be that we were utterly unable to carry on a war and therefore would be less tractable and rise in their demands. William Pulteney ... agreed it was a national concern that we ought to support the ministry in carrying the present negotiations and extricating us out of our difficulties but then we had a right to know how we were drawn into these exigencies which it became the ministers to explain to us and he hoped they would do it for it was his opinion our present misfortunes were owing to their misconduct and blunders. That there were some expressions in the King's Speech which were very remarkable as if some persons from hence had encouraged the Spaniards to stand out. As for himself he despised such insinuations and if any minister of state had given false information of that kind to the King he was the <u>most contemptible of all liars</u> ... our misfortunes were owing in not accepting the mediation proposed to us by Spain at the Congress of Cambrai – he took notice of the late King's speech who said he had repeated advices that the Pretender being set upon the throne of England was part of the scheme of Vienna and Madrid but now that was strangely dwindled and it did not appear there was any foundation for it for the ministers now say they were only <u>apprehensive</u> of it – and it would be for the advantage of their country if they apprehend no more than they comprehended ... Sir Robert Walpole said ... he hoped the ill situation of affairs could not be imputed to the blunders of the ministers ... As to the Pretender what the late King said was true and he had both written and living evidence to prove it, but surely it could not be thought proper now to irritate and widen the wound between us and the Empire, and mentioning this while we were treating of a peace could be of very little consequence to us. As to our refusing the mediation it was notorious the treaty

---

[110] Sir William Strickland, government supporter.
[111] Sir Joseph Jekyll, Master of the Rolls, independent.

between Vienna and Spain[112] was signed before the notification of our refusal of the mediation could arrive at Madrid. Pulteney said there might be accusations and yet not always times proper to produce them, that without doors not one man approved of the present measures and yet when he came into the house the majority here were of another opinion. Therefore to use the noble person's own words he would advise him not to rely too much upon particulars but content himself with triumphing in his majority in the house.

In Winnington's second letter, he dealt with his Chairmanship of the Commons when it met in Committee to discuss the petition against Spanish depredations, and provided an indication of difficulties affecting procedure, particularly the choice of speakers, in such Committees. Winnington only became chairman thanks to the government's use of its majority to block John Barnard, an opposition MP for the City of London who had presented a petition from the merchants of London complaining of the depredations. When Winnington subsequently called upon John Hedges, MP for Bossiney and a former diplomat, to speak rather than Barnard, he was accused by Pulteney of preferring the ministerial side. The opposition proposal that Barnard speak was defeated by the ministerial majority, albeit narrowly,[113] and Pulteney and his allies left the Committee.[114]

Winnington's reports indicate the variety of points at issue and thus the risk of misrepresentation by selective quotation. The immediacy with which topics for debate became issues of competence and confidence helped explain the role of the ministerial majority. This encouraged opposition speakers to highlight their claim that this majority served to compromise national interests. This argument led to a repetitive quality in the debate. However, that characteristic did not define parliamentary discussion. Firstly, it was also necessary for government and opposition to respond to new developments, secondly, it was clear that many parliamentarians were sufficiently independent to respond to debates and events, and, thirdly, there were important tensions within political groupings about foreign policy. In the 1720s and 1730s, those within the ministry, for example between Townshend and Walpole in 1729–30, were not outlined in Parliament. In contrast, in 1743–4, tension within the ministry over Carteret's conduct of foreign policy was to be aired in Parliament.

Although the government was divided about how best to respond to the War of the Polish Succession (1733–5), the opposition was more obviously split, with the Tories against opposition Whig pressure for intervention on

[112] The First Treaty of Vienna, 1725.
[113] Zamboni to Manteuffel, 29 Mar. 1729, Bod. Ms. Rawlinson letters 120 fol. 59.
[114] P. D. G. Thomas, *The House of Commons in the Eighteenth Century* (Oxford, 1971), p. 275.

behalf of the Austrians in accordance with Britain's commitments under the alliance negotiated in 1731. Concerned about the possible domestic consequences, Walpole kept Britain neutral, but he still faced difficulties during the conflict. In the 1734 session, Walpole was pressed hard on the causes and likely consequences of British neutrality, although he won Commons' divisions on 25 January (os) 1734 by 202 to 114 and 195 to 102; as well as good majorities in the Lords. In the 1734 general election, Walpole's majority fell, ensuring that, in the 1735 session, opposition votes were higher than in the previous session – 185 against the Address (29 January (os) 1735) and 208 against an increase of the army (14 February (os) 1735) – but government majorities were still substantial, including, after 'a long debate',[115] ninety-two on subsidies for Denmark. The majorities in the Lords were also large. Newcastle informed Benjamin Keene, envoy in Spain and later an MP, that the Commons had 'owned the greatest satisfaction in the prudence of His Majesty's measures'.[116]

The issue of competence helped explain opposition attempts for the disclosure of papers, in March 1735, for example, instructions sent to British envoys in Poland, France and Spain. This pressure was designed to expose inconsistencies in British policy. The right to call for papers was not contested, but arguments of prudence and caution were employed in order to defend the majorities that blocked such motions.[117] These arguments were made throughout the period, not only in Parliament but also in pro-government publications. Thus, Benjamin Hoadly, Bishop of Hereford and a prominent defender of the ministry in print, writing in the *London Journal* on 27 October (os) 1722, argued that it would be wrong to expose foreign sources in order to provide Parliament with information.

Denied access to papers, opposition speakers had to rely on general charges of incompetence. In 1734, Sir William Wyndham bitterly attacked Walpole for 'in foreign affairs trusting none but such whose education makes it impossible for them to have such knowledge or such qualifications as can be of service to their country, or give any weight of credit to their negotiations'.[118]

The political crisis at the close of the Walpole ministry owed much to foreign policy and to Britain's response to a volatile international situation, although other factors played a role, including divisions in the royal family and among the ministry, both of which related to the succession: to

---

[115] Horatio Walpole to Sir John Clerk, 1 Mar. (os) 1735, NAS.GD. 18/5245/12.
[116] Newcastle to Keene, 12 Feb. (os) 1735, BL. Add. 32787 fol. 14.
[117] George, 12th Earl of Morton to James, Lord Aberdour, 26 Jan. (os) 1734, NAS. GD. 150/3476/42.
[118] Cobbett, IX, 365, 822.

George II and Walpole respectively. The government's failure to produce an acceptable and lasting settlement to the Anglo-Spanish commercial and colonial disputes, which revived in intensity and prominence in 1738, served to strengthen opposition claims that Walpole was unable and unwilling to protect national interests. The opposition forced a call of the Commons in March 1738, and, in a Committee of the Whole House on 28 March (os), Pulteney accused the ministry of doing nothing to protect trade.

The correspondence of MPs from the period indicates the importance of foreign policy alongside domestic politics. The papers of John Campbell are particularly valuable as they offer the perspective of an 'Old Corps' Whig. MP from 1727 until 1761, and 1762 to 1768, Campbell was an active speaker who was selected to move the Address in 1731, 1734 and 1735, and was a Lord of the Admiralty until Walpole's fall. In 1739, Campbell recalled attending meetings at Walpole's where parliamentary tactics were discussed. In March 1739, he seconded the crucial motion on the Convention of the Pardo, by which differences with Spain had been adjusted, writing beforehand to his son, 'I was obliged to be at Sir Robert Walpole's this evening by seven, and stayed there till after nine'.[119] Such meetings were crucial to parliamentary management. That November, Campbell went to the pre-sessional meeting of MPs:

I am just come from Sir Robert Walpole's where we heard the speech that is to be made on Thursday . . . Sir Robert at the same time informed us that the King had given his servants leave to declare his intention to distribute the prizes already taken from the Spaniards between the captors and the merchants who were sufferers by the Spanish depredations.[120]

The Address on the Convention only passed on 9 March (os) 1739 by 244 to 214 votes.[121] Opposition pressure in Parliament in early 1739 accentuated differences within the ministry, directly contributing to a narrowing in the room for manoeuvre that led to the failure to sustain the Pardo compromise and to the outbreak of conflict after the close of the session. The ministry had been pressed towards the close of the session about Spain's failure to pay the compensation agreed under the Convention.[122] Waldegrave, then envoy in Paris, was certain of the interrelationship of the diplomatic negotiations

---

[119] John to Pryse Campbell, 5 Mar. (os) 1739, Carmarthen, Dyfed CRO., Cawdor Muniments, Box 138.

[120] John to Pryse Campbell, 13 Nov. (os) 1739, Cawdor, 138. See also, Sir Philip Parker MP to Perceval, 19 Jan. (os) 1726, BL. Add. 47031 fol. 81. For sessional meetings of pro-government peers, Stanhope to Stair, 17 Feb. (os) 1718, John Drummond to Lord Aberdour, 31 Mar. (os) 1737, KAO. U1590 0145/24, NAS. SRO. GD. 150/3474/57.

[121] Cobbett, X, 1246–1323.   [122] Cobbett, X, 1409–23.

with Spain and the parliamentary situation. In June, he informed Keene, his counterpart in Madrid, that the latter's reports 'I fear will bring our friends at home under great difficulties . . . the warmth which had been expressed in the House of Lords upon the past delay of the payment of the ninety five thousand pounds, will I doubt leave no room for future management in case this last dispatch arrives before the Parliament be up.'[123]

By finally declaring war on Spain, the ministry drew some of the opposition sting in Parliament in late 1739 and early 1740, and ensured that the supplies were readily voted at the beginning of the session.[124] However, it was also exposed to opposition criticism of past policies. In February 1740, Pulteney introduced a motion for an enquiry into the conduct of the authors and advisers of the Convention of the Pardo. As so often, the disclosure of papers was a key issue, but so also was that of consistency, in this case the opposition attempt to demonstrate that Walpole had abandoned the Whig legacy by acting like the Tories had in negotiating the Peace of Utrecht. As did most recorders of debates, William Hay MP noted the heads of the argument:

Mr. Pulteney in a full House made a long and florid harangue; and concluded with a motion to address the King to lay all papers and instructions relating to the Convention before the House. He said his intentions were, that they should be delivered sealed up, and referred to a secret committee to be chosen by ballot, that it might be known whether our right to a free navigation had been insisted on, as it should have been; and whether our minister in Spain had any authority to accept the King of Spain's declaration reserving to himself a power to suspend the Asiento contract, the acceptance of which was made a necessary step towards signing the Convention. He said he followed exactly the precedent in the first year of the late King [George I], when papers and instructions relating to the Treaty of Utrecht were referred to such a secret committee. That the minister [Walpole] was of that committee as well as himself, and therefore he thought he could not now refuse to mete out the same measure to himself which he had before meted out to others . . . It was answered that neither the Treaty of Utrecht and Convention, nor the makers of them were alike . . . that calling for these papers was in some measure impeaching the Convention, which was inconsistent, after both Houses had voted it a good ground-work for a future treaty.[125]

[123] Waldegrave to Keene, 22 June 1739, BL. Add. 32801 fol. 59.
[124] John to Pryse Campbell, 17 Nov. (os) 1739, 26 Apr. (os) 1740, Cawdor, 138, Herbert Mackworth MP to Pleydell Courteen, 7 Jan. (os) 1740, Swansea, University Library, Mackworth papers 1301.
[125] S. Taylor and C. Jones (eds.), *Tory and Whig. The Parliamentary Papers of Edward Harley, Third Earl of Oxford, and William Hay, MP for Seaford* (Woodbridge, 1998), p. 163.

The ministry won on a vote of 247 to 196. The debate illustrated the interweaving of policy, politics and procedure that played such a major role in Parliament.

The outbreak of the War of the Austrian Succession following the invasion of Silesia in December 1740 by Frederick II, the Great, of Prussia, brought on a new situation. The British response was totally different from that of 1733. On 13 April (os) 1741, the Commons passed a motion granting £300,000 'for preventing the subversion of the house of Austria; and for the maintaining the Pragmatic Sanction, and supporting the liberties and balance of power in Europe'. The proposer, Sir Robert Walpole, presented this help as the best way to provide security against France.[126] The decision to help the Habsburg ruler, Maria Theresa, the daughter of Charles VI, led, in the short term, to a marked degree of agreement over foreign policy in Parliament,[127] that also owed something to opposition disunity over the unsuccessful attempt on 13 February (os) 1741 to move for the dismissal of Walpole from George II's counsels.

Walpole was in a far less secure position after the 1741 general election. His problems reflected not so much a shift in public opinion, as the opposition of a number of powerful electoral patrons, especially Frederick, Prince of Wales and John, Duke of Argyll. The new Parliament met on 1 December (os) 1741. During the Commons' debate on the Address, the issue of aid to Hanover in the developing crisis following the outbreak of the War of the Austrian Succession was ventilated by Tory speakers, while Pulteney focused on the less sensitive issue of ministerial mismanagement. He contrasted Parliament and government, and, more specifically, the new and the old Parliament, in arguing that the new Parliament must save the nation. Far from trying to block the principle of parliamentary enquiry, Walpole declared himself ready to support the motion for a day to enquire into the state of the nation. He claimed that disclosure would provide justification, but also commented on the difficulty of influencing the volatile state of European politics, a point already made in the Commons, in April 1741, by his protégé Henry Pelham. Walpole also queried opposition motives:

Sir Robert Walpole replied that the unhappy state of Europe was owing to accidents not in the power of the ministry to prevent. But if we were accountable for it, it was rather to be imputed to the opposition than administration. That a lord in the opposition had lately been received at Paris . . . He desired his [Walpole's] conduct might be examined in a British Parliament: that the whole truth might

---

[126] Cobbett, XII, 168.   [127] Haslang to Törring, 25 Apr. 1741, Munich, Kasten Schwarz 1721I.

appear: which had too often been concealed to his disadvantage; nay, that he had sometimes been obliged out of prudence to conceal it even when the revealing it would turn to his justification.[128]

Reference to present acts of disloyalty served, like discussion of Utrecht, to underline a context of dynastic (Hanoverian versus Stuart) and national struggle. Ministerial speakers claimed that they were not engaged in any abstract discussion about policy, but rather in a political process focused on protecting the Glorious Revolution. Whigs who were opponents of the 'Old Corps' took the same view, and claimed that the Revolution Settlement was challenged not only by the domestic policies of ministerialists, but also by a failure to stand up against the Bourbons. Being in opposition made it far easier to criticise the exigencies and compromises of government foreign policy.

When many of the opposition Whigs entered office in February 1742 after the government was reconstructed following the resignation of the defeated Walpole, they spoke initially in terms of absolutes. Seconding the Army Estimates after the fall of Walpole, Pulteney, now a member of the Cabinet, presented an account of Britain's interests focused on Continental interventionism and opposition to France that looked back to the policies of William III:

He [Pulteney] laid it down as a maxim that this nation was to hold the balance in Europe. There was no supporting it but by a power on the continent able to oppose France: that power was the Queen of Hungary [Maria Theresa]. That we were to proceed in supporting her neither with timidity nor rashness: not so as to engage us in an unnecessary war with France; yet to show France we were prepared: that Flanders [part of the Austrian Netherlands] was a barrier to us, as well as to Holland. Therefore that we should send forces thither . . . if it had no other effect, would occasion a powerful diversion in favour of the Queen of Hungary.[129]

Once Britain had become involved again in a complex and large-scale conflict, then, as with other conflicts, such as the War of the Spanish Succession, issues of foreign policy were closely intertwined with the fate of the war. Success appeared to validate policy choices, and thus debate over the course of campaigns became a way to discuss policy. The dynamics of alliance politics were extensively debated in Parliament.

The shift to this situation, however, involved several stages. The complexities following Britain's entry into war with France in 1743 had been only partly anticipated after war broke out with Spain in 1739. In 1741, it had

[128] *Tory and Whig*, p. 169.   [129] *Ibid.*, pp. 178–9.

been unclear how the developing crisis following Frederick the Great's invasion of Silesia would provide problems (and opportunities) for Britain and, more contentiously, Hanover. Parliamentarians had to adapt to a rapidly changing and unpredictable international situation, and this in a domestic political context made insecure initially by the weakness of the Walpole ministry and uncertainty over the composition of its successor, and then by the divisions within the latter. As a result, it was not surprising that parliamentary discussion of foreign policy has to be carefully related to particular conjunctures.

4

The mid-century crisis, Parliament and foreign policy, 1742–60

The rights of Parliament in the sphere of foreign policy had been extensively discussed during the Walpole years as part of the working out of the Revolution Settlement, and as the opposition reacted to the longevity of the Walpole ministry and to its association with unpopular policies. The constitutional issue was far less present in mid-century, as there were no novel issues to address, although in Scotland the process of amending the terms of the Union continued. In Britain, the fall of Walpole in 1742 was not followed by the political and institutional changes discussed at various times by his opponents. Furthermore, there was no issue of royal prerogative and parliamentary competence comparable to that raised by the territorial cessions at the close of the American War of Independence in 1783. Foreign policy, however, was still a major topic of parliamentary and press contention.

Prior to the death of George II in 1760, the major fault line in the struggle over foreign policy again lay not, as sometimes suggested, between government and people, however defined and represented, with Parliament managed by the former but open to the arguments of the latter, but, rather, within the government. The struggle focused on the apparent needs created by the Hanoverian commitment.

The problems of managing the Commons also reflected the less than clear-cut nature of party allegiances, the consequences of the divided nature of the Whig inheritance, and the limited extent of partisan cohesion and discipline among parliamentarians. The division between Whigs and Tories was, in the majority of cases, readily apparent, and was strengthened by the course of the political crisis of 1742 and, particularly, the reconstitution of a Whig government. In contrast, the division between ministerial and opposition Whigs was porous, a situation demonstrated in 1742 and, again, in 1744–6. The political alignments of the late 1730s had fractured under the strain of the new political world that emerged out of the growing political difficulties that Walpole confronted in 1740–2, and, specifically, as

78

a result, first, of the general election in 1741 and, secondly, of the manoeuvres associated with the fall of Walpole in February 1742. Between then and the reconstitution of a relatively united ministry which was securely in control of Parliament, a process that was not complete until the spring of 1746, political alignments were recognizably different to the position in the late 1730s.

The reconstruction of the ministry in 1742 involved not only the fall of Walpole but also Harrington's replacement as Secretary of State for the Northern Department by John, Lord Carteret. The combination of the two increased the role of the House of Lords in parliamentary discussion of foreign policy. Carteret was the crucial figure in foreign policy, and Walpole's replacement as Commons' manager, Henry Pelham, lacked his predecessor's governmental and political clout. Crucial statements of government policy were made in the Lords, as Carteret's views were of key importance. Pulteney, formerly the most prominent opposition Whig in the Commons, went to the Lords, as Earl of Bath, in the summer of 1742.

The political situation after Walpole's fall was unchanged in some respects: the political world was divided between government and opposition; the ministry composed of Whigs, who supported the Protestant succession; and the opposition divided between opposition Whigs, who similarly backed the Hanoverian dynasty, and Tories, whose loyalty was more uncertain, and whose relations with the opposition Whigs were fraught with suspicion. However, there were also major differences after the fall of Walpole. The composition and policy of the ministry, and the identity of government and opposition Whigs, were unsettled, and the political world was not only volatile, but also seen as such. As Whig politicians manoeuvred to gain advantage, there was a debate amongst the Whigs as to what government policies should be. This was a debate in which the Tories took little role, and it was one that subsided after the consolidation of the Pelhamite regime in early 1746, which explains in part the nature and chronology of the debate.

Although an active and experienced speaker in the Lords, Carteret's foreign policy in 1742–4 was one that could not be defined as parliamentary in the sense of stemming from an awareness of the domestic political constraints upon policy. To a certain extent, the struggle for control between Carteret and the Pelhams (Newcastle, who remained Secretary of State for the Southern Department, and his brother Henry Pelham) revolved directly around the extent to which domestic pressures, as expressed in Parliament and by the constitutional and political role of Parliament, should affect policy. Carteret's general neglect of Parliament as a constraining element demonstrated the extent to which the seventeenth-century constitutional struggle to have policy presented in Parliament did not necessarily lead to political influence for the latter.

As much attention was devoted to what Carteret said in the Lords, the debates there were seen as an opportunity to gain an insight into ministerial thinking. In February 1744, Baron Haslang, the Bavarian minister, sent details of the very strong Lords' protest over expenditure on Hanoverian troops, but added that it would have no consequences other than that of raising tension, because the ministry was certain to gain its point thanks to its secure majority. A week later, Haslang devoted attention to what Carteret had said in a parliamentary speech lasting over two hours.[1] Haslang's views were of consequence because the government was trying to persuade Charles Albert of Bavaria, the Emperor Charles VII, to abandon France and ally with Britain and Austria.

During these years, the debate over policy was especially bitter, a product not so much of the complex and difficult international situation, as of the need for political definition in Britain and the opportunities there for political advancement and advantage. The divisions *within* the government, especially that between Carteret and the Pelhams, interacted with the debate between ministry and opposition to an extent that had not been the case in the 1730s, and thus the parliamentary aspect of this debate commonly had most political importance as an aspect of the related struggles for predominance and over policy within the ministry. More specifically, the arguments of the parliamentary critics of Carteret took on meaning and weight as part of a wider debate amongst the Whigs.

The opposition Whig speakers in the debate on the Address on 1 December (os) 1743, made statements that dramatised the views of Carteret's ministerial opponents as they sought both to exploit divisions within the government and to identify themselves as proponents of an assertive national interest, while, at the same time, responding to the extent to which the nature of the war had shifted during 1742–3. William Pitt the Elder declared 'that the Parliament never engaged but in a defensive war for the house of Austria, not in a war of equivalent, nor in a war of indemnification', the first a criticism of the practice of settling international differences by territorial changes and/or equivalent gains, and the second a criticism of the Anglo-Austrian alliance for seeking gains to compensate for earlier losses by Austria. Both, by implication, sowed doubt about whether Britain was now fighting for the sake of allies including

[1] Haslang to Seinsheim, 4, 11 Feb. 1744, Munich, Gesandtschaft London 211.

Hanover. This resonated in the collective memory of political controversy, both with the critique of Continental interventionism and alliance politics in the last years of the War of the Spanish Succession (1702–13), and with the criticism of British policy under George I in the Great Northern War (1700–21) and, more specifically, the claim that the prime goal was the gain from Sweden for Hanover of the former prince-bishoprics of Bremen and Verden.

Pitt also criticised Carteret: 'that minister who seems to have renounced the British nation. I can never approve of a war of which neither the end or the means have yet been ascertained'. Another opposition Whig, George Dodington, condemned the minister for leading George II 'where he is bewildered in a labyrinth of measures throughout all Europe, from which the whole treasure of this nation cannot extricate him'.[2] This was a reasonable charge, as Carteret's system was overly reliant on other states playing assigned roles, but Dodington also benefited from a general disquiet about complexity. The themes of Europe, interventionism, mismanagement, complexity and cost were all skilfully linked. Carteret's Hanoverianism was depicted as the source of his power, while uneasiness about alliances and allies was also a theme effectively exploited by opposition speakers. A year later, Dodington was appointed to the lucrative post of Treasurer of the Navy, while Pitt joined the ministry in the spring of 1746; both men beneficiaries of the defeat of Carteret.

The argument that parliamentary debate took on significance as part of the struggle by individuals to force themselves into office, and the related conflict within the ministry, can be extended chronologically, although the relationship is not easy to assess. Considerations of parliamentary management certainly played a major role in ministerial discussions in the winter of 1747–8 about the desirability of peace and about what terms would be acceptable. These considerations were also important in the debate between the Duke of Newcastle, still a Secretary of State, and his colleagues in 1748–54 about the feasibility of a costly interventionist diplomacy. Newcastle sought to arrange the election of Joseph (later the Emperor Joseph II), the Habsburg heir, as King of the Romans, and thus heir to the Holy Roman Empire, in order to avoid a contested election and, possibly, a new war of the Austrian Succession when his father, Maria Theresa's husband, Emperor Francis I, died. In contrast, Henry Pelham, First Lord of the Treasury from 1743 until 1754, was committed to economy and uneasy about subsidies.

[2] Warwick, Warwickshire CRO. Newdigate papers CR136B 2530/22.

British envoys saw parliamentary support as crucial to their negotiations. Thomas Villiers, later an MP, reacted from Dresden to the debates following the fall of Walpole as the reconstituted ministry struggled to hold off demands for the punishment of the former minister:

two chief points seem favourable to the best intentioned viz the rejecting of the motion for a Secret Committee and the thanking His Majesty on his endeavours to save the House of Austria which Address will be of weight in foreign affairs yet the decreasing majority in your house [Lords] and the small one in the other makes me apprehend the increase of animosities and confusion and removes out of sight the concord necessary for the interest and honour of our country.

In 1750, Guy Dickens, envoy in St Petersburg, wrote to his counterpart in Vienna:

it would certainly be of great service to the Common Cause, if we could depend at all events on such a respectable corps of troops as is offered to us on this side, and be an effectual means to keep things quiet both North and South. But how our Parliament will relish such great subsidies in time of peace, our great ministers at home are best able to judge.[3]

A parliamentary perspective – the argument that a specific policy could not be proposed as Parliament would never accept it (and the reverse claim) – could, of course, be advanced for tactical political reasons, rather than as an objective assessment of the views of parliamentarians or the exigencies of parliamentary management. This was certainly the case with the rise to office and in influence of Pitt, which was pressed on the grounds of his parliamentary position. In late 1745, indeed, George II argued that the defeat of opposition motions indicated that Pitt's support for the ministry was unnecessary, and the same appeared true in late 1754, and, again, in the winter of 1755–6. However, aside from the degree to which political and parliamentary confidence were not measurable by objective criteria and not simply a matter of the size of majorities, and that this was especially the case in periods of crisis, the resort in ministerial discussion to the issue of parliamentary management in order to advance particular political goals was tactically valuable as it was difficult to deny its importance.

Parliamentary management was a crucial factor in the protracted and serious political crisis of 1754–7, but Newcastle's resignation as First Lord of the Treasury in 1756, when in command of a sizeable majority, indicated that the matter was not simply one of parliamentary arithmetic. A ministry

---

[3] Villiers to his brother, the 3rd Earl of Jersey, 21 Feb. 1742, London, Greater London Record Office Acc. 510/194; Dickens to Robert Keith, 18 Feb. (os) 1750, BL. Add. 35468 fol. 60.

needed a reliable manager in the Commons, but there were serious problems if the ministry was divided or otherwise unable to provide the manager with the firm support he required, factors that helped to account for the difficulties of management in 1754–7 and 1763–7.[4] A divided ministry and a weak manager encouraged attack from politicians who hoped to join and otherwise alter the government, not to overthrow it, although such politicians were quite willing to turn for support to those who sought more substantial changes. Conversely, if the ministry was united, then criticism, whether parliamentary or extra-parliamentary, of its policy was of slight consequence, as the critics of the Pitt-Newcastle administration of 1757–61 came to appreciate and as Pitt himself discovered when he attacked the terms of the Peace of Paris in 1762–3 without success.

This was also the case in the late 1740s and early 1750s when there was a distinct slackening in political tension over foreign policy, a slackening that lasted until the build-up of strife following the unexpected death of Henry Pelham in 1754. This ability to handle the politics of foreign policy reflected both the domestic political situation and the policy being followed. The two were linked. For example, Carteret's fall in 1744 was followed by a less tense parliamentary atmosphere in the discussion of foreign policy. The reconstitution of the ministry that year brought several prominent opposition Whigs into office. The direct payment of Hanoverian troops was ended. George II was forced to be more cautious in his unpopular plans for action, especially those aimed at his nephew, Frederick the Great of Prussia. The general election of 1747 was a success for the government.

Although the War of the Austrian Succession with France (which had come to incorporate the War of Jenkins' Ear with Spain) had been disappointing, and the ministry faced having to win backing for peace terms that were likely to be unpopular, the government benefited from the sense that existing ministerial policies and personnel would continue until the ministerial change that was expected to follow the accession of the Prince of Wales as King Frederick I. Moreover, his opposition to his father's ministers only became evident from 1747 and was, anyway, not very strong; while the example of 1727, when those who had hoped for a change in ministry, following the accession of George II, had been disappointed, seemed instructive. A failure of parliamentarians to attend sessions in the late 1740s was an important sign of a fall in the level of political tension. In March 1748, Charles Wyndham, MP for Taunton and a Tory who had

---

[4] P. A. Luff, 'Henry Fox and the "Lead" in the House of Commons 1754–1755', *Parliamentary History*, 6 (1987), pp. 33–46.

moved over to support the government after the fall of Walpole, wrote to his grand-uncle, Charles, 6th Duke of Somerset:

It is now very near three months since I left London, little thinking I should stay so long out of it: my first design was to stay here three weeks, except anything extraordinary happened in Parliament, in which case I desired my friends to summon me, determined to obey the summons at a day's warning: but instead of any thing happening there, almost every letter I have had, has been to tell me that the house was ill attended, and nothing likely to come on worth attending: so from having no call in town, and a great deal of work going on here, I have stayed on from time to time, till I have brought it so near to Easter that I do not think of leaving this place till after the holidays.[5]

Parliamentary debates were not only significant in terms of relations within the ministry. They were also important in terms of governmental attempts to assert the consistency and stability of British policy. This was particularly necessary in the aftermath of the dissension of Walpole's last years in office. Anthony Thompson, the embassy chaplain left in charge of representation in Paris after Waldegrave died, as relations deteriorated, observed in a letter to an Under-Secretary in December 1742: 'the vigorous resolutions of the Parliament, I have some reason to think, will encourage the King of Sardinia [Charles Emmanuel III] to exert himself more and more'. Five months later, Carteret wrote from The Hague to his fellow Secretary of State, Newcastle, concerning,

a happy change in this country since I was here in October last. First they have a good opinion of the stability of our affairs in England, which they had not when I was here last, but the great majority which His Majesty had in Parliament all the last session had an excellent effect here, and the more because it was not expected; this they have frankly owned to me.[6]

That December, Carteret wrote to James Cope, the Resident in Hamburg and later, on the interest of his uncle, Lord Feversham, an MP, concerning the Commons' debate over the size of the army:

that great point was then likewise settled by so great a majority as has hardly been known . . . 120. As the whole of the measures His Majesty is now pursuing, for the supporting the House of Austria according to his engagements *totis viribus*, for securing the Liberties of the Empire, and re-establishing the Balance of Power, was then professedly under deliberation, you will have a convincing proof in your hands . . . how void of foundation all those malicious reports have been, which have

---

[5] Wyndham to Somerset, 28 Mar. (os) 1748, Exeter, Devon CRO. 1392 M/L18 48/1.
[6] Thompson to Couraud, 11 Dec. 1742, Carteret to Newcastle, 19 May 1743, PRO. SP. 78/227 fol. 465, 43/31.

insinuated, that the conduct of our affairs in pursuit of those great views . . . would be disapproved in Parliament, and from which very sanguine hopes have been formed by our ill wishers abroad of seeing us fall into difficulties in our domestic affairs . . . must recommend to you to make the best use in your power of this very material intelligence.[7]

Hanover was a crucial issue in this period, in part because it served as a way to debate Continental interventionism. The two were related although this was necessarily a complex process as neither was a single option. The relationship between interventionism and Hanoverian interests provided opportunities for opponents to criticize both. However, had there been no Hanoverian link, British ministers would still have had to decide how to respond to the French attempt to remould German, and thus European, politics in 1741–2, just as they would have had to consider in the early 1750s whether to make a major effort by diplomacy to prevent anticipated international crises. It was argued that the British had to accept a European role, whatever their rulership.

In both the 1740s and the 1750s, the government had the parliamentary votes, but the opposition had much of the parliamentary sound and fury. This was an aspect of the political costs of the personal union of Britain and Hanover. Such unions posed the danger that the views of constituent units would be poorly handled, due to insensitivity, a lack of understanding, and pressures arising from the interests either of other units or of the unifying hand represented by the monarch. Furthermore, there was a danger of a conflation of representation, particularism, proto-nationalism and xenophobia to produce opposition to the ruler, or at least a vocal critique.

The representation might be organised in very different ways – the Westminster Parliament and the Polish Sejm were markedly dissimilar to the Hanoverian Council of Ministers – but, in every case of personal union, there was a distancing of the ruler, creating political and governmental problems, pressures and expectations. The consequent gap between ruler and ruled could threaten to become a political vacuum that might exacerbate tensions, or even provoke new ideas about political identity, responsibility and organization. Foreign policy was a crucial source and idiom of political tensions, because it focused concern and debate over the distribution of the profits and costs of power within a political union.

In more specific terms, Hanoverianism was both issue and charge in the contentious questions of how much and how best to respond to France. From the 1740s, the problems of French power, and the response to it, were

7 Carteret to Cope, 7 Dec. (os) 1742, PRO. SP. 82/64 fol. 220.

increasingly seen in Britain more in maritime, colonial and, indeed, global terms, and less in those of Continental Europe. 'Blue water' ceased to be a policy and idiom directed largely at Spain and, instead, was also applied to France. This reflected not only domestic politics and ideology, not least the focus of 'patriotism' on imperial expansion and the displacement of Tory criticism of external entanglements, but also the rapid development of French interests, opposed to those of Britain, in India and North America in the late 1740s and early 1750s.[8] The British monarchs failed to play a leadership role in this new alignment of British concerns. None of the Hanoverians took a positive part akin to that of Charles III of Spain (r. 1759–88). George III's firm response to the demands of the American colonists was the first major royal intervention in imperial matters.

There was therefore a potent tension between the vistas and assumptions of George II, Carteret *and* Newcastle, all of whose ideas were those of an earlier age, and the new intensity of imperial concern and anticipation. Put differently, for George, Carteret and, to a far lesser extent, Newcastle, the Empire meant the Holy Roman Empire and the Imperial Election to its headship, but, in other circles, the Empire was British and spanned the Atlantic, while Imperial election was a providential call of Britain to greatness.

Parliamentary criticism of Hanoverianism combined specific with general points, creating a sense that particular concerns could be accounted for with reference to a more general problem and tendency. The vulnerability of Hanover to Prussian and French attack in the early stages of the War of the Austrian Succession thrust the issue to the fore. In April 1741, Thomas Clutterbuck, a Lord of the Admiralty, moving a Commons' Address, declared 'We ought to pronounce that the territories of Hanover will be considered on this occasion as the dominions of Great Britain, and that any attack on one or the other will be equally resented.'[9] This view, challenged in the Commons by William Pulteney, who referred to the Act of Settlement of 1701, led that summer to the offer of 12,000 British troops for the defence of Hanover against a threatened French invasion. The crisis was in fact settled in the autumn of 1741 by the negotiation, between France and George as Elector, of a neutrality for the Electorate. George II, however, rejected a French attempt to extend the neutrality to include Spain,

---

[8] A. Reese, *Europäische Hegemonie und France d'outre-mer. Koloniale Fragen in der französischen Aussenpolitik, 1700–1763* (Stuttgart, 1988), pp. 228–319; D. Armitage, *The Ideological Origins of the British Empire* (Cambridge, 2000), esp. pp. 182–97; E. H. Gould, *The Persistence of Empire. British Political Culture in the Age of the American Revolution* (Chapel Hill, 2000), esp. p. 42.

[9] Cobbett, XII, 157.

thus ending the Anglo-Spanish war, stating that he was not the master in Britain, that to give his word would be useless, and that he would not be able to sustain what would offend the entire nation.[10]

Public dissatisfaction, as expressed across the range of anti-Hanoverian propaganda, appears to have had an impact on parliamentarians, and, at least, was believed to do so. For example, on 7 December (os) 1742, an estimate, for a pro-government peer, of the ministerial majority in the forthcoming Commons' debate on hiring 16,000 Hanoverian troops for the army designed to help Maria Theresa against France suggested that it would be '100 at least'. In the event, on 10 December (os), the division was 260–193, leading to the conclusion, 'we had greatly the justice of the debate on our side yet pamphlets and popular declamations made several good friends leave us'.[11]

In 1742–4, the Hanover issue in part obscured differences between Tories and opposition Whigs, and thus put the ministry on the defensive, but, at the same time, the issue apparently raised an important distinction between those who supported the Protestant Succession and crypto-Jacobites. To that extent, parliamentary discussion of Hanoverian issues was not totally unsatisfactory for the ministry, as it could expose differences between Tories and opposition Whigs. In December 1741, Lord Charles Noel Somerset, a Jacobite MP, had 'moved that a clause should be added to it [the Address] desiring His Majesty not to engage this kingdom in a war for any dominions not belonging to the crown of Great Britain, but this amendment was disapproved by Mr. Pulteney himself and withdrawn by the proposer'.[12] Pulteney was still in the opposition, but was thinking about how best to rejoin a reconstituted ministry and had no intention of needlessly offending George II.

Hanover became a more serious political issue once Britain was committed to the conflict on the Continent in 1743. Parliamentary concern over commitments to Hanover strengthened the ministers opposed to Carteret. By making it clear that his foreign policy was vulnerable in Parliament, this issue helped force George to turn to the Pelhams in 1744, just as the response to the problems of parliamentary management played a major role in bringing Pitt first to office (1746) and later to power (1756). Both

---

[10] Jean-Jacques Amelot, French foreign minister, to Bishop of Rennes, envoy in Spain, 19 Feb. 1742, AE. CP. Espagne 470 fol. 95.

[11] Anon. to 13th Earl of Morton, 7, 11 Dec. (os) 1742, NAS. GD. 150/3485.

[12] Philip Yorke MP to Marchioness Grey, 8 Dec. (os) 1741, Bedford CRO. L30/9/113/4; Taylor and Jones (eds.), *Tory and Whig. The Parliamentary Papers Edward Harley, Third Earl of Oxford, and William Hay, MP for Seaford* (Woodbridge, 1998), p. 168.

steps were important, in the short term, to the creation of an effective government, but also to the long-term working out of the implications of the
Revolution Settlement. Parliament's position in the field of foreign policy
focused royal concerns and hopes about British assistance for Hanover, and
this ensured that parliamentary management was a sphere in which vital
compromises concerning royal wishes had to be reached.

Foreign policy and, more specifically, the need to manage it in Parliament
also helped produce compromise among Whig politicians. The general
issue was the need to get government business through, while, in the mid-
1740s, the more specific point was the need for the Pelhams to recruit
opposition Whig support if they were to feel secure in Parliament, and an
awareness among many of the latter that co-operation with the Tories in
a dangerous international situation was hazardous. A decade later, in the
face of another hazardous international situation, it was again felt that Pitt
had to be recruited.

Whig realignment and comprehension helped ensure ministerial success
in the 1747 general election, and both contributed to a strong grip on
the subsequent Parliament. This was readily apparent in the muted debate
over the terms of the Peace of Aix-la-Chapelle of 1748. The difficulties
Britain and her allies had faced in the last stage of the War of the Austrian
Succession, particularly in the face of successful French attacks in the Low
Countries in 1745–8, made the terms seem reasonable. William Murray,
the Solicitor General, MP for Boroughbridge, a pocket borough of the
Duke of Newcastle, speaking in the debate on the Address in November
1748, claimed, with reason, that peace had been necessary because of Dutch
vulnerability and the dangerous state of public credit, and that 'we had for
three years preceding met every year with a signal defeat'.[13]

During the subsequent period of peace, the parliamentary opposition
continued to seek issues on which they could attack the ministry for failing
to defend national interests. In 1750, twenty years after Walpole had been
harried on the same topic, the focus was on France's failure to fulfil her
treaty undertaking to destroy Dunkirk's defences. Far from having to com-
pete with the opposition speakers in outrage and xenophobia, Pitt, now as
Paymaster General, replied on behalf of the ministry that the sole alternative to negotiation was war and that Britain was in no state for conflict,
adding that the motion was dangerous as it would incite popular pressure
and, in reply to the claim by John, 2nd Earl of Egmont, MP for Weobley,
who was then the chief political adviser to Frederick, Prince of Wales, that

[13] Cobbett, XIV, 333.

Pitt had formerly adopted the same notion, claimed that it was necessary for nations to follow a prudential course.[14]

The following year, another trusted favourite of opposition attack, subsidies, in this case for the Elector of Bavaria and in order to assist the Imperial Election Scheme, were at issue. The surviving accounts indicate that the Commons was offered both a wide range of information and a reasoned presentation of the advantages and disadvantages of the proposal. Had the historian only the brief account by Sir Robert Walpole's youngest son, Horace, MP for Callington and later a noted writer,[15] it would be possible to say little about the content of the speeches. The far longer account in Cobbett's *Parliamentary History*[16] is much more valuable, although it offers no guidance to the quality of the speeches, and thus of their impact. The report sent to Newcastle by his Under-Secretary and general factotum, Andrew Stone, himself MP for Hastings, provides a useful indication of the importance of employing manuscript sources,

Mr. Pelham opened the debate; he said, that he was no friend to subsidies in time of peace and that he should not have been for this subsidy, if it had not been of a different nature from most others. That the great object with him was the preservation of the peace, and that this subsidy had an immediate tendency to that: that the uniting the Elector of Bavaria to the House of Austria (who had so often been the instrument of France to embroil Europe) and the securing the Imperial dignity to the House of Austria, by the election of the Arch-Duke [later Joseph II], would probably be the effect of this treaty – that he neither knew nor believed, that there would be any other demands of this nature, and that, if these great points could be secured, for so small an expense, as our quota of this subsidy; he could not but think that they would be very cheaply purchased. He entered into the particulars of the treaty – explained the affair of Mirandola – and the transaction with the court of Vienna for bringing them to contribute to the subsidy – and accounted for the Empress Queen's not being a party to the treaty – He said a great deal in defence of the measure – that he believed, France was, at present, sincere for preserving the peace and that he was not at all apprehensive that this would make France alter their system. But possibly, that this great work might, at last, be concluded by the general consent of all parties.

In return, Samuel Martin, MP for Camelford, a follower of Frederick, Prince of Wales, sensibly

represented the success of the Election as doubtful – The ways, by which it was pursued, inconsistent with the laws of the Empire; and the aggrandising the House

---

[14] Cobbett, XIV, 694.
[15] Horace Walpole, *Memoirs of King George II*, ed. J. Brooke (3 vols., New Haven, 1985), 33–4.
[16] Cobbett, XIV, 930–70.

of Austria, as an object, that might be dangerous to this country – But that, supposing it right, the Imperial dignity was nothing but a name – and the real strength of the House of Austria consisted in the hereditary dominions etc,

the last a reasonable point. The speech by George Lyttelton, a Lord of the Treasury and MP for Okehampton, in response to Martin revealed a knowledge of the Imperial constitution:

showed that the election was not inconsistent with the constitutions of the Empire, which he supported by good authorities – that it was a great and useful measure, and that the expense was inconsiderable. That nobody would be more against a subsidiary system [i.e. system focused on subsidies] than himself but that this was not to be considered in that light, but as a means of preserving the peace of Europe, and establishing a system for that purpose.

Murray 'seemed to give general satisfaction' with his speech, which, judging by the account in Cobbett, showed a considerable knowledge of German history and the Imperial constitution. As Stone noted, 'he went into the particulars, that had been mentioned relating to the laws of the Empire, about elections'. In reply, Egmont raised some practical points, and also mentioned the role of Parliament. He asked:

how could we depend upon the Elector of Bavaria? Would not he still be French, in his heart, as his family had always been? . . . would not other Electors, Saxony, Palatine, Mayence [Mainz], and Treves [Trier], expect to be paid also? and who could find money for that? that he acknowledged there would be some utility in this election, if it could be obtained – But that, otherwise, this subsidy would be flung away. If we had subsidies to give, why did not we give one to Denmark? But that his greatest objection to this treaty was that it was made without the consent of Parliament and that (if Parliament could have concurred no other wise) it would have been better to have applied for a vote of credit, with a view to have applied it to this object, than to have taken no notice of Parliament at all.

Egmont's intelligent observations about international diplomacy were countered by Pelham's suggestion that he was opportunistic, and that the government had tried, but failed, to gain Denmark's alliance, 'though he doubted not, if it had been done, it would have been found fault with'.[17]

The following year, on 22 January (os) 1752, similar expertise was presented in the debates over the subsidy to Augustus III of Saxony-Poland. Two former experienced envoys, Thomas Robinson and Horatio Walpole, and one less experienced diplomat, Henry Legge, spoke in the Commons, another speaker, William Yonge, was provided with copies of the

---

[17] BL. Add. 32724 fols. 129–34; Haslang to Preysing, 8 Mar. 1751, Munich, Kasten Schwarz 225.

documents relating to the treaty by Newcastle, and Murray offered the Commons details of French subsidies. Horace Walpole recorded that his uncle Horatio, now a critic of subsidy treaties, 'showed how well he knew where the weakness of such treaties lay'. In other words, both sides could draw on considerable expertise. The government's majority was very substantial, 236 to 54, Newcastle writing of 'a majority of five to one in the House of Commons; and the arguments in favour of this measure were so strong, and so well supported, that I am persuaded it will meet with universal approbation throughout the whole kingdom'.[18] Yonge's account of the debate throws valuable light on the issues raised:

It was opened and the motion for the subsidy moved by Mr. Pelham: who spoke extremely well, and urged the advantage of a King of the Romans very strongly, but I thought rather coolly of subsidy treaties in general, but pressed the compliance with this as a consequential measure of the treaty with Bavaria, which had received the approbation and sanction of Parliament. He was answered by our old friend Horatio Walpole who spoke $\frac{3}{4}$ of an hour against the treaty and exhausted all that could be said on the subject. But I was sorry for his indiscretion, when he spoke against subsidy treaties in to extensive a manner, and put every man in mind of the *preventive* measure of his brother [Sir Robert Walpole], which included many such. But the weakest part of his speech, in my opinion, was his examining seriatim the articles of the treaty . . . However he ended with declaring he should vote for the question . . . His reasons were that as the treaty *was* made he would not subject the king to any disgrace from his Parliament, nor lessen that influence which he *actually* had, and always ought to have with the powers of Europe.

He was answered by the Solicitor General [Murray] who spoke well to the point . . . I got an opportunity of speaking, as I had been desired by the Duke of Newcastle who had enabled me to do so, and in answer to another gentleman who examined the value of the articles of the Treaty, I said, that if we obtained nothing by it, but what was in the Treaty I would not have given my vote for one farthing; but if in consequence we had the word of a king [Augustus III] for what was of the greatest consequence to this nation, explicitly and free from all objectives, it was worth double the sum, and the word of a sovereign prince so solemnly given, was as satisfactory to me, as any treaty, for that one was easily broken as the other. And that I had confidence and reason for that confidence that such assurances were given. This I had foundation for saying, the Duke of Newcastle having put into my hands very kindly all the letters and documents relating to this treaty, from beginning to end both in and out of cypher. And I had a hint, that it was properer

---

[18] Newcastle to Charles Hanbury Williams, envoy to Augustus III, 24 Jan. (os) 1752, Newport, Hanbury Williams papers; Cobbett, XIV, 1152; W. Coxe, *Memoirs of Horatio, Lord Walpole* (1802), pp. 398–405; Horace Walpole, *Memoirs of George II*, I, 166–7.

to come from one who was not a minister than from one who was. The debate was concluded by Mr. Legge, who spoke short, but with great weight, who told us from his own knowledge, that all had been done that could be done to conciliate the King of Prussia, and particularly the obtaining the guarantee of the Empire for his possessions in Silesia, in hopes it might have produced a harmony between him and the House of Austria, without which it could not have been observed, but from the influence of our king on *that court* and on other princes of the Empire. That as the option, which was easy to make, between a very great and permanent power [Austria], and a great power indeed but very precarious, depending on the life of one able man [Frederick II of Prussia], with the support of another great power of an opposite interest [France] and subject to be *reduced* by any one of two shocks which time or accidents might produce . . . Upon the whole the opposition was trifling.[19]

When the Lords debated the treaty on 28 January (os) 1752, the opposition was opened by John, 4th Duke of Bedford, until recently a Secretary of State, and other speakers included a current Secretary, Newcastle, a former one, Granville [Carteret] and a former diplomat, John, 4th Earl of Sandwich. Bedford spoke very well, offering a skilful account of both the international situation and Britain's position. Newcastle's speech, in which he attacked reliance only on 'our wooden walls' [the navy], was muddled, and Granville, who supported the treaty, was criticized for displaying 'much wit but no argument'. On the other hand, he pointed out, with reason, that guarantees were of limited value in international relations, and argued that subsidies would cement an anti-French league. Despite Bedford's able speech, the motion was rejected without a division, a reflection of the government's strength in the Lords, while George II refused to speak to Bedford for some time, itself a valuable help to the ministry.[20]

The following day, the ministry displayed its strength in the Commons, easily defeating a Tory motion for declaring against subsidy treaties in time of peace. The debate revealed Tory concern about taxation and a sense that the financial aspect of foreign policy required scrutiny and could yield them political advantage.

Parliamentary discussion of foreign policy was issue-driven, because crises led to financial demands. This was seen in particular with the collapse of Britain's alliance system in the mid-1750s, as hostilities broke out with France in North America in 1754, while the Seven Years' War began in

[19] Yonge to Hanbury Williams, 24 Jan. (os) 1752, Farmington, Hanbury Williams papers vol. 54 fols. 252–3, a fuller account than that sent the same day by Edward Digby, fols. 244–7.

[20] John Dobson to John Mordaunt, 30 Jan. (os), undated notes, Warwick CRO. CR 136 8/5/6, CR 136 B 3012/44; Walpole, *Memoirs of George II*, I, 167–73; Newcastle to Yorke, 31 Jan. (os) 1752, PRO. SP. 84/458.

Europe in 1756 with Austria allied to France. This collapse in the alliance system could not be treated in the abstract or with reference to general issues of policy. Instead, the government needed to get parliamentary approval for subsidies and other expenditure. Hanover was again at the front of attention, as the British government sought first to take diplomatic measures for its protection and, subsequently, from 1756 to consider how best to prevent French conquest.

In late 1755, a major parliamentary attack was mounted on subsidy treaties with Hesse-Cassel and Russia which, it was, with reason, claimed, were essentially for the defence of Hanover. On 13 November, in the debate on the Address, Pitt, in a declaration of open opposition to the government, spoke for over ninety minutes. He condemned the Hanoverian focus of foreign policy and the past failure to take sufficient note of the defence of North America, stressed the importance of the navy, and offered a very Whiggish account of the royal position: 'the King owes a supreme service to his people'; the people had no such obligation to Hanover. Attacking the subsidy treaties, 'he said that measure would hang like a mill-stone about the neck of the minister who supported it and sink him into disrepute amongst the people'.[21] And yet the government won a clear majority, 311 to 105. On 10 December 1755, Thomas Potter, MP for Aylesbury and an ally of Pitt, told the Commons that the subsidy treaties were

illegally concluded, as being made for the defence of Hanover without consent of Parliament, in violation and defiance of the Act of Settlement, and charged besides the payment of the Hessian levy money in the summer as a criminal misapplication of the public money. And without entering into the expediency or tendency of the treaties, thought for these reasons the House should not given them so much countenance as to prefer them.

In the same debate, Henry Fox, MP for Windsor, who had recently been appointed Secretary of State for the Southern Department and given responsibility for the management of the Commons, attacked Pitt and the attempt to create 'the fatal distinction . . . of Englishman and Hanoverian'.[22] The government's majorities were substantial, with divisions of 318 to 126, 289 to 121, 263 to 69 and 259 to 72 in the Commons, and 85

[21] Gilbert Elliot MP to his father, Lord Minto, 15 Nov. 1755, NLS. Ms. 11001 fol. 15; Walpole, *Memoirs of George II*, II, 69–72; Farmington, Hanbury Williams papers vol. 63 fol. 22.
[22] Fox to Duke of Devonshire, 19 Dec. 1755, Chatsworth House, Devonshire Mss. 330/87; Pryse Campbell to Mr White, 18 Dec. 1755, Carmarthen, Cawdor, Box 138; Walpole, *Memoirs of George II*, II, 95–102.

to 12 in the Lords, but the opposition had accurately focused on an issue that challenged governmental cohesion, especially because of tensions between George II and his ministers. Potter's point about the payment of the Hessian levy money during the summer recess underlined one of the limitations of parliamentary scrutiny and approval: that both might be belated.

The ministry survived Pitt's parliamentary attacks in the session of 1755–6. However, in October 1756, it collapsed as controversy about the failure to prevent the loss of Minorca that June exacerbated tensions within the government. First Fox, and then Newcastle resigned. A ministry led by Pitt and William, 4th Duke of Devonshire took its place, but its weakness led to a sharp bout of ministerial instability that culminated, in July 1757, in the formation of a Pitt-Newcastle ministry.

The formation of this ministry and victories, from 1758, in the Seven Years' War (1756–63) helped ensure that foreign policy debates occurred with few difficulties for the government in the late 1750s. This owed much to Pitt's success in explaining the dispatch of British troops to northern Germany – a new field of operations – in 1758, as designed to help Britain's ally, Prussia, rather than as a measure to assist Hanover. As opposition spokesmen pointed out, there was an inconsistency with Pitt's position in the early 1740s. Then, when intervening on behalf of Austria, it had proved more difficult to avoid charges of Hanoverianism. However, the international situation, that of domestic politics, and also the parliamentary dynamics then had all been different to the position in the late 1750s. Pitt's presence in the Commons in the late 1750s, on behalf of the ministry in whose leadership he had a major role, also played a part in helping ensure the success of the government case. Furthermore, Frederick the Great's role as a Protestant hero, and a successful one at that, defeating the French in 1757, while George II's second son, William, Duke of Cumberland, at the head of a Hanoverian and allied force, was unable to do so, made interventionism seem popular *and* prudent in a way that had not been the case since John, 1st Duke of Marlborough's victories in his heyday in 1704–8.

This, however, was a difficult shift that took time and was accomplished in stages. On 1 December 1757, George II opened the session by acknowledging his concern for Hanover: 'It is my fixed resolution to apply my utmost efforts for the security of my kingdoms, and for the recovery and protection of the possessions and rights of my Crown and subjects in America and elsewhere.' Horace Walpole pointed out that by this '*elsewhere* Hanover was incorporated into the very language of Parliament'. A fortnight later,

however, Pitt queried the use of 'elsewhere' and said he was against sending troops to Germany, although he presented that within a context of
not being against 'Continental measures when practicable'.[23] The caveat,
however, permitted Pitt to change his mind.

Arguments advanced in Parliament and echoed in the press played an
important role in strengthening support for government policy. Although
criticised by some, the reiterated claim that interventionism in Europe
helped Britain to make colonial gains by diverting French resources took
on the characteristics of a given, as well as an important justification of all
aspects of policy; although, in practice, the situation was far more complex.
Both at the time and in retrospect, Pitt very much made this claim his
own, treating it as analysis and armour,[24] and his eager use of Parliament
to propagate his views and to defend governmental policy with vigour
and without apology, helped ensure not only that Parliament's role was
underlined but also that there was not the same air of a grudging and
defensive disclosure of information and views that had characterised much,
although by no means all, of the ministerial discussion of foreign policy
earlier in the century.

Pitt understood the military necessity of supporting allied forces in Germany and sending British troops there, although he took care to have it
appear that he had accepted these moves cautiously or reluctantly, rather
than to have instigated them. In political terms, Pitt covered himself in
1758 by supporting with fresh determination the 'popular' issues before
the Commons: the Habeas Corpus Bill and the Bill introduced by George
Townshend to amend the Militia Act. This conduct in the spring of 1758
angered George II and depressed Newcastle, but it prevented any strong
parliamentary opposition to the decision to commit troops to Germany.
On 19 April 1758, the Commons voted a subsidy to Frederick the Great
and money to support 50,000 men in Duke Ferdinand of Brunswick's army
without a division. George II's and Pitt's ministerial colleagues relied on Pitt
for parliamentary backing. Robert, 4th Earl of Holdernesse, the Secretary
of State for the Northern Department, wrote that the King relied 'on the
signal zeal of his Parliament' to finance the Prussian subsidy, while Henry
Fox, now the Paymaster General and a critic of his former rival, observed

---

[23] Walpole, *Memoirs of George II*, III, 3.
[24] R. Pares, 'American versus Continental Warfare, 1739–63', *English Historical Review*, 51 (1936),
pp. 429–65; M. Peters, *Pitt and Popularity: The Patriot Minister and London Opinion during the
Seven Years War* (Oxford, 1980); R. Middleton, *The Bells of Victory: The Pitt-Newcastle Ministry and
the Conduct of the Seven Years' War, 1757–1762* (Cambridge, 1985); B. Harris, *Politics and the Nation.
Britain in the Mid-Eighteenth Century* (Oxford, 2002), pp. 58–61.

'all this, I hear, Mr. Pitt can get the Common Council [of London] etc. etc. (he thinks) to come into'.[25]

Military success in 1758 greatly helped the government, robbing parliamentary opponents of justification through failure. A return on the massive sums voted by Parliament for the British armed forces and for subsidies to Prussia and Hesse-Cassel was readily demonstrated, and this set up a synergy that made a parliamentary foreign policy seem successful and normative. Indeed, the situation in the middle period of the Seven Years' War was to be looked back to not simply as a pattern for British policy but also of how policy should be expounded and impacted within the political system.

In practice, there were political rifts and tensions, and Parliament recorded them. In the debate on the Address in November 1758, William Beckford, an MP for London who acted as the voice of mercantile opinion in Parliament, warned against subordinating North American to German operations.[26] Pitt was criticized for 'Hanoverizing' in early 1759.[27] To move from the solid votes of parliamentary support to the debates and the correspondence of parliamentarians is to be reminded that bland comments about synergy and the schematic interpretation of Parliament as the pivot of public support for policy, more specifically the spread of empire, are not a total account. For example, 1759 is commonly recalled as a year of triumph abroad and political support at home. In essentials, both are true, but it is necessary to note the uncertain nature of these achievements. A different view was presented in March 1759. Embittered by his exclusion from favour, Charles Townshend, MP for Saltash, could see only a crisis, for which he held Pitt responsible. Characteristically, faction at home was linked to difficulties abroad, although, on this occasion, the critique was directed against a minister and not the opposition. To Townshend, Pitt's opposition, in support of Beckford, to the duty on sugar included in the plans of Henry Legge, MP for Orford and the Chancellor of the Exchequer, for the year's supply, appeared factious, as well as a serious threat to a precarious financial position. Townshend also suggested that Pitt wanted to leave the government in order to return when it collapsed,

The causes of the want of bullion are these. 3 millions in specie exported to pay the army on the Rhine and Prussian subsidy and one million to North America;

[25] Holdernesse to Mitchell, 23 Sept. 1757, PRO. SP. 90/70; Fox to Bedford, 14 Nov. 1757, Bedford Estate Office, London, papers of the 4th Duke of Bedford, vol. 35.
[26] Debate on the Address, 23 Nov. 1758, report by James West MP, BL. Add. 32885 fol. 524.
[27] Walpole, *Memoirs of George II*, III, 55.

at a time when the return of bullion from Portugal has been prevented and no Spanish captures as in the last war: you then broke when your expenses were less, your importation of bullion greater, and therefore how can you expect to survive now, when your charges are so much higher, your resources so much less, and your debt so much increased? Mr. Pitt feels this and has lost all temper. In the House he has lost all parties by his opposition to Mr. Legge, his servile adulation of Beckford, his flattery to Sir Robert Walpole's ashes, his declaration for an excise, and his contempt of the country gentlemen. Yesterday the House groaned as he spoke: your friend Vyner attacked him roughly upon his Martinique expedition and Continental measures: and all, of that party [Tories], stand amazed and disgusted. Northey has retired from the House, Sir John Philipps openly opposes Mr. Pitt. Mr. Legge professes to resign, and all hastens to confusion. I have not seen the Duke of Newcastle: but Pitt gives him no quarter, with the hopes, I believe, of being turned out, that he may run away from present embarrassment . . . and come in again when the storm is passed.[28]

Nevertheless, helped by success in the war, which, in 1759, included the capture of Quebec and the defeat of the French fleet, parliamentary proceedings went very well.[29]

In combination with the political changes that were to follow the accession of George III in 1760, the political framing of, and response to, the foreign policy of the late 1750s transformed the 'party' or partisan approach to policy. This was a complex process, and it would be misleading to underrate the persistence of separate Tory attitudes or of the role of contingency. Had George III sought to maintain the Hanoverian commitments of his grandfather, George II, then it is likely that earlier controversies and alignments would have been recovered. In addition, the short-term nature of Pitt's success in lessening contention should not be neglected.

Yet, at the same time, politics did not stand still. There was a political response to the sweeping character of the naval success and territorial gains of the late 1750s. They affected parliamentarians and others who had not been caught up in earlier enthusiasm for 'blue water' rhetoric and policies. Whereas such attitudes earlier had essentially been associated with opposition politicians keen to criticise government for failing to defend national interests, now they spanned the political world. To that extent, a fundamental assumption about foreign policy in the shape of support for the value of imperial expansion was depoliticised. More specifically, thanks to

---

[28] Charles to George Townshend, 13 Mar. 1759, Bod. MS Eng. hist. d 211 fols. 5–6.
[29] James Wright to Mitchell, 30 Jan. 1759, Richard Potenger to Mitchell, 13 Feb., 22 Dec. 1759, BL. Add. 6823 fols. 55, 60, 73.

Pitt's positive presentation of Continental interventionism, it became far less necessary to defend Hanoverian interests in Parliament, and this also helped to transform the partisan nature of foreign policy debates, and, indeed, to make the debate over this policy less important. Thus, there were important changes underway before the death of George II on 25 October 1760.

5

George III, Parliament and foreign policy, 1760–1800

Parliament played relatively little role in the initial calculations of George III (r. 1760–1820). He wanted peace and ministerial change, and assumed that a new government would be able to manage Parliament. Given the subsequent political instability of the 1760s, this assumption might appear ridiculous, but, in fact, the crucial business of the early years of the decade, most obviously support for peace, was carried through Parliament with few problems. The displacement of Hanover to the margins of British political contention was another change ushered in by the new king. This was not due to any triumph by extra-parliamentary forces, nor, solely, to the impact of, by now widely held, Patriot attitudes. Instead, the change reflected a marked shift in the dynastic dynamic, away from the Anglo-Hanoverian monarchy of Georges I and II, and towards a more clearly British conception on the part of the new king. This helped George III and his ministers to overcome the leading parliamentary challenge to his foreign policy in his first two decades as king, that over ending the Seven Years' War. Despite the earlier hopes of George II, the controversial return of conquests from France and Spain in the peace of 1763 were not accompanied by gains for the Electorate of Hanover. This helped lessen opposition to the peace.

Government unity had already been lost in 1761–2 with the crises that led to the resignations of first William Pitt the Elder and then Thomas, Duke of Newcastle. However, their hesitation in attacking the new ministry led by George's favourite, John, 3rd Earl of Bute, the general desire for peace, the popularity of the new king, and the government's success in both winning the war and negotiating peace, blunted the force of parliamentary criticism. Nevertheless, disagreements over peace terms broadened out into a general discussion of foreign policy. Whereas George III was closely identified with a rejection of the interventionism of his grandfather, George II, Pitt found it impossible to disassociate himself from the policies that had brought wartime success. He pressed for the maintenance of good relations with Prussia and, until the end of the war, of Britain's military commitment to

Germany. The uncertainty that affected government policy until after the departure of Pitt and Newcastle can be glimpsed in the marginal comment on a draft of the royal speech opening Parliament in 1761: 'Q. Whether to say anything and what, of the King of Prussia'.[1] On 12 May 1762, Pitt, who had resigned the previous October, when he had been unable to persuade the Cabinet to back his argument that Britain should declare war on Spain at once, accompanied his affirmation of the value of interventionism in the Commons and of fighting on against the Bourbons, with a restatement of the view of Parliament as a grand council:

When I give my advice to the House I consider myself as giving my advice to the crown ... The Continental Plan is the only plan otherwise all Europe will be interdicted by these haughty oppressions of the House of Bourbon from receiving you whom they affect to treat as an overgrown pirate from their ports. I am convinced this country can raise 12, 13, 14 or even 16 million the next year: I know it without seeking information from bundles of papers and accounts ... The only question is whether grievous and permanent as that tax must be, it is not to be preferred to the perpetual dishonour of the nation, the aggrandisement of the enemy, the desertion of your allies, all which tend to an inglorious and precarious peace ... Think of your greatness in every part of the world.[2]

Pitt's approach was typical of that of many opposition speakers during the century: criticising a ministry trying to follow a prudential foreign policy, and to maintain or, in this case, obtain peace, on the grounds that it was betraying national interests, while failing to consider the implications of this criticism, especially in financial terms.

Partly in response to a request from the French envoy, the opening of the winter session of 1762–3 was prorogued until 25 November, in order to provide time for the arrival of the Spanish response to the peace terms so that the government would better know what to tell Parliament.[3] The Peace of Paris, negotiated in 1762 and signed in 1763, did encounter more parliamentary attacks than that of Aix-la-Chapelle (1748) had done. This was a measure of the stronger sense that Britain had had a bad deal. The return of Martinique and Guadeloupe to France and her retention of a share in the Newfoundland fishery, which was seen as crucial training for sailors, were heavily criticised. However, the political situation was essentially the same as that after the Treaty of Aix-la-Chapelle of 1748. The ministry carried

---

[1] Draft, BL. Add. 57833 fol. 41.

[2] James West MP, report on parliamentary proceedings, 12 May 1762, BL. Add. 32938 fols. 186–8. See also, Walpole, *Memoirs of the Reign of King George III*, ed. D. Jarrett (4 vols., New Haven, 2000) I, 105–7.

[3] Lord John Russell (ed.), *Correspondence of John, 4th Duke of Bedford* (3 vols., 1842–6), III, 142–3.

the Address of Thanks in the Commons by 319 to 65. It was helped by the extent to which the peace terms were favourable, far better than those in 1748, and that there was also a measure of war-weariness. As so often in Hanoverian Britain, it was the parliamentary strength of the government, rather than the vigour of its critics, that was most strikingly apparent to observers, both domestic and foreign.

Once peace came, domestic issues came to the fore in British politics, and the situation remained thus, with the exception of the Falkland Islands crisis of 1770–1, until the outbreak of the War of American Independence, in 1775, was followed, three years later, by French entry into the conflict. The role of domestic issues did not imply that there was not controversy over foreign policy, both over relations with France and Spain, and over the diplomatic strategy Britain should follow on the Continent. However, it was less significant than other political issues, and there was particularly little discussion of foreign affairs in 1764–7. This reflected George III's conscious abandonment of the clear Hanoverian preferences of his two predecessors, a measure that, to a certain degree, helped to 'depoliticise' foreign policy, and the greater role of domestic issues. In addition, the specific competence of Parliament in the field became less relevant, as far fewer treaties were concluded during the period than in the previous half-century.[4]

What George's favourite, and, in 1762–3, first minister, John, 3rd Earl of Bute, called 'the violence of party',[5] owed much to the king's conscious abandonment of party government, as he turned against his two predecessors' policies of trusting all power to Whigs. In addition, the ending of 'Old Corps' Whig cohesion was an important aspect of the instability of the 1760s. It is difficult to imagine Walpole and Pelham losing power as their successors were to do. The dearth of effective governmental leadership in the Commons in the 1760s was also important. Before the time of Lord Liverpool (1812–27), there was not to be a single Lords-led Hanoverian ministry that endured any time. On the other hand, the sole ministry led by someone sitting in the Commons not to have a substantial period in office was that of George Grenville (1763–5). Circumstances were different in the various cases, but it seems clear that dividing the key functions of the Treasury and the leadership of the Commons, as with the Rockingham ministry in 1765–6, the Chatham (Pitt) ministry in 1766–7, and that of

---

[4] H. M. Scott, *British Foreign Policy in the Age of the American Revolution* (Oxford, 1990), p. 20. This is the major work on foreign policy in the period 1763–83.

[5] Bute to Shelburne, 4 Sept. 1763, BL. Bowood 37.

Augustus, 3rd Duke of Grafton in 1767–70, made for weak and unstable government.

Instability in the 1760s was not only a matter of the problems of parliamentary management. It was also the case that both government policies and the atomisation of the political class following George III's break with the 'Old Corps' Whigs were crucial. This atomisation encompassed the entire political system. Parliamentary rifts expressed rather than created it. Diplomats and other foreign observers commented on signs of instability, but, as in the Walpole years, the government sought to counter this impression by stressing its parliamentary position. In 1765, Andrew Mitchell, envoy in Berlin and an MP, was sent

the joint address of the Lords and Commons upon the subject of the libels, which have, for so many months, swarmed in this capital, in defiance of all order and government, and to the great reproach of this country, especially in the eyes of foreigners.

The several addresses, orders, and resolutions of this session, from the beginning carried in both Houses, by so large and respectable a majority, on every point, where the dignity of the Crown has been concerned, as they reflect the highest honour upon H.M.'s measures, so do they incontestably prove the weight and stability of that administration, to which the king has been pleased to trust the execution of his business.[6]

Political division, and the related problems of parliamentary management, owed little to differences over foreign policy. This absence of serious and protracted disputes over foreign policy was further ensured by the generally cautious attitude of the ministries of the 1760s to Continental commitments, and by the unwillingness of Continental governments to respond to British approaches and terms for alliances. In particular, British ministries were reluctant to consider peacetime subsidies as the price of alliances. As a result, Parliament was not faced by demands for support for subsidy treaties, and the government was not split by this issue and by the related consequences of a diplomacy of commitments, as had been the case in 1748–54, the previous period of peacetime diplomacy. The diplomatic agenda had then been dominated by a diplomacy of containment centring on the Imperial Election Scheme, leading to parliamentary contention over subsidies.

Instead, the situation from 1763 on was more comparable to that of the 1730s. Walpolean caution about interventionism was, on the whole, emulated, but, as in 1738–9, trans-oceanic commercial and colonial relations

---

[6] Richard Potenger to Mitchell, 2 Dec. 1763, BL. Add. 6823 fol. 213.

with the Bourbons were a source of particular domestic sensitivity. Naval success and imperial conquest in the Seven Years' War had helped to redefine Britain. The choice in policy was no longer largely seen in terms of Continental interventionism versus a Tory agrarian withdrawal from abroad, albeit one tempered by support for 'blue water' raiding and cheap colonialism. Instead, 'blue water' had been transformed into Britain's destiny. More of the world had been brought within Britain's real and imaginative grasp, and this process continued in the 1760s and early 1770s, with Pacific exploration and thanks to conflict with native peoples and states in North America and India.

In Parliament and public alike, the successes of the middle and closing years of the Seven Years' War had led to the absence of any serious widespread critique of the commitments assumed to arise from Britain's apparent maritime destiny. The glow of success had shadowed the problems and failures of the early stages of the conflict, and there was little public sense that the war had been a risk. This attitude led to a post-war confidence, indeed complacency, that was to have serious consequences for Britain's international position.

While in opposition in the 1760s, Pitt the Elder (Earl of Chatham from 1766) made an effort to sustain and exploit widespread political sensitivity about Bourbon strength and intentions, which were seen as the major threat to Britain's imperial position. Pressing for repeal of the Stamp Act in January 1766, he told the Commons that he feared the potential might of a united House of Bourbon. However, successive ministries in the 1760s saw off criticism of their foreign policy with few problems. In November 1768, on a division of 230–84, the government defeated an opposition motion for diplomatic correspondence with France about the French purchase of Corsica from the republic of Genoa. Thus, the attempt to castigate the ministry of Augustus, 3rd Duke of Grafton for failing to defend national interests failed. Similarly, in the debates on the Address on 9 January 1770, opposition claims that the ministry was failing to defend national interests and was leaving Britain vulnerable failed to shake its majority in either House. In the Commons, Lord North was able to refer to earlier parliamentary support over the Corsica issue. In the Lords' debate of 22 January 1770 on the state of the nation, the opposition use of the issue was again unsuccessful.

Chatham did not succeed in finding a cause with political resonance until a Bourbon power staged a direct attack on British interests. The Spanish expulsion of an English settlement from the Falkland Islands in 1770 provoked eight parliamentary speeches from Chatham between November 1770 and

February 1771. He pressed for a strong navy, a popular administration and the vigorous pursuit of national interests. In his speech of 22 November 1770, in a debate arising from an opposition demand for papers, Chatham cited both the Convention of the Pardo and his advice for war with Spain in 1761. However, there was to be no repetition of the international impasse that had given domestic critics of Walpole their opportunity in 1739. Spain was eventually denied the support from France it had expected and, influenced by a major British naval armament, backed down. As a result, despite opposition claims, the government was able to make it appear that they had got peace with honour. Prior to the Spanish climbdown, the ministry enjoyed support not only because of domestic political considerations, but also, in some cases, because parliamentarians were affected by the issues. Hans Stanley, a supporter of the government in the Commons, observed in November 1770 that he was 'quite out of all patience with the war, which I think cruel and ridiculous'.[7]

Having seen war averted, the opposition still pursued the issue by pressing for an enquiry into the government's conduct of the crisis. Lord North laid before Parliament on 25 January 1771 some papers about the affair and they were soon after published by John Almon, although, in both Houses, opposition speakers called for more papers, not only on negotiations with Spain but also on what the government had earlier known about Spanish designs, and on negotiations with France.

Parliamentary disclosure of papers and their publication were linked aspects of the governmental attempt to propagate favourable impressions, although this was carefully controlled, and the ministry successfully resisted the attempts in both Houses to see more papers. One reason given was that much of the negotiation had been with the French envoy in London and handled verbally. In the early hours of 14 February 1771, at 'the close of the great day of this sessions', the government carried a motion approving its policy and thanking it for communicating the Spanish declaration on a 275–151 division. The Lords division was 107–38.[8]

After the Falklands crisis, attention reverted to domestic issues, though foreign envoys stressed the continued sensitivity of Anglo-Bourbon relations and argued that the British ministry sought to settle disputes so that they did not cause parliamentary difficulties.[9] The debate in the Commons

[7] Hans Stanley to Countess Spencer, 18 Nov. 1770, BL. Add. 75688.

[8] Henry Ellison junior to Henry Ellison senior, 14 Feb. 1771, Gateshead Public Library, Ellison Mss. A16 no. 29. The division figures are those given in Cobbett.

[9] Hanneken, Danish envoy in London, to Osten, Danish foreign minister, 10 Jan. 1772, Copenhagen, Danske Rigsarkiv, England B, Dispatches 1772. I would like to thank Geoffrey Rice for permitting me to cite his transcripts.

on 29 January 1772 on the number of seamen in the navy saw suspicion of the Bourbons and criticism of government policy, but the motion was carried without a division. Parliamentary interest in developments elsewhere in Europe was limited. Although important to Continental power politics, the First Partition of Poland (1772) had little impact on Parliament, while, in the Commons' debate in the Address on 26 November 1772, the mover of the motion applauded, with reference to the Russo-Turkish war of 1768–74, the absence of interventionism in British foreign policy.[10]

British diplomats still noted foreign interest in Parliament. In 1774, David, Viscount Stormont, Ambassador in Paris, reported that Armand, Duke of Aiguillon, the French foreign minister, had spoken

of what Lord North had said in Parliament, with regard to Falkland's Island, with expressions of great pleasure and satisfaction, and added that he had that morning read the account to Monsieur d'Aranda [Spanish envoy], who was much pleased and, took a particular note of it.[11]

Foreign policy became more important again as a domestic political issue as a side-effect of the disputes with the American colonists, for critics of the firm line of the North ministry argued that any conflict would be exploited by the Bourbons. On 20 January 1775, Chatham pressed for the withdrawal of the troops sent to intimidate Boston and warned the Lords about the danger that France would exploit the situation.[12] American independence was seen, both by supporters and critics of government policy, as a threat to the integrity of the British Empire. The political, strategic and economic interdependency of its constituent parts was taken for granted, and it was widely felt that economic and political strength were related, that the monopoly of American trade supported British power, most crucially in any conflict with the Bourbons, and that, without political links, it would be impossible to maintain economic relationships.

Once the War of American Independence had broken out in April 1775, these arguments were adapted into the opposition thesis that Britain should concentrate on reconciliation with the colonists in order to prepare

---

[10] D. B. Horn, *British Public Opinion and the First Partition of Poland* (Edinburgh, 1945); Cobbett, XVIII, p. 521.

[11] Stormont to Earl of Rochford, Secretary of State, 2 Feb. 1774, PRO. SP. 78/291 fol. 77.

[12] R. R. Rea, 'Anglo-American Parliamentary Reporting: A Case Study in Historical Bibliography', *Bibliographical Society of America, Papers* 49 (1955), pp. 224–8; L. D. Campbell (ed.), *The Miscellaneous Works of Hugh Boyd* (1800) I, 247–9; B. Knollenberg (ed.), *Jonathan Williams and William Pitt: A Letter of January 21, 1775* (Bloomington, 1949); see, more generally, R. C. Simmons and P. D. G. Thomas (eds.), *Proceedings and Debates of the British Parliaments Respecting North America, 1754–1783* (New York, 1986), V.

for war with the Bourbons. This was Chatham's argument in the Lords in November and December 1777, and in his last parliamentary appearance on 7 April 1778. As in other periods of conflict, parliamentary considera- tion of foreign policy was focused on the war and related issues. This was accentuated by the personal commitments of parliamentarians. In 1780, twenty-three generals sat in the Commons. The focus on the war was fur- ther encouraged by setbacks. As Burgoyne noted, when called to discuss his conduct, 'where there is miscarriage there must be blame'.[13]

Debate over failure also encouraged counterfactual speculation by speak- ers.[14] Much of this speculation was military in character, but the probable actions of foreign powers also played a role. The possible entry of France and Spain, the second and third most powerful naval powers in the world, was of great concern prior to their actual entry, in 1778 and 1779 respec- tively. In February 1778, Charles, 3rd Duke of Richmond, an opposition peer, declared 'he did not believe we should soon be precipitated into a war with France' as 'he relied on the French king and the French cabinet, who he well knew were adverse to war'.[15] Less than a month later, however, news of a treaty between France and America led to a major parliamen- tary debate. This, and the problems of obtaining victory in America, lent impetus to calls for flexibility in goals. Charles, 1st Earl Camden, another opposition peer, pointed out, in February 1778, that 'ministers who had all along contended for unconditional submission' were forced to consider 'plans of conciliation'.[16] Thus speakers had to consider prudential as well as ideal goals, and these offered contrasting frames of reference which need to be recovered with care.

The political crisis of the early 1780s in the British Isles, which included unrest in Ireland, the Gordon Riots in London in 1780, pressure for con- stitutional and political reform, not least by the Yorkshire Association, and a sustained period of ministerial instability in 1782–4, ensured that for- eign policy was not then at the forefront of parliamentary discussion. In 1782, defeat in America was responsible for the fall of the government. North announced his resignation on 20 March 1782, after the surrender of Cornwallis's army at Yorktown in October 1781 led to a collapse of confi- dence in the war in America as many independent MPs shifted their sup- port. On 27 February 1782, the government had lost a Commons' motion relating to the further prosecution of the war in America. The North min- istry was replaced by one under Charles, 2nd Marquess of Rockingham,

[13] P. Mackesy, *The War for America 1775–1783* (1964), p. 9; Cobbett, XIX, 1187.
[14] Cobbett, XIX, 1163.   [15] Cobbett, XIX, 743.   [16] Cobbett, XIX, 740.

and, after he died in July 1782, by another under William, 2nd Earl of Shelburne.

Failure in war drove foreign policy. However, in Parliament, far from there being any sustained coherent debate about diplomatic strategy in the peace negotiations and for the post-war world, attention was episodic, focusing on specific issues in the peace negotiations of 1782–3. Nevertheless, Parliament's role was important. The sensitivity of peace terms and his weakness there led Shelburne in 1782 to try to settle terms before Parliament resumed at the close of the year:[17] he emphasised the difference between seeking parliamentary approval for an agreement and leaving issues unresolved and public at the start of a session; although he noted that this was also true of the Council.[18] The possibility that the Cabinet would agree to the Spanish demand to cede Gibraltar led to criticism in Parliament that December, although, in fact, the Spanish demand was rejected.

In February 1783, Shelburne was defeated in Commons' debates over the peace preliminaries. They were genuinely unpopular, especially the lack of any guarantees for the Loyalists and for British debts. On 17 February, Charles James Fox and North, the opposition leaders, backed an amendment to the Address on the peace preliminaries, moved by Lord John Cavendish, MP for York, that the Commons would 'proceed to consider' the terms, instead of approving them as the ministry wanted. The opposition won the division by 224 to 208 votes. In the Lords, the opposition amendment was a clearer attempt to present the government as failing to defend national interests. The peace terms were castigated as 'inadequate to our just expectations, and derogatory to the honour and dignity of Great Britain', but the ministry maintained its control of the Lords. Four days later, however, the opposition was again victorious in the Commons. Lord John Cavendish proposed a motion describing the cessions made to Britain's enemies as 'greater than they were entitled to, either from the actual situation of their respective possessions, or from their comparative strength'. Cavendish referred to the treaty as 'degrading and disgusting', claimed that France and Spain were exhausted, and emphasised the strength of the British navy. Having lost the division, 207 to 190, Shelburne resigned on 24 February.[19]

[17] A. Stockley, *Britain and France at the Birth of America. The European Powers and the Peace Negotiations of 1782–1783* (Exeter, 2001), pp. 80–3.
[18] Shelburne to Grantham, 25 Dec. 1782, Bedford CRO. L30/14/306/1.
[19] *Parliamentary Register*, IX, 297–302; Stockley, *Britain and France*, pp. 164–5.

In fact, the defeats were largely blows against the 'universally disliked' Shelburne,[20] who had never sat in the Commons, and not against the peace. A major reason for Shelburne's fall was that the other two competing groups of politicians, the largest parties in the Commons by far, led by Fox and North, were aiming to secure office, and were prepared to do so regardless of any claim by George to choose his ministers. The succeeding Fox-North ministry (1783) in fact accepted the peace preliminaries. Indeed, the power to ratify a treaty was an aspect of the royal prerogative, and the disputed question whether parliamentary approval was required for any agreement to cede territory was avoided by resolving that American independence had been acknowledged by an Act passed the previous session enabling George to settle with the Americans notwithstanding any existing laws. More vividly, Catherine II of Russia declared that rather than accept such a loss, she would have shot herself.[21]

The frequent governmental changes in 1782–3, which were associated with parliamentary instability, made Britain appear a less attractive alliance partner. Alleyne Fitzherbert, envoy in St Petersburg, observed in February 1784,

> It would indeed be unreasonable to expect that when these total changes take place in our government, foreign courts should veer about with the same celerity that we do, and be ready to enter into a cordial and confidential communication with a set of ministers with whose principles and notions they have little acquaintance, and as little reason to rely upon their political stability.[22]

Britain was scarcely alone in having changed ministers, policy and alliance partners in recent decades. The death in 1780 of Maria Theresa had removed her restraining hand on Joseph II and led to a new volatility in Austrian policy. The nature, however, of the British political system, especially the public character of criticism of policy resulting from the parliamentary system, made it easier to dwell on Britain's apparent tendency to change men and measures. British diplomats condemned what they saw as factiousness in Parliament.[23] Such views were shared by members of the British élite. In the summer of 1783, John, 2nd Earl of Buckinghamshire, a former MP

---

[20] BL. Add. 35528 fol. 27.

[21] Cobbett, XXIII, 519–20; Gibbs, 'Laying Treaties Before Parliament in the Eighteenth Century', in R. M. Hatton and M. S. Anderson (eds.), *Studies in Diplomatic History: Essays in Memory of David Bayne Horn* (1970), p. 124. P. Mansel, *Prince of Europe. The Life of Charles-Joseph de Ligne 1735–1814* (2003), p. 105.

[22] Fitzherbert to Sir Robert Murray Keith, envoy in Vienna, 10 Feb. 1784, BL. Add. vol. 35531 fol. 79; John Trevor, envoy in Turin, to Keith, 24 Feb. 1783, BL. Add. 35528 fol. 36.

[23] Joseph Ewart to Keith, 20 Feb. 1783, BL. Add. 35528 fol. 27.

for Norwich and an ex-diplomat, took time off from admiring the scantily clad bathing beauties at Weymouth to reflect on

this unhappy disgraced country surrounded by every species of embarrassment, and without even a distant prospect of establishing an Administration so firm and so respectable as to restore to England any proportion of her defeated dignity. The state is now circumstanced as a human body in the last stage of decline.

Like George III who, in his despair at having to turn to ministers he distrusted, had been driven to consider abdication, the political crisis led Buckinghamshire to question his assumptions, 'Whig as I am and sufficiently vain of my descent from Maynard and Hampden, it sometimes occurs to me that something might be obtained by strengthening the hands of the Crown.'[24]

The British political system, not least parliamentary government, appeared to have failed. Defeat abroad, the crisis of the imperial system, was matched by instability at home. The eventual resolution of the crisis, in the shape of a ministry enjoying active royal support, victory in the general elections of 1784, 1790 and 1796, and, in all bar exceptional circumstances, the support of Parliament, was scarcely prefigured in the chaos and enmity of 1782–3. Indeed, in February and March 1783, William Pitt the Younger had rejected royal invitations to try to form a government.[25]

A sense that Britain was weak and weakening was not new. The instability of 1763–70 had encouraged foreign commentators to discern weakness.[26] As with the Excise Crisis of 1733, the significance of public disturbances was exaggerated, but this perception of failure was itself important. The ministerial changes of 1782–3 were the culmination of nearly two decades of continual harping on British debility, especially the apparent malaise of her political system. The emphasis placed by foreign commentators varied, in accordance with their own perception of Britain and the chronology of crisis there. Nevertheless, the Wilkesite troubles of the 1760s were succeeded by the imperial crisis of the 1770s and then, in 1780–4, first by serious problems in Ireland and England and, secondly, in 1782, by the collapse of the North ministry and a protracted political crisis. Rulers such as Catherine II of Russia, Frederick II of Prussia and Joseph II of Austria argued in the early 1780s that Britain was weak, that this was due to inherent characteristics of her political system, which would probably lead to the dissolution of her

---

[24] Buckinghamshire to Sir Charles Hotham, 12 July 1783, Hull, UL. DDHo/4/22.
[25] Pitt to George III, 25 Mar. 1783, PRO. 30/8/101 fol. 1.
[26] M. Roberts, *Splendid Isolation 1763–1780* (Reading, 1970), pp. 4–7.

empire, and that, in the meantime, this weakness made her an undesirable ally.

In the winter of 1783–4, the focus of ministerial weakness was very much the Commons. Despite having been appointed, by George III in December 1783, to head a new ministry as First Lord of the Treasury, Pitt lacked a majority. Having lost two Commons' divisions on 12 January 1784, he thought of resigning. Distressed to find the Commons 'much more willing to enter into any intemperate resolutions of desperate men than I could have imagined,' George characteristically reiterated his hostility to 'this faction', his readiness to struggle against them until the end of his life, and his willingness to abdicate if they gained office. On 23 January 1784, Pitt's Bill for the government of British India, a crucial piece of legislation, was also defeated.[27]

Parliament was more, however, than the focus of party animosities. An attempt by independent MPs to create a broad-based government of national unity, a frequently expressed aspiration during the century that reveals the danger of simplifying the account of eighteenth-century politics by focusing only on parties, gave Pitt a breathing space in early February 1784. His position was further improved by a swelling tide of favourable public opinion, and this played a role in the government's victory in the general election that spring.

Thus the domestic context of foreign policy changed abruptly in 1784, itself a testimony to the potential importance of Parliament in the political system. Under the Septennial Act, the next election did not have to be held until 1791. And yet the political situation was more complex. Ministries that won general elections could fall soon after: Newcastle's overwhelming success in the election of 1754 and North's success in 1780 did not prevent their fall from office in 1756 and 1782 respectively. The role of party in elections was limited, many seats were not contested on national political grounds, or at all, and independent parliamentarians could prove volatile, as in their desertion of North in 1782. Ministries that had won an election were likely to be longer-lasting than those that had not had an opportunity to do so, but they could also be vulnerable to failure in war, as with Newcastle and North. Such 'external' factors were most important, however, in conjunction with internal division, as with the poor relations between Newcastle

---

[27] George III to Pitt, 23 Dec. 1783, 13 Jan. 1784 (quote), PRO. 30/8/103 fols. 14, 30; Lord George Germain to John, 3rd Duke of Dorset, 27 Jan. 1784, KAO. U269 C192; P. Kelly, 'The Pitt-Temple Administration: 19–22 December 1783', *Historical Journal*, 17 (1974), pp. 157–61; and 'British Politics, 1783–4: the Emergence and Triumph of the Younger Pitt's Administration', *Bulletin of the Institute of Historical Research*, 54 (1981), pp. 62–78.

and Henry Fox in 1756. An even more significant 'internal' factor was provided by an absence or loss of royal favour. This could be fatal to ministries, as Godolphin had discovered in 1710, Newcastle in 1762, Grenville in 1765, Rockingham in 1766, and Fox-North in 1783, and as Pitt was to discover in 1801.

The avoidance of adverse external factors and the need to retain royal support were to play a part in foreign policy in the early years of the Pitt ministry. The government did not want war for political, financial, economic and military reasons, all of which took precedence over diplomatic considerations that might suggest that alliance commitments, and thus accepting the risk of war, were an essential aspect of the search for Continental allies. In addition, Pitt and his colleagues were well aware that, although George III was hardly likely to turn to the opposition, his support had been crucial to the establishment of the ministry, and that he had views that had to be considered.

The government also faced major defeats in the Commons that, although only tangentially related to foreign policy, nevertheless affected the Continental perception of the British situation, and the apparent desirability of Britain as an ally. In March 1785, the government was defeated over the Westminster scrutiny, ensuring that Charles James Fox was returned for such a prominent seat. That August, the ministry withdrew its proposals for a new commercial and financial relationship between Britain and Ireland in the face of serious opposition from the Irish House of Commons. The proposals had earlier been substantially modified in the face of British mercantile and parliamentary hostility. On 27 February 1786, the Commons rejected a plan, sponsored by Charles, 3rd Duke of Richmond, the Master General of the Ordnance, and supported by Pitt, for fortifying the country's leading dockyards, Plymouth and Portsmouth.[28]

These defeats were noted abroad, and commented on by foreign envoys,[29] although it is unclear that they were sufficiently spectacular to do more than underline the sense that Britain was unstable and thus to cast doubts on reports that, under the new government, she was becoming more united and stronger. In January 1784, Samuel Greig, a Scottish admiral in

---

[28] Thomas Orde MP, Secretary to the Lord Lieutenant of Ireland, to 1st Marquess of Lansdowne, formerly Shelburne, 24 Jan., Francis Baring MP to Landsdowne, 20 May 1786, BL. Bowood vols. 27, 9; P. Kelly, 'British Parliamentary Politics, 1784–1786', *Historical Journal*, 17 (1974), pp. 157–61; D. R. Schweitzer, 'The Failure of William Pitt's Irish Trade Propositions 1785', *Parliamentary History*, 3 (1984), pp. 129–45; I. R. Christie, 'The Anatomy of the Opposition in the Parliament of 1784', *Parliamentary History*, 9 (1990), pp. 50–77.

[29] François de Barthélemy, French Minister Plenipotentiary in London, to Charles, Count of Vergennes, French foreign minister, 11 July 1786, AE. CP. 557 fol. 30.

Russian service, warned Sir James Harris, an opposition MP until recently envoy in St Petersburg,

Its now high time that party rage should subside, and people begin to think soberly of the situation of the country; and ministers (whoever they are) be allowed some breathing time, for to apply to public business. For really those intestine broils and dissensions and continual changes of ministers tend greatly to lessen the weight and influence of the nation abroad . . . I know that we abroad look upon those things in a much more serious light, than those at home.[30]

In May 1784, the Austrian Chancellor, Count Kaunitz, wrote to the envoy in London, Count Kageneck, suggesting that chronic instability was preventing the new British ministry from following the Foxite policy of Continental alliances. That August, Joseph II told Emmanuel-Louis Marie, Marquis of Noailles, the French ambassador in Vienna, that Britain was affected by 'toutes sortes de divisions'. Noailles, a former ambassador in London, replied that this would discourage Britain from fighting another war, and that the need to win parliamentary support limited the ministry's ability to mobilise national resources swiftly.[31] Foreign rivals thus used the argument that British power was hamstrung by the role of Parliament.

The parliamentary defeats not only compromised Britain's international position, but also threw light on the nature of parliamentary politics across the century. The defeats occurred not because of the strength of the opposition, but because, on specific issues, the ministry lost the support of the independent MPs. The *Daily Universal Register* declared on 15 January 1785, 'Mr. Pitt has more to dread from the opposition of the independent country gentlemen, than the most formidable avowed opposition in the House of Commons. It is the independent part of the country who feel the taxes.' The defeat of the Fortification Bill was blamed on the independents. Pitt's sister Harriet noted, 'The Opposition brought up all their forces, but they are not very considerable; and the question was lost by the disinclination of the country gentlemen particularly of all the western gentlemen.' Harris was informed that 'the Cornwall gentleman had the weight . . . the friends of ministry are at pains to treat this particular question about these fortifications as one separate from the general system of association on which a

[30] Greig to Harris, 27 Jan. 1784, Winchester, Hampshire CRO. Malmesbury papers, vol. 155.
[31] Kaunitz to Kageneck, 19 May 1784, Vienna, HHStA., Staatskanzlei, Englische Korrespondenz 129; Noailles to Vergennes, 4 Aug. 1784, AE. CP. Aut. 348 fols. 3–4; Dreyer to Count Andreas Bernstorff, Danish first minister, 27 Aug. 1784, PRO. FO. 95/8 fol. 593; Harris to Keith, 8 Feb. 1785, BL. Add. 35533 fol. 213.

party is supposed to act'.[32] James Martin, MP for Tewkesbury, who usually supported the government, opposed the Bill because, he declared, he was too much a Whig to back any increase in the standing army.

Independents in both Houses generally gave their support to the Crown and to the ministers who enjoyed the confidence of the monarch, which was why George III's withdrawal of his backing from the Fox-North government in 1783 had been so crucial in its defeat over the India Bill in the Lords that December. Independents, however, were also willing to withdraw support over particular issues, and this measure of their independence represented an important, but unpredictable, constraint on government policy. It also reflected parliamentary sensitivity to policy choices. In 1786, Thomas, 2nd Lord Walsingham, a former MP, expressed his concern to Pitt about a 'loose House of Commons, whose firm and systematic support is not to be depended upon in the way which it must be had to carry on a war effectually'.[33]

In some crises, such as that posed by the apparent rise of French-inspired domestic radicalism in 1792, the independents would back the Crown, but in 1782 they had withdrawn their support from North and in early 1784 many preferred to pursue the chimera of independent politicians, a broad-based, apparently national government. The latter notion was to recur in 1788–9, when George III's apparent insanity led, in the Regency Crisis, to a serious dispute over the powers of a regent.

In the field of foreign policy, the Pitt ministry, despite its victories in the general elections of 1784 and 1790, could not count on Parliament. William Fraser, Under-Secretary in the Foreign Office, observed in March 1785, 'I hope we are now freer from party than we have been for some time, though the business of Parliament will ever keep it up to a certain degree.[34] This and the governmental failure to secure adequate parliamentary support (as opposed to victory in divisions), were to be demonstrated in the Ochakov Crisis, but the lesson did not have to wait until 1791. It was, for example, by no means impossible that the trade treaty of 1786 with France, the Eden treaty, would go the way of the Irish commercial propositions, and be heavily amended or even defeated. This explains the ministry's care in

---

[32] Harriet Pitt to her mother, the Countess of Chatham, 28 Feb. 1786, Manchester, John Rylands Library, Eng. Mss. 1272 no. 54; Anne Lindsay to Harris, 1 Mar. 1786, Winchester, Malmesbury, vol. 159.

[33] Walsingham to Pitt, 16 July 1786, CUL. Add. 6958; I. R. Christie, 'Party in Politics in the Age of Lord North's Administration', *Parliamentary History* 6 (1987), pp. 47–8, 62, and 'The Changing Nature of Parliamentary Politics 1742-1789' in J. Black (ed.), *British Politics and Society from Walpole to Pitt 1742–89* (1990), p. 122.

[34] Fraser to Keith, 22 Mar. 1785, BL. Add. 35534 fol. 15.

sounding out manufacturing and mercantile opinion and support before and during the negotiations with the French.

Foreign policy returned initially to the partisan political debate as a consequence of the opposition's attempt to exploit an unexpected development, George's negotiation in 1785, as Elector of Hanover, of a *Fürstenbund* (League of Princes) in the Holy Roman Empire that apparently undermined the hopes of his British ministers for better relations with Austria and Russia.[35] The *Fürstenbund* was directed against Joseph II's real and apparent plans in the Empire. This was not an easy issue for British politicians to exploit and the constitutional role of Parliament in foreign policy left scant opportunity for a discussion of it: there was no treaty requiring parliamentary approval, nor any financial demands arising from the negotiations. This contrasted sharply with the controversies over Hanoverian influence in the first half of the century, for then it had been clear that measures that the ministry sought to present as in Britain's interests, most obviously the subsidy treaty with Hesse-Cassel signed in 1726, were in practice designed to further those of the Electorate. Furthermore, the need then to secure parliamentary consent for the voting of funds with which to pay the annual subsidy ensured that the issue was fully discussed, and offered the opposition regular opportunities to criticise foreign policy and the alleged subservience of the Walpole ministry to Hanoverian interests.

The *Fürstenbund* did not provide such a point of access, but the debates over the Address of Thanks in 1786 allowed the opposition to strike a note that would make more contemporary resonance. Fox made it clear in the Commons that the importance of the issue arose from its impact on Anglo-French relations. Freed from the fear of Austrian attack, allegedly as a consequence of Hanover's alienation of Austria, France, he claimed, would be a more formidable naval opponent for Britain.[36] Parliament was a more receptive audience for Fox's statement that France was 'the natural enemy of Great Britain' than for any discussion of the intricacies of German politics. He gave a clear warning of the likely response to any trade treaty with France,

He well knew the fashionable mode of calling treaties commercial, and treaties political . . . ; but he was not to be blinded by any such new-fangled and ill-founded distinctions; treaties of commerce entered into between two countries always had influenced their politics in a very great degree.[37]

---

[35] Cobbett, XXV, 1014; Reginald Pole Carew MP to Harris, 30 Jan. 1786, Winchester, Malmesbury, vol. 146.
[36] Cobbett, XXV, 1006–7.   [37] Cobbett, XXV, 1020, 1007.

In large part thanks to the validating role of Parliament, trade negotiations were a problematic aspect of foreign policy; those with France most so. France was a formidable economic power, Britain's principal political and commercial rival, she was able in 1786 to negotiate from a position of strength, and it was likely that any agreement would affect sectional interests in Britain and worry those concerned about the future of the national economy. More seriously, such terms, and, indeed, all negotiations with France, would provide a clear focus for the customary opposition criticism of any government's foreign policy, namely that it failed to defend national interests; in short, that the country was not safe in ministerial hands. The parliamentary defeat of the last Anglo-French commercial treaty in 1713 was a serious warning about both the sensitivity of such a treaty and the potential for Parliament to play a blocking role. So also were the difficulties in the Westminster Parliament in 1785 over Irish trade, while the role of trade as an issue was highlighted in the debates over the Address in January 1786, when the opposition mentioned recent Austrian and French regulations that affected British imports.[38] It is not surprising that in June 1786 William Eden, then negotiating the trade treaty with France, and himself a MP, was made more optimistic by the imminent end of the session.[39]

In practice, the willingness of the French ministry under Vergennes to offer good terms in order to secure a treaty that it hoped would broaden into political co-operation helped the Pitt government to win parliamentary backing for the terms. The crucial Commons division, at 2 a.m. on 13 February 1787, was 252 to 118, a 'pretty decent' majority.[40] In the debate, Pitt responded to opposition arguments by declaring that 'to suppose that any nation could be unalterably the enemy of another, was weak and childish' and that France's 'assurances and frankness during the present negotiations, were such [as] in his opinion might be confided in'.[41] Such statements, however hedged with qualifications, revealed both the political danger of the Eden Treaty and the problems posed by having to explain policy in Parliament. Not only did such statements conflict with the prejudices and experience of most of the British political nation, but, in 1787, they also clashed with important aspects of British foreign policy, notably

[38] Cobbett, XXV, 993.   [39] Eden to Pitt, 17 June 1786, PRO. 30/8/110.
[40] W. Morton Pitt MP to Harris, 13 Feb. 1787, Winchester, Malmesbury, vol. 163; George Aust, Senior Clerk at the Foreign Office, to Robert Liston, envoy in Madrid, 15 Feb. 1787, NLS. vol. 5546 fol. 41; M. M. Donaghay, *The Anglo-French Negotiations of 1786–1787* (Ph.D. thesis, University of Virginia, 1970).
[41] Cobbett, XXVI, 392–3. For the very different views of Fox and Charles Grey, Cobbett XXVI, 8–9, 285.

concern with the developing Dutch crisis, in which the interests of Britain and her Dutch protégés clashed with those of France.

Thus, Pitt's statements underlined the risk of having to inform Parliament about policy at a time when the international situation was very volatile. Government ministers were convinced that the Eden Treaty would be 'the Anvil de Bataille,' and 'the leading business of the session,'[42] but, once it had been passed, they found themselves publicly committed to a policy that was increasingly undermined by the deterioration in Anglo-French relations. Fortunately for the government, the Dutch crisis of 1787 rose to a peak, and was then resolved satisfactorily, during the recess. Divisions within the Cabinet did not, therefore, interact with parliamentary politics, while it was possible to consider the difficult question of what should be done if Prussia did not act in support of Britain's Dutch allies and, subsequently, to arrange a settlement that did not humiliate France too painfully, without having to consider immediate parliamentary pressures. When Parliament resumed, opposition speakers were to point out that the confrontation with France hardly accorded with Pitt's earlier statement about relations with that country in the debate over the Eden Treaty, but, in the afterglow of success, such arguments had little political resonance.[43]

It was always open to government to adopt, in truth or appearance, the views of opposition, and thus rob them of their arguments. By allying with Austria in 1731 and declaring war on Spain in 1739, Walpole had thus secured quiet parliamentary sessions in 1732 and 1740. By acting firmly in the Dutch crisis of 1787, the ministry had covered itself from any attack on the grounds of failing to defend national interests. In the heady atmosphere of success after the crisis, it was easy to forget or downplay questions over the ministry's changing public statements about France, and the wisdom of committing Britain in Dutch affairs before being certain of Prussian assistance. When the Pittite Thomas, Viscount Bulkeley told the Lords on 27 November 1787 that they had seen 'how all ranks of men pressed forward to support the exertions which the king of a free country alone can make when he reigns in the hearts and affections of his Parliament and of his subjects', he was, albeit with the hyperbole adopted for the occasion, testifying to the singular public success of the British role in the

---

[42] Lord Sydney, Home Secretary, to Charles, 2nd Earl Cornwallis, Governor General in India, 6 Jan., Henry Dundas MP, Commissioner of the Board of Control for India, to Cornwallis, 29 Jan. 1787, PRO. 30/11/1 11 fols. 10, 67.

[43] William Fawkener, Secretary of the Committee of Trade, to Hugh Elliot, envoy in Copenhagen, 17 Oct., Aust to Liston, 2 Nov. 1787, NLS. vol. 12999 fol. 174, vol. 5549 fol. 33; *London Chronicle*, 19 Jan. 1788.

denouement of the Dutch crisis. It had involved the humiliation of the national enemy, and had been quick, bloodless for Britain, and, as was to be shown, not too expensive for her either. Prussia had taken the major role in defeating France's Dutch protégés. The session went very well for the government, and was in fact the quietest the Foreign Secretary, Francis, Marquess of Carmarthen, could remember:[44] he had sat in the Commons in 1774–5 before being summoned to the Lords.

The bolder ministerial attitude in foreign policy, from early 1787 to early 1791, can be seen as arising in part from its greater control of Parliament, certainly in comparison with the sessions of 1784–6. It is notable that the period of the Regency Crisis, the winter of 1788–9, was the significant exception, both in terms of control of Parliament and of boldness in foreign policy. Lord North observed in January 1788, 'if Government are dissatisfied with the present House of Commons, they must have no great inclination to any Parliament whatsoever'.[45] This was to strengthen the ministry's hands in the active Continental interventionism that characterised foreign policy for most of the following three years. In fact, the 1788 session was to become far more difficult for Pitt, culminating in late June and early July when Sir William Dolben's Bill to lessen crowding on slavers was pushed through the Lords despite the vociferous hostility of some senior ministers. In addition, a discontented 'third party' of former supporters emerged to oppose Pitt in the Commons. Nevertheless, there was still a significant contrast with the parliamentary problems of 1784–6.

The next crisis for British foreign policy to excite parliamentary attention, the Nootka Sound Crisis, occurred in 1790 as a result of a clash between British and Spanish interests on Vancouver Island off the Pacific coast of modern Canada. Soon after the crisis broke, Pitt asked the Commons for supplies,[46] but, as in 1787, he was then fortunate that the confrontation with Spain subsequently proceeded when Parliament was not sitting. The government, however, faced the need to act before domestic criticism of naval inaction became too strong, and, also, the need to have something definite, either war or a settlement, to present to the forthcoming session. The claim that the firm British line was influenced by pressure from public

[44] Sydney to George III, Pitt to George, both 27 Nov. 1787, A. Aspinall (ed.), *The Later Correspondence of George III*, vol. 1 (Cambridge, 1962), p. 352; Philip Yorke MP to Philip, 2nd Earl of Hardwicke, 27 Nov. 1787, BL. Add. 35383 fol. 263; Carmarthen to Dorset, 7 Dec. 1787, KAO. C 168A; Fraser to Liston, 6 Dec. 1787, NLS. 5549 fol. 109.

[45] North to Lord Sheffield, 29 Jan. 1788, BL. Add. 61980 fols. 26–7; cf. Barthélemy to Armand, Count of Montmorin, French Foreign Minister, 19 July 1788, AE. CP. Ang., 566 fol. 137.

[46] *The Parliamentary Register* (45 vols., 1780–96), XXVII, 562–6.

opinion and the imminence of a general election has been queried on the grounds that there is no evidence that Pitt held such fears and that his policy can be accounted for without them.[47] Nevertheless, the foreign perception of British policy was affected by the domestic situation. The French envoy argued that the Spanish proposal for mutual disarmament prior to negotiations was unacceptable, because no British ministry would dare to do it in light of the parliamentary agitation over the issue, which he had reported fully. Luzerne also thought the proximity of elections important.[48]

As the summer slipped away, the prospect of any successful naval operations in 1790 receded, and the British ministry was left with the problem of a rapidly approaching session. Were nothing to have been achieved, then the government would be criticised for the expense and lack of action of the naval armament, the same dilemma that had faced the Walpole ministry in 1729. This was doubtless linked to the dispatch of the British ultimatum that formed the basis of the convention signed by the Spanish government on 28 October 1790.

The Nootka Sound Crisis was a repetition of the Dutch Crisis. The opposition was to criticise the terms, as well as the expense of the armament. The rising Whig MP Charles Grey, later the 2nd Earl Grey who was to play such a prominent role in 1832 with the 1st Reform Act, complained in the Commons on 14 December 1790 that British rights to establish settlements were still 'uncertain'. And yet the resolution of the crisis was seen as a triumph for the government. The opposition were unable to capitalise on the dispute. The lack of a clear opposition case was indicated by Lady Palmerston's question, 'we want to know why we ought to dislike the King's speech.' The government was victorious in the Commons' debate on 14 December by a substantial majority, 247 to 123.[49]

The ministry was to be less successful the following spring. Deteriorating relations with Russia arising from Anglo-Prussian pressure on Catherine II to end her war with the Ottoman empire without annexing any of her conquests led the powers to the brink of war in the Ochakov Crisis. The parliamentary aspect of the crisis was certainly followed with attention abroad. Daniel Hailes wrote from Warsaw, whose support would be valuable

---

[47] J. M. Norris, 'The Policy of the British cabinet in the Nootka Crisis', *English Historical Review*, 70 (1955), pp. 572–5; P. Webb, 'The Naval Aspects of the Nootka Sound Crisis', *Mariner's Mirror*, 61 (1975), p. 135; J. Ehrman, *The Younger Pitt. I. The Years of Acclaim* (1969), p. 559 fn. 1.

[48] Luzerne to Montmorin, 8, 15 June, 13 July 1790, AE. CP. Ang. 573 fols. 253, 274–5, 574 fols. 43–4.

[49] Lady Palmerston to Harris, now Lord Malmesbury, 26 Nov. 1790, Winchester, Malmesbury, vol. 162; E. A. Smith, *Lord Grey 1764–1845* (Oxford, 1990), pp. 31–2.

in any war with Russia, concerning 'the King's speech which will be taken to pieces in a most unmerciful manner.'[50] There is an indication that the government wanted the session over before it proceeded to hostile steps against Russia. In February 1791, Joseph Ewart, the bellicose envoy to Prussia, who had recently seen Pitt, wrote to him of the minister's 'wish to have the session of Parliament over before taking any decisive steps'.[51] It is not clear how much weight should be placed on this remark. Recent success over Nootka had definitely led to optimism in government circles, which led to an underrating of the perils of parliamentary discussion. On the other hand, Prussian demands in March 1791 for action left the ministry with little option bar the development of the confrontation with Russia while Parliament was in session. The consequence was serious parliamentary problems, which indicated the potential weakness of any ministry however strong; the 1790 election had been a success for the government and the next general election did not have to be held until 1797.

On 28 March 1791, Pitt presented to the Commons the King's message on the need for further naval armaments, George's approval having been obtained the previous day.[52] The message declared that the failure of efforts to end the Russo-Ottoman war led to the need to lend weight to diplomatic representations by strengthening the navy. The Commons were assured that the expenditure was 'for the purpose of supporting the interests of His Majesty's kingdom, and of contributing to the restoration of general tranquillity on a secure and lasting foundation'. In a brief exchange, Fox, still opposition leader in the Commons, made it clear that the issue would be treated as one of confidence in the ministry, and that he felt that Parliament was receiving insufficient information about the causes of the crisis.[53]

The following day, 29 March 1791, the issue was debated in both houses. In the Lords, the government lost the initiative. Its case was poorly prepared and supported. Expert opposition speakers, such as Viscount Stormont, a former diplomat and Secretary of State, rejected the ministerial argument that it was up to government to decide what was safe to disclose, and moved onto specifics. Nevertheless, the opposition amendment was defeated, and the Address then carried by 97 to 34. George III thought the division 'must give confidence abroad from showing the support given'.[54]

[50] Hailes to Francis Jackson, Secretary of Legation at Berlin, 18 Dec. 1790, PRO. FO. 353/66.
[51] Ewart to Pitt, 11 Feb. 1791, PRO. 30/8/133 fol. 288.
[52] William, Lord Grenville, Home Secretary, to George III, 27 Mar. 1791, BL. Add. 58856 fol. 24.
[53] Cobbett, XXIX, 31–3.
[54] Cobbett, XXIX, 34–52; George III to Grenville, 30 Mar. 1791, BL. Add. 58856 fol. 26.

Ministerial speakers offered more arguments in the Commons, but suffered repeated attacks on the desirability and feasibility of British policy. The government majority on a division of 228 to 135 was substantial and George was pleased by what he saw as a 'very handsome majority,' which he felt would give energy to government policy;[55] but the cohesion and confidence of the ministry had been badly damaged by the debates. The policy of maintaining a bold front and hoping that Russia would back down was not enough for Parliament. There were clearly major problems with the conduct of government business and the presentation of policy; the complexity and seriousness of the diplomatic situation interacted with division and a lack of confidence amongst the ministers and an absence of a sure grasp of the management of both Houses over the issue. The Foreign Secretary, Francis, 5th Duke of Leeds (formerly Marquess of Carmarthen), recorded, on 2 April, a visit from the Lord Chancellor, Edward, 1st Lord Thurlow, who 'lamented with me our being *gagged* in the debates, and thought as I did that it would be better to come forward in both Houses in respect to the measures we were pursuing in our present discussion with Russia'. Henry Addington, the Speaker of the Commons, made the same point a fortnight later.[56]

Public agitation in favour of Russia and against war developed rapidly, encouraged both by the Russian envoy, Count Vorontsov, and by the Russia Company which acted as a powerful commercial lobby. Uncertain, like the ministry, as to what would happen, the pro-government press was hesitant. It was difficult, both in Parliament and in the press, to explain a policy designed both to lead to the intimidation of Russia, but not war with her, and to the retention of Prussia as an ally, but also to her being restrained from going to war. The expectations and nuances affecting foreign policy at this juncture were difficult to convey in a positive fashion, especially as an unwanted war came to seem more likely.

It was Parliament, however, where the crucial pressure was brought to bear on the government. The ministry could try to rely on its majority in both Houses providing support on the grounds of confidence, but that majority was unreliable and the government was split. James, 2nd Earl of Fife, a supporter, noted on 31 March, 'we had a very disagreeable debate yesterday in the House of Lords and not so well for ministers as usual; they also lost 6 in the House of Commons on the debate on the Address'.[57]

---

[55] George III to Pitt, 30 Mar. 1791, Aspinall, *George III*, I, 526.
[56] O. Browning (ed.), *The Political Memoranda of Francis Fifth Duke of Leeds* (1884), pp. 159, 167.
[57] Fife to his factor, William Rose, 31 Mar. 1791, Aberdeen, UL., Tayler papers 2226/131/855a.

The majority was to crumble alarmingly in April 1791, but already there were signs of concern. The government's reduced majority was noted in diplomatic circles and abroad. The absence of some ministerial supporters from the debates was attributed to their reluctance to support the government.[58]

The multifaceted and somewhat unfocused nature of the opposition attack ensured that the views and anxieties of different peers and MPs were catered for, whether concern about the costs of war and consequent taxation, or the loss of the Russian trade, or geopolitical and strategic considerations. Opposition arguments appealed both to those who had doubts about the value of Continental interventionism, and to those who supported the idea but did not like the direction given it by the ministry. The debates of 29 March were also significant, because, as Fox pointed out that day, the opposition had substantially supported the ministry over the Dutch and Nootka Sound crises, or at least had found it inexpedient to press home their criticisms,[59] whereas over Ochakov the attack was full-frontal.

The government was already split over the wisdom of risking war with Russia. Division did not matter greatly while the parliamentary and international situation was favourable, for then ministers did not air or press their doubts about Pitt; but the parliamentary storm on 29 March 1791 revealed that this was no longer so, and there was no compensatory good news from abroad. The parliamentary situation appeared crucial. Richmond told Leeds on the 30th that 'the country would not support' confrontation with Russia. When Leeds threatened next day that he would resign if policy changed, Pitt stressed the loss of support in the Commons, a theme he returned to on 4 April. The government's argument in Parliament that confidence had to be placed in the ministry had been unconvincing; while opposition claims about the inadvisability or danger of confronting Russia were powerful.[60]

Not all ministers, however, were impressed by domestic pressure. Leeds argued that the government should not abandon its policy, adding, 'The language of opposition confirms me in the necessity of not giving way to their clamour at home, or the effects of it abroad.' He warned that a

[58] Luzerne to Montmorin, 1 Apr. 1791, AE. CP. Ang. 577 fol. 88; William Eden, now Lord Auckland, to Francis Drake, envoy in Copenhagen, 5 Apr. 1791, BL. Add. 46822 fol. 170.

[59] Cobbett, XXIX, 61.

[60] J. Lojek, 'British Policy toward Russia, 1790–1791, and Polish Affairs', *Polish Review*, 28, 2 (1983), p. 14; Browning, *Political Memoranda of Leeds*, pp. 152–4, 160; Pitt to Ewart, 24 May 1791, PRO. 30/8/102 fols. 127–33.

climbdown would wreck the reputation of the government and establish 'a Russian party in the House of Commons.' Ewart shared his views.[61] Nevertheless, within the ministry domestic politics was encouraging a sense that policy must be changed. On 11 April 1791, Ewart visited Pitt in London and found him still convinced of the correctness of British policy, but now sure that a majority of the Commons was against him and unwilling to support a Vote of Credit. Ewart reported Pitt as very upset, with tears in his eyes, confessing his mortification, and much affected by the recent parliamentary debate. Ewart later added, 'Mr Pitt was extremely affected by the violent opposition in the House of Commons on Tuesday [12 April], has been much agitated since.'[62]

On 12 April, clearly scenting an opportunity, the opposition had raised the issue of British foreign policy in the Commons. Grey moved eight resolutions which represented cumulatively a major attack on this policy, as both misdirected and inconsistent. The fifth resolution stated that British interests were not likely to be affected by Russian gains on the shores of the Black Sea, while the sixth and seventh drew attention to Britain's obligations to her allies as defensive and argued that no such case then applied. The conventions of eighteenth-century political debate, the fashion for 'enlightened' opinion, and the convenience of being in opposition – if not irresponsibility – combined to allow Grey to set a moral tone. He argued that the maxims of policy which ought to govern foreign policy were clear and evident, that the only just cause of war was self-defence, not political expediency, and that Parliament would never have accepted the Anglo-Prussian treaty of 1788 had it contained provisions which allowed for offensive operations.

Charge provoked counter-charge as the lengthy debate continued, historical precedents and geopolitical speculations both appearing. Power politics and moral issues were both raised. The Foxite Samuel Whitbread, MP for Bedford and a member of a leading London brewing family, argued that the expulsion of the tyrannical Ottomans from Europe by Russia, a move far more radical than any the French revolutionaries were to attempt the following year, would be of universal benefit. It would lead to an economic revival of the Balkans that would help every commercial state.[63]

---

[61] Leeds to Pitt, 9 Apr. 1791, PRO. 30/8/15 fol. 47; Ewart to Pitt, 14 Apr. 1791, Williamwood, vol. 148.

[62] Ewart to Francis Jackson, 14 Apr. 1791, Williamwood, vol. 148. J. Ehrman, *The Younger Pitt. II. The Reluctant Transition*, p. 25 fn. 1 dates the meeting between Pitt and Ewart as occurring after the 12th, but the reference to Pitt's being very affected by the debate on that day occurs after Ewart's account of the interview.

[63] Cobbett, XXIX, pp. 164–217; Smith, *Lord Grey*, p. 34.

The ministry won the division by 253 to 173. Luzerne claimed that, having counted on a majority of 150, Pitt was astonished and embarrassed by the vote.[64] The government could survive such a victory; had indeed overcome worse parliamentary upsets, but Fox declared not only that Pitt must be convinced by the parliamentary agitation that war would be unpopular and that the country was roused from a lethargic state, but also that he must expect to see his majority whittled away by daily motions. After a weak reply by Pitt, William Baker, Foxite MP for Hertfordshire, gave notice that he would bring the subject before the Commons in a new shape on 15 April.[65]

This was the sort of parliamentary pressure that could crack a badly divided ministry. It was underlined by heightened public interest in the debates. The *Leeds Intelligencer*, in its issue of 17 May, reported on the votes of the county MPs on Grey's motion, an unusual step. The domestic situation led Pitt to change the direction of British policy. The Commons adjourned after Baker's motion at 3.30 a.m. on 16 April, the division being 162 to 254;[66] but, already, before that debate, Pitt had begun to draft dispatches that would signal a change. An appearance of firmness towards Russia was to be maintained, but conciliation was to be the policy, compromise the objective. New instructions were drawn up for Ewart, and Leeds, who refused to sign them, resigned.

By abandoning his policy, Pitt rode out the political storm, but the lesson was clear: domestic opinion sought limited objectives for foreign policy in Europe, not direct intervention, and Parliament was able to reflect this opinion. This also affected the governmental response to the growing crisis, from the summer of 1791, caused by deteriorating relations between revolutionary France and her neighbours. In parliamentary terms, Pitt's cautious neutrality over this issue in 1791 and early 1792 was wise.

When, after the French invasion of the Austrian Netherlands (Belgium) in November 1792, the direction of British policy changed towards confrontation with France, this did not create parliamentary problems, because, now, it was the opposition, rather than the ministry, that was divided and vulnerable over the issue. Praise for developments in France, for example by Fox when proposing, on 2 March 1790, the repeal of the Test and Corporation Acts,[67] had already created unease among the Whigs from the 1790 session.

---

[64] Luzerne to Montmorin, 15 Apr. 1791, AE. CP. Ang. 577 fol. 142.
[65] Cobbett, XXIX, 217–18.   [66] Cobbett, XXIX, 218–49.
[67] Cobbett, XXVIII, 397; Fife to Rose, 3 Mar., 27 Nov. 1790, Aberdeen UL. Tayler papers 2226/131/795, 830a.

When the session began on 13 December 1792, Fox attacked the ministry for failing to negotiate with France, and, in order to highlight governmental inconsistency towards international aggression, drew attention to the harsh manner in which Poland was being treated by some of France's bitterest critics. Fox's amendment was, however, heavily defeated by 290 to 50, because, on 11 and 12 December, meetings of prominent Whigs at Burlington House had agreed not to oppose the Address. Their leader, William, 3rd Duke of Portland, had already approved the draft of the royal speech that he had been shown, finding the section on British foreign policy 'particularly satisfactory'. Fox was left to rage impotently 'that there was no Address at this moment Pitt could frame he would not propose an amendment to, and divide the House upon'; a proclamation of opportunism that vindicated earlier press attacks on Fox for holding such views.[68]

Fox was convinced that the Revolution had taken an unfortunate path because it had not been allowed to develop without external threats, and he viewed France's enemies as united in a crusade of despots seeking to suppress liberty. These views, however, enjoyed little support within the political élite. On 15 December 1792, Fox's motion to send an envoy to Paris to negotiate with the French government, a motion keenly backed by Samuel Whitbread, was defeated in the Commons without a division.[69] The previous year, Shelburne, now Marquess of Lansdowne, had praised the French National Assembly for determining that the right of making peace and war came from the nation, not the Crown. As early as 22 May 1790, the National Assembly had resolved, after bitter debates, that the King could not declare war without its approval.[70] Shelburne urged the British government to follow the example of trusting the people, but this constitutional point was of no weight at the close of 1792 as constitutional change, in Britain, had been discredited by its association with the French Revolution, while government policy anyway rested on parliamentary and popular support.

In terms of the politics of the three decades after the Peace of Paris of 1763, the Ochakov Crisis posed the most serious problem of parliamentary

---

[68] 3rd Earl of Malmesbury (ed.), *Diaries and Correspondence of James Harris, First Earl of Malmesbury* (4 vols., 1844), II, 473–6; Lord Loughborough to Pitt, 9 Dec. 1792, PRO. 30/8/153 fol. 71; *Public Advertiser*, 14, 20 Jan. 1792.

[69] L. G. Mitchell, *Charles James Fox and the Disintegration of the Whig Party 1782–1794* (Oxford, 1971), pp. 202–4, and *Charles James Fox* (Oxford, 1992), pp. 125–30.

[70] B. Rothaus, 'The War and Peace Prerogative as a Constitutional Issue during the First Two Years of the Revolution, 1789–91', *Proceedings of the Western Society for French History* (1974), pp. 120–38. This is based on his *The Emergence of Legislative Control over Foreign Policy in the Constituent Assembly, 1789–91* (Ph.D. thesis, University of Wisconsin, 1968).

management. The need to be able to defend foreign policy was clearly at issue during the Falklands Crisis and the early years of the ministry of Pitt the Younger, most obviously with reference to the *Fürstenbund*, the Eden Treaty, the Dutch Crisis, and that over Nootka Sound, but in none of those cases was there a sustained or serious challenge to the government. This was not, however, inevitable. In each case, the issue was serious and there were potentially major challenges to policy. The *Fürstenbund* raised the questions of royal influence allegedly not open to parliamentary scrutiny and the need for better relations with Austria and Russia; the Eden Treaty the possibility of better Anglo-French relations; the Dutch Crisis whether the British government had been misled by the hopes of such relations; and that over Nootka whether the ministry had failed to make precise and sufficient gains.

These challenges were not developed to any serious extent, not because there was no basis for such a critique, but because of the weakness of the opposition, the attraction, greater resonance and relative importance of other issues, for example, the case of Warren Hastings and the government of British India,[71] the ministry's general success in foreign policy in 1787–90, and the fact that divisions within the government did not in these cases spill over into the parliamentary sphere. This is significant, because that had not been the case over a number of other issues, most obviously parliamentary reform, Richmond's fortification bill, the slave trade and the Hastings case. Furthermore, such a spilling over in the field of foreign policy had occurred earlier in the century. That it did not do so in the 1770s and 1780s suggests that foreign policy divisions, though important, were not central to the politics of the period, that ministers were now prepared to restrict their differences to Cabinet and correspondence, and that the political system under the North ministry as well as under that of Pitt prior to the Regency Crisis was less fluid than it had been in 1714–21, 1739–46, 1754–7, 1761–70 and 1782–4.

Aside from these 'structural' features, the ministry was also helped by the extent to which the particular crises prior to Ochakov, including that over the Falklands, were, in parliamentary terms, short-lived, and that it was usually possible to present the government as following a successful policy. This was important because the Foxite Whigs were largely opportunistic in their treatment of foreign policy, and were, therefore, discouraged by signs of ministerial success. As a consequence of the determination of Charles,

[71] Aust to Liston 7, 15 Feb. 1788, NLS. 5550 fol. 53; G. Carnall and C. Nicholson (eds.), *The Impeachment of Warren Hastings* (Edinburgh, 1989).

Count of Vergennes, the French Foreign Minister, to create a new diplomatic alignment, the terms of the Eden Treaty were favourable to Britain, and the ministry's willingness to solicit and win over most manufacturing and mercantile opinion helped to limit the possibility of successful opposition exploitation of the issue.[72] Ministerial sensitivity was also indicated in 1786 when Charles, 1st Lord Hawkesbury, President of the Board of Trade, and formerly an MP for a quarter-century, wrote to William Fawkener, who was negotiating commercial relations with Portugal, 'I have no doubt that when you return to England you will bring with you such an answer . . . or at least such information as will enable us to state a proper case to Parliament and fully to justify the proceedings we shall then be obliged to hold.'[73]

The degree to which the Dutch Crisis was 'close run', and that success was due to Prussian intervention and French financial weakness, and the contrast between the events of 1787 and the analysis and prospectus offered by Pitt during the debates over the Eden Treaty, though mentioned, were not pressed home because of the extent and popularity of British success and the clear endorsement of an anti-French policy by opposition speakers at the time of those debates. Both limited the plausibility of any attack on ministerial policy.

The same was essentially true of Nootka Sound. Spain was a recent enemy. Expansion in the Pacific was seen as a clear national interest, and was not limited by any serious critique of the self-interest of the traders involved; while interest in the possibility of better Anglo-Spanish relations, indeed knowledge of that aspect of the diplomatic world, was generally absent. As over the Falklands in 1770, the government was attacked in a 'domestic' rather than a 'diplomatic' context, not on the grounds that Britain had gone too far, that it had jeopardised diplomatic possibilities by an aggressive stance, but that it had not acted in a firm enough fashion, and that this had led to a belated and unsatisfactory settlement.[74] Indeed, Arthur Young, a supporter of better Anglo-French commercial relations, complained in 1787 that 'to reason with a British Parliament, when her

---

[72] George Pretyman, Pitt's tutor, to Addington, 3 Oct. 1786, 152 M/C 1786 F 47; Sir Francis Baring MP to Lansdowne, BL. Bowood 9; Charles, Lord Hawkesbury, President of the Board of Trade, to Thomas Gibbons, 5 Jan., Hawkesbury to Eden, 19 Jan., John, Earl Wycombe, Lansdowne's eldest son and MP for Chipping Wycombe, to Keith, 6 Feb. 1787, BL. Add. 38309 fols. 134–7, 35538 fols. 11–12; Ewart to William Porter, 2 Feb. 1787, Williamwood, vol. 130; E. A. Smith, *Whig Principles and Party Politics. Earl Fitzwilliam and the Whig Party 1748–1833* (Manchester, 1975), pp. 95–6, 114.

[73] Hawkesbury to Fawkener, 27 Nov. 1786, BL. Add. 38309 fol. 128.

[74] Smith, *Lord Grey*, pp. 31–2.

noisy factious-orators are bawling for the honour of the British lion, for the rights of commerce, and freedom of navigation; that is, for a war – that such a war will cost a hundred millions sterling . . . they are deaf to you'.[75] Honoré, Count of Mirabeau, a prominent politician in the early stages of the French Revolution, reflected current views of the British Parliament when he used the example of the outbreak of the War of Jenkins' Ear to criticise the role of emotion in a popular assembly.[76]

A critique of ministerial moves over Nootka, as earlier over the Falklands, on the grounds that they were not firm enough, was understandable in political terms, but it was vulnerable to the government's ability to present such distant events as it thought most convenient. Furthermore, by early 1791, the developing crisis in relations with Russia offered a better opportunity for the opposition to attack the government and, indeed, seemed to be a more important issue. Parliamentarians knew more about the issue, and the intervention of Vorontsov and the Russia Company ensured that this was even more the case.

The Ochakov crisis was the most abrupt demonstration of the impact of domestic and, in particular, parliamentary factors on foreign policy since the crisis over relations with Spain in 1739. As a result, it was unprecedented in the experience of the politicians of the period. Whatever the undoubted weaknesses of Britain's diplomatic and strategic position in 1791, it was the domestic situation that was responsible for the climbdown over Ochakov. It is clear that the magnitude of the parliamentary crisis seriously affected the ministry, sapping confidence and morale, and exacerbating divisions. Ministerial victories in the divisions were little substitute for the difficulties being faced in Parliament and the strain of sustained public pressure.

The crisis with revolutionary France, on the other hand, was far less serious in parliamentary terms, because Fox and his allies had failed to derive any long-term benefit from the Ochakov Crisis,[77] and, by late 1792, not only lacked the support of independents but also that of much of the now-divided Whig party. Fox pointed out that, 'To declare war, is, by the constitution, the prerogative of the King; but to grant or with-hold the means of carrying it on, is (by the same constitution) the privilege of the People, through their Representatives.'[78] In early 1793, there was little doubt that these representatives would support war with France.

[75] A. Young, *Travels during the years 1787, 1788 and 1789* (2nd edn, 2 vols., 1794), I, 39.
[76] *Archives parlementaires de 1787 à 1860: Recueil complet débats législatifs et politiques des chambres françaises* (127 vols., Paris, 1879–1913), XV, 622.
[77] Smith, *Lord Grey*, p. 35.
[78] *Letter from . . . Fox, to the Worthy and Independent Electors of . . . Westminster* (1793), pp. 23–4.

The aura of imperial power and the imaginative re-creation of Britain as a global state with a maritime destiny that had developed in mid-century did not, however, provide an answer to the diplomatic and military problems that were to face Britain at the close of the century. The successful trans-oceanic amphibious operations of the Seven Years' War (1756–63) had set the tone for discussion of potential military action over the following three decades. As the War of American Independence involved no hostilities in Europe, apart from the unsuccessful Bourbon siege of Gibraltar (1779–83) and their capture of Minorca (1782), and Britain did not intervene in the Austro-Prussian War of the Bavarian Succession (1778–9), the generation of parliamentarians who from 1793 faced the need to discuss the progress of the war with revolutionary France had no relevant recent experience on which to look back.

As with earlier debates, the historical examples cited by parliamentarians were significant. In the Lords' debate of 21 January 1794 on the Address of Thanks, Philip, 3rd Earl of Hardwicke referred back to William III's position at the beginning of the century, claiming 'The events of those times must be so familiar to the recollection of every one, especially from the remarkable analogy which many of them bore to the events of the present day.' In the same debate, George, 2nd Earl Spencer praised the government for creating an anti-French alliance greater than that at the time of the War of the Spanish Succession (1702–13). This period was particularly contested by politicians as government supporters rejected opposition claims that the French Revolution had been anticipated by that of 1688 made glorious in British collective memory. Instead, the two wars with France that sprang from the earlier revolution (1689–97, 1702–13), could serve to validate the idea that opposition to French expansion was integral to British constitutional development as well as national interests. Similarly, in December 1796, in the Commons' debate of censure on ministers for advancing money to the Emperor, Francis II, without the consent of Parliament, Pitt cited precedents from the 1700s and subsequently. He regularly awed his audience with his ability to present large amounts of information from memory, and to deploy his knowledge to effect in unscripted speeches.[79]

Historical analogy was also employed in the Lords' debate of 1794 on the Address in order to discuss whether the revolutionary nature of the French government prevented negotiations with it. Opposition speakers moved an amendment calling for these, but government speakers denied any comparison with Britain's republican government under Oliver Cromwell. David,

[79] Cobbett, XXX, 1079–80, 1074, XXXII, 1327–9; M. Duffy, *The Younger Pitt* (2000), p. 100.

2nd Earl of Mansfield, a former diplomat who had abandoned Fox, distinguished between Cromwell's stable hold on power and the state of France: 'It is as clear a proposition as any in Euclid, that you cannot treat, you cannot make alliance with anarchy.'[80] In contrast, the radical Lansdowne advanced the parallel with the American War of Independence, in which it had been necessary to acknowledge the new republic, while Charles, 3rd Earl Stanhope, also a radical, argued that it was unjust and unnecessary to interfere with France's internal government by making a change in it a war goal. Opposition speakers were clear that Britain had plunged into overly extensive commitments, not simply the 'continental war' decried by Charles, 11th Duke of Norfolk, a keen supporter of Fox, but an unwarranted ideological counter-revolutionary struggle to transform France. William, 3rd Duke of Portland, who had split from Fox, in contrast, pointed out that the amendment would cause the breach of all Britain's treaties. It was defeated by 97 to 12 votes.

The role of Parliament was raised by Banastre Tarleton, Foxite MP for Liverpool, the same day in the Commons. He drew attention to the government's use of the recess and to the clash between Parliament's validating and questioning roles:

After the longest recess which has occurred since the commencement of this Parliament, we are at length assembled to testify our approbation of the measures which have been adopted during so important and critical a period. If Parliaments are made only for the minister, or if a general vote of credit and confidence becomes a customary compliment from this House as often as the minister shall think fit to desire it, Parliament must at last grow despicable in the eyes of the people. Then a proclamation might be easily substituted in its stead, and happy would it be for the nation if that were sufficient: for when Parliament ceases to be a check upon ministers, it becomes a useless and unnecessary burthen on the people.[81]

Burden and foreign policy were directly related in the issue of subsidies to foreign powers which, again, became contentious. In 1794, the subsidy to Prussia was the subject of debate in Parliament, but the ministry convincingly won the division on 30 April by 134 to 33 votes. However, its parliamentary supporters were concerned about the solidity of popular support in the event of a lengthy war.[82]

The role of Parliament in influencing policy was also bound up in the issue of recognising the French republic. On 26 January 1795, Grey presented his motion for peace with France as an opportunity to test Pitt's

[80] Cobbett, XXX, 1078.   [81] Cobbett, XXX, 1100.
[82] Thomas Powys, MP for Northamptonshire, to Addington, 28 Sept. 1794, 152M/C 1794/OZ 20.

opinion that it was impossible to treat with the French government: 'It would be nothing more, if carried, than a parliamentary declaration that the form of government in France was not a bar to a negotiation with this country.' The ministry won the division by 269 to 86 votes.[83] Policy towards France proved a matter for concern for independent MPs who did not share Fox's radicalism but, nevertheless, felt that government policy had united the French against Britain. This was the position of William Jolliffe, the Northite MP for Petersfield, whose autobiography reveals the difficulties he faced in defining an acceptable political stance.[84]

When Grey returned to the charge in February 1796, Pitt, in response, provided a criticism of parliamentary scrutiny and its impact on foreign policy:

I must protest against the practice of being called upon from day to day, from week to week, from time to time, to declare what are precisely our views on the posture of affairs, or what are the steps, which we may think it necessary in consequence to adopt. The progress of the measures, which such a situation of affairs as the present may render necessary, can only be left safely to the conduct of the executive government. If the House are of opinion that the business cannot be safely left in the hands of ministers, the proper step would be to address his majesty to remove them from their situation . . . [and not] to endeavour to interrupt the affairs of government by calling on the House of Commons to interfere with the functions of executive authority . . . whenever this House, adopting a motion like the present, instead of addressing his majesty to remove his ministers, apply in order to take the business into their own hands, they deprive the country of every chance for a successful negotiation. On a question so critical, I am afraid lest I should overstep the line of my duty, by entering too much into detail. It is a subject on which it is impossible to descant so minutely as the hon. gentleman seems to expect, without breaking in upon that principle which has guided every discreet minister in treating subjects of this nature.[85]

Fox countered 'I am not one of those who consider the sitting of Parliament an impediment to negotiation . . . As to the prerogative of the crown of making peace, when and how his majesty pleases, no man doubts of it; but no man, on the other hand, will doubt of the prerogative of the Commons of England to advise his majesty, both as to the time and the terms of pacification.' Highlighting the difference over principle, and with his comments particularly pointed because he had been Foreign Secretary in 1782 and 1783, Fox added that he was opposed to the claim that it was

---

[83] Cobbett, XXXI, 1195; P. Jupp (ed.), *The Letter-Journal of George Canning, 1793–1795* (1991), pp. 194–6.
[84] H. G. H. Jolliffe, *The Jolliffes of Staffordshire* (1892), p. 65.   [85] Cobbett, XXXII, 721–2.

indiscreet for Parliament to comment, as well as to the arguments of the importance of state secrets and the need for parliamentary confidence.[86]

In October 1796, in the Commons' debate over the Address of Thanks, a debate delayed in response to the international situation, the ministerial speakers again stressed the need for a display of unity.[87] In contrast, Fox argued to first principles, claiming that peace with France alone would not suffice, as the 'system' of both British foreign and domestic policy was faulty.[88]

The role of Parliament was very much at issue that December when the Commons debated Fox's motion of censure on ministers for advancing money to Francis II without the consent of Parliament. Part of the opposition critique focused on the fiscal consequences in terms of lessened liquidity in Britain, but there was also much talk of the constitutional position, and as to whether, as a result of such actions, Britain had a limited or an absolute government. John Nicholls, MP for Tregony, baldly stated, 'No minister should have power to send money out of the country, without the previous consent of Parliament'. Richard Brinsley Sheridan, the playwright turned Foxite politician, argued that government policy,

arrogates to ministers a right to judge of the extent, as well as the mode of public expenditure; it is erecting the minister into an absolute dictator; it is a pretension beyond humanity to claim; it is usurping the attributes of the Deity, the power of refusing the desires and disappointing the wishes of those over whom they rule. If they claim the right of landing foreign troops without consent of Parliament, and of paying them, by this delicate process, without application to this House, where is the security left for our liberties and our constitution?[89]

the last an echo of points made earlier in the century when foreign subsidy treaties were discussed. Sheridan's argument had a clear historical resonance. The rights hard-won over the centuries, particularly from the Stuarts, were again at issue.

Fox also called for the defence of constitution, seeking to present this as the battleground with Pitt: 'did he think that it would have degraded his dignity, in the eyes of foreign statesmen, and foreign cabinets, to own that he must consult the British Parliament before he parted with British money'. Fox also suggested that the argument for confidentiality was imprudent: 'The ignorance of the extent of the remittances would increase the terror of the transport of our specie.' He took his defence of the constitution to

[86] Cobbett, XXXII, 729, 732–3.
[87] Pitt to Addington, 21 Sept. 1796, 152M/C 1796/OZ 3; Cobbett, XXXII, 1194.
[88] Cobbett, XXXII, 1197–8.   [89] Cobbett, XXXII, 1334, 1338.

extremes, concluding 'he had no hesitation in saying that occasions might arise, even in a comparatively free country, when the people might be driven to the necessity of resistance'.[90] This was not going to convince parliamentarians or the electorate. The government won the division. One MP left an explanation on the record that reveals concern about precedent rather than principle: 'Colonel Gascoyne said he came down to the House with a determination to vote in favour of the motion; but from the precedents that had been quoted, he was convinced that the transaction was perfectly constitutional.'[91]

In March 1797, the issues of parliamentary rights and royal privilege were returned to when an Address to George III for royal favour to Admiral Sir John Jervis after his victory over a Spanish fleet off Cape St Vincent was opposed as an interference in the role of the executive. Pitt presented government as a matter of different branches with distinct functions. The House accepted this argument and the motion was withdrawn.[92] Jervis, a former MP, was created Earl of St Vincent that June.

However, the opposition pressed hard at the ministry's attitude to the division of government responsibilities, complaining, in April 1797, in a debate over loans to the Emperor that Parliament had not been provided with the necessary papers. They also repeated the habitual cry that the government was failing to defend national interests: 'we shall not deserve to be called the King's Parliament, but the Parliament of the Emperor', claimed Sheridan.[93] The ministry won the division 266 to 87; and, the following month, defeated, by 116 to 31, a motion for withdrawing troops from St Domingo in the West Indies advanced on the basis that their presence there was both costly in manpower and not hitting France hard.

The opposition failure in 1797, led Fox and many of his colleagues to decide at the close of the session to stay away from Parliament. As Fox explained to his electors, 'Nothing useful to this kingdom can take place [in Parliament] until there is an entire and complete change of system.' Pitt thought that Fox's approach was 'so full of insult and defiance to the House of Commons, that with all possible desire to leave him to the insignificance and contempt to which he has doomed himself, I doubt whether it will be possible not to take some parliamentary notice of

[90] Cobbett, XXXII, 1346–7.
[91] Cobbett, XXXII, 1335. Isaac Gascoyne, MP for Liverpool, was a government supporter. For a parliamentarian taking notes on a parliamentary precedent, notes by Francis, 1st Lord Dunstanville, 152M/C 1800/OZ 19.
[92] Cobbett, XXXIII, 2–4.   [93] Cobbett, XXXIII, 230.

it'.[94] Although Fox attended Parliament occasionally, this secession continued until 1801.

The rights of Parliament were raised again in December 1798 when George Tierney, MP for Southwark, an opponent of the government who was unwilling to back Fox's secession from the Commons, moved a motion for peace with France:

> I know it may be said that this motion breaks in upon the undoubted power which the crown has of making war or peace; but I think this is a point which will not be much insisted upon when it is considered that the power of this House is unquestionable with respect to granting supplies. I have, as a member of this House, as good a right to say, that the supplies granted to the crown shall be granted exclusively for England, as to say, what no man doubts I have a right to say, that there shall not be any supply.[95]

Having then raised pragmatic points about the progress of the war on the Continent, the danger of being let down by allies, and the risk of exhausting British finances, Tierney then returned to the constitutional canvas by claiming that becoming an armed nation risked increasing the influence of the Crown. In response, George Canning, a Pitt protégé, who was MP for Wendover and Under-Secretary at the Foreign Office, mixed specific political and military points with constitutional arguments. Canning agreed that the Commons had a right to advise on peace or war, and referred to the Lords' vote of 1707 for no peace with the Bourbons if they retained Spain and the Spanish West Indies. Having conceded this, Canning attacked the opposition for opportunism – arguing that, if France was still a monarchy, they would have condemned the government had it tried to negotiate peace; before suggesting that no real peace was possible if Britain restricted itself to a 'blue water' policy, and deftly continuing to pile up a variety of reasons that would resonate with the different attitudes and assumptions of government supporters. France, for example, was presented as untrustworthy, a source of atrocities, and a threat to British interests and the European balance of power.

The previous May, Tierney had exchanged shots with Pitt, without injury, in a duel fought on Putney Heath that arose from Pitt claiming in the Commons, in a debate on naval manning, that Tierney had deliberately

---

[94] C. J. Fox, *Address . . . to the Electors of Westminster* (1797), p. 13; Pitt to Addington, 16 Oct. 1798, 152M/C 1798/OZ 5. On Westminster politics see also T. Jenks, 'Language and Politics at the Westminster Election of 1796', *Historical Journal*, 44 (2001), pp. 419–39.
[95] Cobbett, XXXIV, 26.

impeded public business. Tierney reported Pitt as saying that 'no man could oppose it in the manner I did unless it were from a wish to impede the defence of the country'. Pitt withdrew the remark when it was judged unparliamentary, but then, as far as Tierney was concerned, repeated the charge. This led Tierney to write to Pitt,

as a public man it cannot be expected that I should submit to it. I know what is due to your particular situation, but I also know and I trust you will recollect what a gentleman, as wantonly provoked as I have been, has a right to require.[96]

The customary governmental call for caution in what was said in debate rested on its alleged impact on the foreign audience. However, at the close of 1798, William Windham, the Secretary at War, MP for Norwich, who had broken with Fox over the French Revolution and joined the ministry in 1794, also warned about the social dimension. He was particularly critical of the impact of press discussion:

By these daily publications the people were taught to look upon themselves as present at the discussion of all the proceedings of parliament, and sitting in judgment on them . . . under the practice of reporting in the newspapers, everything that was said in that House, and which could not be said with safety any where else was, under the cover and authority of parliament . . . scattered all over the kingdom . . . He was not complaining of gentlemen for saying the war was unjust and unnecessary: if they thought so, they were right in so saying. But was it a desirable thing that the public at large, that the lower classes of the community from one end of the kingdom to the other, should, from day to day be told so.[97]

Windham's sense of this social resonance reflected the, to him unwelcome, development of British political culture under the stress of the revolutionary crisis. Lansdowne had urged the case for parliamentary reform in the Lords 'while it could be done gradually, and not to delay its necessity till it would burst all bounds'.[98] This, however, was not only no longer a viable political proposition, but also an attitude towards representation of, and accountability to, the public that no longer played much of a part in the discussion of Parliament's political role.

While MPs carefully noted the extent of 'discontent' among their constituents, ministerialists pressed the equation of national unity with

---

[96] Tierney to Pitt, [25 May 1798], 152 M/C 1798 OZ 11; G. Pellew, *The Life and Correspondence of the Right Honble. Henry Addington, First Viscount Sidmouth* (3 vols., 1847), I, 203–5.
[97] Cobbett, XXXIV, 159–61.   [98] Cobbett, XXXIII, 761–2.

strength. In July 1800, in a debate on subsidies to Francis II, Canning told the Commons,

The one plain question now before the House is whether or not they will enable those ministers, while they have the conduct of affairs, to conduct them in such a manner as may make either war vigorous, or peace attainable? or whether, by the refusal to sanction the engagements which they have entered into with our ally, who has certainly fought the battle manfully during this campaign . . . ministers are to be disabled from either continuing the war with effect, or negotiating with credit or advantage.[99]

Whatever the argument, the ministerialists had the majority on foreign policy. Henry Dundas, an effective debater as well as Pitt's leading supporter in the Commons, responded to an attack by Grey in the Commons in November 1800: 'The hon. gentleman had so often spoken of the incapacity and ignorance of ministers, and of their disgraceful and ignominious conduct of the war, that the repetition of those groundless charges had ceased to make any very disagreeable impression on his mind.'[100] He could more readily take that view because government majorities, ministerial unity and a careful management of Commons' committees ensured a parliamentary stability that contrasted markedly with the situation during the early 1740s. Moreover, as in 1745–8, military failure did not lead to a collapse in the government's position in Parliament. Instead, a far more difficult situation, which encompassed economic downturn, social tension, naval mutiny and fiscal crisis in 1797, and rebellion in Ireland in 1798, was overcome. The opposition was marginalised by its position on foreign policy and the war, to the great benefit of the ministry.

Equally, the themes seen earlier in the century echoed as a result of the international situation. Yet again parliamentarians debated the advisability of foreign subsidies and the value of alliances. The degree of security provided by such alliances, in both the short and the long term, was affirmed by governmental supporters[101] and denied by opponents.[102] International rivalry and war again defined the situation and provided the context for parliamentary politics. There was no equivalent to the situation in France, where, in a context of acute distrust, attempts to restrict executive power in the early 1790s made it difficult for the government to observe

---

[99] Charles Dundas, MP for Berkshire, to Addington, 11 Jan. 1798, 152M/C 1798/OZ 29; Cobbett, XXXV, 452.
[100] Cobbett, XXXIII, 537.   [101] Cobbett, XXXIV, 1160.   [102] Cobbett, XXXIV, 1423.

treaties or conduct foreign negotiations.[103] Conversely, a subsequent move towards authoritarianism in France, which culminated with Napoleon's declaration of imperial status, saw the establishment of rubber-stamp parliaments that were unable to contribute materially to the strength of the regime.[104]

---

[103] Armand, Count of Montmorin, foreign minister, to Noailles, Ambassador in Vienna, 22 Jan. 1790, AE. CP. Autriche 359 fol. 37; J. T. Murley, *The Origin and Outbreak of the Anglo-French War of 1793* (D.Phil. thesis, Oxford, 1959), p. 98.

[104] I. Collins, *Napoleon and his Parliaments, 1800–1815* (1979).

6

Sources and reports

'Upon a careful examination of the former collection of debates during this period [1771–4], it was found that the editor, Mr. Almon,
had not only evinced, in many instances, great partiality, but that he
had – without regard to the character of the speaker or the importance
of the subject – curtailed and mutilated almost every debate, in the
most careless and unwarrantable manner. To remedy these defects,
and to render the work as complete as the nature of it will admit,
it has been found necessary to examine every periodical journal that
was at all likely to contain authentic materials: and by comparing
those materials with the Journals of both Houses, and, in some instances, with manuscript notes taken by members at times when the
standing order for the exclusion of strangers was strictly enforced, the
editor has been enabled, not only to correct the misrepresentations of
Mr. Almon, but to present the reader with many debates, upon subjects of the highest importance, not to be found in the collection above
noticed.'

William Cobbett, *Parliamentary History* XVII (1813), preface,
with reference to John Almon's, *Parliamentary Register*

The discussion of the character and quality of parliamentary debates depends vitally on the sources. Contemporaries largely depended on press
reports, and these were also used in subsequent compilations. However,
such reporting was seen as a parliamentary privilege, and one that should
be restricted, and the consequent restrictions were partly enforced by Parliament. Due to restrictions on note-taking (the oft-ignored order banning
the bringing of pen and paper into the Houses of Parliament)[1] and on
printing reports, and also the conditions in which note-taking took place,
the sources do not provide a complete account of what was said in the debates. Furthermore, difficulties faced those who were permitted to report
debates. Parliament was uncomfortable. Indeed, in 1794, Canning referred

[1] Hayton, I, 23.

to a meeting at the Cockpit 'where was such a crowd, and squeeze and heat, as was sufficient to give one a foretaste of the House of Commons'. Eight years earlier, visiting the Commons, George Huntingford heard two speeches and then 'it grew dark and hot, and I was obliged to retire'.[2] It was not easy for parliamentarians themselves, in their hot and stuffy chambers, that were also sometimes dark, to provide accurate reports of proceedings. Comparisons between different accounts often reveal major discrepancies.

Spectators also faced problems, not least thanks to the limitations of many speakers. In 1727, Harriet Pitt, eldest sister of William Pitt the Elder, watched the new king, George II, open his first Parliament, and wrote to her mother 'I have enclosed the king's speech, which I saw him make today, I can't say heard, for His Majesty was in so much confusion he could not put out his voice to be heard . . . Mylord Lonsdale seconded the motion, but was in such confusion he could make nothing of it and was forced to sit down abruptly and looked very silly.'[3]

Newspaper reporters were faced with additional problems. They were not allowed to take notes until 1783 and, prior to that, had to rely on their memories, William Woodfall excelling so far as to earn the name 'Memory' Woodfall. Reporters were not sure of a place, and from their accustomed position in the back row of the Gallery could not fully see the Commons, which made the identification of unfamiliar voices difficult. Until 1875, the Gallery could be cleared whenever a member on the floor of the House chose to 'spy strangers'. Until 1853, against the advice of Woodfall, the person most conversant with 'Gallery Law',[4] the Gallery was cleared automatically when a division was taken (preventing the drawing up of division lists by strangers), and then not reopened. There were no reliefs for the reporters in the 1770s.

Restrictions did not only affect the newspaper-reading public. In January 1757, Richard Potenger, one of the Under-Secretaries, wrote to Andrew Mitchell, an MP then serving as envoy in Berlin, 'Time and circumstances have not allowed me to have given you what you say you expected from me, the parliamentary history of the session hitherto. Strangers are still excluded.'[5]

[2] P. Jupp (ed.), *The Letter-Journal of George Canning, 1793–1795* (1991), p. 46; George Huntingford, then a Fellow of Winchester, to Addington, no date [endorsed June 1786], 152M/C 1786/F72.
[3] Harriet Pitt to her mother, Harriet, 27 June (os) 1727, BL. Add. 69285.
[4] Woodfall to Addington, 25 Nov. 1790, 152M/C 1790/OZ 22.
[5] Potenger to Mitchell, 25 Jan. 1757, BL. Add. 6823 fol. 33; re 1738, P. J. Mantoux, 'French Reports of British Parliamentary Debates in the Eighteenth Century', *American Historical Review*, 12 (1907), pp. 256, 260; Thorne, I, 368–9.

This situation may lead to the conclusion that it is difficult to assess the content, let alone the quality, of debates, beyond a brief but incomplete recital of the names of speakers, and of the principal heads of debate. In addition, many reports failed to attribute speeches to individual speakers and, instead, offered a consolidated account. As a result, essentially two undifferentiated sides were presented, as was indeed the case with the reports of some debates in William Cobbett's *Parliamentary History*, which was compiled, retrospectively, from 1806.[6] Thus, differences in opinion and emphasis within sides were neglected, while the presentation of debates as essentially an exchange between two sides offered a simplification of the nature of much parliamentary discussion. In addition, such an approach made it difficult to chart the development of an individual's opinions.

As the sources that are readily available are less than comprehensive, it is necessary to cast the net more widely. One major, yet still relatively untapped, source for British political history in the seventeenth and eighteenth centuries is the dispatches of foreign envoys in London.[7] Some use has been made of the dispatches of the envoys of the major powers, particularly France, but such work has been patchy, and does not usually extend to powers of the second rank. There are obvious reasons for this neglect that in no way relate to the value of the material. Most work on British political history in this period has been done by British historians who tend to exhibit a stubborn insularity, being unwilling to use those foreign languages they do possess, unversed in the practices of foreign archives, and seemingly uninterested in investigating them. Thus, much material relating to the reign of James II lies undisturbed in Emilian archives; while the interesting reports of the envoy of Hesse-Cassel in the late 1630s rest unstudied in Marburg. It is no accident that one of the best accounts of British political history in the early eighteenth century, and the only one fully cognizant of the varied links that bound Britain to Europe, is by a German, Wolfgang Michael, who made full use of the diplomatic

---

[6] For his sources, H. H. Bellot, 'General Collections of Reports of Parliamentary Debates for the Period since 1660', *Bulletin of the Institute of Historical Research*, 10 (1932–3), pp. 171–7. For the major problems in using contemporary accounts of debates, see M. Ransome, 'The Reliability of Contemporary Reporting of the Debates of the House of Commons 1727–1741', *Bulletin of the Institute of Historical Research*, 19 (1942–3), 67–79.

[7] J. F. G. Lowe, 'Parliamentary Debates in 1701, from Reports of Foreign Observers' (MA dissertation, University of Liverpool, 1960); Hayton, I, 27. For examples of reports in and with the dispatches of envoys, see those from Palm, the Austrian envoy, in 1727, HHStA. Englische Korrespondenz 65, for example 28 Jan., 4, 18, 28 Feb., 4 Apr. Also see Thom, Wolfenbüttel envoy in London, reports of 31 Jan., 14 Feb. 1727, Wolfenbüttel, Staatsarchiv, 1 Alt 6 nr. 87, and Diemar to Landgrave Karl, 5 Feb. 1727, Marburg, England 195.

archives.[8] Ministers were well aware that such material existed. In November 1761, Henry Fox informed Shelburne that Bute had been upset by what the latter had said in the Lords, and had said that foreign envoys would take note of his remarks.[9]

It is clear that there are major problems with the use of diplomatic reports. Although the reports of the foreign envoys in London can prove particularly illuminating for a study of British foreign policy, there are many hindrances to any uncritical use of them for a study of British domestic politics. Some diplomats wrote reports that were not only inaccurate, but betrayed their ignorance of British government and parliamentary methods. This was certainly the case for some of the foreign diplomats in Britain during the Walpole ministry. Several diplomats were closely identified with those politicians who opposed Walpole, and were themselves heavily influenced by a desire to see the ministry overthrown. Thomas, 3rd Earl of Strafford, one of the leading Tories in the Lords, intrigued with Spain in the mid-1720s and also had links with Benjamin Reichenbach, Prussian envoy in 1726–30. It was from Strafford that Reichenbach sought information on British politics, and the government's interception of his correspondence revealed that, through Reichenbach, the opposition had both been keen to acquire information on Anglo-Prussian negotiations and had urged the Prussians to be stubborn in order to gain concessions. Count Philip Kinsky, Austrian envoy from 1728 to 1736, displayed support for the opposition Whigs, and maintained links with some of their leading members including the Earls of Chesterfield and Stair.[10]

Reflecting the animosity of their home governments and seeking to encourage a hostility to British policies that they hoped would fatally embarrass the Walpole ministry, envoys such as the Austrian Karl Josef von Palm in 1726, the Spaniard Pozzobueno in 1726, Reichenbach in the late 1720s, and the Frenchman Chavigny in the mid-1730s, presented a picture of Britain tottering on the edge of governmental collapse and widespread rebellion. Foreign envoys, however, proved to be particularly inaccurate in their reporting of popular disturbances, and many could only see these as signs of imminent collapse. This was certainly the case in 1733 with the demonstrations attending the Excise Bill. Montijo, the Spanish envoy, who

---

[8] W. Michael, *Englische Geschichte im 18. Jahrhundert* (5 vols., Berlin/Basle and Berlin/Leipzig, 1896–1955).

[9] Fox to Shelburne, 12 Nov. 1761, BL. Bowood 15 fol. 55.

[10] 'James III' to Strafford, 23 Aug. 1726, RA. 96/94; Reichenbach to Grumbkow, 17 Mar., 14, 18 Apr. 1730, Hull UL. Hotham papers 3/3; Townshend to Horatio Walpole, 14 Oct. (os) 1728, Norwich, Norfolk CRO. Bradfer-Lawrence papers; Chavigny to Chauvelin, 16, 28 Apr. 1734, AE. CP. Ang. 385 fols. 194, 285.

had links with the opposition, proclaimed his sympathies by providing free beer to those who demonstrated in London against the Walpole ministry. Three years later, Walpole sought Chavigny's recall.[11]

Allowing for opposition to the ministry is not the sole problem to arise from using diplomatic reports. Aside from general political preferences, diplomats also had more specific links. For example, Chavigny's principal political contacts were among the Tory group led by Sir William Wyndham, whose expert on foreign policy was Bolingbroke.[12] As he was not allowed to take his seat in the Lords, and as the principal critics of foreign policy in that chamber in the 1730s were either opposition Whigs or Tories who were not close to Bolingbroke, it is not surprising that Chavigny's reports concentrated on the Commons where he could show his allies in action. Thus, in 1736, he claimed that the larger-than-expected reduction in the number of sailors was the product of ably conducted opposition pressure, an explanation that ignored government wishes to the same end.[13] Chavigny also briefed his parliamentary allies, for example answering Wyndham's questions about German politics in February 1732.[14] Foreign envoys were indeed an important source of information and opinion for parliamentarians. Chavigny thought it important to prepare the opposition if Francis Stephen of Lorraine became King of Romans.[15] Such briefing was common. Sometimes it related to specific items of legislation. In 1731, Thom discussed the Wolfenbüttel subsidy treaty with MPs.[16]

Envoys differed in their attitudes. If some adopted a markedly anti-Walpolean stance, others were far more sympathetic to the Walpole ministry. This was certainly the case with the Hessian Diemar, the Danes Johnn and Sohlenthal, the Tuscan Pucci, the Russian Cantemir, and, at times, the Sardinian Ossorio and the Prussian Degenfeld. Reading diplomatic dispatches in bulk the overall impression is that they have much to offer, and that individual prejudice is offset by the views of other envoys.

In 1906, Paul Joseph Mantoux suggested that the French archives constituted a significant source for the history of Parliament, and illustrated

---

[11] 'Sulla Crisi Dell' Excise', Appendix 8 of G. Quazza, *Il Problema Italiano e L'Equilibrio Europeo 1720–1738* (Turin, 1965), pp. 455–63; Chavigny to Chauvelin, 18 Feb. 1732, AE. CP. Ang. 376; Chavigny to Bussy, French *chargé d'affaires* in Vienna, 22 Feb. 1732, HHStA. Interiora, Intercepte, 1; Kinsky to Charles VI, 21 Apr., Degenfeld to Grumbkow, 24 Apr. 1733, PRO. SP. 107/11; Walpole to Waldegrave, 21 Mar. (os) 1736, Chewton.

[12] Newcastle to Waldegrave, 3 Mar. (os) 1732, BL. Add. 32776 fols. 150–1.

[13] Chavigny to Chauvelin, 14 Feb. 1736, AE. CP. Ang. 393 fol. 141; William Hay, journal, Northampton CRO. L(c) 1733.

[14] Chavigny to Chauvelin, 4 Feb. 1732, AE. CP. Ang. 376 fol. 162.

[15] Chavigny to Chauvelin, 10 Apr. 1732, AE. CP. Ang. 377 fol. 36.

[16] Thom to Duke of Brunswick-Wolfenbüttel, 13 Feb. 1731, Wolfenbüttel 1 Alt 6 nr. 90 fol. 50.

this by reference to the 1735 debate on the state of the navy.[17] Indeed, in 1786, William Eden reported that he had been shown by a French official 'a long French dispatch regularly numbered as the continuation of a weekly journal of all the proceedings of our Parliament: and it has the appearance of being executed with some ability and accuracy'.[18] In the Correspondance Politique Angleterre series in the French foreign ministry archives, there are indeed many reports of parliamentary debates, although, in 1719, Destouches referred to not sending details of a Lords' debate on Nonconformists' rights as it would waste the Foreign Minister's time.[19] It is possible that some reports, received by the French and other foreign governments, were sent from London by a group of newswriters who produced similar reports for the various governments concerned,[20] although most of such reports were forwarded by diplomats, and there were also many reports written specifically for one government. Reports were sufficiently frequent, and enough attention paid to them, to enable the French foreign minister to comment in March 1727 that each day the opposition speeches were becoming more strident.[21]

Some reports were dispatched by foreign diplomats who had personally attended Parliament. Records of such visits are difficult to find, as foreign diplomats were generally not obliged to seek permission for them, and as there are no registers of important visitors to Parliament. Nevertheless, major debates, such as those over the Excise Bill in 1733, and the voting of increased funds for the Prince of Wales in 1737, were certainly attended by several diplomats.[22] It is unclear, however, how many diplomats attended the still important, though more regular and less exceptional, debates. It seems likely that reporting of such debates was left to hirelings.

Reichenbach certainly attended debates, though it seems that those he attended were the major ones. He had a good command of English, an essential prerequisite for a diplomat hoping to benefit from such a visit. In

[17] P. J. Mantoux, *Notes sur les Comptes Rendus des Séances du Parlement Anglais au XVIIIe siècle, conservés aux archives du ministère des affaires étrangères* (Paris, 1906); and 'French Reports of British Parliamentary Debates in the Eighteenth Century', *American Historical Review*, 12 (1907), 244–69.
[18] Eden to Pitt, 18 May 1786, CUL. Add. Mss. 6958 no. 111. For examples of French reports, Chammorel to Chauvelin, 11 Feb. 1732, AE. CP. Ang. 376 fols. 208–9, and account of debates sent with Chavigny to Chauvelin, 6 Feb. 1736, AE. CP. Ang. 393 fols. 106–9.
[19] Destouches to Dubois, 2 Jan. 1719, AE. CP. Ang. 322 fol. 9.
[20] Gibbs, 'Laying Treaties', p. 127 fn. 48. For reports of debates in 1726, 1730 and 1731 held in Wolfenbüttel, Staatsarchiv, 1 Alt 6 nr. 86, 90–1, and for those sent by Alt to Frederick I of Sweden in 1736, see disputes of 27, 31 Jan., 28 Feb., 2, 6 Mar., Marburg, England, 221.
[21] Charles, Count of Morville to Chammorel, 13 Mar. 1727, AE. CP. Ang. supplément 8 fol. 10.
[22] *Newcastle Courant*, 13 Feb. (os) 1731; *Grub Street Journal*, 22 Mar. (os) 1733; *London Farthing Post*, 3 Mar. (os) 1739.

March 1730, Reichenbach ended a letter to the Prussian statesman General Grumbkow, 'il faut que je finisse pour aller au Parlement ou il sera aujour-dhuy un Debat sur l'Etat de la Nation'.[23] Three years later, Reichenbach's successor as Prussian representative, the Anglophile Count Degenfeld, at-tended the debate in the Commons on the Army Estimates. He reported on the debate to Frederick William I of Prussia, and his dispatch was in-tercepted and deciphered by the British Post Office:[24]

As in a late debate of the House of Commons about the troops of this kingdom, the Dutch reduction was spoke of,[25] Shippen said among other things, that were he of that country, he should rather be for increasing than lessening the troops, for that, if credit was to be given to the newspapers, France would not fail, in case of the death of the Elector Palatine, immediately to light up the flame of war in those parts; but that he hoped England would neither take part in that matter, nor be inclined to keep up the army on that account: that he did not see what all those pompous treaties that had been concluded, and the great sums of money given for several years passed, had been good for, and why people did not rather seek to get into alliance with such powers as had the same religion and forces enough.[26]

Sir William Yonge[27] replied, that though nobody had been named, yet he was satisfied that everybody judged as he did who was meant; that he had all imaginable respect and devotion for that power but that he left it to every well thinking Englishman, whether after this power had rejected the entering into alliance with their Royal Blood,[28] they could bring themselves to expose their money and blood for the said power, unless it should change its ways, and in that case he would not only be the first to promote with all joy whatever could be agreeable to it, but that everybody else would in acknowledgement do the same.

I should not have failed to have demanded an explanation, but that the King himself has right to call anybody to account for what has been said in Parliament, besides which I was admitted into the House out of pure civility, whereas no foreigner was let in the last time.

Under the Second Treaty of Vienna of March 1731, to which the United Provinces had acceded a year later, Britain was bound by treaty obligations to Austria and the United Provinces. Shippen suggested that the death of Karl Philipp, Elector Palatine, an elderly ruler without children, would

[23] Reichenbach to Grumbkow, 21 Mar. 1730, Hull UL., Hotham papers, DDHO 3/3. On 18 Feb. 1729, General Diemar, the Hessian envoy, attended the Commons' debate on the Hessian subsidies: Diemar to Landgrave Karl, 18 Feb. 1729, Marburg, England 197.
[24] Degenfeld to Frederick William I, 20 Feb. 1733, PRO. SP. 107/9.
[25] The Dutch had recently reduced the size of their army.
[26] A reference to Prussia.
[27] Sir William Yonge, MP for Honiton, a Lord of the Treasury. He was noted for his eloquence: R. R. Sedgwick, *The House of Commons 1715–1754* (2 vols., 1970), II, 569.
[28] In 1730, Frederick William I rejected British advances for a double marriage between the two houses: J. Black, *The Collapse of the Anglo-French Alliance* (Gloucester, 1987), pp. 181–3.

produce a Rhenish war. The Elector's dominions included the duchies of Jülich and Berg, as well as the county of Ravenstein, possessions of great strategic importance in and close to the Rhineland and claimed both by the Prussians and by the Sultzbach branch of the Wittelsbach family, the heirs to the Palatinate. The Dutch were very concerned to prevent a Prussian succession in these territories, and in this they were joined by George II, in his capacity as Elector of Hanover. Both had had major clashes with the Prussians over Frederick William's methods of recruiting for his army and over particular territorial disputes.[29]

Shippen's suggestion that the British should seek a Prussian alliance, an alliance with a fellow Protestant power, was therefore a mischievous one, as it could be argued that, for Hanoverian reasons, George had distorted British foreign policy. Shippen's mention of the need for a Protestant alliance was not, however, the repetition of banal, anachronistic views, but a considered response to the international situation. The previous sixteen months had seen the sensational persecution of the Protestants in the archbishopric of Salzburg and their subsequent emigration, as well as widespread attacks upon Protestantism in Austrian-ruled Hungary. These events had been fully covered in the British press,[30] and had been strongly condemned by Prussia. The Jülich-Berg dispute involved confessional factors, as the Wittelsbachs were staunch Catholics, whose rule in the Palatinate had been marked by severe persecution, and thus Shippen could make George II's hostile stance towards Prussia appear to favour Catholicism in the Rhineland, or, at least, lead to the division of the Protestant cause. Shippen's suggestion about the need to improve relations with Prussia was also a public airing of a view held privately by several ministers and diplomats, including Horatio Walpole. It revealed a wide and informed knowledge of European affairs.

In the better-known accounts of the debate, there is no hint of the speeches recorded by Degenfeld. The Jacobite journalist Nathaniel Mist sent an account of the debate to 'James III' at Rome, part of the process by which the Jacobite court obtained frequent reports of debates.[31] The debate is also mentioned in the printed collections both of the Egmont and

---

[29] H. A. Treu, 'De Verhouding tussen Pruisen en Nederland in 1733', *Tijdschrift voor Geschiedenis*, 80 (1967), 486–97; Black, 'Anglo-Wittelsbach Relations 1730–42', *Zeitschrift für bayerische Landesgeschichte*, 55 (1992), pp. 307–22.

[30] For examples of press coverage of persecution in Europe, see *Hyp-Doctor*, 9 Nov. (os) 1731; *St James's Evening Post*, 16 Nov. (os) 1731; *Daily Post Boy*, 10 Nov. (os) 1731; J. Black, 'The Catholic Threat and the British Press in the 1720s and 1730s', *Journal of Religious History*, 12 (1983), 364–81.

[31] Nathaniel Mist to 'James III', 27 Feb. 1733, RA. 159/155. The Stuart Papers contain many useful accounts of debates. For a detailed account of the Commons' debate on the Address, James Hamilton to Graeme, 11 Feb. (os) 1727, RA. 103/80.

of the Carlisle papers, and these contain two accounts by MPs who were present, both on the government side. Sir Thomas Robinson, who spoke in the debate, wrote a letter next day to his father-in-law, Charles, 3rd Earl of Carlisle, himself a former MP for Morpeth, a seat where the family had a strong interest. Robinson's account was brief, concentrating on his own contribution. He noted that fifteen MPs had spoken for the reduction in the armed forces, the opposition stance, and that nine had defended the government. Robinson only named three speakers on each side and these did not include Shippen or Yonge.[32]

Perceval's account, in his diary, was much fuller than Robinson's.[33] He named all twenty-six speakers and summarized their speeches. By the time that Shippen came to speak, Perceval was tired: Robinson noted that the debate was a fairly lengthy one, lasting 'till 8 in the evening', and Perceval was to miss entirely Sir Robert Walpole's speech, which was twenty-fourth in the order he recorded, because he needed to go out to 'refresh' himself.[34] Shippen, speaking twentieth, and Yonge, twenty-first, must have been addressing a House that was already restless and tired. It is clear, nevertheless, that Degenfeld and Perceval were interested in widely different aspects of the debate, and Degenfeld's account throws considerable doubt upon the comprehensiveness of Perceval's reporting. In the Perceval account, very little attention is paid to foreign affairs. He, nevertheless, recorded Shippen's speech at length:[35]

Mr. Shippen. The time is come for us to exert ourselves, and to inspect the expenses of the army, which are become insupportable. He knows the army is a darling point, and the estimates given by the King's direction, but still they are, subject to the inspection of the Commons, and require to be narrowly sifted. He had yet heard no argument of the least weight for the question; for there is not the least probability of danger to his Majesty by a reduction of the army, but there is by keeping up this number of forces, for a standing army is against the foundation of our Government, and whatever saps the foundation, endangers the superstructure. Let them show what government is of value that cannot be supported without a standing army, or how such Government differs from a conquered state. In keeping these up we must be subjected to new taxes for paying them, or to tyrannical methods of collecting the old ones. How little does this demand tally with the King's speech. If it be said we want a body of troops to be ready to fulfil our engagements to foreign princes to assist them according to stipulation, that assistance is either to be by ships, money, or men, but very probably they will least of all desire men, and it were an unreasonable burthen on the subject to keep men perpetually in readiness

[32] HMC. *Manuscripts of the Earl of Carlisle* (1807), p. 100.
[33] HMC. *The Diary of the First Earl of Egmont* (3 vols., 1920–3), I, 313–23.
[34] *Ibid.*, 323.   [35] *Ibid.*, 321–2.

on an account that may not happen, or is not likely soon to happen, from the good situation of affairs on the continent.

He thought 12,000 men were more than enough for entertaining those who delight in military decorations or for quelling religious mutineers, which is all the use they are to be put to, but he will be for 12,000 rather than the 18,000.

Sir William Yonge. It is wrong in gentlemen to argue what may happen in future years, for the debate should be confined to one year, the forces being demanded for no longer time. He believed indeed the hearts of the people would be a sufficient support of his Majesty, had they not been poisoned by acts made use of to disquiet their minds; pains have been taken to give them an ill impression of the Government's designs, and misrepresent them. Some gentlemen think 12,000 only necessary, others think 17,000, he hoped that neither should be thought enemies to their country for their difference of opinion. If gentlemen duly considered how the army is dispersed, they would not be so angry or apprehensive against the greater number moved for, for though we gave the highest number, they will in effect come out but little more than 12,000 men able to defend us in any reasonable time in case of sudden invasion or rebellion, for 1,800 of these are invalids, and 1,800 more at Gibraltar; there are, besides, some thousands in Scotland, some in Guernsey, etc., and as to our safety from the numbers remaining, it is certain that had it not been for the great alacrity used in raising nine regiments, in calling troops from Ireland, and the assistance of the Dutch, the insurrection in the late King's time [the Jacobite rising in 1715, the '15] had proved successful, notwithstanding his standing army. The fear of gentlemen from the number of this army had no weight with him, for he believed in a justifiable and general cause of liberty, the people would easily get the better of them, supposing they would serve ambitious designs, which he could not think they would.

The Degenfeld dispatch suggests that parliamentary knowledge about European affairs and British foreign policy was widespread. Yonge is recorded as stating that, though Frederick William I was not named, 'yet he was satisfied that everybody judged as he did who was meant', and both Shippen and Yonge's speeches rested upon the assumption that the already restless House of Commons would be able and interested enough to follow an exchange upon the subject of a Prussian alliance. Shippen's reference to the press is also important, for it seems clear that the newspapers were the major source of information upon foreign affairs, and that this aided MPs to challenge the government's foreign policy.[36]

Degenfeld's report reflected his interest in the affairs of his sovereign. This was more generally the case with foreign envoys. Thus, in his report

---

[36] G. C. Gibbs, 'Newspapers, Parliament and Foreign Policy in the Age of Stanhope and Walpole', *Mélanges offerts à G. Jacquemyns* (Brussels, 1968), pp. 293–315; J. Black, 'The Press, Party and Foreign Policy in the Reign of George I', *Publishing History*, 13 (1983), pp. 23–40, and *The English Press in the Eighteenth Century* (1987), pp. 197–243.

on the 1731 Lords' debate on the Hessian subsidies, Diemar noted that Carteret had praised the Hessians and Frederick I, King of Sweden and also Landgrave of Hesse-Cassel, and had said that he was only opposed to the cost of the subsidies. During the Falklands Crisis, George, Lord Lyttelton referred to the possibility of Spanish agents listening to debates, and Granville, 2nd Earl Gower made the same point when he successfully moved for the House to be cleared when George, 4th Duke of Manchester claimed, on 10 December 1770, that Gibraltar was poorly defended. In protest, the opposition peers walked out, claiming that the House had been cleared of all honest men as a result of Gower's intervention.[37]

Diplomats stressed an aspect of parliamentary debates otherwise too often ignored or underrated: foreign policy could be discussed in Parliament with knowledge and intelligence. Alongside the perpetuation of outdated concepts by speakers, there was also a willingness to consider developments in international relations and new approaches for British foreign policy. Diplomats also picked up some of the nuances of parliamentary politics. For example, an interesting suggestion of opposition disunity over a Protest can be found in the report of the Saxon envoy on the Army Commissions Protest in 1734. De Löss claimed that the strident tone of the Protest had angered many of the opposition.[38] This underlines the point that the signatories to a Protest did not necessarily represent the strength of opposition sentiment, although the extent to which opposition peers who disliked the terms of a Protest chose not to sign it is unclear.

The accuracy of parliamentary reporting in the press was questioned by contemporaries, but, for the government, it was the opportunities that such reporting created for the opposition that aroused most disquiet. In 1739, Walpole's 'manager' of Scottish affairs, Archibald, Earl of Ilay, told the Lords, 'All the measures of our government are misrepresented to this very day: even the proceedings of this House are libelled, not only in conversation, but in print. Is not every Lord sensible of this?'[39]

Such action was a breach of parliamentary privilege, as both Houses of Parliament had resolved against unauthorised reports of its debates, while, under a Commons' standing order of 1705, strangers were supposed to be taken into custody. Major attempts were indeed made in the 1720s to prevent parliamentary reporting in the press, reporting that spread to the foreign press. In 1726, Jacob Anton van Gansinot, the Wittelsbach envoy

---

[37] Diemar to William of Hesse-Cassel, 15 May 1731, Marburg, England 204; Cobbett, XVI, 1116, 1318; W. S. Taylor and J. H. Pringle (eds.), *Correspondence of William Pitt, Earl of Chatham* (4 vols., 1838–40), IV, 51–3.
[38] De Löss to Augustus III, 5 Mar. 1734, Dresden 638.   [39] Ilay, 15 Nov. (os) 1739, Cobbett, XI, 80.

in The Hague, reported that, as the press reported the most interesting occurrences in Parliament, it was not necessary for him to repeat them in his despatch.[40]

The parliamentary attack on a major provincial paper in 1729 signalled a new situation for press reporting in Britain. Reports in the issues of Robert Raikes's *Gloucester Journal* of 12 March (os) 1728 and 11 February (os) 1729 led to the questioning of Raikes, and, on 28 February (os) 1729, the Commons passed a resolution,

That it is an indignity to and a breach of the privilege of this House for any person to presume to give, in written or printed newspapers, an account or minutes of the debates or other proceedings of this House, or of any Committee thereof. That upon discovery of the authors, printers or publishers of any such written or printed newspaper, this House will proceed against the offenders with the utmost severity.[41]

This move had a definite effect. Newspapers that had hitherto reported parliamentary debates ceased to do so, one such informing its readers,

The publick cannot expect to have an account of the proceedings of the Hon. House of Commons in this or other newspapers, since the printer of Gloucester is taken into custody of the Serjeant at Arms for inserting the same; nay, even those who write, and transmit such accounts, it seems are not excusable, four of whom being ordered to attend the Hon. House of Commons on that account also.[42]

The parliamentary injunction was effective for several years. Manuscript newsletters continued to give details of debates, including quotations from individual speakers,[43] but both the ministry and Parliament had always displayed less concern over newsletters, a luxury product consumed by the wealthy, than over newspapers.[44] The tough stance displayed by the ministry towards opposition newspapers, such as *Mist's Weekly Journal* and the *Craftsman*, in 1728–31, including several prosecutions, could not have encouraged these or other papers to flout the rules over parliamentary reporting. That which survived for the early 1730s was episodic: the King's

[40] Gansinot to Ferdinand, Count Plettenberg, first minister of the Elector of Cologne, 12 Mar. 1726, Münster, NB. 259 fol. 217.
[41] *Journals of the House of Commons*, XXI, 238; G. A. Cranfield, *The Development of the Provincial Newspaper 1700–1760* (Oxford, 1962) pp. 158–9.
[42] *Original Mercury, York Journal; or Weekly Courant*, 2 Apr. (os) 1728.
[43] A surviving example of these newsletters, received by a parliamentarian, are those sent to Viscount Perceval, BL. Add. 27981. For quotation of speech by a named individual, Charles, 3rd Earl of Peterborough's attack on the Treaty of Utrecht, issue of 21 Mar. (os) 1730.
[44] Cranfield, *Provincial Newspaper*, p. 156.

Speech opening and closing each session and the Addresses were printed soon after delivery.[45] They were items of official propaganda and their circulation was probably encouraged. Debates and, even more, accounts of how MPs voted were less common.

The situation was different for the Lords. Opposition peers were out-numbered, but the privilege of registering Protests enabled them to pub-licise their opinions. In 1744, Horatio Walpole complained about the way in which parliamentary news was being published in the Amsterdam press (as had long been the case),[46] and specifically regretted the publication of a translation of the Lords' Protest about the subsidies paid for Hanoverian troops.[47] These Protests were not on the whole available to London read-ers, but were widely disseminated in the provinces. They and the lists of signatories, an item of great political importance, were regularly printed by William Wye in his newsletter, which had, judged by the contents of the provincial press, become, by the mid-1730s, the most influential newsletter. Thus, *Wye's Letter* of 7 March (os) 1734 provided a summary of the debate the previous day in the Lords on the election of Scottish peers to Parliament, in which the speakers were named. Two days later, *Wye's Letter* printed the Protest registered at the end of the debate and the signatories. These reports were regularly reprinted in the provincial press. Protests carried in *Wye's Let-ter* for 21 and 28 March (os) 1734 were printed in the *Newcastle Courant* of 30 March (os) and 6 April (os) 1734. A particular reason for the appeal of the items in *Wye's Letter* was that they were fresh and readers did not have to wait until the summer recess, as they had to do with the magazines or with such newspapers as the *Dublin News-Letter*, which carried its reports on the 1737 session, which finished on 21 June (os), in its issues from 19 July (os) until the end of the year.

However, *Wye's Letter* did not report debates in the Commons and, for these, readers had to turn to the magazines. Until 1735, the *Political State of Great Britain*, and, from 1732, the *Gentleman's Magazine* and the *London Magazine*, all monthly magazines, carried, in the recess, reports of parlia-mentary debates claiming to take advantage of an apparent loophole in reporting. William Guthrie reported for the *Gentleman's Magazine* from the Commons' Gallery, and Thomas Gordon for the *London Magazine*.

[45] *York Courant*, 18 Jan. (os) 1732; *Wye's Letter*, 16 Apr. (os) 1734; *Weekly Oracle or Gentleman's Journal*, 17 Jan. (os) 1736.

[46] E.g. *Amsterdam Gazette*, 1 May 1725.

[47] Walpole to Trevor, 28 Feb. (os) 1744, Aylesbury, Buckinghamshire CRO., Trevor Mss. vol. 37. For printed Lords' Protests in series other than those of foreign ministers, Paris, Archives Nationales, Archives de la Marine B7 330. For Protests, J. E. T. Rogers (ed.), *A Complete Collection of the Protests of the Lords, with historical introductions, edited from the Journals of the Lords* (2 vols., Oxford, 1974).

Promptness in publication, however, was still a problem: in January 1734, Henry Fox, not yet an MP, complained that 'parliamentary affairs' were not 'in print'. Nevertheless, Perceval (from 1733 Earl of Egmont), a former MP, having heard the Commons' debate on the size of the army on 18 February (os) 1737, wrote in his diary, 'I will not set down the debates at length because the *Political State of Great Britain*, the *Gentleman's Magazine* and the *London Magazine*, which come out monthly, has of late years done it.'[48]

The loophole of magazine publication was in theory closed by the Commons in 1738,[49] after a debate in which Sir Robert Walpole had alleged inaccuracy and bias in the reporting.

I have read some debates of this House, Sir, in which I have been made to speak the very reverse of what I meant. I have read others of them wherein all the wit, learning, and the argument has been thrown into one side, and on the other nothing but what was low, mean, and ridiculous...[50]

However, the Commons' resolution of April 1738 did not stop the magazines printing debates. Instead, they resorted to printing the proceedings of imaginary assemblies: 'Debates in the Senate of Lilliput' in the *Gentleman's Magazine*, and a 'Journal of the Proceedings and Debates in the Political Club' in the *London Magazine*. However, they still printed their parliamentary reports in the recess and served therefore more as journals of record than as means of satisfying the public wish for fresh parliamentary news. In May 1741, *The Publick Register: or, The Weekly Magazine*, which was attempting, with little success, to obtain a large share of 'the magazine market', addressed some public queries to the proprietors of the *Gentleman's* and *London Magazine*. In them, it is clear that the prompt publication of parliamentary news was seen as a potentially crucial selling point,

1. Whether through their influence the printers of certain Daily Papers and Evening-Posts, did not refuse to advertise the Publick Register, or Weekly Magazine?
2. Whether this could proceed from any other motive than their being conscious, that they could not procure so early and full an account of the debates, as is, and will be contained in the said Publick Register?
3. Whether their account of the said debates can be looked upon as full, connected, or early, since they have had nothing as yet of what passed in the last session of Parliament; and have, for next month, advertised two debates that happened towards its close?

[48] Henry to Stephen Fox, 19 Jan. 1734, BL. Add. 51417 fol. 44; *Egmont*, II, 350.
[49] *Journals of the House of Commons*, XXIII, 148.   [50] Cobbett, X, 809.

4. Whether, as this is the case, the said Publick Register ought not now to be looked upon as the only paper containing the debates?

5. Whether, from those debates already given in the Publick Register, the world has not reason to believe, they will be published with the most impartial and strict regard to truth, without attachment to any party whatsoever?[51]

Some newspapers resorted to the methods of the magazines in order to report parliamentary news. During the 1742 recess, the most innovative of the Bristol newspapers, the *Oracle: or, Bristol Weekly Miscellany*, printed, under a Bristol bye-line, the text of a Lords' Protest, with an introductory note, 'We hear some persons of great distinction, who have an absolute right to speak their minds freely on any point that shall come before them, have in an authentick manner protested against a late senatorial proceeding, for the following reasons.'[52]

The passage of the Licensing Act in 1737 and its use to enforce theatrical censorship, had encouraged rumours in 1738 that the ministry envisaged press censorship. In fact, nothing was done to strengthen the legal restrictions on the press, bar, significantly, the Commons' resolution of April 1738. Nevertheless, the threat of legal action did indeed help to restrict parliamentary reporting. In March 1739, the *York Courant* informed its readers,

The Publisher of the Lords' Protests relating to the Convention (which were designed to be inserted this day) being taken up hoped the reader will excuse the omission of them, the printer of this paper having no inclination for a London Journey at this snowy season of the year.

A week later, the paper added 'We hear that a strict inquiry is making after the persons, who furnish the coffee houses with written "Minutes of the Proceedings of Parliament", in order to their being apprehended.'[53] The previous year, the first number of a new periodical had addressed the *London Magazine*, 'As it is now rendered unsafe for you to entertain the Publick with any account of the proceedings or debates of those who rule over us . . .'[54]

Nevertheless, the general picture was one of increased press freedom in printing parliamentary news. During the 1739 summer recess, Henry Goreham and John Purser, the printers of the *Craftsman* and *Common Sense*, the leading opposition London papers, both published lists of the Commons' division on the Convention of the Pardo, the controversial settlement of Anglo-Spanish differences negotiated by the ministry. The

[51] *Publick Register*, 23 May (os) 1741.   [52] *Oracle*, 5 June (os) 1742.
[53] *York Courant*, 13, 20 Mar. (os) 1739.   [54] *The Journal of a Learned and Political Club*, No. 1.

York Courant did the same for the northern MPs.[55] The following summer, the *Newcastle Journal* printed in full John, 2nd Duke of Argyll's critical speech on the state of the nation delivered in the Lords on 15 April (os) 1740. The publication of this significant speech by a leading opposition peer was defended by the paper. It is instructive that it felt obliged to defend itself, but it also felt free to print,

As the following speech has not only been printed singly and distributed into a multitude of hands, but has also been offered to the public in several newspapers, it is thought proper by many impartial persons that our readers ought not to be deprived of satisfying their curiosity with the persual of it. We hope therefore that our inserting it in the place of our geography [article], for this week, cannot be construed to our disadvantage, as favouring any particular interest or party. Let the speech and sentiments which it contains, recommend or condemn themselves; we do neither, but leave both to the judgment of the public; and shall, as soon as we can obtain it, offer in like manner the reply to it, according to that impartiality which we have taken upon us to maintain.[56]

The reason for the increased press freedom in the reporting of Parliament is unclear. Much depends upon the interpretation of the last years of the Walpole ministry. The limited governmental response to the opposition propaganda offensive in 1738–41 can be presented as a result of ministerial exhaustion, but it could equally be suggested that ministerial success in surmounting over a decade of serious opposition attacks had bred both a certain confidence and a feeling that the impact of the press and of public opinion was limited. The opposition had admitted their impotence in 1739 by the secession of their members from the Commons, whilst the failure of the February 1741 motion for the dismissal of Walpole from George II's presence and counsels for ever revealed divisions between the opposition Whigs and the Tories.

A pragmatic awareness of the difficult and often counter-productive nature of press prosecutions may also have played its part. The prosecutions of the 1720s and early 1730s were closely associated with two men, Sir Philip Yorke, Attorney-General from 1724 to 1733, and Charles Delafaye, an Under-Secretary from 1717 to 1734. Delafaye in particular had considerable knowledge of the press, having served as Writer of the *Gazette* from 1702 to 1707. In the 1720s, he kept the opposition press under close surveillance.[57] Neither Yorke's replacements, Sir John Willes (1734–7) and

[55] *Daily Gazetteer*, 23 June (os) 1739; Cranfield, *Provincial Newspaper*, p. 162.
[56] *Newcastle Journal*, 7, 14 June (os) 1740.
[57] Delafaye to Stanhope, 16, 20 Oct. (os), 3, 6 Nov. (os) 1719, Delafaye to Townshend, 25 June, (os) 19, 26 July (os), 6, 30 Aug. (os), 13 Sept. 1723, PRO. SP. 43/63, 66, 67: Delafaye to Poyntz, 27 Feb. (os) 1729, BL. Add. 75451.

Sir Dudley Ryder (1734–54), nor Delafaye's, Andrew Stone (1734–51), also an MP from 1741 until 1761, displayed comparable interest in the press. Willes struck a definite note for caution in 1734. Asked for his advice on a specific issue of the *Craftsman* by Newcastle, he replied,

prosecutions of this sort ought to be avoided as much as possible. For papers of this kind, if not taken notice of, seldom survive the week, and fall into very few hands; but when a prosecution is commenced, everybody is enquiring after them, and they are then read by thousands, who otherwise would never have heard of them. Besides upon trials of this sort, His Majesty's enemies always take an opportunity of spiriting up the mob against the Government . . .

Ryder as a young man used to read and discuss newspapers in coffee-houses, while Willes had been caught 'scribbling libels' during Anne's reign.[58] Of Stone's colleagues as Under-Secretaries, George Tilson, Edward Weston, John Couraud and Thomas Stanhope, none displayed Delafaye's interest in press surveillance. Couraud feared that a prosecution of the *Daily Post* in 1738 would simply revive its sales, and observed 'it is difficult to know how to deal with those fellows . . .'[59] Pragmatic considerations, coupled with the different attitudes of a new generation, can be seen behind the decrease in government action in the 1740s. Henry Pelham responded to suggestions in 1747 that the Commons act against reporting of their proceedings with the reported phrase, 'Let them alone; they make better speeches for us, than we can make ourselves.'[60]

This attitude did not mean that the government completely abdicated from its role as supervisor of the press. Ministerially sponsored and funded newspapers appeared, especially Henry Fielding's *True Patriot* and his *Jacobite's Journal*. Moves were made against particularly virulent opposition newspapers, such as the *National Journal or Country Gazette*, a tri-weekly with Jacobite sympathies suppressed in June 1746 within three months of its launch. There is also evidence of attempts to restrict the publication of parliamentary debates. In December 1742, the vociferous opposition weekly the *Westminster Journal* noted: 'My last paper has produced a very strong representation against the liberty I have taken of inserting any proceedings of the worthy society of INDEPENDENT SCALD-MISERABLE-MASONS, but more especially against the impropriety of publishing any speeches

[58] Willes to Newcastle, 23 Dec. (os) 1734, PRO. 33/33 f. 147; Transcripts from the shorthand journal of Dudley Ryder, 12 July, (os) 6 Sept. (os), 3, 28 Dec. (os) 1715, Sandon Hall, Staffordshire. The items cited were omitted from the published edition of the journal; H. Walpole, *Memoirs of George II*, ed. J. Brooke (3 vols., New Haven, 1985), I, 111.
[59] Couraud to Waldegrave, 4 Sept. (os) 1738, Chewton.
[60] W. Coxe, *Memoirs of the administration of the Right Honourable Henry Pelham* (2 vols., 1829), I, 354–5.

made to that august body.'[61] In addition, the publication of recent parliamentary debates in book form led to the imprisonment of the printer.[62]

The relative laxity of the government approach to printing clearly did not suit all ministerial figures. In 1744, the Lord Chancellor, Philip, Lord Hardwicke, who had, as Sir Philip Yorke, been Attorney General, apparently on his own initiative, attempted, without success, to use the press in order to restrain the reporting of parliamentary news. His attempt can be documented to an unusual extent. The relevant documents consist of three letters from Thomas Harris, an agent of Hardwicke's, to Hardwicke and a draft item for the *Gazette*. No reply from Hardwicke survives. The first letter was sent on 12 July (os) 1744,

I have punctually obeyed your commands, and I hope, executed them to your mind; I went in the first place to the Printer of the "General Evening Post" and he did not care to insert your paper, Sir, because the authors of the magazines and he are friends, and was afraid it would prejudice him in his business at the same time. From hence I went to the "Daily Advertiser" and left it there with eight shillings, but the printer of the paper could not assure me that the author would permit the insertion of your letter until he had seen it, but added that he thought matters did not stand so nicely without the author as to make him refuse it, since the truth of what yours contained was but too notorious. However, Sir, if I find tomorrow that it is not inserted (for he told me it should be approved) I will go and take it from the printer's hands and will be careful, and expeditous to get it into some of the other papers if possible.[63]

Two days later, Harris wrote again

I am very sorry that the account I am going to send you is different to that you have already received; for when I went, the morning after I left the Paper with the Printer of the Daily Advertiser, (not seeing it inserted as I expected and wished) to enquire what was the reason of his not printing it; he told me that the author was afraid that the Magazine Gentleman would be displeased, and that they might proceed against him to his detriment, and therefore thought it best not to meddle with the affair. So that of five papers I have tried, not one of them is willing to insert it

The General Evening Post
Daily Advertiser
Daily Post
Champion
and Daily Gazetteer[64]

---

[61] *Westminster Journal*, 11 Dec. (os) 1742.
[62] William Bentinck to the Dowager-Duchess of Portland, 21 Mar. (os) 1741, BL. Egerton Mss 1712 fol. 212.
[63] Harris to Hardwicke, 12 July (os) 1744, BL. Add. 35587 fol. 263.
[64] Harris to Hardwicke, 14 July (os) 1744, BL. Add. 35587 fol. 264.

Judging from Harris's next letter, Hardwicke told him to approach Edward Owen, who had printed the *Gazette* since 1734. Owen made it clear that he would do nothing unless instructed by the Secretaries of State, Carteret and Newcastle.[65] Harris enclosed with his last letter the item he had attempted to place in the *Gazette*:

To the author of the Gazette.
Sir,

The unjustifiable Liberty, which has for some time been taken by the Compilers of the Magazines, of publishing for the most part without the least authority, and in direct contradiction to the Resolutions of both Houses of Parliament, what they are pleased to style accounts of the Debates and Proceedings there, is at last grown to so scandalous an excess, as to call aloud for a Remedy. To go no further back, then the last London Magazine, (tho by no means intend to exclude his worthy rival of St. John's Gate) the Performances which its authors have thought fit to give the Public, under the names of three Honourable Persons, are so far from bearing the least mark of authenticity, that I have been assured by some who were present in the House during the whole Debate, and took notes of the Principal Heads of it, there is not a single expression or turn of thought, which those Gentlemen really used, and many things ascribed to them, which they would be ashamed to own. This is a Licence taken with an assembly of the highest Authority in the Kingdom, which the lowest Court of Judicature would punish with severity. That such dull and impudent Forgeries should be published every month uncensured, is indeed so incredible, that it is not to be wondered, if people at a distance from London are so generally imposed upon by them, and mistake the forced Declamations of miserable Garreteers, for the masterly eloquence of the greatest men in the nation.

The Injury this does to the characters of the Gentlemen, and the ill consequences these lessons of Politicks may have upon the public, induce me to believe a Piece of news, which I have from very good hands, that several members of the first distinction are determined to attempt the supressing of this insolent practice by authority of the Legislature at their next meeting.

Whites July 27th 1744   I am Sir
                                    Yours
                                    A.Z.[66]

The threat of parliamentary action against the *London Magazine* and its 'worthy rival of St. John's Gate', the *Gentleman's Magazine*, reveals that Hardwicke lacked Pelham's tolerant attitude. Indeed, in February 1739, he had made in the Lords 'an excellent speech to explain the true meaning of the liberty of the press, which he said he found was not at all generally

---

[65] Harris to Hardwicke, 28 July (os) 1744, BL. Add. 35587 fol. 268.
[66] A. Z. to the *Gazette*, 27 July (os) 1744, BL. Add. 35587 fol. 269.

understood, that it was not a liberty to defame and libel, but that it was opposed to previous restraints put upon the press, as had been formerly done by licencers and other methods.'[67]

Discerning such a middle way in practice was difficult, whatever the legal situation. It was particularly so in the case of parliamentary reporting where the privileges of the two Houses conflicted with a public appetite for news and comment. The relationship between Parliament and the press was a complex one, for it was not only opposition figures who sought to insert material in the press. For example, Thomas Sherlock, then Bishop of Bangor, sought to have the substance of a speech he had made in the Lords published in the *Daily Courant* in 1731.[68] In addition, as the obligation on the government to provide information to parliamentarians was limited, the latter were often forced to a variety of sources, particularly the press, to gain information, and they sometimes mentioned this in debate.[69]

The ministry had tried to employ the law against newspapers in the late 1710s, 1720s and early 1730s, and, although it had been successful in some respects, particularly in largely destroying the Jacobite press, the difficulties of using the law had been amply revealed. Reasonably effective against those whose ideology was clearly different from Court Whiggery, the law was of limited use in the high-political conflicts of the late 1730s and 1740s which centered around the attempt by one group of Whigs to supplant the 'Old Corps' Whigs through parliamentary means. Similarly, the major commitment of the ministry to the press in 1742–8 was in financing Fielding's newspapers which sought to confront and benefit from the Jacobite challenge. In political terms, the Pelhamite decision not to use the legal tactics of the 1720s against the press was a sensible one. To do so would have been to provide issues over which Tories and opposition Whigs, a dangerous political combination, could unite.

The net effect was to leave contemporaries and historians with more information about parliamentary debates than would otherwise have been the case. Possibly the ministry was simply prepared to accept press abuse and reporting as one of the tribulations of office, rather as they accepted opposition in Parliament. A similar attitude was revealed, in 1753, by Joseph Yorke, an MP and one of Hardwicke's sons, when he commented on Henry Fox's attack on his father in the Commons, 'all the dirt he can throw upon that Person, will never stick, though it may bespatter himself'.[70]

[67] Frances Hare, Bishop of Chichester, to Francis Naylor, 15 Feb. (os) 1739, HMC. *Hare Mss*, p. 43.
[68] Sherlock to Weston, 1, 8 May (os) 1731, Iden Green, Kent, papers of Edward Weston.
[69] Cobbett, IX, 699, 701, XIII, 479–80, 7 Feb. (os) 1735, 18 Jan. (os) 1744.
[70] Yorke to Hugh Jones, Under-Secretary in the Northern Department, 8 June 1753, BL. Add. 35432 fol. 90. For Fox's attacks on Hardwicke, Walpole, *Memoirs of George II*, I, 228–9, 233–5.

The mid-1740s was a period when opinion 'out of doors' had singularly little impact on parliamentary majorities. Hardwicke's attempt to insert a warning in 1744 would therefore seem to reflect an attitude no longer common within the ministry. Suppressing reporting 'by authority of the legislature' was not the method supported by Pelham, who would probably have agreed with the first, though not the second, part of a reflection by the experienced diplomat and MP Benjamin Keene in 1739, 'I find by experience that he who cannot despise noise is not fit for a public employment. But let him despise it as much as he pleases it must disgust him at the long run and make him weary of public business.'[71]

The most significant action against press reporting of parliamentary debates did not occur as a result of ministerial action. Parliament appointed printers to print items such as the Addresses, and, in 1747, these printers, angry at what they regarded as an illegal infringement of their privileges, instigated action by the Lords against the printing of Jacobite treason trials conducted in that House. The printers of the *Gentleman's* and *London* magazines were brought before the Lords and only released on condition they did not repeat the offence. Action was also taken against the *Ipswich Journal*. The effect of these moves was to induce caution into the provincial press, end parliamentary reporting in the *Gentleman's Magazine* until 1752, and end the attribution of speeches to individual members in the *London Magazine*.[72]

In mid-century, more leniency was shown to the magazines than newspapers in parliamentary reporting, and in 1760 four newspapers that breached the regulations were punished. In 1762, the Commons reaffirmed its right to control the publication of its proceedings, and printers were accordingly punished in 1764, 1765, 1767 and 1768. Paul Langford has referred to a striking paucity of sources for much of the 1750s and 1760s that, in part, 'reflects the failure of contemporary journalists to break through the secrecy and suspicion which marked the legislature's treatment of early parliamentary reporting'.[73] Nevertheless, the role of the Commons in expelling John Wilkes in 1764 and subsequently, in 1769, denying him election for Middlesex, the political *cause célèbre* of the age, made the newspapers more determined to report Parliament. This led, in 1771, to a clash in which the City of London gave shelter to printers who refused to answer

[71] Keene to Waldegrave, 23 Mar. 1739, Chewton.

[72] Cranfield, *Provincial Newspaper*, pp. 163–5. For the limited state of mid-century reporting, preface to Cobbett, XI.

[73] P. Langford, review of R. C. Simmons and P. D. G. Thomas (eds.), *Proceedings and Debates of the British Parliament Respecting North America 1754–1783*, vols. 1–2 (New York, 1982–3), *Parliamentary History*, 4 (1985), p. 238.

charges in the Commons. The clash between the two jurisdictions vindicated the Commons, but made the political dangers of suppressing reports of debates all too clear. From 1771, little attempt was made to limit reports, and they swiftly became a major feature of the newspapers. Press coverage of the Lords also became relatively easy, and therefore prominent, from 1775.[74]

Once papers had developed the practice of printing reports during the session, it was difficult to substitute other material speedily, it was easier to fill space by this means than by any other, and, after the papers had gone to the expense of obtaining parliamentary reports (for long the sole specialized reporters were the parliamentary ones), it was necessary to use the copy. However, a freedom to report debates did not necessarily mean that Parliament was kept informed by the government. Indeed, the sense of information as a weapon was captured by Lord North when, speaking about the French treaty with America, he told the Commons in 1778 'If it was in the interests of France to publish it, it was in the interests of England to conceal it'.[75]

The *Morning Chronicle* of 8 January 1787 stated that 'the first aim of the reporter of parliamentary debates in this paper is, and ever has been, to evince the most unquestionable impartiality and fairness'. Aware of the importance of a reputation for accuracy, newspapers competed to stress their reliability, although a candid note could be struck, as by the *Oracle* of 29 January 1795: 'The person who objects to our not having given Mr. Pitt's amendment on Mr. Grey's motion verbatim, will, however find that our account contains the substance and purport of it, which are all that can be expected in a daily paper'.

There were frequent charges of inaccuracy about the press reporting of Parliament, and the Gallery, which housed the reporters, was known as a place for drinking. In 1788, William Grenville told the Commons that 'newspaper misrepresentations of the proceedings of that House had of late been very frequently complained of'.[76] The following year, Lady Chatham distinguished between speech and report, but felt able to write on the basis of the latter: 'the opinion expressed by Mr. Fox (or at least that the newspapers make his)'. Canning argued that the *True Briton, Sun* and

[74] P. D. G. Thomas, 'The Beginnings of Parliamentary Reporting in the Newspapers, 1768–74', *English Historical Review*, 74 (1959), pp. 623–36, and 'John Wilkes and the Freedom of the Press (1771)', *Bulletin of the Institute of Historical Research*, 33 (1960), pp. 86–98; W. C. Lowe, 'Peers and Printers: the Beginning of Sustained Press Coverage of the House of Lords in the 1770s', *Parliamentary History*, 7 (1988), pp. 241–56.
[75] Cobbett, XIX, 912.   [76] Cobbett, XXVI, 1429.

Morning Herald provided the best accounts in 1794, but that the *Morning Chronicle* 'treats me ill on purpose'. In 1798, Tierney complained about a misrepresentation in the *Times*, although he made allowances for the errors arising from the need for haste in reporting. His complaint provided an opportunity for Pitt and Windham to argue that misrepresentation was a widespread problem.[77]

On the other hand, newspapers challenged this view, while, at the same time, revealing that they focused on leading speakers and subjects; an understandable preference but one that left open the question of the accuracy of their other coverage. The *Morning Post* of 4 January 1798 stated that its arrangements for reporting the debate of the previous night 'were made upon the supposition that Messrs. Fox, Pitt, and Sheridan would rise late, and we therefore reserved some of our reporters and a part of this paper for their speeches'. The *True Briton* of 2 February 1799 announced:

We have great satisfaction in having received from various quarters, and, particularly from several Members of Parliament, who were present at the debate on Thursday night, the highest commendations of our report of it; and particularly of Mr. Pitt's speech. Our reporters were peculiarly attentive to his statement, as we thought it essential that both Ireland and this country should know what were the precise grounds upon which it was intended the union should be established.

Sometimes, newspapers made it clear that they were providing a less than full coverage, and explained why. The *Public Advertiser* of 21 February 1792 chose not to report a debate over papers on the Ochakov affair as it felt it 'an uninteresting recapitulation of those arguments for and against confidence in ministers' that it had already repeatedly given.

The greater volume of newspaper reports provided more material for the compilers of parliamentary debates, but they were not the sole source. Many parliamentarians provided texts of their speeches or corrected those that were sent for emendation. Thus, William Shippen sent his speeches to the monthly *Political State of Great Britain*, Edward Cave, the founder of the *Gentleman's Magazine*, and its publisher until his death in 1754, took steps to have speakers check reports, and Cobbett noted that 'all the principal speeches which appear in this work' under the name of Sir Philip Francis 'were carefully corrected by himself'. Fox spoke without notes, but was sometimes willing to revise reports of his speeches for publication. John Debrett, the printer of the *Parliamentary Register*, provided Canning

---

[77] Lady Chatham to Edward Eliot, 18 July 1789, Belfast, Public Record Office of Northern Ireland, papers of Edward Gibson F2/17; P. Jupp (ed.), *Letter-Journal of George Canning*, p. 62; Cobbett, XXXIV, 148–55.

with copies of his speeches for correction. This led to differences between the accounts in the *Parliamentary Register* and those in the *Parliamentary History*.[78]

Some parliamentarians had their speeches printed in pamphlet form as Thomas Pownall did with his attacks on the government over the Falklands dispute. The role of the press did not lead to the end of the market for the publication of speeches in pamphlet form.[79] Thus, the pamphlet of Fox's *Speech ... in the House of Commons, 3rd of February 1800, on a motion for an address to the throne, approving of the refusal of ministers to treat with the French Republic* (1800) was reprinted at least twice that year. Pamphlets provided a completeness that appeared lacking in newspaper accounts. In 1784, for example, Debrett published a pamphlet of *Fox and Pitt's speeches in the House of Commons, on ... June 8, 1784. These speeches, which are an abridgement of all the arguments of both parties, upon the business of the Westminster Scrutiny ...*

Facilitating publication was an aspect of the more general process by which parliamentarians wrote accounts of debates for their own edification or, more usually, for the benefit of others. The best were those based on notes taken in the chambers, although parliamentarians rarely clarified the process by which they drew up their accounts. In 1730, however, Thomas Winnington recorded that he 'took notes' during Commons' debates in order to be able to send 'a particular account' to his friend Henry Fox. Sarah, Duchess of Marlborough had accounts of debates in Parliament sent her by parliamentarians and, on at least one occasion, 'an officer who belongs to the House of Lords'. Alexander Hume Campbell, MP for Berwickshire, sent his brother, Hugh, 3rd Earl of Marchmont, an account of his speech on 14 April (os) 1746 in favour of abolishing hereditary jurisdictions in Scotland, but added a caveat:

The substance as near as I can recollect it I have scrawled over as well as I am able and sent it to you by this post. You will do with it what you think proper and add or abridge what you please so as to quiet the minds of our friends.[80]

[78] A. Boyer, *The Political State if Great Britain* (60 vols., 1711–40), XXXVII, vii; Cobbett, preface to XI, and XXXIV, iii; L. D. Reid, *Charles James Fox. A Man for the People* (1969), p. 378; P. Jupp (ed.), *Letter-Journal of George Canning*, pp. 61, 63, 65, 176.

[79] *Two Speeches of an Honourable Gentleman on the late Negotiation and Convention with Spain* (1771). This was used as the source for the reports beginning on Cobbett, XVI, 1368 and 1385; Hayton, I, 26; Thorne, I, 369.

[80] Stephen to Henry Fox, 17 Jan. (os), 14 Feb. (os) 1730, BL. Add. 51417 fols. 34, 38–40; C. Jones and F. Harris, '"A Question ... Carried by Bishops, Pensioners, Placemen, Idiots": Sarah Duchess of Marlborough and the Lords' Division over the Spanish Convention, 1 March 1739', *Parliamentary History*, 11 (1992), pp. 258–9; HMC. *Polwarth V* (1961), p. 237.

The account of the Lords' debate on the Address on 9 January 1770 published by Cobbett 'was taken by a gentleman, who afterwards made a distinguished figure in the House of Commons; and by him it has been obligingly revised for this work'. The same source provided other accounts.[81] Sending accounts for publication represented an attempt to ensure an accurate record, as well as an appeal for support to contemporaries and posterity.

Press reports were treated as accurate by some parliamentarians, not least when they wanted to criticise opponents, although also when they made reference to speeches in letters to correspondents. John Campbell recorded in December 1742: 'Mr. Carew had got a magazine in which Mr. Sandys' speech upon the motion for removing Sir Robert Walpole from His Majesty's person and councils was printed. He held it in his hand and read most of it very distinctly as part of his own speech.'[82] Thus, the hypocrisy of Samuel Sandys, a former opposition Whig, who had bitterly attacked Walpole in April 1741, but who now, as Chancellor of the Exchequer, had voted against reviving the secret committee established to investigate the Walpole ministry, could be clearly demonstrated by Thomas Carew, Tory MP for Minehead. Later that month, John Tucker informed his brother that he had been greatly impressed by the debates on the Hanoverian subsidies, adding 'I shall not endeavour to particularise them because I expect one side at least of them if not both will be soon in print from whence you will see what has been said'. Seventeen months later, however, Tucker struck a different note:

I am with you equally surprised at the publication of our Weymouth affairs in the Magazine and am at a loss to find out the reason for it . . . The author is mistaken in the setting out of the debate for it was begun by Lord Romney and Lord Aylesford, Lord Talbot spoke but once and that speech was not longer than the first that is there given him. The Chancellor's speech may be pretty near what he said in this 2d speech of Lord Talbot. There is a good deal of what was said by others.

Campbell found himself misrepresented in 1740:

Upon your telling me that I had the name of C. Calpurnius Piso from the Appendix to the London Magazine I bought that pamphlet, and there I found a speech under that name, but indeed my dear they have mended it so much that I can by no means call it mine, I can only acknowledge one sentence vis: nothing can be honourable that is not just, and no war can be just that is not necessary. This they have transposed, and introduced it in a very different manner from what I did for

---

[81] Cobbett, XVI, 647, 741, 1091.   [82] John to Pryse Campbell, 2 Dec. (os) 1742, Cawdor, Box 138.

I was not so sanguine in my expectations of the Spaniards doing us justice as C. Calpurnius Piso seems to be.[83]

There were also more positive views. In 1775, Horace Walpole wrote of 'the newspapers, which are now very accurate in recounting debates';[84] although he had ceased to be an MP in 1768. In 1787, Henry Addington sent his father both a letter and two *Morning Chronicles* in order to meet his interest in the Warren Hastings' debates. William Coxe, a thorough scholar, concluded that the printed accounts available in 1798 were in general accurate. He came to this conclusion as a result of reported comments to this effect by Sir Robert Walpole and William Pulteney, a comparison between printed accounts and available manuscript sources, and a consideration of the means by which the magazines acquired their reports.[85] Since 1798, these magazine accounts have been supplemented by the printing of additional sources, as well as the making available of important manuscript collections, for example the correspondence of Campbell and Tucker. As a consequence, it is now possible to have a fuller picture of the debates, while, in addition, the accuracy of individual accounts may be more readily checked.

It is still the case that there are significant gaps, for example for the period 1747–53, which is also when the debate in print over foreign policy appears to have been lacking in vigour, and for 1757–68.[86] In addition, comparisons between surviving accounts and what was reported as the length of speeches suggest that there are still major discrepancies and that verbatim accounts of what was said were not provided.[87] Major speeches were frequently long. Lord North, for example, spoke for one and three-quarter hours in the Commons' debate on 17 February 1783 on the peace at the end of the War of American Independence, and Stormont spoke for two hours the same day in the Lords. Fox spoke for two and a half hours four days later.[88] Printed accounts do not always measure up to what could be anticipated

---

[83] John to Richard Tucker, 14 Dec. (os) 1742, 10 Apr. (os) 1744, Bod. Ms. Don. c. 105 fol. 197, 107 fol. 24; John to Pryse Campbell, 3 Apr. (os) 1740, Cawdor, 138.

[84] Horace Walpole to Countess of Upper Ossory, 1 Feb. 1775, W. S. Lewis (ed.), *The Yale Edition of Horace Walpole's Correspondence* (48 vols., New Haven, 1937–83), XXXII, 235.

[85] Anthony to Henry Addington, 15 Feb. 1787, 152M/C 1787/F13; W. Coxe, *Memoirs of the Life and Administration of Sir Robert Walpole, Earl of Orford* (3 vols., 1798) I, xxxxii. See also preface to Cobbett, XI.

[86] K.W. Schweizer, *Statesmen, Diplomats and the Press – Essays on 18th Century Britain* (Lewiston, 2002), p. 55. See, however, for example, the valuable account by Sir James Caldwell in K. W. Schweizer, 'The Bedford Motion and House of Lords Debate 5 February 1762', *Parliamentary History*, 5 (1986), pp. 107–23.

[87] Thomas, 'Beginnings of Parliamentary Reporting', pp. 632–4.

[88] George, Viscount Althorp MP to his mother, Countess Spencer, 17 Feb. 1783, George, 4th Earl of Jersey to same, 17 Feb., Charles, 1st Earl of Lucan to same, 21 Feb., BL. Add. 75689.

from such timing, in large part because reporters did not have enough space until the 1820s to reproduce speeches verbatim,[89] although, in addition, the speed of speaking varied, and rhetorical flourishes were best delivered in a stately fashion.

Parliamentary sources are best for periods of volatility and marked tension. It was then that parliamentarians were both most likely to attend and most likely to report on proceedings, or at least to seek to supplement the printed sources. It was also then that these sources were likely to be most comprehensive as the pressure of public interest was strongest. It would be misleading to expect an unvarying degree of activity, interest or treatment.

[89] Thorne, I, 369.

7

Character and quality of parliamentary discussion

I look upon the several princes of Germany at this juncture as to many
Members of Parliament. Almost all have their private interest in view,
few regard the general good of the [Holy Roman] Empire.[1]

Despite William Sturrock's observation, and the fact that most parliamentarians did not speak in foreign policy debates, many, in both Houses,
had opinions on foreign policy and were not simply manoeuvring to their
personal or factional advantage. As Parliament was the public forum in
which the ministry formally presented and defended its policy, and also
was criticised in a fashion that obliged it to reply, it was Parliament where
the public debate over foreign policy can be seen as most intense and most
effective. There was an obligation to respond to criticism that was lacking
in the world of print, and also an immediate linkage between the debates
and the taking of decisions, the debates themselves being occasioned by
the discussion of these very decisions. Nevertheless, as the writer George
Gordon asked in 1741, 'how shall gentlemen be judges of the conduct of
our ministers, with regard to foreign affairs, unless they understand, as far
as possible for one in a private station, the interests and views of foreign
nations, and attend to every public transaction that happens in Europe'.[2]

The provision of information and opinion in the debates by ministers
and diplomats, present and past, was crucial to this understanding. In
February 1735, during the War of the Polish Succession, at a time when the
government was uncertain about how best to respond to Bourbon successes
against Austria, Sir Robert Walpole felt able to defend its unwillingness to
say much in Parliament by referring to public knowledge:

When facts are notoriously known to the whole world, where consequences are
obvious to every man of common capacity, surely gentlemen do not expect that

---

[1] Sturrock to Richard Neville Aldworth, 19 Dec. 1740, Chelmsford, Essex, CRO., D/D By C1.
[2] G. Gordon, *The Annals of Europe for the Year 1739*, II (1741), p. iii.

His Majesty, either in his speech, or by particular message, should give this House a long and particular detail of such fact or consequences: the bare mention is enough, and that His Majesty has sufficiently done.

In 1783, when peace terms were to be debated in Parliament, Thomas, Lord Grantham, the Foreign Secretary, and, himself, a former envoy, felt able, when writing to the 3rd Earl of Harrington, to assume that it would be possible for the latter to speak without the information Grantham was happy to provide:

As it is of the utmost consequence that the consideration of the Preliminaries in the House of Lords should be opened and supported by peers of the most independent and respectable characters and abilities, I cannot address myself with more propriety than to your Lordship in hoping that you will undertake to move or support an address, which, agreeably to the usual forms, will accompany that deliberation. Should your Lordship do me the honour to wish for any information from me on this important subject, I should have the greatest satisfaction in communicating to your Lordship without reserve everything which is within my knowledge.[3]

Despite the mass of information and opinion available to the public about international affairs, much of it in the press, one of the most valuable points to emerge from a consideration of parliamentary correspondence is the uncertainty of parliamentarians concerning likely developments. This uncertainty was most marked in times of war, reflecting the general volatility of these periods, but was in no way restricted to them. Uncertainty was particularly acute for ministers, who needed to know what to tell Parliament at the beginning of each session.[4]

This uncertainty throws light on the public, particularly printed, debate over policy which can suggest a false clarity over policy, in which diplomatic and military strategies were apparently predetermined by partisan political traditions, the weight of history interacting to this end with specific and clashing partisan viewpoints. Thus, particular views could readily be regarded as Tory, Whig, Country or Patriot, and could be associated with distinct policies.

Such an analysis, however, was (and is) misleading, and was usually employed to serve partisan points, frequently in terms of arguments about consistency or, more commonly, inconsistency. In fact, the striking feature of much parliamentary correspondence is the extent to which it was by no means clear to parliamentarians what policy would be followed, or how

---

[3] Cobbett, IX, 712; Grantham to Harrington, 12 Feb. 1783, Bedford, CRO., Lucas papers, 30/14/363/1.
[4] Chavigny to Chauvelin, 24 Dec. 1735, AE. CP. Ang. 392 fol. 226.

policies and policy options were related to political groups. This was most apparent at points of discontinuity, which were both domestic (changes in ministry) and international (the outbreak of war and the negotiations for peace).

A consideration of the most apparently consistent group, the Tories, reveals the extent to which their attitudes towards foreign policy were, in fact, affected by circumstances. These, both international and domestic, were considerably more unpredictable and volatile than the discourse of national interests on the international scale, and the debate over Court and Country, Whig and Tory, on its domestic counterpart, might suggest. As a consequence, it is not surprising that positions shifted. This has been concealed by the habit of discussing the public debate in general terms and over a broad sweep, so that it becomes, in large part, a question of 'Blue Water' versus Continental interventionism, a rift supposedly healed to brilliant effect in the late 1750s by Pitt's policy of conquering America in Germany. Such an interpretation fails both to note the shifts and discontinuities within the debate, and to place sufficient weight on them, not least in terms of their relationship with domestic and international developments. If, in 1717, Tory MPs praised Charles XII of Sweden and said that his fall would jeopardise 'the Balance [of Power] in the North' and British trade in the Baltic,[5] they did so essentially because they sought to oppose what was presented as a Hanoverian tilt to British policy, rather than because of any interest in Sweden. Indeed, in 1739, Newcastle drew attention to major changes in opposition arguments over the previous five years, which, with reason, he attributed to the opposition's determination always to oppose governmental policy.[6]

Such remarks focus attention on the neglected topic of the quality of parliamentary discussion of foreign policy. Comments on this issue are scanty. Without explaining the basis for his statement, J. R. Jones claimed in 1980 that 'wilful misrepresentation of facts, sensationalism and pandering to popular prejudices, partisanship and appeals to xenophobia characterised most parliamentary debates'. Referring to the response to the Quadruple Alliance in 1718, Graham Gibbs stated, 'The debates in Parliament added little to the existing public discussion except heat.' When studying Commons' debates, Sir John Fortescue was 'absolutely nauseated by their hollowness and cant'. More generally, it has been argued that 'by definition both formally and informally, the legislative approach to foreign affairs is more partisan

---

[5] Perceval note on Commons' debate on 8 Mar. (os) 1717, BL. Add. 47028 fol. 183.
[6] 15 Nov. (os) 1739, Cobbett XI, 29–30.

and less intellectual than the executive approach'.[7] Many sources, however, particularly newspapers and magazines, certainly or probably simplified the arguments in Parliament in order to present two clear-cut positions, and deliberately stressed rhetorical stances (the 'sensationalism' noted by Jones) at the expense of cautious discussion, and the use of other evidence.

It is difficult to evaluate the quality of debate in eighteenth-century Parliaments, not only because of the scanty nature of the surviving evidence, discussed in the previous chapter, but also because conventions of behaviour and speech, as well as standards of argument and proof were different, and indeed developed, not least as Parliament became a more regular feature of the political system. Speeches that may appear reasonable today were not always acceptable to many contemporaries. Partisanship appears to have been more interesting to many than detail. George, Viscount Althorp MP reported of the debate on the peace preliminaries at the end of the War of American Independence:

Mr. Powys has made a speech against the resolution which tends to censure the peace, in which he again exercised his wit on the state of parties and brought up Lord John [Cavendish] who entered into a full vindication of his creed and conduct very warmly . . . and now Mr. Richard Sutton has put an end to the warmth by entering into the detail of the peace without being much listened to by the House.

Thomas Powys, MP for Northamptonshire 1774–97, was unlike most country gentlemen in being a powerful and effective speaker. Sutton, MP for Sandwich, a Lord of the Treasury under North, and an opponent of the preliminaries, was an able man, who had considerable knowledge of foreign affairs: the son of a diplomat, he had been an Under-Secretary, first in the Southern and then in the Northern Department, from 1766 until 1772.

Humphrey Minchin, MP for Okehampton and a Foxite opponent both of North and of the peace preliminaries, provided another clue to what was considered desirable when he wrote of debates in the Lords 'carried on with a spirit and cleverness' lacking in the Commons. He was soon, however, able to comment on better speeches. Minchin reported of the debate on 21 February 1783 that Charles James Fox started with

the question of the peace which deviated as many others had done into the causes, reasons and consequences of the late ministerial changes and those which were likely

---

[7] J. R. Jones, *Britain and the World, 1649–1815* (1980); G. C. Gibbs, 'Parliament and the Treaty of Quadruple Alliance', in R. M. Hatton and J. S. Bromley (eds.), *William III and Louis XIV Essays 1680–1720 by and for Mark A. Thomson* (Liverpool, 1968), p. 301; H. Strachen, *The Politics of the British Army* (Oxford, 1997), p. 6; J. N. Rosenau, 'Private Preference and Political Responsibilities: The Relative Potency of Individual and Role Variables in the Behaviour of U.S. Senators', in J. D. Singer (ed.), *Quantitative International Politics: Insights and Evidence* (New York, 1968), p. 49.

now to follow. A babbler or two then followed before Pitt rose who began as Fox had done by sticking close to the arguments for the Peace from the comparative view of the state of this country and that of her enemies in navy, army and finance. He then came into the ministerial debate following and combating Mr. Fox's arguments stating his own conduct and that of his friends, painting the ill consequences he foresaw from the change attacking vehemently Lord North but concluding with a very fine and pathetic description of his own sentiments and feelings as to being in or out of office. Upon the whole both as to matter of business and flow of eloquence at the last I think one of his most capital performances. Lord North is now speaking in reply, confuting his arguments and showing that a union between the two parties now supposed to be on the point of uniting is the most likely to effect that harmony and strength which can alone give hopes or probability of a firm and stable administration . . . Mr. Secretary Townshend is now speaking with his usual perspicuity and elegance,[8]

the last a reference to Thomas Townshend, MP for Whitchurch and Home Secretary. During the Shelburne ministry, he was the leading government spokesman in the Commons, and, in defending the preliminaries, argued that the terms were the best way to maintain good relations with the Americans. Townshend also argued that the lands ceded to France and Spain were not crucial possessions.

Powys was unusual. Most country gentlemen were less competent and active in debate. Many indeed rarely or never spoke, and they had their counterparts in the Lords. This led to a certain amount of disdain, expressed, for example, by Thomas Villiers, envoy to Augustus II of Saxony-Poland, and later first MP for Tamworth and then a peer, initially as Lord Hyde and eventually as Earl of Clarendon; Villiers wrote to his brother, the 3rd Earl of Jersey, in 1745:

The independent country gentleman (I speak as I suppose you did without meaning any individual) must not take it amiss if those, labouring for the public good, don't always give the great attention he thinks his lamentations deserve: I look upon him as one of the happiest animals, when he keeps himself clear of politics; but if once infected, he is more miserable than if he had the plague, he is almost incurable . . . The interests of states and princes, and the care of preserving and destroying of birds and beasts (which is properly his department) are occupations of no connection; and a man taking up a 11 hours and $\frac{3}{4}$ out of the 12 that he don't sleep by the latter can be but a very incompetent judge of the former. The few confused notions he can collect only perplexes his mind, and make him more wretched than a valetudinarian with a smattering of physick or anatomy. His first step towards recovery is to have recourse to somebody more skilfull than himself,

[8] Althorp to Countess Spencer, 19 Feb., Minchin to same, 18, 21 Feb. 1783, BL. Add. 75689. For Powys's ability and reputation, P. Jupp (ed.), *The Letter-Journal of George Canning, 1793–1795*, (1991), p. 56.

and to let nature alone, which is the humble advice I offer to your independent country gentleman.[9]

Given such attitudes, it is scarcely surprising that independent parliamentarians could be very suspicious of government policy, as well as resentful of its presentation. Villiers was reflecting the approach taken by Carteret, whose department he had served in.

Given the difficulty of establishing what was said in Parliament and of assessing its relevance to contemporaries, it might be suggested that it is futile to judge the quality of the speeches. However, the neglect of this issue also reflects a historiographical difficulty. Most British political historians lack the detailed knowledge of foreign policy and international relations that would enable them to assess the degree of knowledge and the sophistication of analysis displayed by speakers. Furthermore, most diplomatic historians lack the necessary knowledge of domestic history, and, in particular, of parliamentary practices.

More serious is the relative neglect of the issue by these historians. There is a tendency to present foreign policy in a monolithic interpretation in which the actors are the 'British', 'French' *et al.* and either to ignore or to simplify the diplomatic consequences of domestic pressures. In contrast to the ordered series of diplomatic papers, the material for assessing domestic pressures is diffuse, fragmentary and difficult to judge. Another inevitable problem is the subjectivity implicit in any assessment of quality.

In assessing speeches, it is necessary not only to have an understanding of the conventions of parliamentary behaviour and debate, and the factors affecting the surviving record, but also an ability to assess the circumstances of the day, including the relationship between speakers and the topography of the chambers,[10] and, more significantly, the political context. For example, William Pitt the Elder's speeches are frequently cited by historians without any understanding of context. Instead, it is necessary to appreciate the political strategies motivating Pitt's expression of views on foreign and military policy, and the way in which these views responded to specific conjunctures, which were, moreover, more those of domestic politics than of the international system, although the latter also changed greatly and frequently during his period in politics.

The discussion of Pitt the Elder is an instance of a more general failure in which domestic politics and foreign policy specialists simplify issues

---

[9] Villiers to Jersey, 19 July 1745, London, Greater London Record Office, Acc. 510/219.
[10] C. Wilkinson, 'Politics and Topography in the Old House of Commons, 1783–1834', in C. Jones and S. Kelsey (eds.), *Housing Parliament. Dublin, Edinburgh and Westminster* (Edinburgh, 2002), pp. 154–6.

and pressures in the other sphere. The explanatory process thus breaks down or atomizes. Furthermore, an underrating of the external or internal implications of policy decisions and debates ensures a difficulty in assessing their consequences.

One of the more impressive features of parliamentary debates was the knowledge of international relations displayed by some parliamentarians. Expert opinion could be presented in Parliament. Both chambers contained several diplomats or former diplomats, and some of these contributed their knowledge to the debates. In 1728, Horatio Walpole began his Commons' speech in defence of the maintenance of the size of the army, a step seen as crucial to sustaining Britain's international position, by 'an account of the proceedings of several courts of Europe and the ministers employed at them'. In the debate on the Address in November 1742, Edward Finch gave 'an account of all his negotiations, and the interest as well as the views of every court in Europe'.[11] Expertise was clearly valued by parliamentarians. In 1770, Hans Stanley observed 'Death has thinned our ranks in the House of Commons, I think unfortunately, for Mr. [George] Grenville was a great repertory of knowledge, though in my opinion he did not prove an able minister when he was tried, or at least his measures were unsuccessful.'[12]

Not all who had been diplomats revealed the same knowledge or made an equal contribution, while diplomat parliamentarians, such as Thomas Robinson in the early 1730s, were frequently out of the country. William Blathwayt, Secretary at War from 1683 until 1704, acting Secretary of State in 1692–1701, and a MP in 1685–7 and 1693–1710, was a crucial figure in military and diplomatic administration, but he was never prominent in Parliament and made only brief interventions in debate.[13] William, 1st Earl of Harrington, a Secretary of State in 1730–42 and 1744–6, and earlier a successful envoy to Spain, was not prominent in the Commons in 1715–22 and 1727–30, much of which period he was abroad. However, from 1730, when he was in Britain for most of the time, he also did not take a role in the Lords comparable to that of Carteret, a former diplomat, nor of his colleague as Secretary of State, Newcastle, who lacked any experience of foreign diplomacy. Chavigny thought Carteret very well informed when he

[11] HMC. *The Diary of the First Earl of Egmont* (3 vols., 1920–3), III, 338; Duncan Forbes MP to John Forbes, 1 Feb. (os) 1729, H. Duff (ed.), *Culloden Papers* (1815), p. 104; Henry Finch MP to Lord Malton, 18 Nov. (os) 1742, Sheffield, Public Library, Wentworth Woodhouse papers M3-122; Thorne, I, 298.

[12] Stanley to Countess Spencer, 18 Nov. 1770, BL. Add. 75688. For the contrast between oratory at the bar and in Parliament, H. Walpole, *Memoirs of the Reign of King George III*, ed., D. Jarrett (4 vols., New Haven, 2000), II, 198.

[13] Hayton, III, 237.

discussed German developments with him in 1732. This was not simply a matter of past knowledge from Carteret's period in office, as he was also able to complain about current Bavarian policy.[14] On the other hand, Chavigny felt that Bolingbroke's Tory colleagues lacked his ability to explain foreign developments; and the government's refusal to let Bolingbroke sit in the Lords when he was allowed to return to Britain deprived Parliament of a major talent.[15]

A lack of contribution to debate did not mean an absence of informed opinion. Richard, 1st Viscount Cobham, who had spent six months in Vienna in 1714–15 as envoy, did not make an impression in Parliament comparable to that of Daniel Pulteney, who had been envoy in Copenhagen in 1706–15 and was active as an opposition Whig in debates on foreign policy in 1726–30, or Philip, 4th Earl of Chesterfield, who was envoy at The Hague in 1728–32. Both Carteret and Chesterfield spoke in the Lords' debate on the Convention of the Pardo in 1739. Yet, Cobham's letter to Newcastle in December 1743 explaining the resignation of his commission, reveals that his opposition to Hanoverian commitments was not derived from ignorance or xenophobia. He wrote of:

the extreme difficulty and hazard of supporting the Queen of Hungary [Maria Theresa] by an English army in Upper Germany, or of attacking France in her almost impenetrable barrier of Alsace, Lorraine, or the Netherlands, without the concurrence of the Dutch upon the foot of the last war. The first of these cases existed last year, and the last in the natural course of events must be the question for the ensuing campaign . . . I cannot say, as things are circumstanced, that it is fit for this country to engage in making conquests on the Continent, I mean upon France, for I know no other ground where our army can set their feet but on her territories, unless they will avowedly remain in a state of inaction. Things appearing to me in this light, I must give my opinion against all measures which naturally lead us to take so dangerous a step unsupported as we seem to be at present . . . I have already felt severe marks of His Majesty's displeasure for differing in opinion with his ministers in Parliament.[16]

Cobham's assessment was a reasoned one, based on a grasp of Britain's military and diplomatic position, and it was to be vindicated by the campaign of 1744 when it became rapidly apparent that talk of the prospects for a successful invasion of eastern France was misplaced.

It was not only those who had served as diplomats or generals who could offer informed opinions in Parliament. Robert Harley, a formidably

[14] Chavigny to Chauvelin, 11 Feb. 1732, AE. CP. Ang. 376 fol. 219. For earlier praise, Destouches to Dubois, 23 Nov. 1718, AE. CP. Ang. 311 fol. 60.
[15] Chavigny to Chauvelin, 13 Apr. 1732, AE. CP. Ang. 377 fol. 51.
[16] Cobham to Newcastle, 9 Dec. (os) 1743, BL. Add. 35587 fol. 205.

detailed parliamentarian, acquired considerable expertise on diplomatic negotiations. William Pulteney was able to discuss international developments intelligently with Chavigny. Lord North, then Chancellor of the Exchequer, provided an assessment of French finances when he told the Commons in April 1769 that France was not in a state to go to war with Britain.[17] Material from the offices of the Secretaries of State and, later, the Foreign Secretary could be used to prepare other ministers for debates, as in 1790 when Charles, Lord Hawkesbury, the President of the Board of Trade, was provided with information on Anglo-Spanish relations.[18]

The speeches of many parliamentarians indicated a considerable amount of information and thought. So also did their writings, including publications. For example, in 1756, Samuel Martin MP published *Thoughts on the System of our Late Treaties with Hesse-Cassel and Russia, in regard to Hanover*, a vindication of his opposition to the Hessian subsidy treaty which had led to his dismissal as secretary to the Chancellor of the Exchequer, Henry Legge, who had refused to sign a warrant under the treaty. In these *Thoughts*, Martin offered an intelligent warning against system-builders:

The future conduct of states is not the subject of mathematical certainty, and who shall presume to foreknow the resolutions of politicians, a species of men that know their own minds as little as the vulgar world do theirs? . . . therefore kingdoms, as well as individuals, must be content to provide against the probable injuries of each other; not waiting for unattainable certainty on the one hand, nor on the other, outrunning the appearance of danger, to bestow, vain, impracticable, and endless endeavours, to be secure from mischiefs barely possible.[19]

Parliamentarians based their views on reading,[20] discussion and assumptions. Discussion included frequenting the world of the coffee houses, where information was exchanged and opinions moulded. Some MPs, such as Sir John Miller, MP for Newport 1784–90, were noted for this.[21] It was possible to mug up on subjects as Henry Addington was urged to do when war seemed likely over the United Provinces in 1787.[22] Domestic correspondents offered both information and opinion, Dr. Charles

---

[17] Hayton, IV, 276–7; Chavigny to Chauvelin, 13 Apr. 1732, AE. CP. Ang. 377 fols. 59, 61; Cobbett, XVI, 609. See also North in 1774, Cobbett, XVII, 1330–4.

[18] Hawkesbury to Burges, 12 Dec. 1790, Bod. Bland Burges papers 37 fol. 55.

[19] S. Martin, *Thoughts on the System of our Late Treaties with Hesse-Cassel and Russia, in regard to Hanover* (1756), p. 38.

[20] K. W. Schweizer, 'The Bedford Motion and House of Lords Debate, 5 February 1762', in Schweizer, *Statesmen, Diplomats and the Press – Essays on 18th Century Britain* (Lewiston, 2002), pp. 73, 84, re I. Mauduit's *Considerations on the Present German War* (1760).

[21] Namier, III, 139.

[22] James Williamson to Addington, no date, Exeter CRO. D 152 M/C 1786 F52.

Blagden, Secretary of the Royal Society, providing Henry, 2nd Viscount Palmerston, MP for Newport, Isle of Wight, and a critic of the government in 1790, with information on the weakness of the Nootka Convention, especially relating to British whaling.[23] Parliamentarians also had their own correspondents abroad, enabling Lord North, for example, in 1788 to doubt reports that William V of Orange was in firm control of the United Provinces.[24]

In some cases, travel also helped. Whereas Sir Robert Walpole, George III and, until 1748, Newcastle had never been abroad, many parliamentarians travelled for pleasure and interest. Shortly before he became MP for Rye, Robert Jenkinson, later 2nd Earl of Liverpool, witnessed the chaos in Paris during the early stages of the Revolution. Parliamentarians did not only travel as young men. In January 1770, Sir Edward Hawke, MP for Portsmouth and 1st Lord of the Admiralty, responded to opposition claims that the government was concealing the risk of war with the Bourbons, by telling the Commons 'I was in France last summer, and that I know certainly by the observations I made, that they are not in a condition to go to war'. Four years later, however, in the Commons' debate on the Budget, North criticised Isaac Barré, MP for Calne, when he told the House that it was difficult to know the details of French finances, 'but it is easy for a gentleman of quick parts to travel into France, and gain that kind of information, to hold forth, and to persuade people who know nothing of the matter, that he knows something of the matter'.[25]

In 1787, Sir John Sinclair, the pro-government MP for Lostwithiel, had an audience of one and a half hours with George when he returned from a seven months' tour of northern Europe that he had taken to distract himself after his wife Sarah died.[26] Before becoming an MP in 1780, Nathaniel Wraxall had travelled extensively, including to Scandinavia and Russia. In 1775, he published the favourably received *Cursory Remarks made in a tour through Northern Europe*. John, 2nd Lord Boringdon, who took a role in Lords' debates from the 1790s, had travelled extensively in 1792–4.

Prominent tourists were indeed able to mingle at the highest ranks of Continental society. In a Commons' debate of 1741 on foreign policy, Charles, 5th Lord Baltimore, a supporter of Frederick, Prince of Wales, then in opposition, who held an Irish peerage and sat for Surrey, 'said he knew the King of Prussia (Frederick II) personally and he was sure that a

---

[23] Blagden to Palmerston, 22 Nov. 1790, New Haven, Beinecke Library, Osborn Shelves c 114.
[24] North to John, Lord Sheffield, 1 Feb. 1788, BL. Add. 61980 fols. 29–30.
[25] Cobbett, XVI, 682, XVII, 1331.
[26] Sinclair to Charles Jenkinson, 2 July 1787, BL. Add. 38222 fols. 90–1.

precipitate resolution of this House at the end of the last session lost the King of Prussia to the Emperor',[27] in other words that parliamentary backing for Austria had led Frederick to ally with Charles Albert of Bavaria, the newly elected Emperor Charles VII. This argument exaggerated the role both of Britain and of Parliament, as Frederick was primarily motivated by the opportunities for territorial gains from Austria. In 1731, Thomas Robinson, MP for Morpeth, who had dined recently with Cardinal Fleury, the leading French minister, commented on French hostility to Britain. Charles Emmanuel III of Sardinia discussed international relations with George, Lord Euston three years later.[28] In 1737, Euston was to become MP for Coventry (where his father Charles, 2nd Duke of Grafton was Recorder), but was noted as a callous bully, not a parliamentarian. The press suggested that foreign travel contributed to the quality of parliamentary debate. Accepting the criticism of tourists as gleaning 'every vice and folly they meet with', the *Universal Spectator* of 3 April (os) 1742, nevertheless, declared:

we have, however, some exceptions, and some young noblemen who have done an honour to their country abroad; and by acquiring a knowledge of men, of commerce, of the interests and tempers of foreign courts, with the different policies of different nations, will be of service to their country at home. Lord Halifax, in the House of Peers, and Lord Quarendon, in the Commons, are illustrious examples for the young British gentry.

George, 2nd Earl of Halifax, was to be an important minister and prominent parliamentarian, as President of the Board of Trade and Secretary of State. George, Viscount Quarendon, MP for Oxfordshire 1740–3 and 3rd Earl of Lichfield 1743–72, in contrast, was denied a ministerial career by his Tory sympathies, but he was an able and active speaker in 1740–2. The value of travel to parliamentarians was also emphasised later in the century. The *Public Advertiser* of 3 March 1792 stated: 'it must give great pleasure to the impartial observer, that the debate on Wednesday turned upon the great questions of the Laws of Nations, and of the interests of Europe, which were treated so ably by young travellers, who have acquired their information upon the large scale of the Continent of Europe'.

In light of Cobham's arguments, it is instructive to reconsider Gibbs's assessment of the parliamentary debates over Hanover in the early 1740s. He concluded that opposition 'arguments were at best grossly over-simplified

---

[27] Diary of Dudley Ryder MP, 18 Dec. (os) 1741, HP.
[28] HMC. *Manuscripts of the Earl of Carlisle* (London, 1807), pp. 89–90; Arthur Villettes, envoy in Turin, to Duke of Newcastle, 25 Dec. 1734, PRO. SP. 92/137.

and exaggerated, and at times totally misplaced'.[29] Much of the parliamentary language over Hanover in the early 1740s was certainly aggressive, the Hanoverian issue being used to discuss fundamental questions of constitutional propriety, dynastic legitimacy and national interest. In January 1744, John, 4th Earl of Sandwich, then an opposition Whig, urged the Lords to heed the general national opposition he discerned to Hanover, and, specifically, to payment for Hanoverian troops:

It may be hoped that these sentiments will be adopted, and these resolutions formed by every man who hears, what is echoed through the nation, that the British have been considered as subordinate to their own mercenaries; mercenaries whose service was never rated at so high a price before, and who never deserved even the petty price at which their lives used to be valued; that foreign slaves were exalted above the freemen of Great Britain, even by the King of Great Britain, and that on all occasions, on which one nation could be preferred to the other, the preference was given to the darling Hanoverians.[30]

Rhetoric in modern representative assemblies, however, is not incompatible with an intelligent assessment of the situation, although the former commands more attention; and there is no reason to believe that the situation was different in the eighteenth century.

Opposition parliamentarians claimed that their views corresponded with those of the public, and were therefore more worth stating. This view extended to peers. In January 1744, Charles, 3rd Duke of Marlborough told the Lords,

It is not possible to mention Hanover, or its inhabitants, in any public place, without putting the whole house into a flame, and hearing on every hand expressions of resentment, threats of revenge, or clamours of detestation. Hanover is now become a name which cannot be mentioned without provoking a rage and malignity, and interrupting the discourse by a digression of abhorrence.[31]

Alarmist generalisations were not restricted to this instance of parliamentary discussion of foreign policy. In November 1739, Daniel, 3rd Earl of Winchilsea, an experienced opposition speaker, gave his view of policy over the previous two decades:

tame submissions to pacific negotiations, which have, as was long since foretold, at last ended in an open and declared war; and that at a season, which, if we consider the present situation of affairs in Europe, we must allow to be the most unlucky

---

[29] G. C. Gibbs, 'English Attitudes towards Hanover and the Hanoverian Succession in the First Half of the Eighteenth Century', in A. N. Birke and K. Kluxen (eds.), *England und Hannover* (Munich, 1986), p. 44.
[30] Cobbett, XIII, 562.   [31] Cobbett, XIII, 564–5.

for this nation, of any we could have chosen, ever since Spain began to insult and plunder, and we to negotiate and submit.[32]

Alarmist sentiments, and a stress on the general rather than the particular, were also expressed by pro-government speakers. In December 1743, for example, Robert, 2nd Lord Raymond told the Lords that the opposition were 'the favourers of France, and the betrayers of the great cause of universal liberty'.[33]

In judging opposition rhetoric, it is necessary to consider the particular problems their parliamentarians faced. George, 3rd Earl of Lichfield, a Tory and formerly, as Viscount Quarendon, an MP, told the Lords in December 1743, 'as this House has not of late years been let into any secrets relating to our foreign transactions . . . we can judge from nothing but public appearances'.[34] It was not therefore surprising that, as Philip, Lord Hardwicke pointed out that day, opposition speakers offered little proof in support of their arguments.[35] Furthermore, criticism of the role of the monarch had to be indirect, helping to ensure that the Hanoverian issue was treated both as a very significant matter and in a very general way. The opposition were also appealing to a wider public, most obviously in their Protests, and this encouraged a rhetorical approach.

This public was that of the British public nation, European powers, and posterity. The Lords' Protest over the Hanoverian troops, ending the great debate on 9 December (os) 1743, stated that

the willingness of the States General [Dutch] . . . or any other power in Europe, to enter into a closer conjunction with us, at this critical time, most chiefly depends upon the idea they shall conceive of the state of this nation at home, especially with regard to the greater or lesser degree of union and harmony, which shall appear to subsist between His Majesty and his people . . . as our votes have, we hope, proved us to the present age, our names in the books may transmit us to posterity Englishmen.[36]

In appealing to such an audience it was possibly felt best, either by the speakers, or by the reporters whose accounts we are substantially dependent upon, to adopt a broad and rhetorical approach. Furthermore, it is possible that the euphoria of public speaking, the conceit of conviction, and the sense that, once in opposition, there was no harm in embarrassing the government as much as possible, all combined to encourage a strident style and an aggressive approach.

---

[32] Cobbett, XI, 64.   [33] Cobbett, XIII, 305.   [34] Cobbett, XIII, 379.   [35] Cobbett, XIII, 344.
[36] Cobbett, XIII, 382–3.

It is also necessary in evaluating speeches to make allowance for the increasing preference for real, or apparent, spontaneity, as parliamentarians, with their developing standards of expertise and demands for a particular style of rhetoric, became more critical of 'set speeches', and, indeed, the use of notes; although there was still much preparation at the close of the century, a period that has been described as the 'apogee of oratory'.[37] It is clear from contemporary comments that responses to the style of particular speakers varied greatly. In the case of most speakers, there is no indication about such responses, or the reasons for them, but prominent speakers were considered at length.

William Pitt the Elder aroused particular controversy because of the vigour of his criticism. On 2 December 1755, William Murray, MP for Boroughbridge, Attorney General, and an able but uncombative speaker, distinguished between Pitt's 'florid eloquence' and 'the talent of a solid judgment'. In the debate on the Army Estimates three days later, Richard Rigby, the bold, if not destructive, MP for Tavistock, noted 'a most violent, abusive, but very fine, declamation from Mr. Pitt', but Major-General Lord George Sackville, MP for Dover and a supporter of the ministry,

made an excellent speech, and very unlike anybody's else, for it was quite to the question; disapproved of Mr. Pitt's present style of debating, that if our country is in such a deplorable condition, we ought to be considering how to remedy it. If he has accusations against any minister he ought to appoint a day for the purpose of hearing them; but all ministers are unworthy our consideration in comparison of relieving the public, which seemed to be forgot, and abuse or defence of our ministers to engross our whole thoughts.[38]

Pitt's style was vulnerable to mockery. In January 1751, in a debate over the number of seamen, which was linked to the ability of the navy to support British policy, John Hampden 'brought him [Pitt] lower than the most able and serious disputants with all their power could ever effect'. Hampden, according to Horace Walpole, 'drew a burlesque picture of Pitt and Lyttelton under the titles of Oratory and Solemnity, and painted in the most comic colours what mischief rhetoric had brought upon the nation and what emoluments to Pitt'.[39] Another critic, John, 2nd Earl of Egmont,

---

[37] Thorne, I, 343; P. D. G. Thomas, *The House of Commons in the Eighteenth Century* (Oxford, 1971), pp. 203–4.

[38] Cobbett, XV, 606; Rigby to John, 4th Duke of Bedford, 6 Dec. 1755, Lord John Russell (ed.), *Correspondence of John, 4th Duke of Bedford* (3 vols., 1842–6), II, 179–81; Campbell to his wife, 16 Dec. 1755, Cawdor, Box 138; Bayntum Rolt diary, 4 Feb. 1754, Bristol UL.

[39] H. Walpole, *Memoirs of King George II*, ed. J. Brooke (3 vols., New Haven, 1985) I, 13.

wrote of Pitt:

his rhetoric and power of speech was in abuse only, and his project and ideas were such as suited only with the superficial ideas of the lowest understanding and were strangely defective to a degree of contempt, with men of judgement and experience in business . . . his fame as an orator depended upon his total defect as to an argumentative understanding. Incapable of induction or ratiocination, to deduce a long chain of consequences, or to survey with accuracy all the parts of a question so as to draw a just conclusion . . . But possessed of a wonderful power of words and a pompous diction, improved by the study of the poets, of rhetoric, the speeches of old orators . . . he not only cast alternatively a cloud or a glare about his absurd propositions . . . but even triumphed over common sense within himself.[40]

The sense of Pitt as spectacle was captured by Horace Walpole, who wrote that his speech of 15 December 1755 was 'accompanied with action that would have added reputation to [David] Garrick', a reference to the leading actor of the period. Horace Walpole claimed that Pitt was one of the few speakers to study eloquence, but that set speeches were no longer in vogue. He also argued that invective in debate was a necessary way to achieve attention. Pitt certainly excelled in this field, but he also employed verbal devices that Walpole claimed had fallen into disuse. Nevertheless, as Walpole pointed out, 'the grace and force of words were . . . natural to him'. In May 1762, when Walpole referred to Pitt speaking 'in very capital style', he distinguished between speaking as an orator, as Pitt did, and being thought a bully who relied on illiberal invectives.[41] Henry Harris wrote of Pitt's performance in the subsidy treaty debates in 1755, that he

was born for opposition – more excelling in his manner, in his language, and in high invective, than all the public speakers I ever heard of . . . Mr. [Henry] Fox behaved just as a great man, and a minister, I think, should always behave: with the utmost spirit, but with no loss of temper – setting plain facts, and fair argument against all this imposing eloquence – he did not affect, nor would it become his station to imitate the splendid verbiage of his rival.[42]

Pitt was not alone in his methods, nor was he the sole MP compared with London actors. James Harris, MP for Christchurch from 1761 to 1780 and a poor speaker, noted in 1779: 'I have seen [Charles James] Fox and [Edmund] Burke (the last in particular) so vociferate and so gesticulate in the House of Commons, that had a [Thomas] Weston or a [Edward] Shuter done so at Covent Garden or Drury Lane, they had been hissed off the stage for most

---

[40] BL. Add. 47012 B fols. 182–4.
[41] H. Walpole, *Memoirs of George II*, III, 116–17; *Memoirs of George III*, I, 105–7.
[42] Farmington, Hanbury-Williams papers, vol. 63 fol. 61, vol. 271, fol. 20.

unnatural extravagance'.[43] The theatrical mood climaxed with Edmund Burke's dagger speech on 28 December 1792 when he threw a dagger on the floor of the Commons in order to warn of pro-French revolutionary subversion, only to be greeted with laughter.[44] In judging both rhetoric and reason, it is necessary to consider the impact of physical presence. It is difficult, if not impossible, to recover the impression made by gesture, energy and presence from the available sources.[45]

Whether or not they had presence, many parliamentarians resorted to bold rhetoric. In 1726, Nicholas, Lord Lechmere, an effective lawyer and MP, who had become an opposition Whig and had a fiery temper, was described as having 'flamed in the House of Lords'.[46] In 1786, Philip Francis, MP for Yarmouth, Isle of Wight and a member of the Foxite opposition, 'nauseated' George Huntingford 'with his virulence, false painting, and tautology'. William Grenville, MP for Buckinghamshire and a member of the government, in contrast, he found 'sensible' and 'manly'.[47] In 1781, Hugh Elliot wrote from his embassy in Berlin:

Mr. [Nathaniel] Wraxall has thought proper to deliver a philippic against this court and its sovereign [Frederick the Great]. It is much to be regretted that a sense of dignity in the House does not put a stop to personal invective against foreign princes ... Wraxall's speech has been translated into all foreign newspapers and the abusive parts of it distinguished with italics. In England where that species of writing is as usual to us as our daily bread it is scarcely remarked, here the shoe pinches and a tight shoe upon a gouty foot is apt to raise ill humours.[48]

Bold rhetoric was also contested. During the Falklands crisis, Wills, 1st Earl of Hillsborough replied to the opposition argument that British 'naval power is able to give the whole universe laws ... A language of this nature may be very fine in romance, but men of business experimentally know, and laugh at the absurdity'.[49] Similarly, in 1762, George Grenville asked whether William Beckford, MP for London and a vociferous ally of Pitt, thought that 'great words, blustered in Parliament, constituted resolution'.[50]

---

[43] Harris memorandum, 20 Mar. 1779, HP.
[44] Cobbett, XXX, 189; L. W. Jennings (ed.), *The Correspondence and Diaries of John Wilson Croker* (3 vols., 1885), I, 409.
[45] P. J. Waller, 'Laughter in the House. A Late Nineteenth and Early Twentieth Century Parliamentary Survey', *Twentieth Century British History*, 5 (1994), p. 8.
[46] George Clarke to Edward Nicholas, 20 Jan. (os) 1726, BL. Eg. 2540 fol. 561.
[47] Huntingford to Addington, June 1786, 15M/C 1786/F 72.
[48] Elliot to Philip Yorke, 3rd Earl of Hardwicke, 1 Mar. 1781, Belfast, Public Record Office of Northern Ireland, Caledon papers.
[49] Cobbett, XVI, 1039.   [50] Walpole, *Memoirs of George III*, I, 104.

Humour was a valuable tool for many parliamentarians, helping to defuse tension and win support. It was seen as an alternative to rhetoric. Barré claimed in 1761 that he could not 'rouse, animate or divert, has no arts to deceive with'.[51] Humour also helped to alleviate boredom,[52] which was a particular problem for many parliamentarians as their interest in politics was less than that of the professional politicians who dominate modern representative assemblies. In January 1730, Stephen Fox was clearly discouraged by the nature of the debates. He wrote to his brother on the 17th (os), a Saturday, 'I have been at the House of Commons but once (which was the first day [13th os] we had so long and unentertaining [sic] a debate that the House did not rise till a quarter after twelve.' Stephen Fox was not the most assiduous of MPs. Born in 1704, he had become MP for Shaftesbury in 1726, but had spent much of 1728–9 in Italy. On 24 January (os) 1730, Stephen Fox was still not a fund of information, 'We had two pretty pert debates in the House yesterday and the day before, that of yesterday I came rather too late for, having stayed very long at the masquerade the night before.' That was all he recorded.[53] Nevertheless, Fox moved the Address in 1734, 1736 and 1738. Horace Walpole was another parliamentarian who became bored, and he preferred the glittering *salons* of Paris to being an MP.[54] Walpole was greatly impressed by Charles Townshend's ability to speak in a witty fashion, and compared him to Garrick acting extempore scenes from Congreve.[55]

Humour, however, led to charges of levity, as in 1773 when Thomas Townshend upbraided Lord North for forsaking argument and endeavouring 'to divert the House with some of that wit of which he had such an abundant share'.[56] Some humour appears to have been unintentional. In January 1736, there was much laughter in the Commons when John, Viscount Tyrconnel, MP for Grantham, announced that he loved peace as much as the pictures of Claude Le Lorrain.[57]

The quality of individual speakers and speeches was assessed very differently by contemporaries. In part, this involved partisanship; although that was not the sole reason. When Burke was criticised by a newspaper reporter for a 'violent; rambling; flimsy; figurative; laboured' hour-long speech on 13 November 1770, attacking government policy in the Falklands Crisis,

[51] P. D. Brown and K. W. Schweizer (eds.), *The Devonshire Diary. William Cavendish Fourth Duke of Devonshire. Memoranda on State of Affairs 1759–1762* (1982), p. 153.
[52] Thorne, I, 345.   [53] Stephen to Henry Fox, 17, 24 Jan. (os) 1730, BL. Add. 51417 fols. 34, 36.
[54] R. W. Ketton-Cremer, *Horace Walpole, A Biography* (3rd edn, 1964), p. 239.
[55] Walpole, *Memoirs of George III*, III, 131.
[56] *The History, Debates and Proceedings of Both Houses of Parliament from 1743 to 1774* (7 vols., 1782), VII, 53.
[57] Report sent with Chavigny to Chauvelin, 6 Feb. 1736, AE. CP. Ang. 393.

another writer challenged each of these descriptions, in part by praising the facets criticised. Thus 'rambling' became 'large and extensive . . . line of argument'. Nineteen years later, Henry Addington thought him 'violent to madness'.[58]

Rhetorical manner, a strident style and/or humour was not incompatible with the discussion of affairs in an intelligent fashion, a point that was, and has been, made about Pitt the Elder.[59] John Hungerford, Tory MP for Scarborough in 1692–5, 1702–5 and 1707–29, was one of the most frequent non-ministerial speakers of those years and was known for 'his easy and popular eloquence'.[60] This did not preclude important contributions, as in December 1718 when he opposed the Address of Thanks to George I for declaring war on Spain: 'said he had carefully looked over all the treaties before them but found not one article in them for security of the English commerce and desired that in this Address they would mention it to his Majesty'.[61] This Hungerford did as a result of information that the Austrians planned, with the connivance of the British government, to create an East India Company based on Ostend. Charles James Fox had charm, but was also capable of vigorous and forensic oratory that cut through problems in order to provide a clear exposition of the opposition view.[62] His animated style was recorded in Karl Anton Hickel's 1793 painting *Charles James Fox Speaking in the House of Commons*.

Alongside style, status was important. What was said, and how it was said carried weight, but who said it carried more. Thus, in the vote for measures against Sweden in 1717, the opposition of John Smith, MP for East Looe, a long-established Whig politician and former Speaker, who was then Teller of the Exchequer, was important: 'gave great weight to the opposition because he as well as the Speaker [Spencer Compton] was known a person extremely well affected to the King, and to be a master of rules of Parliament'.[63] A different type of status was derived from a reputation for speaking. Reporting on the Commons' debate on the Address in November 1742, Henry Fox reported that Thomas Winnington and Henry Pelham had spoken well for the ministry and William Pitt for the opposition, but

---

[58] F. P. Lock, *Edmund Burke, Volume I, 1730–1784* (Oxford, 1998), pp. 299–300; Addington to his father, 5 Feb. 1789, 152M/C 1789/F 12.

[59] K. W. Schweizer, 'The Elder Pitt and British Strategy: An Unpublished Parliamentary Speech, 9 December 1761', in *Statesmen, Diplomats and the Press*, p. 61. P. D. G. Thomas, ' "The Great Commoner": The Elder William Pitt as Parliamentarian', *Parliamentary History*, 22 (2003), pp. 145–63.

[60] A. Boyer, *The Political State of Great Britain* (60 vols., 1711–40), XXXVII, 620–1.

[61] Hugh Thomas to John, 11th Earl of Mar, 22 Dec. 1718, RA. 41/13.

[62] J. Wright (ed.), *The Speeches of the Rt. Hon. Charles James Fox in the House of Commons* (6 vols., 1815).

[63] Perceval note on Commons' debate of 8 Mar. (os) 1717, BL. Add. 47028 fol. 184.

he added 'upon the whole it was a bad debate'.[64] The degree to which only a small number of parliamentarians were regarded as good speakers gave them particular status.

Whatever their style or status, many speakers made sensible speeches. Newcastle, who was not a natural orator, offered the Lords in November 1739 an interesting assessment of the French system of government:

notwithstanding the great age of the present prime minister of that Kingdom [Cardinal Fleury], notwithstanding his present peaceable disposition we cannot entirely trust to it; we know he can alter that disposition, when he finds it proper or necessary so to do; we know the animosity that has so long subsisted between that nation and this: we know the regard the people of France have for the royal family of Spain; and therefore the prime minister of that Kingdom, notwithstanding the arbitrary form of their government, may, like the ministers in other countries, be forced to chime in with the general inclinations, perhaps the general whim, of his countrymen. Many things may induce the French to alter their present measures, and as their king is absolute master within his dominions, the effects of that alteration may, and probably will be, instantaneous.[65]

Newcastle was to be proved correct. In 1741, with Fleury still in office, France attacked Austria. In 1736, the Lords had listened to an informed and sensible discussion of how far British armaments had led the French to end the recent War of the Polish Succession. In response to opposition comments on the failure to send squadrons to the Baltic and Mediterranean, it was claimed that the very act of preparing a major naval armament had an impact on the French. Furthermore, opposition comments about the threat posed by the French gain of the reversion to Lorraine were countered, reasonably enough, by the argument that France had in recent wars always been able to overrun the Duchy.[66]

Part of the problem in discussing foreign affairs was the nature of the international system. Dynasticism provided the principal theme and idiom of the system, and the monarchical control of foreign policy in most states kept it secretive. In the volatile, indeed kaleidoscopic, international system of the period, it was difficult to assess, let alone predict, the policies of other states. Dramatic reversals of policy, such as the Prussian abandonment of France in 1742, or the negotiation of an Austro-French alliance in 1756, and surprise attacks, such as the Bourbon and Sardinian attacks on Austria in 1733, the Prussian invasion of Silesia in 1740, and the Danish attack on Sweden in 1788, produced an atmosphere of uncertainty in which rumour

---

[64] Henry to Stephen Fox, 18 Nov. (os) 1742, BL. Add. 51417 fol. 94.   [65] Cobbett, XI, 29.
[66] *A Collection of the Parliamentary Debates in England from 1668 to the Present Time*, XIII (1740), p. 197.

flourished and conspiracy was believed in, because sometimes true. The opposition was wrong-footed in the 1736 session[67] when the War of the Polish Succession suddenly ended at a time when it was preparing to attack the government for a failure to act.

In such a situation, it was necessary, in judging the policies of other states, to confront their apparent nature as frequently unclear or ambivalent and difficult to establish. As a result, it was simpler to discuss policy in terms of innate history and national interests, and to assess intentions in the same terms. The plans of France could, it was argued, be gauged by considering her past policy, an analysis aided by the belief that for each state there was an obvious natural interest dictating a particular course of policy. Parliamentarians who discussed international relations in such a fashion were simply sharing in the common terminology and analytical methods of the day, devices used by statesmen as much as journalists.

Furthermore, the strong historical bent of parliamentary discussion, the frequent reference to past events in British foreign policy, accorded with the general fashion in which international relations were discussed. Just as early seventeenth-century English discussions of foreign policy were greatly influenced by the recent experience of sustained conflict with Spain in 1585–1604, so discussion after 1713 took place in the shadow of the struggle with France: the Nine Years' War (1689–97) and the War of the Spanish Succession (1702–13). This experience was crucial not only because of its role in British foreign policy, but also because of its significance in domestic history, not solely political, but also social, economic and fiscal, the war having represented a major burden in all spheres. Many British politicians of the subsequent decades served in these wars, either as diplomats or generals. The future George II displayed great bravery at the battle of Oudenaarde in 1708. James, Viscount Stanhope fought in Spain, where he was captured, while his two brothers were killed in the War of the Spanish Succession. John, 2nd Duke of Argyll, John, 2nd Earl of Stair, and William, 1st Earl Cadogan had all been among Marlborough's generals. Party politics had played a major role in the conduct of war. The Peace of Utrecht, negotiated by the Tories in 1713, was, both at the time and subsequently, a central topic of political debate, defended by Tories, such as Thomas, 3rd Earl of Strafford and Thomas, 1st Lord Trevor in 1718, and by opposition Whigs wooing Tory support, such as Argyll in 1740, and vilified by Whigs, such as Charles, 3rd Earl of Peterborough in 1730.

---

[67] Chavigny to Chauvelin, 24 Dec. 1735, AE. CP. Ang. 392 fol. 227.

The frequent discussion in Parliament of past events, such as Utrecht, the Quadruple Alliance of 1718, the Hanoverian acquisition of Bremen and Verden, and the Alliance of Hanover of 1725, reflected, in part, the limited amount of information available concerning current diplomacy. In addition, these events were held to be instructive. Thus, the subsidy treaty debate in 12 December 1755 included reference to Edward III, a noted hammer of the French, and to Elizabeth I's use of German troops. In the Commons' debate on the Address on 13 November 1770, Sir William Meredith, MP for Liverpool and a supporter of the Marquess of Rockingham, warned of the need to end tyranny at home if the country was to fight for liberty abroad, adding 'our ancestors abandoned King John, in consequence of which he lost all his foreign dominions', and followed up with a reference to Edward II and Scotland.[68]

However, reference to the past was also a function of a political society where legitimacy derived essentially from past events, and the nature of the response to them. This was crucial in a country where the succession had been and was contested. Thus the response to the Glorious Revolution and the Hanoverian Succession, both events located concretely in the recent past, 1688–9 and 1714 respectively, defined or could be held to define dynastic loyalty and political affinity. The categories might be rejected by some, for example Tories seeking to avoid the imputation of Jacobitism, but this forced them to define their own view of the past and to challenge the arguments advanced by others. Foreign policy played a central role in the debate, because it could be used to defend or criticise the monarch, and because dynasticism served as a common theme linking constitutional and international affairs.

Another parallel that was more pertinent to the question of speaker quality was that of threats to Britain with the challenge that Philip of Macedon had posed to Classical Greece. This made it possible to compare speakers who used that example to the great orator Demosthenes, who had warned about Macedon. Sir Grey Cooper, a former supporter of Lord North when a MP, who had moved to support Pitt in response to the French Revolution, made the comparison in 1799, referring to Pitt's 'sublime understanding', although Sylvester Douglas, MP for Midhurst, who made the same point, laconically pointed out that the speeches 'of Demosthenes were not able to save Athens'.[69]

---

[68] Cobbett, XVI, 1038–9.
[69] Cooper to Addington, 9 June, Douglas to Addington, 20 Feb. 1799, 152M/C 1799 OZ8, OI 12.

In making qualitative judgements about speakers, it is necessary to note such (and other) aspects of the extent to which foreign policy debates could raise both general and specific points. If it is assumed that all speakers should have offered a detailed account of the international situation in order to throw light on the foreign policy problems and choices facing Britain, then it is possible to adopt a critical attitude. However, it is necessary to avoid any assumption that parliamentarians should adopt a uniform approach. Instead, speakers presented issues in different lights, not least in order to make very different political points. Thus, subsidy debates raised both general questions of the purposes of foreign policy and specific points about the value or otherwise of particular alliances in different conjunctures. Given the similarities between some of the crises facing Britain, it is also not surprising that many speakers returned to the same themes, such as the respective importance and value of 'blue water' and Continental approaches, and the impact of Hanover.

The public discussion of policy, in Parliament as much as in the press, was intended to illuminate foreign policy in terms that could be readily understood, and there was frequently the obvious wish to transform it into ammunition for use in political debate. It was precisely because foreign policy was not separated from such debate but was an integral part of it, that it is necessary to judge diplomacy, in part, in terms of its political context, and also to suggest that because the parliamentary discussion of foreign policy was designed to serve a political purpose that does not imply that it was without standards or quality. Precisely because of the contentious nature of the subject, and the particular experience and knowledge of individual speakers, debate tended to be well informed. For example, although the Lords' debate in early 1730 on the Treaty of Seville only lasted one day and although it was a contentious issue in a highly charged session, the debate was of a high quality and well informed:

The Lords Strafford, Bathurst and Gower objected that it was a manifest violation of the Quadruple Alliance by stipulating Spanish instead of Swiss troops,[70] that the lives of the present possessors might be in danger from them and that the King of Spain[71] might perhaps be for keeping these countries for himself, and not to give them up to Don Carlos,[72] that a Spanish garrison in Leghorn[73] would be a further security in the hands of Spain for the good behaviour of England, and would make our trade to Italy lie at their mercy.

---

[70] As garrisons in Parma and Tuscany in order to protect Don Carlos' claims on their successions.
[71] Philip V.   [72] Elder son by Philip's second marriage. Later Charles III of Spain.   [73] Livorno.

The Court said it was not a violation, only an immaterial alteration, the substance and design being preserved, which was the securing of the successions to Don Carlos; that if the Emperor was sincere as to those successions going to Don Carlos he could not object to it; and that our trade to Italy would be as secure as it is now . . .

My Lord Gower said that the Quadruple Alliance stipulated the introduction of Swiss troops only to secure the successions to Don Carlos but also to preserve the feodalite of the Empire against any violation, and that in the Letters of Expectative for securing the eventual succession to those countrys the Emperor says he grants . . . Letters upon consideration . . . of the Quadruple Alliance and that in cases of any deviation from it he says *nec velle nec posse teneri.*

Lord Abingdon said he took every alteration of a Treaty without the consent of all the contracting parties to be a violation of that treaty . . . The Duke of Newcastle said that the Queen of Spain finding that the Swiss had not been introduced though 10 or 12 years had passed since the stipulation for introducing them, feared they never would be introduced, and therefore insisted upon the alteration to Spanish troops.[74]

Recently discovered, this account is far fuller than that in Cobbett. It is also clear that the speakers were very well informed and made cogent points. There is no reason to doubt that a similar disparity between Cobbett and actual debates would be perceived if fuller accounts of the latter could be found. Hopefully, progress will be made in this direction, although, as very few domestic collections that are known to exist remain inaccessible or unexamined, it is likely that discoveries will be limited.

Complaints suggest that the quality of debates was affected by difficulties in gaining access to diplomatic papers. Sir Robert Walpole himself remarked in 1738 that no MP could claim any real knowledge of international developments if he knew no more than what he had learned by being in the Commons.[75] When papers were disclosed, this was frequently long after the event. The trade treaty with Spain of December 1715 was only laid before the Lords in June 1717, and was not laid before the Commons. The Anglo-Austrian Treaty of Westminster of May 1716 was not laid before Parliament until 1718: February for the Lords and November for the Commons, although the secret article was not disclosed. Other treaties, such as the Triple Alliance of January 1717, were announced to Parliament far more promptly (although it was not fully laid before the Commons until February 1730), but the extent of delay and secrecy encouraged conspiracy theories. These were not only advanced by opposition speakers.

---

[74] The Queen of Spain was Elisabeth Farnesse. Anon. to Mylord, 8 Mar. (os) 1729 [1730], Gosforth, Northumberland CRO., 650/c/18/1.
[75] Cobbett, X, 675.

In the debate over the opposition motion in January 1734 calling for the instructions to the envoy in Saxony-Poland to be laid before Parliament, Walpole suggested that the opposition had 'heartened to every little whisper of some of the foreign ministers at this court, which is, I believe, the only foundation they have for what they have asserted'.[76]

Government majorities ensured that the ministry controlled the process of public disclosure. Opposition attempts to take control, such as Samuel Pargiter Fuller's in the Commons on 2 January (os) 1719 to draw attention to reports of a willingness to cede Gibraltar, or the move twelve years later to highlight Spanish dissatisfaction with the Treaty of Seville, could be thwarted, but they helped compromise the reputation of the government.[77] In the Lords' debate of March 1734 over a royal message seeking the means to augment forces during the recess, Carteret, then in opposition, complained that the House had been given no information, and asserted, 'it cannot be expected that I, or any other lord who has not had the honour to be admitted into that secret, should speak so fully to the present question as we might otherwise have done . . . I cannot speak properly to it, in any other way than as relates to our constitution'. Chesterfield, then in opposition, also complained that the House had been kept in ignorance.[78] A Protest in George I's last session, that of 1727, noted,

The papers hitherto laid before the House in order to the consideration of his Majesty's speech, are such as only as concerned the accession of the States-General to the treaty of Hanover, and the letters and memorials since the arrival of the British fleet on the coast of Spain in America; but none of the negotiations or measures (which we suppose to have been made) that have been carried on between the courts of Great Britain and Vienna, and the Northern powers, which his Majesty's speech and the resolution also may have relation to, have as yet been communicated to this House; but all those measures, and many others unknown (as we believe to this House) are in our opinions, intended to be approved and justified by this resolution; to which therefore we cannot concur, no more than if it had declared the measures honourable, just, and necessary.[79]

As government speakers did not generally reveal more information, parliamentarians remained handicapped. In the Commons' debate on the Address on 13 November 1770, Lord North denied that the French had been

---

[76] Gibbs, 'Laying Treaties Before Parliament in the Eighteenth Century', in R. M. Hatton and M. S. Anderson (eds.) *Studies in Diplomatic History: Essays in Memory of David Bayne Horn* (1970), esp., pp. 122–3, 131–2; Cobbett, IX, 229.

[77] Destouches to Dubois, 1 Feb. 1719, AE. CP. Ang. 322 fols. 172–3; Gibbs, 'Newspapers, Parliament, and Foreign Policy in the Age of Stanhope and Walpole' *Mélanges offerts à G. Jacquemyns* (Brussels, 1986), pp. 307–12.

[78] Cobbett, IX, 522, 632.   [79] Cobbett, VIII, 543.

asked to mediate over the Falklands dispute, and criticised the opposition for getting its news from the press, but he did not provide any reliable information at this junction, and on 22 November, in a debate in the Lords on an opposition demand for papers, the government argued that to provide them would jeopardise negotiations.[80]

The lack of such information made the material and news provided to parliamentarians by foreign envoys particularly valuable, although it was impossible to confirm its validity. At the same time, the government also provided information less formally. In January 1727, Thomas Robinson, then Secretary of Embassy in Paris, and soon to be MP for Thirsk, told the French foreign minister that, although George I did not doubt French intentions,

> yet the repetition of these assurances at this particular time of day, were in some measure necessary, at the opening of the Parliament, when, to satisfy more the curiosity, than the diffidence of some of the chief members, (who being themselves once assured of it, might convey the same thing to others,) His Majesty's ministers might, as it proved necessary, talk to those gentlemen with the greater readiness, and persuasion of the firmness, and fidelity of France, not only from the constant, and uniform behaviour of this Court, but even, were there occasion for more proofs of it, from the latest, and freshest renewals of their promises to abide by their engagements.[81]

In 1767, Grafton, the First Lord of the Treasury, informed Shelburne, then Secretary of State for the Southern Department,

> as it has been thought most expedient to divide among the different persons the persons best qualified to take a part in the debate on Friday he has desired to see as many of them himself as the time will allow and begs his Lordship will lose no time in seeing Lord Clare, Mr. Dyson and Colonel Barré and communicating to them the sentiments of the Cabinet on the paper he had the honor to send his Lordship a copy of today.[82]

Yet even had material about British policy been disclosed, there was still much room for debate over the intentions and strength of foreign powers, and over the advisability of British responses. Both were probed, with considerable skill, by parliamentarians. There was a major difference between the peacetime situation and that during war. In the latter case, there was an immediacy of focus on current operations. This military dimension,

[80] Cobbett XVI, 1050, 1082.
[81] Robinson to Newcastle, 23 Jan. 1727, BL. Add. 32749 fol. 36. For ministers lobbying MPs in 1727, newsletter, Osnabrück 294 fol. 23.
[82] Grafton to Shelburne, 4 Mar. 1767, BL. Deposit 9516 Bowood papers, vol. 15 fol. 3.

nevertheless, also involved issues of foreign policy for it apparently served to demonstrate the strength or weakness of alliances. Wartime operations and alliance politics could also be used to debate the extent to which government policy was intended to secure national interests.

Discussion of such operations could broaden out to include a more far-flung consideration of foreign policy. For example, Sheridan, in his attack on the mishandling of the 1799 invasion of the Netherlands, moved from the specific point, of a lack of clarity as to whether the ministry had sought to seize the Dutch navy or to remove the French from the Netherlands, to ask what the ministry had decided to do if the latter had been successful. Sheridan argued that it would have been mistaken to seek to restore the house of Orange.[83] Aside from the importance of this issue, it offered a parallel to the related question of the advisability of seeking to restore the Bourbons. The debate underrated one of the primary aims of the expedition: the demonstration by Britain to her allies that she was taking an active role in the war. The opposition, however, was handicapped by what the government chose to reveal. In this case, Sheridan accused the ministry of deceiving the Commons by withholding facts, and thus of covering up failure. He declared 'a more flagrant deception of Parliament was never practised'.[84]

A different form of deception was alleged by government speakers who claimed that, far from outlining consistent views, opposition spokesmen sought to take advantage of circumstances, and also opposed whatever the government proposed for the sake of opposing. Lord North made this point in 1770 with reference to opposition criticism of the government for failing to stop the French acquiring Corsica. Sir Robert Walpole claimed in the Commons in 1739 that

gentlemen, in their opposition to the administration, make it their business to collect precedents and examples from our neighbours, and if they can find anything parallel to them practised by the government, let it be never so reasonable, then it is always the universal clamour that the government immediately designs to reduce the whole constitution to the French form, that they make themselves arbitrary. But if some gentlemen have a favourite measure in view which corresponds with anything practised by the French government, that agreement is so far from being a reproach to it, and a reason why it ought not to be pursued that it is recommended solely on that account.[85]

The international context thus served to provide a basis for judgement. This was a matter not only of foreign policy, but also of a frame of reference for

---

[83] Cobbett, XXXIV, 1401–3.   [84] Cobbett, XXXIV, 1406.   [85] Cobbett, XVI, 1049, XI, 207.

domestic developments. For example, the opposition press could suggest in 1732–3 that the Parlement of Paris was readier to display independence than the Westminster Parliament.[86] Similarly, a London item in the *Bristol Gazette and Public Advertiser* of 12 September 1771 argued that there were similarities between the two countries: 'in both their Parliaments have been essentially suppressed, the one by force, the other by fraud'.

To move between 1732–3 and 1771 in successive sentences testifies to the extent to which attitudes were longstanding. These can indeed be seen as part of the 'structure' of parliamentary politics. At the same time, it can be argued that there were shifts in the emphasis and quality of parliamentary discussion. This was most forcefully asserted by Hamish Scott in his important study of British foreign policy in the period from the Peace of Paris in 1763 to the end of the War of American Independence:

The standard of parliamentary discussion about foreign affairs was very low: a reading of the debates indicates that there was less knowledge of Europe and less concern with the state of British diplomacy than during the reigns of the first two Hanoverians.[87]

This important assertion requires unpicking. There were certainly fewer debates, but this reflected the nature of British foreign policy in the period and, more particularly, the move away from subsidy treaties and the lesser role of Hanover in discussion of foreign policy and domestic politics. As there were fewer debates, it was less possible for parliamentarians to display knowledge of Europe in either House, but that is not the same as having less knowledge. Scott's view of the standard of discussion may in part be attributed to his assessment of the direction that foreign policy should have taken. By arguing that this should have been different to what was generally seen as politically acceptable, Scott emphasised the role of Parliament as a constraining mechanism:

Parliament's influence after the Seven Years War was fundamentally negative. It inhibited and, on occasions, actually prevented ministers from adopting novel policies, particularly towards the Bourbons. In 1772–3 Rochford abandoned attempts at Anglo-French reconciliation, principally because of his fear of a hostile reaction from the House of Commons. Even relatively minor concessions to France, for example over the fortifications at Dunkirk or the Newfoundland Fisheries, were made all but impossible by the hostility of the Commons towards the national enemy. This was even more true of the major Anglo-Bourbon dispute of the first decade of peace over the Falklands Island . . . [Parliament] confirmed ministers in

[86] *Craftsman*, 22 July (os) 1732; *Fog's Weekly Journal*, 24 Mar. (os), 21 Ap. (os) 1732.
[87] H. M. Scott, *British Foreign Policy in the Age of the American Revolution* (Oxford, 1990), p. 21.

their pursuit of an essentially traditional and orthodox diplomatic strategy and was a major obstacle to innovation.[88]

This approach very much reflects Scott's analytical and empirical emphases: he looks at foreign policy from the diplomatic context and from his reading of the international situation, and repeats the emphasis and attitudes seen in the dispatches from envoys. Such an approach is indeed an important one, and Scott's particular interest in the rise of Austria, Prussia and Russia lends it further emphasis. His critical comments about the 'tone of parliamentary debates and the divisions revealed',[89] which also reflect the views of Michael Roberts,[90] are ones that diplomats were happy to repeat. In 1779, shortly before he became a Secretary of State, David, Viscount Stormont

> . . . condemned loudly the frequent indiscretions which noble lords were guilty of in mentioning matters of state in that House. While he was in a public character at Paris, he had almost daily reason to experience it . . . he believed that newspaper accounts, and other publications, in pamphlets etc. of their lordships' debates, containing angry and indiscreet expressions, either respecting the French court or the French king, had worse effects than anything else whatever in bringing matters to their present state. He was very sorry to hear Spain brought into the present debate; the conduct of crowned heads, and the spirit and ability of great nations, were subjects of a very delicate nature, and ought to be mentioned with great caution.[91]

Yet it is necessary to qualify this approach by paying more attention to the role of Parliament in British politics, to understand the place of adversarial debate, and, more specifically, to note that there are very different views on the best direction for British foreign policy after 1763. To turn first to the last point, the need for, and advisability of, a new diplomatic strategy after 1763, as suggested by Scott, is unclear, and therefore it is unsatisfactory to present Parliament as a foolishly negative element. Parliamentarians were well attuned to domestic circumstances and the relationship between these and foreign policy needs underlining. As a result of the Seven Years' War, the national debt had almost doubled, from £74 million in 1756 to £133 million in 1763, and, as a consequence, debt charges as a percentage of revenue had risen. The consequent political and governmental strains were considerable. Critics of British foreign policy in this period, and, in particular, of the reluctance to make concessions in order to win alliances, have failed to explain why this sphere should have been immune from the general governmental and political pressure for restraint in terms of

---

[88] *Ibid.*, pp. 21–2. [89] *Ibid.*, p. 22. [90] M. Roberts, *Splendid Isolation 1763–1780* (Reading, 1970).
[91] Cobbett, XX, 45.

commitments and expenditure. As taxpayers concerned about the level of public debt, parliamentarians were committed to restraint. Similar restraint was to be displayed from 1815 in response to the indebtedness built up during the French Revolutionary and Napoleonic Wars.[92]

Linked to this was the question as to whether in 1763–74, even had Britain been able to afford interventionism, it would have been a sensible policy. This was a two-way question. Aside from British interests, there was the degree to which Britain had little to offer as an ally, particularly to Austria, Prussia and Russia. This was partly because, as France played a lesser role in central and eastern Europe than she had done, and sought to do, in the 1730s and 1740s, so the attraction to powers there of allying with Britain in order to counter France decreased.

From the British point of view, there was little reason to expose the country to the financial, diplomatic and domestic political costs of alliance with a major European power. Although claims of fostering a stable and benign European order, especially against France, had accompanied interventionism from 1689, domestic, not least parliamentary, critics, had claimed, with much reason as well as force, that the centrepiece of much interventionism after 1714 had been Hanoverian interests, both expansionism and a collective security system that would protect Hanover. Scholars who treat Parliament as an encumbrance are apt to underplay this charge, or treat it as irrational, but it had considerable weight, and, indeed, was frequently expressed by ministers and diplomats concerned about the direction and implications of policy.

When, after George III's accession in 1760, Hanoverian interests became less central, then ministers adopted a more circumspect approach to possible commitments, and one that took greater note of the facts of British capabilities, political and financial. Ministers sought alliances, but with greater caution when events moved from expressions of good will to negotiations. As Austria, Prussia and Russia were at, or close to, war in 1768–74, 1778–9 and 1782–3, ministerial caution was vindicated. Not only were these conflicts in which Britain had little close interest, but it was also unlikely that these powers would have been able or willing to provide appropriate support to Britain in her confrontations with the Bourbons.

After 1763, Britain was both a 'satisfied' power and one that was not greatly interested in organising diplomatic combinations in order to sustain the international status quo. It is possible to see this as the triumph

---

[92] J. Hoppit, 'Checking the Leviathan, 1688–1832', in D. Winch and P. K. O'Brien (eds.), *The Political Economy of British Historical Experience, 1688–1914* (2002), pp. 276–86.

of Treasury and Parliament over Secretaries of State and Hanover, to argue that such a struggle had characterised relations between Walpole and
Townshend, and between Pelham and Newcastle, and that the principle
of fiscal retrenchment and, therefore, caution in diplomatic commitment
triumphed with the Grenville (1763–5) and North (1770–82) ministries,
and was revived in the early years of that of Pitt the Younger (1783–6).
North told the Commons in May 1778 that Continental connections 'cost
Great Britain a vast deal, and the return they made was not adequate to the
expense'.[93]

Yet, alongside this view of domestic restraint on foreign policy, and
irrespective of the question of whether or not this restraint was appropriate,
comes an 'external' or diplomatic rationale for the disengagement from the
interventionist tradition. This would focus on a number of factors that
reflected lesser need or opportunity. In the former case, there was the decline
in the threat to Hanover from French or Prussian attack, and, in the latter,
the practical disadvantages of alliances. For example, the incompatibilities
presented by the earlier attempts to strengthen the status quo by seeking
co-operation with powers – Prussia in 1740, Austria and Russia in 1755 –
that wished to overturn it were appreciated more readily in the 1760s. In
1730, such a situation had led to the abandonment of the Anglo-French
alliance. After 1763, it ensured there was no real value in seeking alliances
unless relations with France markedly deteriorated.

It has been suggested that hostility with the Bourbons was redundant,
as international relations had been transformed by the rise of Austria,
Prussia and Russia, and as French ministers were eager to co-operate with
Britain in order to preserve the European system. Such an approach puts
parliamentary expression of hostility and suspicion towards France and
Spain in the category of unhelpful, if not anachronistic. In 1763, the
French envoy sounded the British government on co-operating to protect Poland from its neighbours. This was taken forward by Emmanuel-
Armand, Duke of Aiguillon, foreign minister in 1771–4, who believed
that the two states must co-operate to limit Russia's rising power in eastern Europe. To woo Britain, he adopted a more conciliatory attitude towards Anglo-French relations than that shown by Etienne-François, Duke
of Choiseul, who had dominated French foreign policy in the 1760s.
The First Partition of Poland in 1772, led to a resumption of French
approaches and, eventually, to a favourable response by George III and
one of his Secretaries of State, William, 4th Earl of Rochford. The latter,

[93] Cobbett, XIX, 1173.

however, was well aware that an alliance was impracticable for domestic reasons.

Yet, it would be misleading to argue that the alliance was rejected simply because it was too innovative for the political nation, whose representatives in Parliament were indeed kept in the dark about such a possible transformation in policy. In fact, such a realignment would have committed Britain to opposition to the partitioning powers, the most powerful alliance in Europe. As parliamentarians would have pointed out had an alliance been negotiated, it was unclear what could have been done to protect Poland from partition, while Hanover would also have been seriously exposed in the event of war. Furthermore, the threat of British naval attack had little effect on Russia in 1720 or 1791. Thus, in the short term, an Anglo-French alliance would have been implausible diplomatically and unsuccessful militarily, and, in Parliament, the ministry would have risked an anticipation of the Ochakov debates of 1791; debates that serve as a worthy comment on criticism of the quality of parliamentary discussion.

In the longer term, in 1772–3, it was reasonable to hope that the mutually suspicious partitioning powers would divide, as indeed happened, and to fear that D'Aiguillon would be replaced, especially as Louis XV was elderly. The British ministry did not wish to surrender its diplomatic independence to France. If distrust had not prevented an Anglo-French alliance in 1716, there was in 1772–3 no longer an impetus comparable to an endangered Protestant succession and a threatened Hanover to make a French alliance desirable.

British security clearly rested on naval power and that was threatened by the Bourbons, not the Russian fleet. For parliamentarians to be concerned about naval and colonial issues was not due to a failure to appreciate opportunities and threats on the Continent, but, rather, a reflection of an appropriate sense of national interest. In both Britain and France, it was assumed that the Peace of Paris of 1763 would not last. Choiseul had begun considering a future war with Britain even before the close of the Seven Years' War,[94] and, in April 1763, the French began to gather information that might help in an invasion. For Choiseul, naval reconstruction and diplomacy were both aspects of his preparations for a war of revenge.[95]

[94] AE. CP. Espagne 536 fol. 32, 537 fol. 224.
[95] M. C. Morison, 'The Duc de Choiseul and the Invasion of England, 1768–1770', *Transactions of the Royal Historical Society*, 3rd ser., 4 (1910), pp. 83–115; R. E. Abarca, 'Classical Diplomacy and Bourbon "Revanche" Strategy, 1763–1770', *Review of Politics*, 32 (1970), pp. 313–37; H. M. Scott, 'The Importance of Bourbon Naval Reconstruction to the Strategy of Choiseul after the Seven Years'

Although Choiseul fell in 1770 in the Falklands Crisis, it was scarcely surprising that British parliamentarians lacked any confidence in French intentions. The French annexation of Corsica against British wishes in 1768, and their initial support for Spain in the Falklands dispute, appeared to indicate the essential thrust of French policy. Furthermore, the habit, in both Parliament and the press, of placing colonial and naval issues before Continental power-politics as topics for concern was both in keeping with traditional assumptions and a reasonable reflection of what appeared to be current national interests. It was more important to Britain that she became the foremost European power in South Asia and the Pacific than that she took a leading role in the fate of eastern Europe. This was also a reflection of commercial interests and of the role of trade in the assessment of British power.

Thus, two very different attitudes can be adopted towards the expression of anti-French opinion in Parliament in the 1760s and 1770s. On the one hand, it can be argued that this was a foolish and outdated response that failed to take note of developments in European power-politics, and, on the other, that it was based on an acute perception of national interests and one that also ensured that parliamentary opinion was in accordance with that of the political nation. The last point underlines the political character of the issue; it was not simply a question of an intellectual response. This adds another dimension to the problem facing scholars, as it is unclear how sensible it is to abstract the intellectual response that 'should' have been made from the political context.

It is important to confront the issue explicitly as it is of direct importance to any judgement of quality. If warnings about French intentions and moves are presented as paranoid and/or a failure to understand the major developments in Europe, then many speakers and much of the ambience and ethos of parliamentary discussion of foreign policy will be seen as unsatisfactory. So also for criticism of interventionism, which will be presented as small-minded and penny-pinching. Conversely, if these approaches are treated as worthy of consideration, then the situation will be very different. In part, this is a matter of recovering the relevance of contemporary criticisms of interventionism, what Chavigny in 1736 termed the spirit of opposition to all engagement,[96] and of restoring what might be termed the Tory tradition of foreign policy to rightful attention; although it is necessary to underline that such attitudes were held, indeed frequently expressed, by many who

---

War', *International History Review*, 1 (1979), pp. 17–35; M. M. Escott, *Britain's Relations with France and Spain, 1763–1771* (Ph.D. thesis, University of Wales, 1988).

[96] Chavigny to Chauvelin, 16 Feb. 1736, AE. CP. Ang. 393 fol. 146.

were clearly not Tories, particularly Sir Robert Walpole, Henry Pelham, and George Grenville. Thus, it is necessary to appreciate the debate within government and the political establishment about national interests and goals, and to realise that contention and criticism were not restricted to the opposition, or even a margin of political outsiders.

This contention involved attitudes as well as interests and goals, and these attitudes were directly relevant to the question of 'best policy' and 'best practice'. In simple terms, and again allowing for a failure to conform to party political alignments, there was a tension between 'Whig' and 'Tory' attitudes towards the international system, with most parliamentarians conforming to the latter. The 'Whig' attitude assumed that through human action, it was possible to create a more benign international system. It was a mechanistic viewpoint in thrall to Newtonian physics, with clear-cut national interests that could be readily assessed and balanced, and one that sought the safety of collective security systems and believed that they could be made to work. These views made sense of, and demanded, interventionism. This was the approach of many British diplomats, of some Secretaries of State, most obviously Stanhope, Carteret and Newcastle, and of several influential scholars of the last half-century, such as Graham Gibbs and Ragnhild Hatton. From their perspective, the Tory attitude, which was dubious about all of these views, was misguided and dangerous, and its frequent expression in Parliament demonstrated the limited quality of debates.

The 'Tory' attitude, in fact, drew on a coherent intellectual and moral philosophy. It was inherently pessimistic about the possibilities of creating trust and workable collective systems, and inclined to assume that any settlement of differences would be precarious, if not short-term. This attitude was lapsarian, rather than Newtonian, and with a stress on the human volition of rulers and ministers, not the mechanics of the balance of power. This approach had considerable merit, not least because it appreciated the limitations of the schematic understanding of national interests and international relations. If the 'Tory' approach is understood, then it is possible to take a more optimistic account of the quality and ethos of debates.

To take one apparently minor example, parliamentarians were correct to draw attention to Dunkirk. The agreement to prevent Dunkirk from acting as a naval base, imposed on the French at Utrecht, and repeated in peace treaties signed in 1748 and 1763, justifiably captured the imagination of the British 'political nation'. Crucially, it was seen as a litmus test of French intentions, and this ensured that it had a domestic weight separate from its international relevance. British ministries continually stressed this domestic issue when discussing the subject. After the opposition raised the matter in Parliament in 1732, in order 'to inflame matters between us and France', James, 1st Lord Waldegrave, the envoy in Paris, was ordered to act in order to stifle the

nest-egg for clamour next sessions . . . Your Excellency sees how necessary it is, if your Court is as desirous as ours is, to keep up friendship and good harmony, that something be done, this summer, to remove that bone of contention, by finishing what would put the harbour of Dunkirk into the condition it ought to be by treaty . . . The affair of Dunkirk is indeed a national concern, and must be brought to the Parliament . . . requires your Excellency's serious thoughts and application, for every step that is taken here and with you upon it, must be laid before the Parliament, and this affair should therefore be pressed with that view.[97]

The last remark came from Thomas Pelham, both MP for Hastings and Secretary of Embassy at Paris, and reflected the wisdom of his joint position. In June 1732, Newcastle, who spent much time on Parliament,[98] complained to the French envoys that the commissioners who were supposed to discuss Dunkirk had never met, 'and I hinted what might be the consequence if it was not done before the next session of Parliament'.[99] The issue did not go away. In 1774, instructing Stormont to complain about new works at Dunkirk, Rochford wrote, 'As this affair is likely to be agitated in Parliament, the sooner I hear from your Excellency . . . the more satisfactory it will be.'[100]

This was not foolish 'clamour'. Dunkirk had served as an invasion port in 1708 and was to do so again in 1744. To treat such agitation as foolish is to misunderstand both Britain's strategic situation and the role of Parliament, alongside the press, as the point of articulation of the views of the political nation. The latter encouraged a focus on relations with France in parliamentary discussion of foreign policy, particularly after 1739, a year in which Anglo-Spanish relations had dominated attention. Other powers were often discussed only in so far as they could or should be included in an anti-French alliance. This reflected the concern France aroused and the degree to which it was easier *and* appeared more appropriate to attack ministries over relations with France than those with other powers. The latter did not strike the same chords of public anxiety, and parliamentarians were well aware that their debates would be reported.

Parliamentary concern about the financial cost of interventionism has received insufficient attention. This reflects a lack of sympathy for, and interest in, the views of taxpayers, but there is also a failure to grasp the

---

[97] Delafaye to Waldegrave, 4 May (os), 6 July (os) 1732, Thomas Pelham MP to Waldegrave, 29 Jan. (os) 1733, Chewton.
[98] Delafaye to Waldegrave, 18, 29 May (os) 1732, Chewton.
[99] Newcastle to Harrington, 9 June (os) 1732, PRO. SP. 43/82.   [100] PRO. SP. 78/291 fols. 1–3.

political value of peace. This value was captured by Edmund Gibson, Bishop of Lincoln, in July 1718 when he wrote to a fellow bishop,

all things seem to concur abroad to make it a cheerful meeting and an easy session: though many things are talked of by way of perplexing; which I hope will not be attempted if we have peace abroad. The disbanding of 4 or 5,000 men and 2 shilling in the pound on land is what the ministry give out.[101]

Accusations of folly in discussion of foreign policy sometimes had a socio-political tinge in the eighteenth century, with an attitude expressed, or implied, as if comments by those outside the élite, let alone their having a role, were misguided and deleterious. Chesterfield definitely adopted a tone of social criticism when, as envoy in the United Provinces, he condemned its system of government, 'by the happiness of this form of government it is in the power of any linen draper of Harlem, woollen draper of Leyden, or fishmonger of Amsterdam . . . in short to determine the state of foreign affairs'. James, 2nd Lord Tyrawly, a military figure who served as envoy in Lisbon and St Petersburg, 'had little reverence for Parliaments, and always spoke of them as the French do of the long robe: he even affected not to know where the House of Commons was'.[102]

Although such attitudes were manifested in Britain, it was more common to treat opposition not with reference to social criteria, but, rather, as an inherent aspect of the political system, albeit one made harmful by factious politicians. Harrington compared the opposition to 'mad dogs' in 1730.[103] With the long experience and jaundiced perspective of a bureaucrat, Delafaye wrote in 1732,

the opposers dispute the ground inch by inch about the Salt Bill. There is nothing in it but parliamentary play of offering clogging clauses, cavilling etc. which protracts the debates but do not abstract the passing of the Bill as you may see by the divisions.[104]

In 1730, a similar assurance was given to the Landgrave of Hesse-Cassel over the Dunkirk issue.[105] On the whole, Delafaye was accurate in specifics, but inclined to downplay the extent to which the prospect of opposition affected the formulation, execution and presentation of policy.

---

[101] Gibson to Nicolson, 29 July (os) 1718, Bod. Ms. A 269 fol. 77.
[102] Chesterfield to Harrington, 15 Jan. 1732, PRO. SP. 84/316 fol. 84; Walpole, *Memoirs of George II*, III, 15.
[103] Harrington to Newcastle, 25 Mar. 1730, BL. Add. 32768 fol. 232.
[104] Delafaye to Waldegrave, 9 Mar. (os) 1732, Chewton.
[105] D'Ilten to Landgrave, 5 Mar. 1730, Marburg, 4f Kur-Braunschweig.

As ever, it is too easy when discussing the role of Parliament to neglect the feel of the House. The Dunkirk issue amply demonstrated the unpredictable character of debate. In the debate on the state of the nation in 1730, Stephen Fox recorded that when Sir William Wyndham said that he had witnesses ready, 'there was a great cry in the House call 'em in call 'em in'. In response, Horatio Walpole, seconded by Henry Pelham, claimed that it would be irregular to examine witnesses when the House had not been given prior notice, as it would give one side an unfair advantage. Wyndham pulled forward an older concept of Parliament. In 'a very warm way and . . . a very artful and clever speech', he expressed surprise at the ministry's fear or unwillingness to hear evidence, adding

as for desiring to hear evidence on tother side he could not imagine what was meant by tother side, he thought nobody could be on tother side but those that lived on tother side the water [Jacobites] . . . when he had done there was again a prodigious noise of call 'em in call 'em in,

a dimension of debate not captured by Cobbett. Sir Robert Walpole's speech was explained by Fox as responding to the House. He spoke

very artfully. He endeavoured very often to put everybody in good humour . . . joked and laughed but upon feeling the pulse and temper of the House, who made a great noise to have the witnesses called in he said he knew what it was to contend against gentlemen's curiosity and love of news, and so in a manner consented to the thing and gave up the question of his brother and Pelham for which some blame him, but I think he did right for I am persuaded the clamour would have been as strong as it is at present if the witnesses had been refused a hearing.[106]

This sense of responding to a House is not captured by accounts that focus solely on the interplay of ideas, but was part of the texture of debate and crucial to the quality of speeches and speakers. The varied nature and role of Commons' leadership was captured by Hans Stanley in 1763:

Mr. [Henry] Fox is said to have managed ably the secret and personal applications, which have rendered the majority for the Court so ample as you have seen in the Votes, but in public debate never any man made so poor a figure in point of ability, or even of discretion, nor did there even from the first subsist between him and the other part of the ministry that confidence which forms a system of strength.[107]

[106] Stephen to Henry Fox, 14 Feb. (os) 1730, BL. Add. 51417 fols. 38–9.
[107] Stanley to Buckinghamshire, 6 June 1763, BL. Add. 22359 fol. 64.

8

A parliamentary foreign policy?

that firmness, beauty, and magnificence of our excellent Constitution, founded on the mutual consent of Prince and People; both moving, as it were, in one orb, reciprocally influencing, attracting, and directing each other; whose united power may be compared to a machine for the determining the equality of weights; the Sovereign, and the representative Body, counterpoising each other, and the Peers preserving the equilibrium.

This summary of the classic thesis of the British constitution appeared in 1791 as part of an 'Address to the Public' at the beginning of the first volume of the *Senator*, a new periodical devoted to reporting parliamentary debates, and the appearance of which indicated continued strong public interest in such reports.[1] The image was appropriate, for the existence and nature of parliamentary government was regarded as both expressing and securing the fundamental character of the British constitution. The use of mechanistic language was also appropriate. It reflected the spirit of part of the political culture of the period and, in particular, an optimistic assessment of the possibility of establishing a political order that was consistent, predictable and stable, proof against the fallibility of human ambitions and schemes.

The reality of parliamentary government was somewhat different, not least because of the tension expressed in the *Senator*'s simile, a tension that led John Dunning, MP for Calne and, then, a supporter of Shelburne in opposition, to tell the Commons in 1771 that 'our whole constitution is a political kind of chaos, and depends upon the preservation of opposing elements: the king has his prerogative, the peers their jurisdiction, and we our privileges'.[2] In the *Senator*, the comparison to a machine, in which separate bodies balanced each other, was matched by the image of reciprocally influencing and directing bodies moving in the same orbit. This apparent contrast provides much of the key to the different ways in which the position of Parliament can be approached: alongside a stress on co-operation

[1] *Senator*, I (1791), iii.   [2] Cobbett, XIII, 142.

or conflict between Parliament and royal government, there was a considerable measure of interdependence. In addition, the crucial political disputes usually occurred within the government, and Parliament's most important direct political role generally centred on its relationship to these disputes.

The futility of most opposition storm and thunder was readily apparent (blatantly so on 29 April 1794 when the ministry refused to speak in reply to opposition attacks), although more so to British than to foreign commentators. In the case of the latter, it was not only the views of envoys in London that were important, but also those of their governments, as well as the diplomatic world elsewhere. Thus, in 1735, when the British government was trying to negotiate an end to the War of the Polish Succession, Horatio Walpole, the key negotiator, wrote to his brother that the Austrians had decided

to hearken to nothing that shall be advised from England and even to let things to continue upon the same foot they are whatever may be the consequence until our Parliament shall meet, in hopes that the English nation is so alarmed with the pushes of the House of Bourbon that the Walpoles will be obliged to declare publicly in favour of the Emperor or to resign their places.[3]

In fact, although they had been advised to follow such a course, the Austrian government was about to settle directly with France, but this report indicated the concern that foreign views were affected by the possibility that ministries might be overthrown, that, by its very existence, the hopes and fears that the parliamentary process gave rise to challenged the stability of British foreign policy. This had apparently been demonstrated in 1733 when the Excise Crisis had led to expectations about the fall of the Walpole ministry that may well have influenced responses to Britain's likely position in the international crisis that developed that year; as well as encouraging a more general sense that domestic problems would vitiate Britain's position on all issues.[4]

In December 1740, the Sardinian envoy in The Hague noted the widespread belief that Parliament and the nation would oblige George II to stop French schemes by a formal declaration of war.[5] Like many others who wrote or talked about the impact of Parliament, the opinion-formers in The Hague were wrong. British commentators were more acute in

---

[3] Horatio Walpole to Robert Walpole, 1 Oct. 1735, BL. Add. 23796 fols. 1–2.
[4] Gansinot, Wittelsbach envoy in The Hague, to Count Törring, Bavarian foreign minister, 23 June 1733, Munich, Kasten Schwarz 17323.
[5] Chavanna to Charles Emmanuel III, 1 Dec. 1740, AST. LM. Ollanda 37.

understanding the distinction between pressure and impact. When, in 1776, Charles James Fox launched an attack on the ministry, Thomas, Lord Pelham reported:

Lord North after having been abused and bated for twelve hours got up in the highest good humour. Told the House he was there to be bated and for them to fire their darts at but that what he had done or advised proceeded from an honest heart, that he would support the measures he had advised, and that he would never give up, until he had seen his king and his country relieved from the horrid situation they were now in. It pleased all parties and he was much applauded.[6]

In December 1782, Charles, Lord Camden, the Lord President of the Council, focused on what he saw as the impotence of an opposition faced by governmental control of Parliament; ironically so, in view of the ministry's defeat the following February:

As to the foreign politics and the war it is almost impossible to make a reputable opposition upon that ground as things are circumstanced. The war must proceed, and all that can be done, is to remark from time to time upon the negligence and mismanagement of the ministers, and that always ends in a parliamentary approbation of their conduct and operates as a pardon against all future impeachments.[7]

Despite the weakness of opposition in Parliament, no alternative structure to Parliament could feasibly be advanced in what was a profoundly legitimist and, in many respects, conservative society. Radicals could propose alternatives, but their very radicalism condemned them. Christopher Wyvill's attempt to establish an alternative structure in 1779–80 failed, as did radical projects for 'conventions' in the 1790s. There was a desire to work within Parliament, rather than an alienation from it. One sure sign of an incipient transfer of power is the slipping away of authority from the established institutions of state to new unofficial bodies. This had been at issue in the seventeenth century, but was not in the eighteenth, with the exception of the Thirteen Colonies in North America prior to the outbreak of revolution in 1775 and Ireland in the early 1780s.

Although Parliament did not sit for much of the year, and, due to the role of government and the Court, was not the sole national focus of political activity, it was nevertheless clear that an ability to perform well in debate was still seen as an important aspect of political life at the close of the century. Charles, 2nd Earl and 1st Marquess Cornwallis, who had briefly been an MP (1760–2) before becoming a peer (though he spent most of his

[6] Lord Pelham to Thomas Pelham, 25 Feb. 1776, BL. Add. 33126 fol. 301.
[7] Camden to Earl of Shelburne, 14 Dec. 1782, BL. Bowood papers, Box 38.

two and a half years as an MP on active service in Germany), wrote after thirty years as a member of the Lords,

I have always been of opinion that no man who has a regard for the consideration in which he is to stand with his country, should produce himself, even in the House of Lords as an efficient member of Administration, without possessing such powers and habits of Parliamentary Debate as would enable him to do justice to a good cause, and defend his measures as well as those of his colleagues.[8]

Thus, an ability to explain and defend foreign policy in Parliament could still be very important. In 1791, the ministry suffered in the Ochakov crisis from the disaffection of the Foreign Secretary, Francis, 5th Duke of Leeds, who was not, himself, the best of parliamentarians, as well as from the absence of a minister who could lead expertly for the government in the Commons on foreign policy. In 1754–5, the ministerial position in the Commons had been similarly weakened because Thomas Robinson, the Secretary of State, although an experienced ex-diplomat, was no orator.[9]

Parliamentarians could be relied upon to complain. Cornwallis wrote in 1790 to Henry Dundas about arrangements for the government of India,

you will be sufficiently aware that the opposition in Parliament will spare no pains or exertions to throw ridicule and odium upon any system that you or Mr. Pitt may bring forward, without thinking it incumbent upon them to propose any remedies for the errors or imperfections which they will lay to its charge.[10]

The following year, Cornwallis, then commanding against Tipu Sultan of Mysore, was angered by attacks on his policies in India which he saw as politically inspired, rather than based on true knowledge of the situation,

What is it that we astonished Indians do not read in your debates? We there see that Tippoo is our barrier against the Marattas; The Tiger a barrier against the Deer! As well might it have been said to the Elector of Saxony during the Seven Years' War, how fortunate are you to have so noble a barrier as the great Frederick [II of Prussia] against the power of Sweden, which some years ago threatened the ruin of your dominions.[11]

And yet, rather than simply emphasising the negative dimensions of parliamentary scrutiny of foreign affairs, it is also pertinent to note the positive aspect of Parliament's role. In 1715, Horatio Walpole attributed a more flexible French diplomatic stance to 'the influence of the new elections which

---

[8] Cornwallis to Pitt, 23 Jan. 1792, PRO. 30/11/175 fol. 21.
[9] J. C. D. Clark (ed.), *The Memoirs and Speeches of James, 2nd Earl Waldegrave* (Cambridge, 1988), pp. 160–1.
[10] Cornwallis to Dundas, 4 Apr. 1790, PRO. 30/11/151 fol. 36.
[11] Cornwallis to Lansdowne, 9 Oct. 1791, BL. Bowood, Box 40.

will certainly give great credit and weight to His Majesty's affairs in all parts it being the best Parliament that was ever chosen for the good of our country since the [Glorious] Revolution'.[12] Despite criticism, Cornwallis was confident of parliamentary support.

Governmental control of Parliament was crucial to the equation of Parliament and foreign policy. A small majority in a Commons' division in 1732 led the hostile Chavigny to argue that Britain would be unable to fulfil international commitments in a letter that was intercepted by Britain's Austrian ally.[13] In contrast, when the two powers had been allies, French envoys had reassured their superiors that, irrespective of opposition agitation, the government would dominate Parliament;[14] although there could also be concern that this would make Britain a difficult ally.[15]

There were attempts to circumvent at least some aspects of Parliament's role. Contentious policies led monarchs to keep ministers in the dark or to ignore their opinions, helping to provoke the parliamentary storm over the Partition Treaties and also to precipitate the Whig splits of 1717 and 1743–4. These policies also led ministries to refuse parliamentary requests for papers. The demand for papers was frequently a highpoint of parliamentary contention. The debate raised issues of confidentiality and secrecy that were readily politicised. On 18 December (os) 1741, when Walpole was reeling after the general election and much of Europe was succumbing to war, William Pulteney attacked on the issue.

The first motion was for all memorials, declarations, etc. etc., and letters that had passed between the King of England and the Queen of Hungary [Maria Theresa] or between their ministers relative to the state of the war in Germany. We [the ministerial side] objected only to such letters as might have passed between the King himself and that Queen which it was neither decent, nor respectful in us to desire to see, nor honourable in the King to show; nor could possibly be of any use to us. This bore a long debate, and on the question for amending the question so as only to exclude such letters, we were ayes 237, nos 227. Then the very same question was moved with regard to France, and, the same amendment passed without opposition. Then the same with regard to Prussia, and it was then insisted on that such letters were necessary because that Prince [Frederick the Great] wrote his own dispatches and did much business by personal correspondence with other crowned heads. Sir Robert Walpole begged them to postpone this question, which amended, as the others were, might pass some time hence, but then was an affair

---

[12] Walpole to Stair, 12 Mar. 1715, NAS. GD. 135/141/2.
[13] Chavigny to Bussy, 22 Feb. 1732, HHStA. Stk. Interiora Intercepte I fol. 45.
[14] E.g. Chammorel's reports of 14, 17, 21 Nov. and Destouches of 17 Nov. 1718, AE. CP. Ang. 311 fols. 39, 44, 54, 52. cf. Diemar to Landgrave of Hesse-Cassel, 8 Apr. 1732, Marburg, England 202.
[15] Destouches to Dubois, 9 Nov. 1722, AE. CP. Ang. 343 fol. 121.

which was to be kept secret by stipulation, till a day very near at hand; but if it was understood that no answer should be expected to this address till after that day, it might go now. This was readily consented to, but Sir Robert finding himself misunderstood told them fairly, that he did not answer for it when such answer did come, that the King might not be advised to say that *all* contained in that question was not proper for their view. Then Mr. Pelham deprecated the question itself now, and desired that it might be postponed till such time (which was understood to be immediately after the holydays) as the answer could be given to it, putting his credit and reputation upon it that when they should know the reason those who were most eager for it now would wish they had been of this opinion. This made great impression, and many of their side; as Lord Chetwynd, Mr. Sydenham, Mr. Bowes, Lord Cornbury, Mr. Rutherford, spoke for postponing the question, and many more cried out for the withdrawing it; which they were very unwilling to do, and confounded to see so many of their party show little implicit faith in their leaders. At length, Sir John Rushout, forced to it, got up to withdraw his motion, on condition that it was understood, that the ministers would agree to and comply with such question immediately after the holydays; then Mr. Pelham got up and explained himself, till indeed there was no condition left at all; and believed that this question so improper now, would, thus worded, *always* be improper; then the House was in uproar, and first Lord Chetwynd in a passion, and then almost all who had declared for withdrawing the question, rose and recanted; and much altercation ensued. The case was, that the ministers were at first extremely willing that all their negotiations with Prussia should be laid before the Parliament; but when they considered a little better the extent of the question and the temper of the King of Prussia, they found that some were asked for by it which we had no right to see; and others, I believe, which the King of Prussia could not suffer to be shown without having recourse to the strongest resentment, by way of justification of the most villainous conduct. And at last I fancy the Parliament must be content (as indeed with regard to very recent and unfinished negotiations they always ought to be) with as much as those who have seen all think proper to be laid before them.

The ministry won that division by 232 to 208 votes,[16] whereas, four days later, it lost divisions on the contested Westminster election. Henry Fox's account makes it clear that the range of relevant issues was raised, that individual MPs changed their views, and that the contentious atmosphere of debate played a part.

Although opposition critics found it difficult to obtain papers they wanted, there was criticism from a very different direction, with the argument that the practice of providing papers affected the conduct of government, specifically the style of instructions to envoys. Hans Stanley, MP for Southampton, a former envoy to Paris and then Ambassador designate to St Petersburg, commented in 1766, 'I know not whether this way of

---

[16] Henry to Stephen Fox, 19 Dec. (os) 1741, BL. Add. 51417 fols. 79–81.

writing has arisen from the very ill custom of communicating negotiations to Parliament but they have the air of manifestos, much more than of the confidential intercourse which ought to subsist between ambassadors and their courts, they are ambiguous, obscure, and full of an hauteur' that even the proud Louis XIV would not have employed.[17]

Ministerial speakers could argue that exposition of the general direction of policy obviated any need for full disclosure. This line was taken in the Commons in 1717 when funds were demanded for confrontation with Sweden:

that indeed the particular application to which the sum demanded was intended, was not communicated to the House because that would destroy the service designed by it, yet the letter informed them twas to defeat the invasion threatened from Sweden, and to put the kingdom in peace and safety. That forms ought to give way to necessity . . . that the refusing it now would be a great slight to His Majesty, and encourage his enemies.

The ministerialists continued by presenting parliamentary support as the alternative to a more risky option of royal prerogative action, and of the parliamentary option therefore as a valuable control on commitments, an approach that sought to rally Whig support,

finally that the King could have entered into treaties if he had pleased by his prerogative which would have been effectual to preserve his dominions, yet because that might have been expensive to his subjects for such treaties must have provided a mutual defence to both the parties, and that might have engaged England in a war for their defence who articled to defend him, but His Majesty chose rather to apply this way to his loyal Parliament as the quickest, cheapest, and safest way to settle them in peace.[18]

Aside from papers, there was also a search for information by means of summoning witnesses. In 1739, the government defeated two opposition attempts in the Lords to summon the Directors of the South Sea Company for questioning, although the opposition did succeed in having merchants, protesting about Spanish depredations on trade, heard and questioned.

The refusal to provide Parliament with information did not prevent the reiteration of the constitutional conventions of co-operation, conventions that could be maintained because government majorities could defeat

[17] Hans Stanley to John, 2nd Earl of Buckinghamshire, 18 Aug. 1766, BL. Eg. 22359 fol. 52.

[18] Perceval notes, BL. Add. 47028 fol. 184. For the weeding of what was presented the following century, V. Cromwell, 'The Administrative Background to the Presentation to Parliament of Parliamentary Papers on Foreign Affairs in the Mid-Nineteenth Century', *Journal of the Society of Archivists*, 2 (1963), p. 306.

opposition requests for papers, while royal discretion and secrecy helped, in general, to reduce the political significance of differences between monarch and ministers. Thanks in part to the practice of secret diplomacy by monarchs and ministers, Parliament could be ignored, especially if peace prevailed and subsidy treaties or commercial agreements were not being considered. If a parliamentary foreign policy, in the sense of a policy over which Parliament, even if it had no executive functions, was, nevertheless, fully considered, did not pertain, the term was still applicable with regard to a policy that had to take note of parliamentary views and of Parliament's constitutional and political role. This political role created a sense of parliamentary competence, responsibility and validation greater than the constitutional one. Thus in 1725, Townshend wrote to his fellow Secretary of State, Newcastle, about the need to win parliamentary approval for Dutch accession to the recent Treaty of Hanover between Britain, France and Prussia:

If the Dutch accede to our treaty, there will be a necessity of laying it before the Parliament for they will certainly, in consequence of their accession, not only insist upon his Majesty's joining with them in measures for stopping the Ostend trade, but likewise that our [East India] Company shall act in concert with theirs for destroying the Ostend ships in the Indies, which I believe will not be ventured upon by our Directors unless the treaty has the approbation of Parliament.[19]

Irrespective of constitutional requirements, the sense that government had to ensure parliamentary validation was part of the currency of European diplomatic correspondence.[20] Within Britain, monarchs and ministers had to respond to this belief and to political and constitutional circumstances, although the extent to which policy was affected as a consequence is open to debate.

This state of affairs was not the result of the Glorious Revolution. In so far as Parliament became an annual feature, the Glorious Revolution was obviously important, but, prior to the Revolution, Britain already had a reputation abroad for political and ministerial instability that was not dependent on Parliament's constitutional position. Indeed, the problems of post-Revolutionary parliamentary management helped eventually to produce a measure of political stability by encouraging monarchs to turn to ministers who could manage, and by leading the latter, in 1716, to pass the Septennial Act, extending the period between elections and thus decreasing the volatility of parliamentary politics.

[19] Townshend to Newcastle, 2 Oct. 1725, PRO. SP. 43/7 fols. 148–9.
[20] Solaro di Breglio to Charles Emmanuel III, 2, 9 Sept. 1733, AST. LM. Austria 63.

For the century after the Revolution, the situation was similar to that of the century before: in some circumstances and particular contingencies, Parliament was of considerable influence, if only through its existence, but, on other occasions, this was not the case. If the history of the breach between Britain and Russia in the late 1710s, and their subsequent reconciliation in the early 1730s, can be written without any significant reference to Parliament, the same was not the case with the failure to create an alliance between the two powers after the Seven Years' War or, even more, with the collapse of the Pitt ministry's confrontation with Russia in 1791.

The role of Parliament also had a dynastic context. Theoretically the vast accretions of strength represented by the acquisitions of the crowns of Sweden, Poland and Britain by the rulers of Hesse-Cassel, Saxony and Hanover respectively should have enabled them to dominate northern Europe. Other German rulers attempted to emulate them. Duke Leopold of Lorraine laid the basis for the eventual marriage, in 1736, of his eldest son, Francis Stephen, with the heiress of the Austrian dominions, Maria Theresa, because he hoped this union would give Lorraine the strength to break free from French tutelage. Frederick William I of Prussia considered a marriage between his heir, the future Frederick the Great, and Anne of Mecklenburg, the niece of the childless Czarina Anna, a move that could have produced the dynastic union of Prussia and Russia.

These schemes did not produce lasting gains in power. In the cases of Britain, Poland and Sweden, the limitations of the constitutional and political powers of the Crown thwarted the German monarchs. Augustus II and Augustus III drew little benefit from Poland apart from the glory of a crown. George I and George II failed in their attempts to use British power to strengthen the Hanoverian position in the Empire. Although Parliament paid for the British fleets that served the Hanoverian diplomatic strategy in the Baltic in the late 1710s and 1720s, and for the Hessians, George I and George II had to respond to the constraints of their situation. The Prussian claim in 1729 (see p. 67) that Parliament would not back George II as Elector in a war fought on behalf of Hanover accorded with the thrust of the Act of Settlement. The claim was also an instance of the argument that a state's strength was related to its constitutional and political ability to mobilise support. In considering the strength of the new dynastic conglomeration of Britain–Hanover, it was necessary to assess the relationship between ruler and British Parliament. Sasstroff, the Prussian Resident in Cassel, was inaccurate in his assessment of what Parliament would do, but correct in arguing that it had to be considered. Had Parliament refused to pay the Hessians, George would have been forced to yield to

Prussia in the struggle for the domination of northern Germany prior to the 1740s.

Nevertheless, despite Parliament's support over the Hessians in 1729, attempts to create an alliance with the Wittelsbachs in 1729–30 foundered on the unwillingness of the British government to provide the necessary subsidies, the Hessians were paid off in 1732, and, in the War of the Austrian Succession (1740–8), George was forced to watch while his hated nephew, Frederick II, pushed Prussia into a dominant position. Hanoverian influence in Mecklenburg was eroded, Prussia acquired East Friesland in 1744 despite Hanoverian protests, and the British ministers insisted on focusing on sustaining a coalition against France rather than creating one against Prussia. Thus, the attempt to use the Anglo-Hanoverian dynastic union to foster Hanoverian territorial interests failed. The later eighteenth century witnessed nothing to parallel the Hanover–Britain, Hesse–Sweden, and Saxony–Poland unions. Instead, states that had pursued a measure of internal consolidation and had acquired territory and interests through war, such as Russia, Prussia and Austria (which had had to fight hard to enjoy the benefits of dynastic diplomacy) dominated central and eastern Europe.

Hopes that Hanover could act as a major power had failed to overcome its weakness and vulnerability and the independence of the British political structure. There was a tension between the wish of George I and George II to develop military strength and parliamentary views.[21] The Hanoverian issue was one in which opposition parliamentarians could deploy both rhetoric and more prudential considerations; although, at least in so far as passing motions was concerned, they were up against government majorities. In the debate on the Address in January 1730, Thomas Wyndham, an opposition Whig MP for Dunwich,

past ten o'clock made a motion (in favour of the King of Prussia) which if it had been attended to would have prolonged the debates till sunrising: it was to confine whatever assurances the Parliament should give His Majesty of making good his engagements, and of standing by him to attempts upon his Britannic dominions.

In the event, as Perceval noted, 'no reply was made to him'.[22] On 4 February (os) 1730, Wyndham followed up by condemning the Hessian subsidy as an infringement of the Act of Settlement.

The parliamentary opposition to subsidy treaties with Hesse-Cassel is an apt example of the problems the Crown faced. Although the treaties were

---

[21] Chavigny to Chauvelin, 24 Nov. 1735, AE. CP. Ang. 392 fol. 179.
[22] Robert Trevor to Poyntz, 15 Jan. (os) 1730, BL. Add. 75450; HMC. *The Diary of the First Earl of Egmont* (3 vols., 1920–3), I, 5.

never defeated in Parliament, the continued strength and vigour of the opposition on this point, combined with Walpole's determination to cut government expenditure, and thus taxes, led the British ministry to a shift in policy. The attempt by George I and George II to use British money to weld together a Hanoverian and Hessian bloc capable of defying the Prussian attempt to dominate northern Germany had to be abandoned.

In general, Parliament featured more as a factor, active or passive, in commercial issues and Anglo-Bourbon relations, than in those with the powers of central, eastern and northern Europe. In 1732, when Britain and Austria were allied, Harrington instructed Robinson in Vienna to use the domestic situation in order to prompt Austrian concessions,

observing that it will be absolutely impossible for the King, however well inclined to their interests, to secure the affections of this nation to them, or even to make the guaranty he has already given [of the Pragmatic Sanction] of so much use to the Emperor's descendants, as His Majesty himself would wish and desire, if some facility be not shown in points wherein our commerce is concerned.[23]

While taking this position, the government was also keen to dispel the idea that it was subject to opposition pressure, Delafaye writing in 1732 about 'these little mortifications, and however foreigners may on this account fancy the government here is weak, they will always find that whilst it pays a due regard to the laws and constitution, it will ever be strong enough to support itself at home and to have weight and influence abroad'.[24]

This analysis was challenged the following year in the Excise Crisis. In the eyes of foreign commentators, domestic problems prevented the Walpole ministry from fulfilling its commitments at a time of international crisis. Chavigny and his Sardinian and Spanish counterparts, Ossorio and Montijo, the envoys of the three powers that attacked Austria in the War of the Polish Succession in 1733, presented Britain, which had treaty commitments to Austria, as on the brink of civil war, and these reports had an impact in European courts.[25] This would apparently present a major instance not of parliamentary views on foreign policy swaying British diplomacy, but of the very existence of legislative contention as incapacitating this diplomacy. In practice, such a simple reading of the situation can be challenged,[26] while the issue is also important as it indicates the

[23] Harrington to Robinson, 1 Feb. (os) 1732, PRO. SP. 80/84.
[24] Delafaye to Waldegrave, 7 Feb. (os) 1732, Chewton.
[25] Guy Dickens (Berlin) to Edward Weston, 12 May, Walter Titley (Copenhagen) to Weston, 12 May, Villettes (Turin) to Delafaye, 26 May 1733, PRO. SP. 90/34, 75/61 fols. 140–1, 92/35 fols. 106–7.
[26] J. Black, '1733 – The Failure of British Diplomacy?', *Durham University Journal*, 74 (1982), pp. 199–209.

methodological difficulties of assessing the impact of Parliament. Indeed, in 1733 the impact of domestic considerations was more subtle than that of weakness stemming from opposition pressure. Indeed, as an instance of the variety in diplomatic views, Degenfeld, the Prussian envoy, argued that British neutrality was due to governmental promises of low taxes, and a resulting reluctance to demand new ones until such time as French moves had so angered the public that they pressed for action,[27] in other words a repetition of the situation in 1701.

This was a perceptive analysis, as the experience of the later 1720s was indeed as, if not more, important than that of the Excise Crisis in accounting for British policy in 1733. The years of expensive and indecisive confrontation that had marked the conflict between the Vienna and the Hanover Alliances in the late 1720s had produced much discontent. To a substantial extent, British policy after the fall of Townshend in 1730 was characterized by a reaction against the policy of the preceding years, a reaction expressed in terms of a wish to minimise entanglements and avoid expense. This was the foreign policy of Sir Robert Walpole, and it prefigured the policy followed by Bute and his successors from 1762.

It is not helpful to present this in terms of parliamentary pressure on British diplomacy, as that underplays the ability of ministers to advance and pursue their own ideas on policy. Furthermore, throughout the century, government speakers advanced the theme of the rightful prerogatives and sway of lawful authority, in response to opposition criticism in Parliament about the conduct of foreign policy. This view was supported by the size of government majorities. The jaundiced Tory George Clarke complained in 1726 to a fellow MP, Edward Nichols, 'there seems to be little occasion for Parliament, for it is a sort of resolving all power into one hand'.[28]

Later in the century, however, from a different political background, Philip Yorke, MP for Cambridgeshire, an independent supporter of the Pitt ministry, and later 3rd Earl of Hardwicke, expressed his disillusionment with current parliamentary politics, and also his view that publication of debates was dangerous. Significantly, he was writing to Sir Robert Murray Keith, a diplomat, who had himself been a mostly absent MP for Peebleshire: 'no great advantage can be expected from long sessions, when no questions but those which relate to party are ever attended. The publication of the debates and opposition speeches have lost America, and the fewer there are

[27] Degenfeld to Frederick William I, 10 Feb. 1733, PRO. SP. 107/9.
[28] George Clarke to Edward Nicholas, 26 Mar. (os) 1726, BL. Eg. 2540 fol. 610. Inaccurately dated in Sedgwick, I, 555.

to be published, the better the business will be done, if in good hands.'[29] Given such claims, and impressed by the fuss that parliamentarians could create, it is not surprising that foreign diplomats and, albeit less consistently, foreign ministers arguably exaggerated its influence. They were products of a political culture that, while often accepting the existence of representative institutions, believed that they should not debate foreign policy, and that it was an essential prerogative of royal authority. These diplomats fail to appreciate 'the difference in opinion which is incident to all numerous assemblies'.[30] Thus, in 1732, Kinsky, the Austrian envoy, was urged to bring up his new child in Germany so that he did not suck in with his milk 'cet air parlementaire'.[31] In 1790, Luzerne, French envoy in London, wrote to criticise the impact of the development of public politics in Paris:

le mal que nous a fait la discussion qui vient de s'élever dans l'Assemblée Nationale. Tel qu'en soit la fin, nous serons perdu dans l'opinion publique, à moins que par une décision pure et simple on ne donne au Roi le pouvoir de faire la guerre et la paix; et que l'on ne vote directement un subside pour faire les premiers frais de l'armement.

Noting that the speeches in the National Assembly were accurately trans-lated in London, Luzerne added 'Leurs injures personnelles les rendent encore plus vils, et le résultat de toutes les réflexions, est que la nation ne peut rien faire, representée par une pareille assemblée'.[32]

Concern about the uncertainty resulting from Parliament's position, combined with their professional desire for stability, and the particular interests of the representatives of Britain's allies, ensured a measure of sup-port from foreign diplomats for the Peerage Bill in 1719. This was designed to strengthen the Stanhope-Sunderland ministry by restricting the mem-bership of the House of Lords, and thus preventing the future George II, then in opposition, from creating fresh peers when he came to the throne. France was then an ally and Destouches approvingly reflected that this would make British foreign policy more consistent and solid.[33] The Bill, which was defeated in the Commons, also served as a reminder both of the constitutional importance of the Lords and of the close relationship between the politics of both Houses. Such a measure would have made it impossible to push through contentious changes in policy such as the abandonment of the Grand Alliance by Anne's Tory ministers.

[29] Yorke to Keith, 16 Dec. 1784, BL. Add. 35533 fol. 101.
[30] Delafaye to Waldegrave, 25 May (os) 1732, Chewton.
[31] Pfütntmury to Kinsky, 4 Mar. 1732, PRO. SP. 100/11.
[32] Luzerne to Montmorin, French foreign minister, 25 May 1790, AE. CP. Ang. 573 fols. 157–9.
[33] Destouches to Dubois, 13 Apr. 1719, AE. CP. Ang. 323 fol. 246.

Variety between representative institutions in Europe extended to that between the two Houses of Parliament. At times, there was competition, not least to ensure that important business was brought forward. In April 1726, Strafford complained that George I had sent a message to the Commons the previous month asking for funds to increase the number of sailors in the fleet, and thereby give additional strength to foreign policy, and that the message had not been communicated to the Lords.[34] The debate sparked off by Strafford's complaint provided a fine display of the view of some of the peers concerning the prerogatives of their house. It also clearly touched a nerve in many peers, for the division preceding the Protest was 59–31, a substantially better opposition vote than their last Protest, in February 1726, when the division had been lost by 94–15.

In April 1726, Strafford also told the Lords that they were 'the grand standing council of the sovereign; the hereditary guardians of the liberties and properties of the people, and, next to the king, the principal part of the legislature, and who therefore have a right to be consulted in all matters of public concern'. He was supported by the opposition Whig Nicholas, Lord Lechmere, who argued 'that it must be for the service of the crown, upon all occasions, to have the advice of both House of Parliament', and 'that it was the undoubted and inherent right of the House of Peers, to alter and amend all Money Bills which came from the Commons', a view that was contrary to accepted conventions. Lechmere, who had sat in the Commons for thirteen years and been both Solicitor-General and Attorney-General, also claimed 'that, according to ancient usage, all demands of supply should come from the throne in the House of Peers'. According to the account in Cobbett, Lechmere corroborated all his assertions, 'by several precedents upon record, which, at his desire, were ordered to be read'. No details were provided, so that a speedy reading of the account suggests that it was restricted to fine sentiments, when it is clear that detailed and informed arguments were advanced.[35]

It was clear from its debates that the Lords were an active and vigilant House. This does not imply that the House dominated the politics of the age, however much many of its individual members took a prominent role in government and opposition. Indeed, as Chesterfield pointed out in the House in 1740, 'Kings are generally for consulting with such as are of their own choosing, and these are often such as have no dignity, privilege or right by their birth.'[36] Furthermore, it was generally easier to manage the Lords: it contained fewer members and most of the clerical and Scottish

---

[34] Cobbett, VIII, 511.   [35] Cobbett, VIII, 518–19.   [36] Cobbett, XI, 732.

representatives tended to support the government. Henry Fox noted in October 1742, 'the Duke of Argyle's low spirits and repeated approbation of foreign measures, Hanover troops etc. makes opposition in the House look faint and weak, till ours, at least, shall have prepared domestic matter for it'.[37]

The importance of financial considerations helped ensure that the role of the Lords was more limited than that of the Commons. There was no clear constitutional convention as to which minister should be regarded as the principal one, but the four most successful in the eighteenth century, Walpole, Pelham, North, and Pitt the Younger, were all First Lords of the Treasury sitting in the Commons. In comparison, the Secretaries of State, who were more commonly peers, were generally less influential. This can be attributed in large part to the need to relate the requirements of policy, which in the case of foreign policy could be very expensive, to parliamentary exigencies and possibilities. In 1758, Lord Chancellor Hardwicke suggested that there would not be any debate in the Lords over the issue of a subsidy to Prussia, 'As this will be a message of supply, Your Grace knows better than anybody that the return of the House of Lords can only consist of assurances of support.'[38] In practice, the Lords' importance depended on circumstances, especially the success of government management, much of which involved patronage, but also the extent of ministerial cohesion and the issues in dispute. Irrespective of this, it is worth pondering the observation of the Tory Allen, Lord Bathurst, a former MP, who told the Lords in 1726, 'that the appellation of Parliament being given to the Commons separately from the Lords was entirely unprecedented'.[39]

A focus on particular crises leads to an episodic account of the role of Parliament. It is, however, important to see this role as more than a summation of these individual crises, important as they were. In general, successive governments enjoyed the support of Parliament, and foreign policy was no exception. This ensured a degree of financial support that was crucial. The British system of public finance rested on a parliamentary-secured public national debt, and this enabled successive governments to finance war expenditure by borrowing at a rate denied their rivals. Furthermore, British tax rates were higher than those in France, and the ability to sustain these was a consequence both of the strength of the economy and of the degree to which the role of Parliament facilitated consent.[40] Parliament, therefore,

---

[37] Henry to Stephen Fox, 19 Oct. (os) 1742, BL. Add. 51417 fol. 88.
[38] Hardwicke to Newcastle, 2 Apr. 1758, BL. Add. 32879 fols. 27–8.   [39] Cobbett, VIII, 519.
[40] P. Mathias and P. K. O'Brien, 'Taxation in England and France, 1715–1810: A Comparison of the Social and Economic Incidence of Taxes Collected for the Central Governments', *Journal of European Economic History*, 5 (1976), pp. 601–50.

helped to enlarge the power of government,[41] not least in the field of foreign policy which it supported by funds for the military and by subsidy treaties.

This capacity to give effect to decisions was important if the latter were to have weight. In late 1725, Townshend explained that he wanted Parliament to back the Treaty of Hanover,

> will when approved by both Houses, discourage our enemies and let our friends see that we are in earnest and that they may depend upon their engagements with us provided the resolutions of the Parliament are followed with the fitting out a strong fleet, without which I can assure you (according to the notion at present universally entertained of us abroad) all the Parliament can say will make very little impression in our favour.[42]

As a result of parliamentary support, a strong fleet was indeed fitted out and employed to intimidate Britain's opponents in European and Caribbean waters. It is instructive to contrast the British mobilisation in the Dutch Crisis of 1787 with the problems that France faced that year. Not only was the French government affected by serious financial problems,[43] but, in addition, the attempt to introduce reform by calling a nominated Assembly of Notables had failed earlier in the year.[44] More generally, the ability of the British state to provide subsidies to other powers was an indication of the fundamental strength provided by the combination of parliamentary government and burgeoning commerce.

Commercial interests were well represented in the Commons. Of the 2041 MPs elected from the dissolution of 1715 to that in 1754, there were (there is some overlap of categories) 198 'merchants', 43 principal industrialists, 31 London aldermen, 27 directors of the Bank of England, 29 directors of the East India Company, 28 directors of the South Sea Company, and 27 owners of estates in the West Indies. In large part, this representation gave force to the alignment of the Whig system with the moneyed interest of the financiers and leading merchants of the City of London. Of the 1964 MPs returned between the dissolutions of 1754 and 1790, there were 10 directors of the Bank of England, 16 of the South Sea Company, 31 London aldermen

---

[41] P. K. O'Brien, 'Fiscal Exceptionalism: Great Britain and its European Rivals from Civil War to Triumph at Trafalgar and Waterloo', in D. Winch and O'Brien (eds.), *The Political Economy of British Historical Experience 1688–1914* (2002), p. 258.

[42] Townshend to Newcastle, 27 Nov. 1725, PRO. SP. 43/8 fol. 80.

[43] A. Young, *Travels during the years 1787, 1788 and 1789* (2nd edn, 2 vols., 1794), I, 72–3; B. Stone, *The French Parlements and the Crisis of the Old Regime* (Chapel Hill, 1986), pp. 84–5; C. C. Sturgill, 'The French Army's Budget in the Eighteenth Century. A Retreat from Loyalty', in D. G. Troyansky, A. Cismaru and N. Andrews (eds.), *The French Revolution in Culture and Society* (Westport, 1991), p. 125.

[44] V. R. Gruder, 'Paths to Political Consciousness. The Assembly of Notables of 1787 and the "Pre-Revolution" in France', *French Historical Studies*, 13 (1984), pp. 323–55.

and 9 colonial agents. Of the 558 MPs in the Parliament of 1784–90, there were 45 'East Indians' (directors of the Company or 'nabobs' who had returned from India with wealth) and 9 West Indians.[45] The representation of 'East Indians' helped ensure that debates on developments in India could draw on considerable expertise.

The influence of merchants was frequently referred to by MPs. In May 1762, when the Commons considered support for Portugal against the Bourbons, Richard Glover, an MP for Weymouth who had a background in the world of London merchants, criticised the Portuguese government for its treatment of British trade and merchants, and the Pitt-Newcastle ministry for failing to protect them, and, when Pitt disagreed, referred to information from 'some nameless merchants'.[46] Such pressure did not always reflect the particular interests of the MPs' constituencies. In 1692–3, Foot Onslow, MP for Guildford 1689–1700, played an active role in the successful opposition to a proposed bill to lessen restrictions on the import of fine Italian silk. He presented this as a threat to the Levant trade; in which, indeed, he had earlier taken a role at Smyrna.[47] Diplomats were pressed on the need to help the government defend its position in Parliament on commercial issues, as William Fawkener was when he was sent to Portugal in 1786, and William Eden when he negotiated a trade treaty with France the same year and during subsequent negotiations.[48]

Commercial interests and the concerns of the economy were brought to bear on government, not only in Parliament but also by lobbying from parliamentarians. Sir Ellis Cunliffe, MP for Liverpool, as the corporation's candidate, from 1755 until 1767, is recorded as speaking only once in the Commons, on the prize bill in 1759, but that was not the limit of his political activity. In 1763, Cunliffe gave a firm warning to Bute about postwar colonial arrangements:

Being informed a message from His Majesty would come to the House of Commons 'for granting seven thousand pounds for the maintenance of the forts and settlements in the River Senegal' my duty to my constituents, as well as their instruments to me engaged me to take the liberty to enquire of the Chancellor of the Exchequer how; or under whose management this money was to be employed; suggesting at the same time it was the sense of the commercial part of the nation

[45] Sedgwick, I, 148–53; Namier I, 131–62.
[46] H. Walpole, *Memoirs of The Reign of King George III*, ed. D. Jarrett (4 vols., New Haven, 2000), I, 104.
[47] Hayton, V, 21–2.
[48] Hawkesbury to Fawkener, 27 Nov. 1786, Hawkesbury to Eden, 19 Jan. 1787, BL. Add. 38309, fols. 128, 136.

that 'The Committee of the Company of Merchants trading to Africa' who had been appointed and approved by Parliament in the care of the other forts, were the properest persons to have the care of these. The Chancellor answered 'He did not doubt they would be the persons employed, but wished me not to make any motion, or mention anything about it in the House'. Now, My Lord! as I am desirous always to concur with government, and have the greatest confidence in your Lordship's administration, I am content to remain silent on this occasion, provided proper assurances be given that the forts and settlements in Senegal will not be put into private hands, but placed under the direction of the African Committee; But should a contrary measure be intended, this appears to me so destructive of the commerce of this nation in general, and of that of my constituents in particular, that I must think myself obliged to oppose it.

Cunliffe informed Bute that he would wait on him in order to ascertain his views 'and to give any farther information I can'.[49] Not all MPs were as eager to lobby for their constituents' interests. Indeed, the relationship between MPs and their constituencies varied greatly, in large part in response to the views and local and national political position of the MPs.[50] In 1790, James Martin, MP for Tewkesbury 1776–1807, suggested that the process of election, specifically expenditure by the candidates, compromised the reputation of MPs. Seven years earlier, the *Edinburgh Advertiser* of 17 June 1783 had directed the harsh gaze of social exclusion at the practice of instructing MPs: 'The constituents of a certain senator, who declared he spoke their sentiments by their instruction, consist of a tinker, a taylor, a hog-feeder, and the returning officer, who is an old Highland serjeant.' The interests of constituents could also conflict, as over wool export, which benefited particular landowners and merchants but harmed the cloth industry.[51]

Mention of Cunliffe serves as a reminder that the influence of parliamentarians on all aspects of policy cannot be measured from their contribution to debate. Instead, it was their impact in the complex, interrelated world of government, politics and society that was at issue. The role of parliamentarians in commercial and colonial policy is underrated because so much was a matter of lobbying, not debate. This begs the question of how far this role should be seen as an aspect of Parliament's importance. The case of commerce is an apt example of the prior importance of parliamentarians and of their continuing role outside Parliament. Nevertheless,

---

[49] Mount Stuart, papers of John, 3rd Earl of Bute, papers from Cardiff 9/93.
[50] D. Eastwood, 'Parliament and the Locality: Representation and Responsibility in Late-Hanoverian England', *Parliamentary History*, 17 (1998), pp. 68–81.
[51] Martin to John Parsons, 8 May 1790, Gloucester CRO. D214 F1/99; George Huntingford, Warden of Winchester, to Addington, 9 Apr., 9 May 1788, 152M/C 1788/F53, 49.

the existence of the Commons lent weight to such lobbying, just as it ensured that there was a wealth of expertise available if required for debates.

Ministers could also lobby parliamentarians on foreign policy. In January 1727, Thomas Robinson, Secretary of Embassy in Paris, reported that the French foreign minister had told him he hoped the British government did not doubt French assurances. In reply,

> I told Monsieur de Morville that the King could not and certainly did not doubt of it, yet the repetition of these assurances at this particular time of day were in some measure necessary at the opening of Parliament when, to satisfy more the curiosity than the diffidence of some of the chief members (who being themselves once assured of it might convey the same thing to others) His Majesty's ministers might, as it proved necessary talk to those gentlemen with the greater readiness and persuasion of the firmness and fidelity of France, not only from the constant and uniform behaviour of this court, but even were there occasion for more proofs of it, from the latest and freshest renewals of their promises to abide by their engagements.[52]

Parliament's role in raising money ensured that parliamentary support for the government helped both the ministry's international situation[53] and the confidence of the monied interest, and thus public credit. The favourable session of 1726 led Daniel Dering to report from London, 'This has given a spirit in the City [of London] where everything rises, and they seem there not to be afraid of a war.'[54] Conversely, Britain's opponents saw Parliament's role in raising funds as a potential weakness for Britain. In 1728, the Sardinian envoy in Vienna reported Austrian hopes that a prolongation of the international crisis would exhaust parliamentary willingness to finance British military preparations.[55]

Finance was particularly important in wartime. Then, parliamentary taxation played a crucial role in the mobilization of resources. This links to the competitive advantage of states and governmental systems, an issue that was of concern to contemporaries, as in their comparisons of Britain with France. More recently, comparative state development has been probed by political scientists seeking an explanatory model that can differentiate between polities, as well as a political *longue durée* that replaces that of

[52] BL. Add. 32749 fol. 36.
[53] Charles, Count of Morville, French foreign minister, to Richelieu, envoy in Vienna, 19 Jan. 1727, Paris, Bibliothèque Victor Cousin, Fonds Richelieu, vol. 31 fol. 205.
[54] Dering to Egmont, 28 Mar. (os) 1726, BL. Add. 47031 fol. 126.
[55] Solar de Breille to Victor Amadeus II, 12 Mar. 1728, AST. LM. Austria 58.

economics.[56] In such an approach, Parliament's role is significant to Britain's strength and success.

In contrast, a stress on the short term and on the role of contingency in policy formation and execution leads to a qualification of the role of Parliament in the governmental system, and, more specifically, a denial of any simple relationship between parliamentary consideration of policy and a diplomacy that was largely outside of parliamentary control and knowledge. Such a stress on the short term also directs attention to the episodic quality of parliamentary debate, as parliamentarians responded to circumstances. Indeed, in 1758, Pitt 'called on any who disapproved the measures taken or taking, to speak out, to discuss them, or to propose others *then*; not to lie in wait in hopes of distresses, and then find fault; though for himself he hoped he should never be judged by events'.[57] This stress on the short term, similarly, precludes any simple answer to the question of why ministries enjoying substantial parliamentary majorities, should, nevertheless, be greatly concerned about the parliamentary implications of foreign policy, and about the debates themselves. The particular issue in dispute, the natural desire of politicians to avoid trouble, the need to exercise persuasive powers, and the fiscal implications, real and perceived, of policy all played a part in answering this question, but any detailed study of particular episodes reveals both variations in the weight of these factors and the play of contingency.

This provides a significant clue to the nature and consequences of the Revolution Settlement. The settlement was not simply a matter of the events and resolutions of 1688–9, but also of developments over the following years and, in particular, the political and fiscal impact of William III's war with France. This process is commonly regarded as finishing in 1701, the date of the Act of Settlement and of a shift towards the parliamentary disclosure of foreign policy. The shift encouraged a stress on Parliament as the opening forth of policy to nation and world; at once a glorious counterpoint to Versailles and an agency and forum that were more potent than the latter. In February 1713, Bolingbroke wrote 'The Queen will open the true state of the negotiation to her Parliament and to the world'.[58]

What is possibly not sufficiently stressed is that the resulting political and constitutional conventions and arrangements, summarised in terms

---

[56] See, for example, B. Downing, *The Military Revolution and Political Change. Origins of Democracy and Autocracy in Early Modern Europe* (Princeton, 1992); T. Ertman, *Birth of the Leviathan: Building States and Regimes in Medieval and Early Modern Europe* (Cambridge, 1997).

[57] H. Walpole, *Memoirs of King George II*, ed. J. Brooke (3 vols., New Haven, 1985), III, 38.

[58] Bolingbroke to Strafford, 3 Feb. (os) 1713, BL. Add. 73508.

such as the Revolution Settlement and parliamentary foreign policy, were far from fixed and were indeed very varied in their impact. Combined with an understanding of the absence of consensus that lay behind contemporary and modern claims of eighteenth-century British national interests, this offers a vision of flexibility and debate that enables us to appreciate that issues were indeed at stake in foreign policy, that political skills and management could be of great importance, and that a detailed attention to specific conjunctures is required if the effects of Parliament's existence and prerogatives, and of parliamentary views and politics, are to be appreciated. The extent to which informed commentators regarded Parliament as an important sounding board for government policy helped to ensure its active role in the working out of the Revolution Settlement.

The ministry was made fully aware of this through interceptions. In 1717, the French foreign minister instructed the envoy in London to report on the parliamentary reception of the Triple Alliance. In 1730, ministers could read a letter from the Austrian envoy, in which he admitted being in the dark about the likelihood of a reconciliation between the two powers, and note that he added 'The meeting of the Parliament will probably make the thing out more clear to us.'[59] Important political speeches were, indeed, only delivered in Parliament and British diplomats took pains to communicate them to foreign governments.[60]

Yet intercepts also revealed that foreign envoys were prepared to look beyond parliamentary support for the ministry in order to present that backing as precarious and/or as no reflection of national attitudes. In 1726, the ministry intercepted and decyphered a despatch from Karl Josef von Palm, the Austrian envoy, who had close links to the opposition Whigs:

It is true they have the Parliament on their side; but that is not to be wondered at, for upon the foot that matters are and have been carried on within these few years, when the members, and consequently the majority are bought with great pensions and employments, it is no great skill to have gained the Parliament. But then I have been assured from a very good hand, that if it should be once perceived that the ministry are not deep in the king's favour and that His Majesty should out of dislike to them, make some show of changing them, in that very moment there would be a turn, and most of those upon whom the ministry *chiefly* depend, would pull off the mask and declare against them. But as long as this does not happen, it is not so much as to be supposed, that the Parliament will oppose the government unless the kingdom should come to be plunged into some visible ruin

---

[59] Nicolas, Marshal Huxelles to Iberville, 23 Jan. 1717, Kinsky to Seckendorf, 29 Dec. 1730, PRO. SP. 107/6, 11.

[60] Charles Whitworth (St Petersburg) to Carmarthen, 3 Apr. 1789, PRO. FO. 65/17 fol. 84.

or danger, for though more than the third part have actually opposed and will still oppose it, yet this can have no effect, because the ministers will always get the better by their purchased majority. The nation itself is not satisfied with the Parliament, because every body knows that there has not been one, time out of mind, in which the members have been so corrupted and devoted to the Court. For though the Parliament has approved the measures and engagements taken with foreign powers, and particularly with France, yet the nation in general, high and low, are of a contrary opinion . . .[61]

This approach was a threatening one as it questioned the validity of Parliament and the electoral process as the representation of the nation, and thus denied the importance of governmental success in parliamentary management. Palm himself was expelled in 1727 for making public a memorial he presented to George I which accused George of falsely impugning Austrian conduct in his speech to Parliament. The Austrian government was receptive to Palm's views about British politics. Johann Pentenriedter, one of its senior diplomats, wrote from Vienna to the Austrian envoy in Paris that the government's triumph in Parliament was due to corruption, and that such a situation could not last for long.[62] Opposition parliamentarians propagated the same view, as did Jacobite agents.[63] In 1727, Sarah, Duchess of Marlborough, an opposition Whig, wrote that the ministers had 'been miserably exposed lately in the debates in Parliament; but gold continues still a great majority'.[64] In contrast, ministers claimed that parliamentary backing was matched by popular support.

Irrespective of this question, there was a widespread feeling that parliamentary decisions were of great importance for international developments.[65] As diplomats reported the views of ministers, so news of the impact of Parliament spread throughout Europe. Thus, in 1727, Frederick William I of Prussia was informed by his envoy in Paris that the French government was very pleased that Parliament was willing to vote subsidies. In turn, the French intercepted the dispatch.[66]

[61] Palm to Charles VI, 13 Dec. 1726, CUL. Cholmondeley Houghton corresp. no. 1379.
[62] Pentenriedter to Baron Mark de Fonseca, 22 Mar. 1727, HHStA. Nachlass Fonseca, vol. 21 fol. 341. For the responses of Sinzendorf and Eugene to the Jacobite envoy, Graeme to Hay, 29 Mar. 1727, RA. 105/75.
[63] Charles Caesar MP to 'James III', 9 Feb., Graeme to Hay, 22 Feb. 1727, RA. 103/52, 104/11.
[64] Sarah Marlborough to Humphrey Fish, 13 Mar. (os) 1727, BL. Add. 61444 fol. 110.
[65] Dehn, Brunswick-Wolfenbüttel envoy in Vienna, to Duke Ferdinand-Albrecht of Brunswick-Bevern, no date [early 1727], Wolfenbüttel, Staatsarchiv, 1 Alt 3 nr. 27 fol. 60.
[66] Chambrier to Frederick William, 8 Feb. 1727, AE. CP. Prusse 83 fol. 190; Welderen, Hesse-Cassel envoy in The Hague, to Prince William of Hesse-Cassel, 25 Feb. 1727, Marburg, Niederlande 661.

'In Parliament our things go tolerably well, we have been strongly attacked in the House of Commons.'[67] With this remark, Newcastle captured, in 1740, the need to distinguish carefully between assaults by opposition and its success. Allowing for this, the very need to respond gave British ministers a very different experience to that of Continental counterparts. Their officials were also affected. Horatio Walpole left his Paris embassy to attend sessions. Charles Delafaye, an Under-Secretary to Newcastle, referred in 1730 to the need to prepare for opposition attacks in Parliament:

so busy are we in looking over 15 or 16 years correspondence with France, to pick out all that relates to Dunkirk or Mardyke, to St. Lucia and any other complaints we may have had of the French. For we may expect to hear of Oswego, of Canceaux, of the French smugglers, and what not? and we must show that we have not been selling our country to buy the friendship of our neighbours. The condescension of the ministry, when they have friends enough [a majority of MPs] to have stopped these impertinent demands of papers, meant for nothing but to amuse people without doors and create jealousies and clamour, is certainly noble and generous, and so frank a proceeding as laying everything fairly before the House, ought to satisfy all those who are not determined never to be satisfied, till they have obtained what I hope never will come to their share.[68]

Due to such work, there were delays in handling diplomatic business before and during sessions,[69] and in seeing envoys.[70] In 1727, Diemar reported that the ministry was too busy with Parliament to deal with the succession to Hanau. Six years later, Delafaye explained to Waldegrave, 'The hurry of business does still engross my Lord Duke of Newcastle's time to such a degree, that it is impossible for him to finish, as yet, the despatches that have been some days preparing for his foreign correspondents.' Joseph Yorke, envoy in The Hague and a long-serving MP, successively for East Grinstead, Dover and Grampound, was angry about the consequences of parliamentary disputes over policy in 1755 and complained to Philip, one of his three MP brothers,

It is hard to be fighting your cause as I am in a manner without instructions, but they say that your House calls for so many papers, they have no time to do anything

---

[67] Newcastle to Waldegrave, 27 Feb. (os) 1740, Chewton.
[68] Delafaye to Poyntz, 21 Feb. (os) 1729, 16 Feb. (os) 1730 (quote), BL. Add. 75449–50.
[69] Draft to Mor. de Grimaldi, 2 Apr. (os) 1729, PRO. SP. 100/32; Thomas Pelham to Waldegrave, 21 May (os) 1733, Chewton.
[70] Diemar to Landgrave Karl, 5 Feb. 1727, Marburg, England 195; Pollon, Sardinian envoy, to Victor Amadeus III, 27 Mar. 1787, AST. LM. Ing. 88; Carmarthen to Keith, 7 Mar. 1788, PRO. FO. 7/15 fol. 90.

but copy old things and consequently the new must be neglected . . . brick without straw is difficult to make . . . get me instructions.[71]

The political crisis in late 1783 also greatly hit diplomatic business, and thus left British diplomats in the dark. More generally, in March 1792, William, Lord Auckland, MP for Heytesbury and envoy at The Hague, wrote to his brother Morton Eden, envoy in Berlin, 'You seem to think it odd that you have so few official letters since your arrival at Berlin: but this is always the case with respect to all the missions during a session of Parliament'.[72]

Elections were another dimension of the parliamentary commitment. In August 1733, Newcastle wrote to William, 3rd Earl of Essex, envoy in Turin,

pity me; no sooner was the bustle of the session over, but the forwardness of the gentlemen in opposition, with relation to the elections for a new Parliament, made it necessary for us to be equally active, and those affairs take up so much of our thoughts and time, that we are obliged to neglect everything else, even our best friends.[73]

In January 1730, Delafaye had tried to capture the balance of parliamentary influence in a private letter to a diplomat,

By one [question] put this day, for the communicating to the House any engagements for subsidies to foreign princes or for the hire of foreign troops not yet laid before the House, which was rejected by 200 against 107, Your Excellency will find this is not a season to apply for a subsidy beyond what we already pay: unless a most evident occasion should make it necessary. In that case, the same majority will always make good their address upon His Majesty's speech.[74]

Much depended on the international context. Thus, the return of peace to Europe at the close of 1735 helped the Walpole government with the 1736 session, as it undercut opposition claims that British neutrality was threatening Europe's balance of power and British interests,[75] and enabled the ministry to take the initiative by cutting the size of the army and navy, rather than being seen to do so in response to criticism.[76] Sir Robert Walpole

[71] Diemar to Eugene, 4 Mar. 1735, HHStA. GK. 85(a) fol. 574; Delafaye to Waldegrave, 19 Apr. (os) 1733, Couraud to Waldegrave, 13 May (os) 1736, Chewton; Joseph to Philip Yorke, 9 Dec. 1755, BL. Add. 35364.
[72] Fox to Keith, 21 Nov. 1783, PRO. FO. 7/7; Fraser to Keith, 21 Nov. 1783, Auckland to Eden, 1 Mar. 1792, BL. Add. 35530 fol. 192, 34441.
[73] Newcastle to Essex, 27 Aug. (os) 1733, BL. Add. 32782 fol. 162.
[74] Delafaye to Poyntz, 26 Jan. (os) 1730, BL. Add. 75451.
[75] Ossorio to Charles Emmanuel III, 12 Dec. 1735, 26 Jan. 1736, AST. LM. Ing. 42–3.
[76] Couraud to Waldegrave, 19, 29 Jan. (os), 5, 9 Feb. (os) 8 Mar. (os) 1736, Chewton; Bolingbroke to Robert Knight, 5 Feb. 1736, BL. Add. 34196 fol 97.

himself emphasised parliamentary considerations when he discussed policy. In a draft of 1730, he wrote

In what a light will the friendship of France stand in our Parliament, if they do not only fail in the execution of the Treaty of Seville, and appear at last to desert us there, but at the same time violate their own treaties and act so infamously with regard to the demolition of Dunkirk? . . . France must give England satisfaction, ample satisfaction in the affair of Dunkirk, if they hope to continue the union betwixt the two Crowns.

Two years later, Harrington told Chavigny that the 'mauvaise humeur' of Parliament was one reason why it had been necessary to abandon the French alliance in 1730. In a ministerial meeting in 1738 to discuss Spanish depredations, 'Sir Robert said it was necessary not to attempt to extenuate or alleviate the depredations; the temper of the House would not bear it'.[77] This argument had also been used in 1726 when Townshend responded to Dutch pressure for financial assistance for military preparations. He claimed that MPs 'would fly into strange extremes', and pointed out that Daniel Pulteney, a prominent opposition Whig, had already claimed in the Commons that the British always had to pay for troops that they were obliged to furnish by treaty. Townshend added that, if the ships of the Austrian Ostend Company were not intercepted on their way home, the next session would be troublesome: 'the Parliament will be disgusted'.[78]

Townshend had also captured the multi-faceted role of parliament, as both threat and opportunity, the previous autumn, when referring to the 'game . . . designed to be played at the instigation of the Court of Vienna in England this next session', namely revealing George I's letter about the return of Gibraltar. He, however, saw Parliament in this case as having acted as a welcome restraint on ministerial exuberance:

after the unwary engagements Lord Stanhope had without orders made, as to Gibraltar, both in Spain and in France, his Majesty could not give any way a more advantageous turn to that unhappy affair, than to say he could not do it without our consent of Parliament; and that he would endeavour with their consent to satisfy his Catholic Majesty which answer did at that time not only stop the mouths of both the French and Spanish courts.[79]

At the same time, the Gibraltar issue led to a possible restriction of Crown power with the rumour that Parliament might in some way formally

---

[77] BL. Add. 74065 no. 1; AE. CP. Ang. 376 fol. 145; Sandon, Harrowby papers, vol. 432 doc. 30B.
[78] Townshend to William Finch, 29 Mar. (os) 1726, PRO. SP. 84/289 fols. 228–31.
[79] Townshend to Newcastle, 8 Nov. 1725, PRO. SP. 43/77 fol. 385.

incorporate Gibraltar and Minorca into the dominions of the Crown and thus lessen the King's ability to dispose of them.

A similar sense of context was (and is) necessary when considering whether Britain should, or could, send troops to the Continent during the Seven Years' War. Robert, 4th Earl of Holdernesse, Secretary of State for the Northern Department, offered the then government line in December 1757, when he wrote to Andrew Mitchell, envoy in Berlin, and himself MP for Elgin Burghs,

of the unanimity with which the present session of Parliament has been opened; the zeal with which the Protestant cause is supported; and the cheerfulness with which people, in general, will bear the heavy load, that must necessarily be laid upon them, for the support of the war, this year. An attempt to send British troops abroad would put the continuance of this happy situation of things at home to the greatest hazard, and it is past doubt that a unanimity in Parliament is, in this critical session, of much more consequence to the interests of Germany, than a few British troops joined to the armies there could possibly be.[80]

His fellow Secretary of State Pitt the Elder's sense of what was acceptable to Parliament was helping direct government policy, although, looked at differently, it was only an important element in the formation of policy while, more significantly, a disunited ministry groped its way forward in an uncertain international and domestic context. Furthermore, political memory weighed heavy on the government. Here it was not a case, as earlier in the century, of the political legacy of Utrecht, but rather a wish to distance moves from those taken by Carteret in 1742–4. As a consequence of his manner and attitudes, Carteret's interventionism had apparently been separated from parliamentary considerations, and this had led to the storm of criticism in Parliament about Hanoverian influences. Pitt, and his colleagues, wished to avoid a repetition of such attacks, and this helped shape policy. In this respect, parliamentary influence was cumulative.

This again was an aspect of the working through of the Glorious Revolution. The inclination to co-operate with Parliament competed with a reluctance to accept the resulting compromises. The pro-government *Honest True Briton* declared, in its issue of 8 May (os) 1724,

If generally, or in most sessions of Parliament since the Revolution, needless trouble had not been given to those who had had the administration of affairs, or that opposition had not been made more to men than things, this nation had, no doubt, appeared with greater lustre abroad than at some periods of time it did, and have been much richer and more powerful than at present.

---

[80] Holdernesse to Mitchell, 12 Dec. 1757, PRO. SP. 90/70.

'Needless trouble' was not the same as enforced policy decisions. Instead, opposition attacks suffered not simply as a consequence of government majorities, but also because of timing. Once decisions had been taken and implemented, then it was very difficult for Parliament to have any impact, but, conversely, if Parliament debated issues early, their implications and consequences were frequently unclear. In the debate on 17 February 1783 about terms with America, 'the Duke of Richmond thought any opinion upon the peace premature'.[81]

Nevertheless, there was a clear sense of public scrutiny, both through and of Parliament, with the latter becoming increasingly prominent from the 1760s, and not only with the rise of criticism by radicals. Hans Stanley captured this scrutiny in 1773, referring, with respect to the Commons' discussion of the East India Company, to 'the very great fatigue we have undergone . . . Our materials are so far collected and prepared that I think we shall be able to satisfy the curiosity of the public, and some better purposes before the end of the sessions'.[82]

Elections were also seen as a form of scrutiny, although many MPs and all non-Scottish peers had nothing to fear on that head. Bolingbroke felt certain that the imminence of elections would lead MPs to support the Treaty of Utrecht and the end of the War of Spanish Succession. He wrote, in April 1713, that MPs 'have their new elections before their eyes, they are desirous to make the burden as light this year as possible . . . and to do nothing which may have an unpopular view among those who are to choose them'.

In this same letter, Bolingbroke offered another reason for his confidence in parliamentary support, specifically the role of prior agreement:

I take it for granted that none of the princes concerned, nor all of them joined together can hope to obtain from this Parliament the least complaisance on the head of subsidies. A Parliament which sat during the last summer, which had its share in the transactions of that time, looks on itself as a party to a great degree in all that was then done.[83]

Bolingbroke's letter was addressed to Thomas, 3rd Earl of Strafford, a peer and political ally who was a diplomat, and, as with other documents, should be seen as involving more than dispassionate analysis. Nevertheless, there was a clear sense that parliamentary support strengthened the government, not least with regard to allies. Earlier that year, Bolingbroke had referred to

---

[81] George, 4th Earl of Jersey to Countess Spencer, 17 Feb. 1783, BL. Add. 75689.
[82] Stanley to Countess Spencer, 14 Apr. 1773, BL. Add. 75688.
[83] Bolingbroke to Strafford, 28 Apr. (os) 1713, BL. Add. 73508.

Parliament 'from whom I dare prophecy that such allies as hang back will receive little encouragement'.[84]

British diplomats repeatedly stressed foreign interest in Parliament, both for signs of information about government policy and for evidence of political stability. The argument that the former was important in effect downplayed the role of diplomacy as a means of penetrating into royal 'designs with certainty'.[85] Indeed, the government sought to assist this focus on the Crown in Parliament. In 1735, Diemar, the envoy of Hesse-Cassel, forwarded to Prince Eugene a translation of George II's speech which he noted had been made in the office of the Secretaries of State and given to the foreign envoys, although he added that he had been told that the real version was more energetic, the last welcome news for Austrian ministers seeking more robust opposition to the Bourbons. Royal speeches to Parliament, and the Addresses in response, were carefully drafted,[86] and an appropriate gloss was placed on them when they were discussed with foreign powers.[87] The presentation of treaties to Parliament can be located in this context. The process continued throughout the century. Thus, a recent Anglo-Russian subsidy treaty was communicated in 1799.[88]

The resulting emphasis on public diplomacy posed problems not simply with reference to putting the best spin on parliamentary dissension, but also as to how best to relate Parliament to other aspects of public politics, particularly the press, at least part of which was usually very critical of the ministry. On the eve of the battles in the 1729 session, Delafaye observed to one of the British envoys in France,

I do not doubt but before they [Parliament] have sat many days, our ill wishers both at home and abroad will be convinced that any expectations they may have had from that quarter were entirely vain and groundless. I must own that to those who do not thoroughly understand our constitution, and have no notion of the excess to which the liberty of the press may be carried here, the weekly insults upon the King and his ministry carried on with impunity, may give an opinion of the administration being very weak. But they are quite out in their judgement who reason thus, for never was greater hopes of a good session.[89]

---

[84] Bolingbroke to Strafford, 3 Jan. (os) 1713, BL. Add. 73508.

[85] Keene to Newcastle, 17 Feb. 1734, PRO. SP. 94/119.

[86] Diemar to Eugene, 4 Feb. 1735, HHStA.GK. 85(a) fols. 554–5. For drafts of royal speeches in 1761–70, BL. Add. 57833 fols. 40–53.

[87] Thomas Pelham to Waldegrave, 19 Jan. (os) 1736, Chewton. For French satisfaction with that year's speech, Chavigny to Chauvelin, 26 Jan. 1736, AE. CP. Ang. 393 fol. 79. See also Harrington to Robinson, 16 Jan. (os) 1736, PRO. SP. 80/120. For the Austrian and Dutch response, Trevor to Robinson, 25 Feb. 1736, BL. Add. 23797 fol. 204.

[88] Copy of Russian treaty, Cobbett, XXXIV, 1174.

[89] Delafaye to Poyntz, 14 Jan. (os) 1729, BL. Add. 75451.

Debate also served the purpose of outlining opposition views, and therefore of setting the parameters of political discussion and the options that foreign governments had to respond to.[90] Aside from actual foreign interest, parliamentarians believed that there must be such attention as they were convinced that their decisions and debates were of great 'importance to the affairs of Europe'.[91] This could lead to a portentous rhetorical self-consciousness.

Aside from that audience, there was, also, a definite attempt to appeal to British public opinion. Thus, in response to a vote of credit, on 25 March (os) 1726, to provide funds during the international crisis created by the formation of the hostile Alliance of Vienna, 'the Tories had their design in obliging the ministry to publish to the nation that there was so great a sum yet unaccounted for'. The sense of Parliament as a potential threat to the constitution as a consequence of its role in strengthening government power was also brought forward:

much was said on our constitution and the granting such a power might destroy it . . . Mr. Snell [John, Tory MP for Gloucester] said that in King Charles the Second's time though the House of Commons had addressed the King to enter into a treaty with the States of Holland they would not give the King any money till they were sure that His Majesty had entered into that treaty, but this was giving immense sums without knowing for what, Sir Robert Walpole closed the debate by fixing it as the others had done on the necessity there was to give the King such a power at this juncture and assured the House that what they had already granted this session had such good effects abroad that he believed and was morally sure, with several expressions to this purpose, would prevent a war, that nothing but the folly of the Court of Spain to act against their own interest would bring on a war.[92]

The greater role of Parliament after the Glorious Revolution is only part of the parliamentary and political history of the century. As far as the former is concerned, the failure to stage a successful counter-revolution in Britain was important. Counter-revolution was attempted by and on behalf of the Stuarts on a number of occasions, including 1692, 1708, 1715, 1744, 1745, 1746 and 1759, and it is worth considering what the success of any of these would have entailed for Parliament. The Stuarts claimed that they would respect the constitution had they returned, but it is easy to appreciate

[90]   Diemar to Eugene, 4, 8, 22 Feb. 1735, HHStA. GK. 95(a) fols. 555, 557, 564–5, 569–70.
[91]   St John Brodrick MP to his father Alan, another MP, 15 Jan. (os) 1726, Guildford, Surrey CRO. Brodrick Mss. 1248/6 fol. 359.
[92]   James Hamilton to 'James III', 25 Mar. (os) 1726, RA. 92/44; Thomas Brodrick MP to Alan Brodrick MP, 26 Mar. (os) 1726, Guildford, Brodrick Mss. 1248/7 fol. 1.

contemporary scepticism about such claims. The growth in parliamentary power that followed the Glorious Revolution had become an integral part of the Williamite political settlement, and overthrowing the succession by force would have entailed rejecting the parliamentary legislation of 1689 and 1701, as well as the whole structure of post-1688 practices, conventions and attitudes within which this growth in power had taken place and had meaning.

Thus, a Stuart restoration would, at the very least, have led to a challenge to the position of Parliament. There would have been a determination to bring Parliament and Crown into accord, rather than to rule without Parliament, but this would probably have entailed a process of 'packing' similar to that attempted by James II before he was removed in 1688. There is evidence that the Tories enjoyed more popular support than the Whigs, but that is not the same as providing a Parliament to support the measures that 'James III' might have pursued. In the case of foreign policy, there would have been a tension between well-established public anti-Bourbon views and likely Jacobite client status towards France. It is clear that a Jacobite Britain may not have been a French client or pro-French for long. In 1678, Charles II had turned against Louis XIV. Aside from his poor relations with the Papacy, James II was neither ally nor client of Louis in 1688. Instead, George I and George II were allied to France in 1716–31, and accused by critics of being overly pro-French. However, it was less contentious for Protestant monarchs committed to the Glorious Revolution to follow such a policy than it would have been for a Jacobite monarch. This was an important aspect of the impact of the suppositions of the political nation.

Parliament might well have served as the basis for criticism of the foreign policy of a Jacobite monarch, but it would have been able to achieve little. Had the policy not involved military expenditure, then the Crown would have had little direct need for parliamentary support. Constitutionally, foreign policy was still the Crown's, and Parliament's role was advisory, restrictive and supportive, but not prescriptive. In addition, a second Stuart restoration might have led to the re-establishment of a Parliament in Edinburgh, as well as to the strengthening of the powers of the Dublin Parliament. Both would have had a consequence for the confidence and role of the Westminster Parliament.

The establishment of the Revolution Settlement after the Glorious Revolution, followed by the subsequent history of Jacobite conspiracy, helped ensure that no other counter-revolution was attempted. There was nothing equivalent to the Regent's stringent definition of the *parlements'* right to remonstrate in 1718 or his exiling of the Parlement of Paris in 1720, to

Fleury's exiling of many of the Parlement of Paris's members in 1732, to renewed troubles in the 1750s, and to the remodelling of the *parlements* in the 'Maupeou Revolution' in 1771,[93] or to Gustavus III's suppression of the Swedish Age of Liberty in 1772. Contemporaries claimed to discern the same process of counter-revolution in Britain under George III,[94] but this comparison lacked weight, and it was only in the Thirteen Colonies of North America that there was a violent response to what was seen as George's counter-revolution. In practice, the nearest approach to a counter-revolution directed against parliamentary power in the British Isles was the Union of Scotland and England in 1707, which ended the recent independent tendencies of the Edinburgh Parliament. George Lyttelton, an opposition Whig, warned the Commons in 1740, 'It is not Spanish or French arms, but Spanish and French maxims of government, that we should have most to fear . . . Let the Cortes of Spain, and the Parliament of Paris be a warning to this,'[95] but such claims tell us more about the usefulness of foreign comparisons for opposition rhetoric than they do about government policy.

In the absence of any suppression of the powers of the Westminster Parliament, its role developed without any marked discontinuity. Nevertheless, the context was not unchanging. The attitudes, competence, and character of the monarchs were significant for the workings of parliamentary monarchy. Much of the credit for Britain's constitutional monarchy rests with those who redefined the royal position between 1689 and 1707. The 'limited' or 'parliamentary' monarchy that was a product of the Glorious Revolution was successful because it was flexible: it could respond to changes in the political world, not least in the interests and abilities of individual monarchs. These changes also included the world of 'public opinion' which, in Britain, was increasingly important in disputes involving Parliament, as it also was in France with the *parlements*.[96] The sense of representation through such bodies was focused and articulated in response to governmental pretensions and initiatives, although, in many respects, this was a return to the medieval and sixteenth-century ambiguity of parliaments and estates as at once bodies designed to enhance governmental power and to make representations to it.

[93] D. Echeverria, *The Maupeou Revolution* (1985).
[94] D. Jarrett, *The Begetters of Revolution: England's Involvement with France, 1759–1789* (1973).
[95] Cobbett, XI, 338.
[96] B. R. Kreiser, *Miracles, Convulsions, and Ecclesiastical Politics in Early Eighteenth-Century Paris* (Princeton, 1978); D. Van Kley, *The Damiens Affair and the Unraveling of the 'Ancien Regime', 1750–1770* (1984); J. Swann, *Politics and the Parlement of Paris under Louis XV, 1754–1774* (Cambridge, 1995), p. 85.

An unpopular foreign policy was one field of tension. In Britain, this was most acute in controversies over Hanoverianism, and in France over the alliance with Austria concluded in 1756 and finally extinguished by war in 1792. Had the chronological order been reversed, then, in Britain, the rise in domestic radicalism in George III's reign would have been accompanied by a profound challenge to foreign policy, comparable to that seen in 1743–4 and 1755–6. The separation of these two was important to the *relative* political harmony of the entire period, although concerns about Hanoverianism were serious in the reigns of George I and George II as they challenged support for the monarchy in the face of Jacobitism. After the Jacobite threat was crushed in 1746, Pitt the Elder in the late 1750s had increased expectations about the influence of popular and City opinion,[97] and also made Commons' leadership more politically central and controversial than it had been under Henry Pelham. Both of these developments looked towards the political instability of the 1760s, but that did not focus on foreign policy. Empire, not Europe, was the subject of strife.

In Britain, hostility to Hanoverian concerns and influences was less divisive socially than the appeal of Revolutionary France was to be. In Britain, the revolutionary crisis of the 1790s led to attempts to extend the flexibility of the limited monarchy, as, in 1795, when Charles James Fox argued that Britain was truly a republic because it was a monarchy founded on the good of the people. From the other side of the political divide, concern about revolutionary sentiment led to anxious calls for a restriction of parliamentary discussion. *A Letter from a Magistrate to Mr. William Rose, of Whitehall, on Mr. Paine's Rights of Men* [sic], a conservative publication of 1791, criticised such discussion of the French Revolution, as it was feared that it would influence the public and lead them to apply such ideas to the government of Britain.[98] This tension was captured in 1793, after war was declared, when the *Morning Herald* of 30 March responded to opposition criticisms that excluding strangers from the Commons had denied their speakers 'necessary publicity' by stating that this proved that the opposition was seeking a wider audience, with speeches not 'for the sake of an influence upon their hearers, but . . . addressed to persons less capable of detecting their fallacy, and are meant for repetition in their own prints'. As early as February 1790, Charles, Lord Hawkesbury, the President of the Board of Trade, had linked relations between British Dissenters and France with developments in Parliament, particularly the quarrel between

---

[97] B. Harris, *Politics and the Nation. Britain in the Mid-Eighteenth Century* (Oxford, 2002), p. 61.
[98] P. J. Corfield, E. M. Green, and C. Harvey, 'Westminster Man: Charles James Fox and his Electorate', *Parliamentary History*, 20 (2001), p. 182; Anon., *A Letter* (1791), p. 152.

Burke and Sheridan in the debate on the Army Estimates on 9 February. Hawkesbury wondered whether the cause of the latter was a disagreement over introducing 'the principles of the French Revolution here'.[99]

There was also concern, from the other end of the political spectrum, that Parliament no longer represented public views. Just as Jacobites had claimed, earlier in the century, that Parliament's composition and opinion reflected government corruption, so now radicals challenged its role. This led Britain's allies to express fears about the country's stability. In May 1792, Auckland sent a private letter to William, Lord Grenville, the Foreign Secretary, from The Hague, 'I found great uneasiness in the minds of the Dutch ministers respecting the Associations in London, Norwich, Sheffield etc. for the pretended purposes of constitutional reform. They learned from me with great pleasure that the English nation collectively considered is fully sensible of the unexampled prosperity which it enjoys under its laws, sovereign and government.'[100]

Thus, in the crisis of the 1790s, as in that of 1745–6, the question of weaknesses stemming from the existence and role of Parliament was subordinated to the general issue of political stability. To foreign observers, Parliament was one element in this consideration, and, for them, stability was the crucial aspect of foreign policy; because, if the political system was unstable, the intentions of the government, and indeed the parliamentary discussion of foreign policy, were of limited consequence. In this perspective, politics was not contained within Parliament, which was seen as an arm of government, rather than as a representation of national stability and views. This serves as a potent reminder of the contingent and controverted character of parliamentary government, and thus of the relationship between Parliament and foreign policy.

---

[99] Hawkesbury to John, 3rd Duke of Dorset, 10 Feb. 1790, KAO. U 269 C182.
[100] Auckland to Grenville, 15 May 1792, BL. Add. 58920 fol. 86.

9

Conclusions

The 'Glorious Revolution' involved a period and process of testing new arrangements. As far as Parliament was concerned, this entailed consultation and review, with the monarchy retaining the initiative over foreign policy. Parliament could debate and fund proposals, but it did not make policy. Furthermore, parliamentary debates and complaints were predicated on the expectation that the executive would use its power to remedy failures. The somewhat uncertain use of royal authority under William III gave way to a more 'managed' approach under Anne and George I. Conventions by which Parliament could participate in policy formation developed. This was not so much a product of Parliament, or, more particularly, politicians able to manage it, seizing the initiative, as in conventional Whig interpretations of British political development,[1] but rather a new stage in the longstanding relationship between Crown and Parliament.

This relationship should not be in adversarial terms. Co-operation and even harmony were traditional goals. Furthermore, the challenge to this co-operation was seen to stem as much from Parliament as from the Crown. Carteret, now Earl Granville and Lord President of the Council, presented an account of 'the people' as an active player, capable of scrutinising both Crown and Parliament, and of the constitution as mutable, when he addressed the Lords in 1752 during a debate about entering into subsidy treaties. He agreed that 'both Houses of Parliament, and more particularly this House, have a right to interpose with their advice against concluding any treaty which may then be supposed to be upon the anvil', but, added,

that the most certain way of preserving this most important right is to avoid making use of it in an unjust, immoderate, or suspicious manner; for as the people are highly interested in supporting the prerogatives of the crown, in order to prevent their being oppressed, and their country sacrificed by the artful and ambitious schemes

[1] C. Roberts, *The Growth of Responsible Government in Stuart England* (Cambridge, 1966) and *Schemes and Undertakings: A Study of English Politics in the Seventeenth Century* (Columbus, 1985).

of a faction in parliament, if an opinion should once generally prevail among the people, that we are making use of any of our privileges in a manner inconsistent with the true prerogatives of the crown, it would be easy for the king then upon the throne to put an end to all our privileges, and indeed to our existence . . . the present is not a proper time for pushing our privileges to any great extent, because the people do not seem inclined to patronise what has been usually called an opposition in parliament: the people are sensible of the danger they are in, and they now begin to judge . . . that their relief cannot come from a contest, but from a cordial union between king and parliament.[2]

Parliament did not sit each year for anywhere near as long as its modern successor. It sat for only about 100 days in the year and its business was dominated by local issues – turnpikes, canals, enclosures, bridges – and, latterly, improvement commissions and even divorce bills. Thus any stress on a continuum of opposition focused on Parliament creates the misleading impression that Parliament was perpetually involved in huge set piece, government-versus-opposition battles. A consideration of the number of days in each session devoted to such occasions would remove any such impression. Just as politics remained, for most of its practitioners, a part-time concern, the same was true of foreign policy, for all but a few specialists. George Canning remarked in 1795 on the occasion of Grey's call for negotiations with France, that 'beyond all things else the greater part of the House – anxiously wishes, a speedy conclusion of the debate'.[3] Nevertheless, Parliament, in and out of session, was an ever-present factor.

As Parliament came to meet every year from the 1690s, so management became more important, although the periods when majorities were so small that 'every question depends in a great measure upon accident',[4] or, at least the pressures of particular moments and issues, were short. At the same time as it posed problems, Parliament also gave the government opportunities to defend its position. This was clearly seen in the diplomatic correspondence of the period. In February 1727, Thomas Robinson reported that he had told French ministers about the government's success in Parliament, 'to acquaint them with the happy state of His Majesty's affairs in England, to find so unusual an unanimity in one house, so great a majority in the other, and so much applause from all sorts of persons without doors, that the measures lately taken, may be said to have been universally concurred in, and approved by the whole nation'.

---

[2] Cobbett, XIV, 1184–5.
[3] P. Jupp (ed.), *Letter-Journal of George Canning, 1793–1795* (1991), p. 195.
[4] Henry to Stephen Fox, 19 Dec. (os) 1741, BL. Add. 51417 fols. 81–2.

Parliament and public were thus pushed together by the government. Robinson saw parliamentary news as important to the battlefield in opinion:

by the most unaccountable industry, and artifices imaginable of the Muscovite, Imperial, and Jacobite factions, there have been raised here the idlest and most short-lived stories of discontent, opposition, and tumults in England, that their utmost malice, and invention could produce . . . how well the last news from England has confounded and destroyed them.[5]

Very different accounts were offered by opposition figures. In 1726, Sir John Graeme, the Jacobite envoy in Vienna, used parliamentary proceedings to depict the government as weak when he saw Count Sinzendorf:

'I found Dr. Friend's speech in the debates upon treaties laid before the House of Commons so full of good sense and solid reasoning, that I carried my letter along with me . . . which I translated to him, and wherewith he was extremely satisfied.'

Graeme also told Sinzendorf what Strafford and other opposition figures had said in the Lords,

but he [Sinzendorf] added the court . . . carried all before them . . . I begged of him to consider of what consequence the Emperor's declaring openly for the King [Pretender], would be, in embarrassing the present ministry, and thwarting their measures, since even without any assurances of that kind, and in spite of the threatenings of the government, there are some brave patriots who dare venture to speak their mind freely.[6]

A decade later, 'James III' was similarly hopeful of both international problems and parliamentary difficulties for the ministry.[7]

The relationship between parliamentary and popular support was one that was probed repeatedly throughout the century. The highpoint of harmony occurred at the close of the 1750s; not uncoincidentally, a period of great military success. The *Monitor* declared, in the summer of 1758, that Pitt had brought unanimity.

The immense sums granted by Parliament this year are a proof of it . . . The unanimity, with which the great sums necessary for answering these great ends were granted, is a proof that a minister, whose actions entitled him to the confidence of the people, is alone capable of carrying this nation happily through such a war, as we are now engaged in.[8]

---

[5] Robinson to Newcastle, 4 Feb. (os) 1727, BL. Add. 32749 fols. 69–72.
[6] Graeme to Hay, 6 Apr. 1726, RA. 92/110.   [7] James to Duke of Ormonde, 11 Jan. 1736, RA. 185/48.
[8] *Monitor*, 13 May, 17 June 1758.

The following year, Pitt's fellow Secretary of State, Holdernesse, was confident 'we shall have a most unanimous session'.[9]

In practice, even then, there were rifts and tensions. These were not simply among policy makers and parliamentarians. Instead, as one of Newcastle's correspondents noted in 1759, there were social tensions which were linked to policy issues, 'a sort of a murmur at the expenses of Continental connexions . . . the landed interest is now allowed to crouch under the load of the war, while the merchants who contribute so small a share of it grow more and more prodigal', a reminder of the sensitivity of taxation and of the continued resonance of the longstanding Tory theme that war benefited the merchants at the expense of the oppressed landed interest.[10] Nevertheless, in comparison to 1754–7, the domestic political situation appeared harmonious. Hans Stanley referred to the impact in the Hampshire parliamentary election of the 'false though popular doctrines so often repeated in Parliament that there no longer remains any difference of political opinion among His Majesty's subjects'.[11]

At other times, domestic tensions were more acute and diplomats privately warned, what ministers publicly proclaimed, that discord affected Britain's international position. Shortly before Walpole fell, Villiers wrote to his brother from his Dresden embassy,

neither do I reflect so much on the possession of power, as on the use of it. No pains must be spared to reestablish a better concord, and our reputation abroad; for believe me, notwithstanding what I have heard to the contrary, one is connected with the other; contempt begats contempt, and if it is as great against us, that which some of us have for other nations, our discord will be encouraged and increased at home for a consequential ill success in foreign affairs. Experience demonstrates what I advance.

Villiers indeed would have preferred a coalition, but, sensibly, pointed out that William III's unsuccessful efforts to that end had proved it to be almost impracticable.[12] In 1743, a pamphleteer contrasted the national need to deal with European affairs with the opposition's parliamentary pressure for domestic changes, and asked if foreign powers would enter into alliances 'with us, let it be ever so necessary or pressing, when they could not be certain of our continuance in it from year's end to year's end'.[13] Concern about Parliament helped lead to an instinctive response to keep it in the

[9] Holdernesse to Robert Keith, 2 Nov. 1759, BL. Add. 35483 fol. 40.
[10] John Gordon to Newcastle, 28 Nov., 1759, BL. Add. 32899 fol. 168.
[11] Hans Stanley to Newcastle, 24 Nov. 1759, BL. Add. 32899 fol. 83.
[12] Villiers to Jersey, 24 Jan., 28 Mar. 1742, London, Greater London Record Office, Acc. 510/192, 198.
[13] Anon., *A Letter to a Great Man in France* (1743), p. 16.

dark in moments of crisis. On 11 January (os) 1744, George Grenville, an opposition Whig MP, complained in the Commons, then meeting as a Committee of Supply to debate continuing forces in Flanders, that it was the practice then not to let Parliament know anything of public measures. In the winter of 1782–3, the government refused to divulge the details of the preliminary peace articles, the *Morning Herald* stating on 23 January 'To the utter astonishment of the peace-proclaiming politicians, who yesterday thronged the gallery of the House of Commons not a syllable fell from the lips of his Majesty's ministers.'

Such behaviour led to the repeated conviction that Parliament was being kept in the dark; a major qualification to any notion of parliamentary government. By their nature, these suspicions could not be disproved. It was alleged in 1730, for example, that not all the Treaty of Seville was laid before Parliament, although, in fact, the secret clauses attributed to the treaty, providing for the restoration of Gibraltar and Minorca within six years, and for bringing this measure before Parliament within three,[14] did not exist. In January 1744, Richard Tucker wrote from Weymouth to his brother John, one of the MPs for the constituency:

had the opportunity to entertain our friends at the Club, with your accounts of debates on the Hanover troops...I find the people at the helm go on in the old way of refusing the people the satisfaction of knowing what treaties are formed and this will give the world room to conclude that the worst which is suggested of their purport is true.[15]

If the management of Parliament was a central task of government, an awareness of the likely response of Parliament to particular proposals was as important as patronage in retaining control of the legislature. This helped make Britain a functioning parliamentary monarchy, one in which, despite problems, Parliament and Crown sought to operate in harmony, while policies were considered in light of the likely response of Parliament. When, in 1745, the Bavarian envoy told Harrington, who sought an alliance, that Bavaria would not allow her troops to be used to invade France, Harrington wrote to Newcastle in a letter not intended for disclosure, 'I see no great prospect of our being able to conclude anything with that Prince, which will be justifiable in Parliament'.[16] Bavaria sought a subsidy treaty, and Harrington was correct. No treaty was negotiated.

---

[14] Anon., *A Letter to a Member of Parliament, relating to the Secret Article concluded and ratified by the Treaty of Seville, concerning Gibraltar and Minorca* [1730], French manuscript translation, AE. CP. Ang. 370 fols. 96–8.
[15] Bod. Ms. Don. c. 106 fol. 161.   [16] Harrington to Newcastle, 29 July 1745, PRO. SP. 43/36.

Consideration of the likely parliamentary response was not, however, the same as direction. Furthermore, consideration was more the case for some ministers than others, and was more pertinent in the case of relations with some states (France, Spain) and over some issues (trade, colonies), than others; although this differentiation essentially arose from an awareness of parliamentary attitudes. In the case of these states and relations, consideration was further limited as a result of the actions of those on the spot. The India Act of 1784 might declare that conquests in India were 'repugnant to the wish, the honour, and policy of this nation', but the government was affected, if not constrained, by the attitudes and actions of officials on the spot.[17]

More generally, the role of the Crown remained central. Monarchs chose ministers, and Lord North told the Commons on 27 February 1782:

the King had a right to admit and dismiss from his councils whomever he pleased: and he might, without assigning any cause, or without fixing any guilt upon the person, recall that confidence which he had been graciously pleased to bestow upon any one of his servants.[18]

Furthermore, many of the possibilities of greater parliamentary power were never pursued. Parliamentary enquiries into accounts lapsed after 1714, estimates of annual military expenditure were generally passed without detailed scrutiny, and successive ministries ignored appropriation clauses. As a sign of what could be envisaged, Chavigny reported in 1733 that the opposition wished to see a permanent committee of the two houses to administer the finances.[19] This never happened. Instead, there was the process mentioned in the *Morning Post* of 17 March 1786, 'Mr. Pitt has acted very prudently, in selecting the members of the committee, for the inspection of public accounts, from among his own friends'.

More generally, the ability of Parliament to overthrow ministries was limited. There was no equivalent in Britain to the situation in Bohemia, where the Estates collected taxes and, in 1714, created a permanent executive body, or in Württemberg, where the Estates used their own officials to supervise tax collection,[20] although, in the 1774 Commons' debate on the Budget, Lord North declared 'it is the glory of this country that all the world knows what England owes, and what England can pay; but in France all is

[17] B. E. Kennedy, *Anglo-French Rivalry in India and in the Eastern Seas, 1763–93: A Study of Anglo-French Tensions and of their Impact on the Consolidation of British Power in the Region* (Ph.D. thesis, Australian National University, 1969), p. 342.
[18] *The Parliamentary Register*, 6 (1782), p. 324.
[19] Chavigny to Chauvelin, 17 July 1733, AE. CP. Ang. 381 fol. 121.
[20] J. A. Vann, *The Making of a State: Württemberg, 1593–1793* (Ithaca, 1984).

private'.[21] Ironically, British diplomats and ministers complained about the consequences of limited government in other states, especially Sweden and the United Provinces. Successive British ministries bemoaned the impact on Dutch policy of the consultative and decentralised nature of its government, arguing that this limited the value of the United Provinces as an ally.[22]

In Britain, monarchs needed to appoint and, if necessary, sustain, a ministry that could get government business through Parliament. This was a shifting compromise, one subject to contingency and the play of personality. Conventions developed, but were subject to strain and debate. Understanding of the situation in Westminster can be enhanced by considering the Dublin Parliament. There, also, developments in the reigns of William and Anne were crucial, not least growing government expenditure as a result of war, and Parliament's refusal to vote any more hereditary revenues. As a consequence, in a context of political strife as well as compromise and negotiation, new constitutional and political conventions developed. A new process of revenue supply was linked to the advent of regular parliaments:

> By 1714 there was a clear understanding of what the various principles were. Parliamentary provision of money was based on a two-year duration of taxation, thereby dictating that Irish parliaments would meet every second year. The ways and means of raising taxation in Ireland was the preserve of the Commons, which in itself gave control of the purse-strings to Parliament. The government was accountable to Parliament in relation to public income and expenditure, given that the Commons, and the Committee of Public Accounts in particular, could wreck the supply should they so choose.[23]

Conventions and assumptions played a major role in politics on both sides of the Irish Sea, but there were still shifts of emphasis. These were generally in favour of Whig dominance and the consolidation of 'Old Corps' control over government during the reigns of George I and George II. However, there was a growing willingness to challenge the executive during the reign of George III. Paradoxically, the non-interventionist character of foreign policy, during the first three decades of his reign, ensured that this willingness was less apparent in that field. Indeed, the Ochakov crisis was the first occasion during the reign when parliamentary considerations helped force a reversal in policy towards other European powers. Significantly, this involved Russia, a state with which the parameters of acceptable policies were less clear than in the case of France and Spain.

---

[21] Cobbett, XVI, 1331.

[22] Horatio Walpole to Trevor, 23 Jan. (os) 1736, Aylesbury CRO. Trevor papers I, 41.

[23] C. I. McGrath, *The Making of the Eighteenth-Century Irish Constitution. Government, Parliament and the Revenue, 1692–1714* (Dublin, 2000), p. 288.

The far less threatening international situation in the 1760s and early 1770s had meant that there was little apparent need for a quid pro quo of royal explanation of the need to request assistance and parliamentary promises of support. John, Lord Hervey, who had been MP for Bury St Edmunds from 1725 to 1733, had written of George II's need for just such an approach:

The King was forced to meet his Parliament with a sort of hereditary speech, for it was just in the same strain with the last half-dozen of his father's, the topics of which were the uncertain state of Europe, the intricacy of affairs, the natural protraction of treaties, the hopes of a happy conclusion being at hand, and the dependence he had in the loyalty and goodwill of his Parliament for supporting him with money and troops.[24]

George III was in a very different situation, and this is a reminder of the extent to which the circumstances of parliamentary management owed much to the course of foreign policy. This was true both of the general need for parliamentary support and of the ability to sustain criticism in particular crises. Thus, the disastrous early stages of the Seven Years' War led to demands for a parliamentary investigation. Henry, 2nd Duke of Chandos wrote to his heir that 'the spirit of the kingdom' seemed 'to demand . . . a strict scrutiny'.[25] In practice, greater skill in managing commitments from then on in the war and the creation of the Newcastle-Pitt ministry removed such pressures.

Towards the close of the Seven Years' War, Elizabeth Montagu wrote to William Pulteney, now Earl of Bath, in June 1762, 'I hope, as your Lordship does, that a peace which will secure us from disasters and make government more easy, will render popular discontents and murmurs of little consequence'.[26] This was certainly not true of the Wilkesite issue and other domestic, or imperial, controversies of the decade, but was the case for foreign policy. Once the war had ended, it proved easier to manage the parliamentary consequences of foreign policy than had been the case in the two previous periods of peace: 1713–39 and 1748–56. There was less political interest in Europe and less governmental concern about Hanover than had been the case. Thus, critics of George III did not need to push for an extension of parliamentary competence in the field of foreign policy.

The absence of a linear progression towards modern constitutional and political practices is readily apparent. It was matched by marked variations

[24] R. R. Sedgwick (ed.), *Some Materials towards Memoirs of the Reign of George II by John, Lord Hervey* (1931), I, 75.
[25] 2nd to 3rd Duke of Chandos, 26 Aug. 1756, HL. Stowe manuscripts, Box 10 (29).
[26] Montagu to Bath, 5 June 1760, HL. Montagu papers no. 4523.

in the perception of international challenge. These variations affected both government policy and public attitudes. In 1729 and, even more clearly, 1738–9, there had been pressure for war with Spain, but, after this conflict ended in 1748, anxiety about her never again reached this pitch. A sense of being excluded from maritime destiny by Spain had been overcome. Attention shifted to France, which was conclusively defeated in 1758–62. After 1763 there were anxieties about French and Spanish challenges to British imperial interests and a feeling that they had to be protected from attack, as in 1770 over the Falklands, but the sense that the Bourbons had to be overcome in order to secure these interests was far weaker than prior to 1758. As this had been the positive drive for action (frequently corresponding to the negative fear about interests being subordinated to Hanover), the abating of this pressure helped the government. The Bourbon challenge during the War of American Independence changed the situation, leading to a period of concern that ended in 1790 when Spain backed down in the Nootka Sound Crisis and France, riven by crisis, was unable to help her ally.

Although there were concerns about developments in Continental Europe, they did not reach the pitch of pushing government towards war. In 1727, the Marquis de Silly suggested to a political ally, Louis, Duke of Richelieu, French envoy in Vienna, that the British nation was so inflamed that the two Houses of Parliament might ask George I to declare war on the Emperor.[27] This was a mistaken assumption. In practise, successive governments were able to respond to developments on the Continent, such as the First Partition of Poland in 1772, without feeling pressed to fight by domestic opinion. Indeed, the principal problem they faced occurred when, as in 1791 over Ochakov, the governmental desire for confrontation or conflict clashed with parliamentary reluctance to offer backing.

The case of Ochakov, as of Dunkirk in 1730, suggests that Parliament was not a negative encumbrance to the role of the executive in national government. Instead, it provided an important sounding board for political anxieties and, in moments of crisis, a system for checking the relationship between government and political nation. Moreover, as the sessions of 1730 and 1791 showed, a willingness to challenge on a particular issue did not necessarily extend to a preparedness to overthrow the government.[28] On the whole, this system worked to the benefit of the government, but, when it did not do so, it should not be assumed that Parliament was somehow a negative factor. Instead, it is necessary to move from the authoritarian perspective

[27] Silly to Richelieu, 28 Mar. 1727, Paris, Bibliothèque Victor Cousin, Fonds Richelieu vol. 31 fol. 43.
[28] E. A. Smith, *Lord Grey 1764–1845* (Oxford, 1990), p. 35.

sometimes voiced by ministers and diplomats and assert the value of an institution able to act as a check, if not a balance. This was not Parliament's sole role, but it was an important function, and one that was valuable to the political system, however irritating it might be to government. This value was not lessened by the nature of the debates within Parliament. Instead, parliamentarians understood the domestic political context and consequences of foreign policy, and used this appreciation with skill and effect.[29]

So also did those who cited parliamentary considerations. When, in 1725, Townshend proposed to divide the Austrian Netherlands between Britain, France and the Dutch and to maintain a garrison of 10,000 troops, Horatio Walpole, MP for Great Yarmouth as well as envoy to France, sensibly replied that 'the people' would oppose the step. He also stressed the manner in which public attitudes did not change as fast as those of the ministry in response to international circumstances: a willingness to keep the French out of the Low Countries had not yet been transformed into a readiness to drive the Emperor, Charles VI, out.

> The raising of eight or ten thousand men in England to garrison the places your Lordship mentions, without costing the nation a farthing would not have met with much difficulty at a time when it was visible that the Netherlands must otherwise have fallen into the power of France; and I much doubt whether the present behaviour of the Emperor, although very apparent to those that are in the secret of affairs, is yet become so notorious, and of such a dangerous consequence in the eye of the nation as to outweigh the popular objections of having 10,000 men kept in the neighbourhood of England, and to be raised at this time before a rupture break out . . . I am afraid the people of England and Holland must see in a clearer light than I apprehend they do at present, how dangerous the Emperor's views are like to be to the liberties of Europe, before they will relish a disposition which will interfere with some popular notions of their own.[30]

Fortunately, those in 'the secret of affairs' did not prevail. A permanent military presence in the Austrian Netherlands would have been a major burden on British policy.

A positive portrayal of Parliament should not, however, be offered without qualification. In the case of foreign policy, there are several elements to consider. First, there is the specific issue of the role of Parliament in facilitating military preparedness, and, therefore, both the wartime effectiveness

---

[29] For an instructive stress on compromise in France, J. M. J. Rogister, 'Parlementaires, Sovereignty, and Legal Opposition in France under Louis XV', *Parliaments, Estates and Representation*, 6 (1986), pp. 27–31. See, more generally, his *Louis XV and the Parlement of Paris, 1737–1754* (Cambridge, 1995).

[30] Townshend to Horatio Walpole, 27 Aug., reply 10 Sept. 1725, BL. Add. 48981 fols. 105–14, 115–24; quotes fols. 119, 122–3.

of Britain and the peacetime sense that Britain's military potential deserved consideration. Philip Francis was expressing the general view in the debate on the Mutiny Bill on 16 March 1786 when he 'laid it down as a maxim, that the great security which this country had for its liberty, was the dependence of the army for its subsistence on that House'.[31] Secondly, there is the more general question of the influence of Parliament's existence on the mechanics and content of foreign policy. In the case of the mechanics, it has been argued that parliamentary-backed public finance was a crucial political and governmental advantage in international competition.[32]

More generally, Parliament served to incorporate the powerful social groups and political interests in the country, and to ensure that the government, answerable to them in Parliament, was in some way theirs. This was more a process of combination of interests and views than simply a matter of consent.[33] The combination of interests and views avoided the possibility of political division arising from differences in the social structure, specifically between land and trade. An important aspect of the success of the Commons was its openness to the new emergent mercantile and industrial interests of the period: both in membership and in the House's consideration of commercial views. Commercial growth did not lead to serious social tension or political problems. Parliament provided an opportunity for commercial groups to exert influence and to seek to define public support for commerce, and in both cases more so than any forum available in France.

The stress on parliamentary-backed public finance, however, neglects or underplays the problems created by Parliament's position, while it also exaggerates the extent to which warfare is primarily a matter of resources and domestic political circumstances. Parliament did not always accept what the government felt necessary. More generally, the absence of a reliable party unity on which governments could rest left ministers feeling vulnerable to attack, and this caused particular problems in wartime. Carteret's inability to secure the management of the Commons led to his fall in 1744 and his failure to regain power in 1746. The approach of the 1756 session destroyed the Newcastle ministry, and, in the subsequent political crisis, the creation of a viable leadership in the Commons was the key issue. Furthermore, the large proportion of government expenditure met by borrowing, rather than

---

[31] *Morning Post*, 17 Mar. 1786.
[32] Brewer, *The Sinews of Power. War, Money and the English State, 1688–1783* (1989); N. A. M. Rodger, *The Safeguard of the Sea. A Naval History of Britain, I, 660–1649* (1997), p. 432.
[33] For a skilful discussion, P. Langford, *Public Life and the Propertied Englishman, 1689–1798* (Oxford, 1991).

taxation, can be presented in part as a response to the known reluctance to raise taxation.

In addition, even if Parliament did support government proposals, that did not necessarily imply that popular consent was gained. Despite parliamentary backing in 1738 for a pacific policy towards Spain, public agitation helped to create a political crisis that led to war with Spain the following year. After the Seven Years' War, the governmental attempt to ease the burden of its debts was hit when the Stamp Act duties and cider excise were both repealed in 1766 in response to popular opposition. The danger of a parliamentary system, whether democratic, quasi-democratic or neither, was clearly reflected in this episode, because those who cannot prevail in the assembly, or who feel under- or unrepresented in it, will not necessarily accept its injunctions.

The role of parliamentary opposition can be seen in two ways. For example, the wartime critical stance of Pitt the Elder in 1745 and 1756 can be presented as cynical opportunism, needlessly threatening political and governmental stability at a time of national crisis. Alternatively, it can be argued that the existing government could not cope, that war accentuated a central feature of the political system, namely that successful parliamentary management required competent leadership and acceptable policies, as well as patronage, and that such policies had to take note of the wider political world, especially in periods of real and apparent crisis. Furthermore, the difficulty of managing Parliament could lead to the rise of a more competent leadership, as in the War of the Austrian Succession and, even more, the Seven Years' War.

Thus, the existence of Parliament caused serious difficulties, as well as the advantages that are generally stressed in schematic accounts. The same was true of the other representative bodies within the British empire; and this argument can be extended to their counterparts on the Continent, although their disadvantages tend to be stressed in a teleology focused on the development of strong states and employing the concept of Enlightenment Despotism.[34]

It is unclear how much weight should be placed on the problems posed by Parliament. Much clearly depended, and depends, on an obviously subjective response to the issues of stability, continuity and order. This mirrors the role of debates over foreign policy, strategic needs and military capability. Once it came to be necessary to translate rhetoric into policy,

---

[34] J. Black, *Eighteenth-Century Europe* (2nd edn, 1999), pp. 455–68, and *Kings, Nobles and Commoners: States and Societies in Early-Modern Europe* (2004).

there was little sense of generally agreed steps, more particularly of how to respond to adversity and difficult circumstances. Public finances were certainly crucial to the resources available for the pursuit of security and gain. 'A Parliament always ready to grant supplies' was seen as one of the factors enabling Britain to take a leading role against the Bourbons by an anonymous writer in 1736–7.[35] Resources were particularly important to the ability of Britain to take part in sustained warfare, and also permitted the state and country to recover between conflicts. The success of British public finances lay in their permanence and acceptability, allowing the shifts from war to peace and from peace to war to be made, in fiscal terms, quite effectively. As so many contemporaries acknowledged, access to funds lay at the heart of Britain's success, and British envoys were provided with details about the ability of the government to get its financial business through the Commons.[36]

Resources, however, were no more than the enabler of success. Their conversion into effective military units, and the use made of these units, were both crucially important, and each, indeed, attracted parliamentary attention. Domestic political pressures anyway played a major role in discouraging ministries from seeking a large peacetime standing army. Conversely, in the 1650s, Oliver Cromwell was able to build up an effective military in the absence of parliamentary supervision, although at heavy fiscal cost, and in a way that challenged the stability of the Protectorate. Thus, the relationship between Parliament and military effectiveness was more ambiguous than is frequently appreciated.[37] Success was also an independent variable. Just as it did not simply stem from parliamentary support and resources, so it contributed to them. This was captured, in December 1759, by Richard Potenger, an Under-Secretary, when he also introduced an apt comparison with France:

the series of successes with which His Majesty's arms have been blessed in the course of the last summer, and which have carried this nation to the highest pitch of glory . . . Every thing passes in the quietest manner in the House of Commons; there is scarce more than one voice there upon affairs of the most national consequence. Eight millions were voted the other day; the money is already found, and the subscription quite full . . . the interest of it is to be paid by a new tax of three pence per bushel upon malt. How happily different is this situation from that of our enemy who is endeavouring to get money by the last and most contemptible resources,

[35] Anon. memoire, 'A few observations humbly submitted to consideration' (no date), CUL. Cholmondeley Houghton collection, manuscripts 73/53.
[36] John Couraud, Under-Secretary, to Robinson, 6 Feb. (os) 1736, BL. Add. 23797 fol. 178.
[37] See, more generally, Black, *Britain as a Military Power 1688–1815* (1999), especially 1–5, 270–2.

those of smelting their plate, and proclaiming their bankruptcy by putting a stop to the payment of bills drawn upon their country.[38]

At the same time, it is necessary to move aside from any simple definition of effectiveness, or, indeed, therefore, success, and, instead, to appreciate that the issue of 'fit for purpose' was central in political and military institutions and decisions, and that effectiveness, purpose and success were politically constructed and debated.

This debate linked Parliament's wartime influence to the peacetime situation. Diplomatic and military priorities, or what is now termed strategic culture, did not stem from an obvious assessment of clear-cut national interests, however much the language of the latter might be employed.[39] Instead, policy choices were debated and, indeed, changed. The extent of the debate challenges the emphasis in some of the recent literature on a national mood or identity, however manufactured, and the tendency to give explanatory force to this new version of the *Zeitgeist*.[40] By challenging this interpretation, it is possible to present Parliament as playing a major role as a sphere in which the debate over policy was conducted. A schematic approach that treats national interests as flowing from the nature of the international system[41] will have little time for domestic debate, and will treat Parliament rather as an institutional enabler serving to secure resources. In contrast, an analysis that focuses on such debate accepts a mutability of interests, in which Parliament's continuing role appears not as a hindrance, but as a powerful addition to mechanisms within the executive that encouraged exchanges over policy. This helps answer the question of whether democratic states are less effective than authoritarian rivals. The capacity of the former both to enhance governmental effectiveness and to engender ideas did not, and does not, ensure success, but it is an important strength.

[38] Potenger to Mitchell, 22 Dec. 1759, BL. Add. 6823 fol. 73.
[39] H. Kleinschmidt, *The Nemesis of Power: A History of International Relations Theories* (2000); Black, *European International Relations 1648–1815* (2002).
[40] L. Colley, *Britons. Forging the Nation 1707–1837* (New Haven, 1992); Black, 'Confessional State or Elect Nation? Religion and Identity in Eighteenth-century England', in T. Claydon and I. McBride (eds.), *Protestantism and National Identity. Britain and Ireland, c.1650–c.1850* (Cambridge, 1998), pp. 53–74.
[41] For example, P. W. Schroeder, *The Transformation of European Politics 1763–1848* (Oxford, 1994).

Select bibliography

Place of publication London unless otherwise stated.

PRINTED SOURCES

Almon, J., *The Debates and Proceedings of the British House of Commons, 1743–74* (1766–75).

Almon, J. (ed.), *The Parliamentary Register* (1775–80).

Aspinall, A. (ed.), *The Later Correspondence of George III*, vol. 1 (Cambridge, 1962).

Blackstone, Sir William, *Commentaries on the Laws of England* (5th edn, Oxford, 1773).

Brown, P. D. and Schweizer, K. W. (eds.), *The Devonshire Diary. William Cavendish Fourth Duke of Devonshire. Memoranda on State of Affairs 1759–1762* (1982).

Browning, O. (ed.), *The Political Memoranda of Francis Fifth Duke of Leeds* (1884).

Chandler, R. (ed.), *The History and Proceedings of the House of Commons* (1742–4).

Clark, J. C. D. (ed.), *The Memoirs and Speeches of James, 2nd Earl Waldegrave* (Cambridge, 1988).

Cobbett, W. (ed.), *Parliamentary History of England* (36 vols., London, 1806–20).

Davis, H. *et al.*, *The Prose Works of Jonathan Swift* (16 vols., Oxford, 1939–68).

Debrett, J. (ed.), *The History, Debates and Proceedings of both Houses of Parliament* (1792).

Duff, H. (ed.), *Culloden Papers* (1815).

Gordon, G., *The Annals of Europe for the Year 1739*, II (1741).

Gordon, M., *The True Crisis* (1730).

Graham, J. M. (ed.), *Annals and Correspondence of the Viscount and the First and Second Earls of Stair* (2 vols., 1875).

Hayton, D. (ed.), *The Parliamentary Diary of Sir Richard Cocks, 1698–1702* (Oxford, 1996).

Horwitz, H. (ed.), *The Parliamentary Diary of Narcissus Luttrell, 1691–1693* (Oxford, 1972).

Ilchester, Earl of (ed.), *Lord Hervey and His Friends 1726–38* (1950).

Jennings, L. W. (ed.), *The Correspondence and Diaries of John Wilson Croker* (3 vols., 1885).

Jones, C. and Holmes, G. (eds.), *The London Diaries of William Nicolson Bishop of Carlisle 1702–1718* (Oxford, 1985).

Laprade, W. T. (ed.), *Parliamentary Papers of John Robinson, 1774–1784* (1922).

Malmesbury, 3rd Earl of (ed.), *Diaries and Correspondence of James Harris, First Earl of Malmesbury* (4 vols., 1844).

Newman, A. N. (ed.), *The Parliamentary Diary of Sir Edward Knatchbull 1722–1730* (1963).

Rogers, J. E. T. (ed.), *A Complete Collection of the Protests of the Lords, with Historical Introductions, Edited from the Journals of the Lords* (2 vols., Oxford, 1974).

Russell, Lord John (ed.), *Correspondence of John, 4th Duke of Bedford* (3 vols., 1842–6).

Sedgwick, R. R. (ed.), *Some Materials towards Memoirs of the Reign of George II by John, Lord Hervey* (1931).

Tayler, A. and H. (eds.), *Lord Fife and his Factor* (1925).

Taylor, S. and Jones, C. (eds.), *Tory and Whig. The Parliamentary Papers of Edward Harley, Third Earl of Oxford, and William Hay, MP for Seaford, 1716–1753* (Woodbridge, 1998).

Taylor, W. S. and Pringle, J. H. (eds.), *Correspondence of William Pitt, Earl of Chatham* (4 vols., 1838–40).

Walpole, Horace, *Memoirs of King George II*, ed. J. Brooke (3 vols., New Haven, 1985).

Walpole, Horace, *Memoirs of the Reign of King George III*, ed. D. Jarrett (4 vols., New Haven, 2000).

Warrana, D. (ed.), *More Culloden Papers*, III (Inverness, 1927).

Wright, J. (ed.), *The Speeches of the Rt. Hon. Charles James Fox in the House of Commons* (6 vols., 1815).

Young, A., *Travels during the years 1787, 1788 and 1789* (2nd edn, 2 vols., 1794).

SECONDARY SOURCES

Abarca, R. E., 'Classical Diplomacy and Bourbon "Revanche" Strategy, 1763–1770', *Review of Politics*, 32 (1970).

Barker, H. and Burrows, S. (eds.), *Press, Politics and the Public Sphere in Europe and North America 1760–1820* (Cambridge, 2002).

Bellot, H. H., 'General Collections of Reports of Parliamentary Debates for the Period since 1660', *Bulletin of the Institute of Historical Research*, 10 (1932–3).

Black, J., '1733 – The Failure of British Diplomacy?', *Durham University Journal*, 74 (1982).

Black, J., 'The Press, Party and Foreign Policy in the Reign of George I', *Publishing History*, 13 (1983).

Black, J., *The English Press in the Eighteenth Century* (1987).

Black, J., *The Collapse of the Anglo-French Alliance* (Gloucester, 1987).

Black, J., 'Anglo-Wittelsbach Relations 1730–42', *Zeitschrift für bayerische Landesgeschichte*, 55 (1992).

Black, J., 'Confessional State or Elect Nation? Religion and Identity in Eighteenth-century England', in T. Claydon and I. McBride (eds.), *Protestantism and National Identity. Britain and Ireland, c.1650–c.1850* (Cambridge, 1998).

Black, J., *Eighteenth-Century Europe* (2nd edn, 1999).

Black, J., *Britain as a Military Power 1688–1815* (1999).

Black, J., *European International Relations 1648–1815* (2002).

Black, J., *Kings, Nobles and Commoners: States and Societies in Early-Modern Europe* (2004).

Black, J., 'The Catholic Threat and the British Press in the 1720s and 1730s', *Journal of Religious History*, 12 (1983).

Blanning, T. C. W., *The Culture of Power and the Power of Culture. Old Regime Europe 1660–1789* (Oxford, 2002).

Bogle, E. C., *A Stand for Tradition: The Rejection of the Anglo-French Commercial Treaty of Utrecht* (Ph.D. thesis, University of Maryland, 1972).

Brewer, J. *The Sinews of Power. War, Money and the English State, 1688–1783* (1989).

Carnall, G. and Nicholson, C. (eds.), *The Impeachment of Warren Hastings* (Edinburgh, 1989).

Childs, J., *The British Army of William III* (Manchester, 1987).

Christie, I. R., 'Party in Politics in the Age of Lord North's Administration', *Parliamentary History*, 6 (1987), pp. 47–68.

Christie, I. R., 'The Changing Nature of Parliamentary Politics 1742–1789', in J. Black (ed.), *British Politics and Society from Walpole to Pitt 1742–89* (1990).

Christie, I. R., 'The Anatomy of the Opposition in the Parliament of 1784', *Parliamentary History*, 9 (1990).

Coleman, D. C., 'Politics and Economics in the Age of Anne: The Case of the Anglo-French Trade Treaty of 1713', in Coleman and A. H. John (eds.), *Trade, Government and Economy in Pre-Industrial England: Essays Presented to F. J. Fisher* (1976).

Colley, L., *In Defiance of Oligarchy: The Tory Party, 1714–60* (Cambridge, 1982).

Colley, L., *Britons. Forging the Nation 1707–1837* (New Haven, 1992).

Collins, I., *Napoleon and his Parliaments, 1800–1815* (1979).

Coombs, D., *The Conduct of the Dutch. British Opinion and the Dutch Alliance during the War of the Spanish Succession* (The Hague, 1958).

Corfield, P. J., Green, E. M. and Harvey, C., 'Westminster Man: Charles James Fox and his Electorate', *Parliamentary History*, 20 (2001).

Coxe, W., *Memoirs of the Life and Administration of Sir Robert Walpole, Earl of Orford* (3 vols., 1798).

Coxe, W., *Memoirs of Horatio, Lord Walpole* (1802).

Coxe, W., *Memoirs of the administration of the Right Honourable Henry Pelham* (2 vols., 1829).

Cranfield, G. A., *The Development of the Provincial Newspaper 1700–1760* (Oxford, 1962).

Cromwell, V., 'The Administrative Background to the Presentation to Parliament of Parliamentary Papers on Foreign Affairs in the Mid-Nineteenth Century', *Journal of the Society of Archivists*, 2 (1963).

Cruickshanks, E., *Political Untouchables. The Tories and the '45* (1979).

Davies, G., 'The Control of British Foreign Policy by William III', in *Essays on the Later Stuarts* (1958).

Dickson, P. G. M., *The Financial Revolution in England: A Study in the Development of Public Credit, 1688–1756* (1967).

Donaghay, M. M., *The Anglo-French Negotiations of 1786–1787* (Ph.D. thesis, University of Virginia, 1970).

Downie, J. A., ' *The Conduct of the Allies*: The Question of Influence', in C. T. Probyn (ed.), *The Art of Jonathan Swift* (1978).

Downie, J. A., *Robert Harley and the Press* (Cambridge, 1979).

Downing, B., *The Military Revolution and Political Change. Origins of Democracy and Autocracy in Early Modern Europe* (Princeton, 1992).

Eastwood, D., 'Parliament and the Locality: Representation and Responsibility in Late-Hanoverian England', *Parliamentary History*, 17 (1998).

Echeverria, D., *The Maupeou Revolution* (1985).

Ehrman. J., *The Younger Pitt*. (3 vols., 1969–96).

Ertman, T., *Birth of the Leviathan: Building States and Regimes in Medieval and Early Modern Europe* (Cambridge, 1997).

Escott, M. M., *Britain's Relations with France and Spain, 1763–1771* (Ph.D. thesis, University of Wales, 1988).

Gauci, P., *The Politics of Trade: The Overseas Merchant in State and Society, 1660–1720* (Oxford, 2001).

Gibbs, G. C., 'Parliament and Foreign Policy in the Age of Stanhope and Walpole', *English Historical Review*, 77 (1962).

Gibbs, G. C., 'Newspapers, Parliament and Foreign Policy in the Age of Stanhope and Walpole', *Mélanges offerts à G. Jacquemyns* (Brussels, 1968).

Gibbs, G. C., 'The Revolution in Foreign Policy', in G. Holmes (ed.), *Britain after the Glorious Revolution 1689–1714* (1969).

Gibbs, G. C., 'Laying Treaties Before Parliament in the Eighteenth Century', in R. M. Hatton and M. S. Anderson (eds.), *Studies in Diplomatic History: Essays in Memory of David Bayne Horn* (1970).

Gibbs, G. C., 'English Attitudes towards Hanover and the Hanoverian Succession in the First Half of the Eighteenth Century', in A. N. Birke and K. Kluxen (eds.), *England und Hannover* (Munich, 1986).

Gibbs, G. C., 'Parliament and the Treaty of Quadruple Alliance', in R. M. Hatton and J. S. Bromley (eds.), *William III and Louis XIV. Essays 1680–1720 by and for Mark A. Thomson* (Liverpool, 1968).

Glete, J., *Navies and Nations. Warships, Navies and State Building in Europe and America, 1500–1860* (2 vols., Stockholm, 1993).

Graves, M. A. R., *The Parliaments of Early Modern Europe* (Harlow, 2001).

Gregg, E., *Queen Anne* (1980).

Gruder, V. R., 'Paths to Political Consciousness. The Assembly of Notables of 1787 and the "Pre-Revolution" in France', *French Historical Studies*, 13 (1984).

Hanley, S., *The Lits de Justice of the Kings of France* (Princeton, 1983).

Harkness, D. A. E., 'The Opposition to the 8th and 9th Articles of the Commercial Treaty of Utrecht', *Scottish Historical Review*, 21 (1923–4).

Harris, T., *Politics under the Later Stuarts: Party Conflict in a Divided Society 1660–1715* (Harlow, 1993).

Harris, B., *Politics and the Nation. Britain in the Mid-Eighteenth Century* (Oxford, 2002).

Hattendorf, J. B., *England in the War of the Spanish Succession: A Study of the English View and Conduct of Grand Strategy, 1701–1712* (New York, 1987).

Hayton, D., 'The "Country" Interest and the Party System, 1689–c. 1720', in C. Jones (ed.), *Party and Management in Parliament 1660–1784* (Leicester, 1984).

Hayton, D., 'The Country Party in the House of Commons 1698–1699: a Forecast of the Opposition to a Standing Army?', *Parliamentary History*, 6 (1987).

Hayton, D., 'Contested Kingdoms, 1688–1756', in P. Langford (ed.), *The Eighteenth Century 1688–1815* (Oxford, 2002).

Hayton, D. (ed.), *The House of Commons 1690–1715* (5 vols., Cambridge, 2002).

Holmes, G., 'The Commons' Division on "No Peace without Spain", 7 December 1711', *Bulletin of the Institute of Historical Research*, 33 (1960).

Holmes, G., *British Politics in the Age of Anne* (2nd edn, 1987).

Holmes, G. and Jones, C., 'Trade, the Scots and the Parliamentary Crisis of 1713', *Parliamentary History*, 1 (1982).

Hoppit, J., *A Land of Liberty? England 1689–1727* (Oxford, 2000).

Hoppit, J., 'Checking the Leviathan, 1688–1832', in D. Winch and P. K. O'Brien (eds.), *The Political Economy of British Historical Experience, 1688–1914* (2002).

Horn, D. B., *British Public Opinion and the First Partition of Poland* (Edinburgh, 1945).

Horwitz, H., *Parliament, Policy and Politics in the Reign of William III* (Manchester, 1977).

Hurt, J. J., *Louis XIV and the Parlements. The Assertion of Royal Authority* (Manchester, 2002).

Jarrett, D., *The Begetters of Revolution: England's Involvement with France, 1759–1789* (1973).

Jenks, T., 'Language and Politics at the Westminster Election of 1796', *Historical Journal*, 44 (2001).

Jolliffe, H. G. H., *The Jolliffes of Staffordshire* (1892).

Jones, C., 'The House of Lords and the Growth of Parliamentary Stability, 1701–42', in Jones (ed.), *Britain in the First Age of Party 1680–1750* (1987).

Jones, C. and Harris, F., '"A Question . . . Carried by Bishops, Pensioners, Placemen, Idiots": Sarah Duchess of Marlborough and the Lords' Division over the Spanish Convention, 1 March 1739', *Parliamentary History*, 11 (1992).

Jones, D. W., *War and Economy in the Age of William III and Marlborough* (Oxford, 1988).

Jones, J. R., *Britain and the World, 1649–1815* (1980).

Jupp, P. (ed.), *The Letter-Journal of George Canning, 1793–1795* (1991).

Kamen, H., *Philip V of Spain* (New Haven, 2001).

Kelly, P., 'The Pitt-Temple Administration: 19–22 December 1783', *Historical Journal*, 17 (1974).

Kelly, P., 'British Parliamentary Politics, 1784–1786', *Historical Journal*, 17 (1974).

Kelly, P., 'British Politics, 1783–4: the Emergence and Triumph of the Younger Pitt's Administration', *Bulletin of the Institute of Historical Research*, 54 (1981).

Kennedy. B. E., *Anglo-French Rivalry in India and in the Eastern Seas, 1763–93: A Study of Anglo-French Tensions and of Their Impact on the Consolidation of British Power in the Region* (Ph.D. thesis, Australian National University, 1969).

Kenyon, J. P., *Revolution Principles: The Politics of Party 1689–1720* (Cambridge, 1977).

Ketton-Cremer, R. W., *Horace Walpole, A Biography* (3rd edn, 1964).

Klaits, J. F., *Printed Propaganda under Louis XIV: Absolute Monarchy and Public Opinion* (Princeton, 1976).

Kleinschmidt, H., *The Nemesis of Power: A History of International Relations Theories* (2000).

Van Kley, D., *The Damiens Affair and the Unraveling of the 'Ancien Regime', 1750–1770* (1984).

Kreiser, B. R., *Miracles, Convulsions, and Ecclesiastical Politics in Early Eighteenth-Century Paris* (Princeton, 1978).

Langford, P., review of Simmons, R. C. and Thomas, P. D. G. (eds.), *Proceedings and Debates of the British Parliament Respecting North America 1754–1783*, vols. 1–2 (New York, 1982–3), *Parliamentary History*, 4 (1985).

Langford, P., *Public Life and the Propertied Englishman, 1689–1798* (Oxford, 1991).

Lewis, W. S. (ed.), *The Yale Edition of Horace Walpole's Correspondence* (48 vols., New Haven, 1937–83).

Lock, F. P., *Edmund Burke, Volume I, 1730–1784* (Oxford, 1998).

Lojek, J., 'British Policy toward Russia, 1790–1791, and Polish Affairs', *Polish Review*, 28, 2 (1983).

Lowe, J. F. G., 'Parliamentary Debates in 1701, from Reports of Foreign Observers' (MA dissertation, University of Liverpool, 1960).

Lowe, W. C., 'Peers and Printers: the Beginning of Sustained Press Coverage of the House of Lords in the 1770s', *Parliamentary History*, 7 (1988).

Luff, P. A., 'Henry Fox and the "Lead" in the House of Commons 1754–1755', *Parliamentary History*, 6 (1987).

Mackesy, P., *The War for America 1775–1783* (1964).

Mahon, Lord, *History of England from the Peace of Utrecht 1713–83* (7 vols., 1858).

Mantoux, P. J., 'French Reports of British Parliamentary Debates in the Eighteenth Century', *American Historical Review*, 12 (1907).

Mathias, P. and O'Brien, P. K., 'Taxation in England and France, 1715–1810: A Comparison of the Social and Economic Incidence of Taxes Collected for the Central Governments', *Journal of European Economic History*, 5 (1976).

McGrath, C. I., *The Making of the Eighteenth-Century Irish Constitution. Government, Parliament and the Revenue, 1692–1714* (Dublin, 2000).

McGrath, C. I., 'Parliamentary Additional Supply: The Development and Use of Regular Short-Term Taxation in the Irish Parliament, 1692–1716', in D. Hayton (ed.), *The Irish Parliament in the Eighteenth Century: The Long Apprenticeship* (Edinburgh, 2001).

McJimsey, R. J., 'A Country Divided? English Politics and the Nine Years War, 1689–1697', *Albion*, 23/4 (1991).

McJimsey, R. J., 'Crisis Management: Parliament and Political Stability, 1692–1719', *Albion*, 31 (1999).

McJimsey, R. J., 'Shaping the Revolution in Foreign Policy: Parliament and the Press, 1680–1730', unpublished paper.

McMains, H., *The Parliamentary Opposition to Sir Robert Walpole 1727–31* (Ph.D. thesis, Indiana State University, 1970).

Michael, W., *Englische Geschichte im 18. Jahrhundert* (5 vols., Berlin/Basle and Berlin/Leipzig, 1896–1955).

Middleton, R., *The Bells of Victory: The Pitt-Newcastle Ministry and the Conduct of the Seven Years' War, 1757–1762* (Cambridge, 1985).

Mitchell, L. G., *Charles James Fox and the Disintegration of the Whig Party 1782–1794* (Oxford, 1971).

Murley, J. T., *The Origin and Outbreak of the Anglo-French War of 1793* (D.Phil. thesis, Oxford, 1959).

Myers, A. R., *Parliaments and Estates in Europe to 1789* (1973).

Namier, L. B. and Brooke, J. (eds.), *The House of Commons 1754–1790* (3 vols., 1964).

Norris, J. M., 'The Policy of the British Cabinet in the Nootka Crisis', *English Historical Review*, 70 (1955).

O'Brien, P. K., 'Fiscal Exceptionalism: Great Britain and its European Rivals from Civil War to Triumph at Trafalgar and Waterloo', in D. Winch and O'Brien (eds.), *The Political Economy of British Historical Experience 1688–1914* (2002).

Pares, R., 'American versus Continental Warfare, 1739–63', *English Historical Review*, 51 (1936).

Peters, M., *Pitt and Popularity: The Patriot Minister and London Opinion during the Seven Years War* (Oxford, 1980).

Plumb, J. H., *The Growth of Political Stability in England 1675–1725* (1967).

Ransome, M., 'The Reliability of Contemporary Reporting of the Debates of the House of Commons 1727–1741', *Bulletin of the Institute of Historical Research*, 19 (1942–3).

Reid, L. D., *Charles James Fox. A Man for the People* (1969).

Roberts, C., *The Growth of Responsible Government in Stuart England* (Cambridge, 1966).

Roberts, C., *Schemes and Undertakings: A Study of English Politics in the Seventeenth Century* (Columbus, 1985).

Roberts, M., *Splendid Isolation 1763–1780* (Reading, 1970).

Rogers, N., *Whigs and Cities. Popular Politics in the Age of Walpole and Pitt* (Oxford, 1989).

Rogister, J. M. J., 'Parlementaires, Sovereignty, and Legal Opposition in France under Louis XV', *Parliaments, Estates and Representation*, 6 (1986).

Rogister, J. M. J., *Louis XV and the Parlement of Paris, 1737–1754* (Cambridge, 1995).

Roosen, W., 'The Origins of the War of the Spanish Succession', in J. Black (ed.), *The Origins of War in Early-Modern Europe* (Edinburgh, 1987).

Rosenau, J. N., 'Private Preference and Political Responsibilities: The Relative Potency of Individual and Role Variables in the Behaviour of U.S. Senators', in J. D. Singer (ed.), *Quantitative International Politics: Insights and Evidence* (New York, 1968).

Rothaus, B., 'The War and Peace Prerogative as a Constitutional Issue during the First Two Years of the Revolution, 1789–91', *Proceedings of the Western Society for French History* (1974).

Schaeper, T. J., 'French and English Trade after the Treaty of Utrecht: The Missions of Amisson and Fénellon in London, 1713–1714', *British Journal for Eighteenth-Century Studies*, 9 (1986).

Schroeder, P. W., *The Transformation of European Politics 1763–1848* (Oxford, 1994).

Schweitzer, D. R., 'The Failure of William Pitt's Irish Trade Propositions 1785', *Parliamentary History*, 3 (1984).

Schweizer, K. W., *Statesmen, Diplomats and the Press – Essays on 18th Century Britain* (Lewiston, 2002).

Schwoerer, L. G., *No Standing Armies: the Antiarmy Ideology in Seventeenth-Century England* (Baltimore, 1974).

Scott, H. M., *British Foreign Policy in the Age of the American Revolution* (Oxford, 1990).

Scott, H. M., 'The Importance of Bourbon Naval Reconstruction to the Strategy of Choiseul after the Seven Years' War', *International History Review*, 1 (1979).

Sedgwick, R. R. (ed.), *The House of Commons 1715–1754* (2 vols., 1970).

Smith, E. A., *Whig Principles and Party Politics. Earl Fitzwilliam and the Whig Party 1748–1833* (Manchester, 1975).

Smith, E. A., *Lord Grey 1764–1845* (Oxford, 1990).

Stockley, A., *Britain and France at the Birth of America. The European Powers and the Peace Negotiations of 1782–1783* (Exeter, 2001).

Stone, B., *The French Parlements and the Crisis of the Old Regime* (Chapel Hill, 1986).

Swann, J., *Politics and the Parlement of Paris under Louis XV, 1754–1774* (Cambridge, 1995).

Symcox, G. J., *The Crisis of French Seapower, 1688–97: From Guerre d'escadre to Guerre de Course* (The Hague, 1974).

Symcox, G., 'Britain and Victor Amadeus II: or, the Use and Abuse of Allies', in S. Baxter (ed.), *England's Rise to Greatness, 1660–1763* (Berkeley, 1983).

Thomas, P. D. G., 'The Beginnings of Parliamentary Reporting in the Newspapers, 1768–74', *English Historical Review*, 74 (1959).

Thomas, P. D. G., 'John Wilkes and the Freedom of the Press (1771)', *Bulletin of the Institute of Historical Research*, 33 (1960).

Thomas, P. D. G., *The House of Commons in the Eighteenth Century* (Oxford, 1971).

Thomas, P. D. G., '"The Great Commoner": The Elder William Pitt as Parliamentarian', *Parliamentary History*, 22 (2003).

Thomson, M. A., 'Parliament and Foreign Policy, 1689–1714', *History*, new series, 38 (1953) reprinted in R. M. Hatton and J. S. Bromley, (eds.), *William III and Louis XIV. Essays 1680–1720 by and for Mark A. Thomson* (Liverpool, 1968).

Thorne, R. G. (ed.), *The House of Commons 1790–1820* (5 vols., 1986).

Turner, E. R., 'Parliament and Foreign Affairs, 1630–1760', *English Historical Review*, 34 (1919).

Vann, J. A., *The Making of a State: Württemberg, 1593–1793* (Ithaca, 1984).

Waller, P. J., 'Laughter in the House. A Late Nineteenth and Early Twentieth Century Parliamentary Survey', *Twentieth Century British History*, 5 (1994).

Webb, P., 'The Naval Aspects of the Nootka Sound Crisis', *Mariner's Mirror*, 61 (1975).

Whyman, S. E., *Sociability and Power in Late-Stuart England. The Cultural Worlds of the Verneys 1660–1720* (Oxford, 1999).

Wilkinson, C., 'Politics and Topography in the Old House of Commons, 1783–1834', in C. Jones and S. Kelsey (eds.), *Housing Parliament. Dublin, Edinburgh and Westminster* (Edinburgh, 2002).

Wollman, D. H., *Parliament and Foreign Affairs, 1697–1714* (Ph.D. thesis, University of Wisconsin, 1970).

Woodfine, P. L., *Britannia's Glories. The Walpole Ministry and the 1739 War with Spain* (Woodbridge, 1998).

Index

Printed in the United Kingdom
by Lightning Source UK Ltd.
124376UK00002B/241-243/A